AFRICAN OR AMERICAN?

African or American?

*Black Identity and Political Activism
in New York City, 1784–1861*

LESLIE M. ALEXANDER

UNIVERSITY OF ILLINOIS PRESS

URBANA AND CHICAGO

Library of Congress Cataloging-in-Publication Data
Alexander, Leslie M.
African or American? : Black identity and political activism
in New York City, 1784–1861 / Leslie M. Alexander.
p. cm.
Includes bibliographical references and index.
ISBN 978-0-252-03336-0 (cloth : alk. paper)
1. African Americans—New York (State)—New York—History.
2. Free African Americans—New York (State)—New York—Political
activity—History. 3. Free African Americans—New York (State)—New
York—Social conditions. 4. African Americans—Race identity—New
York (State)—New York. 5. African Americans—New York (State)—
New York—Intellectual life. 6. Free African Americans—Legal status,
laws, etc.—New York (State)—New York. 7. Citizenship—United
States—History. 8. New York (N.Y.)—History—1775–1865.
I. Title.
F128.9.N4A44   2008
305.896'0730747—dc22   2008002160

Dedicated to the memory and spirit of my father,

John D. Alexander

1942–1994

And to my mother,

Sandra M. Alexander

CONTENTS

ACKNOWLEDGMENTS

There are so many people to thank for their support and assistance during the long, arduous, yet exciting, process of writing this book. First, my family: Sandy Alexander, Michelle Alexander, Carter Stewart, Nicole Marie Stewart, Jonathan Carter Stewart, Corinne Alexander Stewart, and Sasha Alexander for their patience, encouragement, and words of inspiration. In the midst of major changes in your own lives, you unselfishly recognized my need to focus on completing this project. I am humbled by your sacrifice; it means more to me than I can ever adequately express. Mostly, to my mom and my sister, I want to thank you for your love. It is hard to describe the warmth and sense of peace that comes with receiving unconditional love and total acceptance, but yours is with me all the time.

I would also like to honor the memory of my father, John Donald Alexander. In many ways, this research project has been shaped by his sudden absence. Thank you for giving me life, love, and the passionate desire to dream big dreams. The world is a little emptier without you. I miss you every day.

Thank you also to my grandparents, Delbert and Ruby Alexander and Jack and Grace Huck, for providing a legacy and a source of inspiration.

I find myself at a loss for words when I try to express my deep appreciation and affection for my dissertation chair, Margaret Washington. I am so grateful for her unwavering commitment to my scholarship and her shining example over the years. Under her guidance, I became a Black historian, an uncompromising researcher, and a better person. Even more, I am thankful for her friendship; she offered solace in times of tremendous adversity. Only we can understand the joys and sorrows that we shared together, but we stood by each other in good times and bad; I carry that with me always. Thank you for being a true mentor and a true friend.

There will always be a special place in my heart for Robert L. Harris Jr. for his service on my dissertation committee, and his invaluable advice to this very day. He is an amazing example of how to be a compassionate scholar and teacher, and he has inspired me in so many ways. Thank you for all your support over the years, your influence has made all the difference to me.

I would also like to thank Thomas H. Holloway and R. Laurence Moore for participating on my dissertation committee and taking the time to review my work. I will always remember and appreciate your generous willingness to extend yourselves on my behalf.

My life has been profoundly shaped by the years I spent at Cornell University, mostly due to the love and support from all those who have agitated within the walls of the Africana Studies and Research Center, Ujamaa Residential College, and the Southside Community Center. Thank you all for touching my life and shaping the person I have become.

More personally, I would like to express my love and appreciation to my "other" mentors, James Turner, Abdul Nanji, Jacqueline Melton-Scott, and the late Don Ohadike. James Turner taught me so many important lessons, and remains a constant source of inspiration to me; he has been a father, mentor, and comrade. Dr. Turner, I do not think you will ever know how often I think of you and strive to model my political and intellectual life after yours. Thank you so much for the love and life lessons you have given me over the years. Abdul Nanji brought me into the "Africana Family" and introduced me to some of the most important events of my life: the African Heritage Studies Association conferences, the twenty-fifth and thirtieth Africana celebrations, and the Wednesday Nighters that lasted until dawn. I learned more from conversations with him and the brothers and sisters in those rooms than I ever learned in a classroom. I hold those moments in my heart. Jacqueline Melton-Scott, my "pocket mommy," has been a mother to the entire Africana community, and I feel so lucky that she chose me as one of her "daughters." Thank you for sharing your enduring spirit and powerful energy, mostly, for the love. To the "Chief," Don Ohadike, thank you for your passionate energy, I know your spirit continues to watch over us all.

I would also like to thank all those comrades who stood beside me during my graduate years and beyond. I am listing you alphabetically so no one gets mad! It feels like a mere mention of your names does not begin to do justice to the love, respect, and gratitude that I have for you all, nor to the myriad of beautiful ways in which you have brought joy to my life, strength to my convictions, and inspiration to my work. I hope you know I keep each one of you in my heart: Jim Akins, Ayele Bekerie, Chris Bischof (and Eastside College Preparatory School), Thelvia Bonano, Scot Brown, Rosa Clemente, Rhea Combs, Daniel "Keith" Hayes, Frances Henderson-Louis, Erica Fuller-Briggs, Ken Glover, Nicole Guidotti-Hernandez, Moon-Ho Jung, Jean Kim, Kwasi Konadu, Susie Lee, Aegina Adams Martin, Adin Michelen, Vernon Mitchell Jr., Joaquin Morante, Angel David Nieves, Elizabeth Stordeur Pryor, Carina Ray, Shamiso Rowley, Brian Sales, Gabriela Sandoval, Michelle Scott, Fanon Che Wilkins, Thabiti Willis, and the Brothers of Simba Wachanga.

Thank you, also, to all my friends and colleagues, who since my arrival at the Ohio State University, have offered gifts of friendship and academic encouragement. Most especially: Ernest L. Perry Jr., Derrick White, Jelani Favors, Demetrius Eudell, Robert Bennett III, Hasan Kwame Jeffries, Walter Rucker, Zawadi

Barskile, Cicero Fain, Jason Perkins, Tony Gass, Ousman Kobo, Judy Wu, Mytheli Sreenivas, Ahmad Sikainga, Beverly Moss, Maurice Stevens, Wendy Smooth, Cheria Dial, Jahi Dial, Jermaine Archer, Jeffrey O. G. Ogbar, Jennifer Wilks, Sara Johnson, Candace Katungi, Carol Anderson, Tiffany Preston, Tiwanna Simpson, Kevin Boyle, Debra Moddelmog, Lucy Murphy, Leila Rupp, James Genova, Kate Haulman, and Cathy Koch.

Very special thanks go to Hasan Kwame Jeffries, Vernon Mitchell Jr., and Ernest L. Perry Jr. Their keen insight shaped the argument and content of this project, and I am deeply thankful for their friendship, vision, and commitment to my work. My deepest gratitude goes to Lilia Fernandez and Stephanie Smith; their support, encouragement, hours of phone calls, laughter, patience, and willingness to accept my frail humanity are not only tributes to genuine friendship, but are the very things that have seen me through this process. I will be eternally grateful.

I am deeply indebted to those who provided intellectual and financial support: the Ford Foundation, the Anonymous Donor Fellowship, the Sage Fellowship, the Cornell Graduate School, the New York Historical Society (especially Cynthia Copeland), the New York Municipal Archives, and the staff of the Cornell Library. I am especially thankful for the Ford Foundation's annual conferences, where I gained strength and encouragement from the multitude of scholars engaged in inspiring research.

I will close by extending my heartfelt appreciation to Sterling Stuckey, for reviewing early drafts of this manuscript, and to the anonymous readers, whose invaluable comments transformed the development of this book. I am also especially grateful to Leslie M. Harris, who shares my passion for Black New York City; her support and encouragement are testaments to the vision of real intellectual collegiality. Finally, sincere gratitude goes to my editor, Joan Catapano, for her patience and commitment to this project.

ILLUSTRATIONS

PREFACE: "ONWARD FOREVER"

> . . . they will see that we are men, and men with a determined spirit
> to go on to victory; no favors, or frowns, or obstacles of any kind are
> to deter or awe us, until our object be gained . . . our motto, with all
> of us, should be "onward and onward forever" . . . until our object be
> accomplished.
> —New York State Convention of Colored Citizens, 1841

On January 2, 1815, William Hamilton, a revered leader in New York City's Black community, delivered a passionate appeal urging the "descendants of Africa" to deeply reflect on their African heritage and their potential role in shaping Africa's political destiny. For Hamilton, claiming an African identity was critically important to his vision of racial advancement in the African Diaspora; a move he hoped would inspire Black people in the United States to assist in establishing Africa as a potential "seat of authority."[1] Yet just twenty-five years later, when Black New Yorkers gathered for a statewide convention, they proudly affirmed "we are Americans" and pledged their commitment to agitate in the United States for abolition and the rights of full citizenship.[2] This range of political thought embodied the ideological tensions and dramatic shifts among New York City's Black leadership in the nineteenth century and demonstrates that, as activists sought to solve the problems plaguing their community, they battled over critical questions of strategy and identity. Indeed, emancipated Black New Yorkers faced an array of social, economic, and political challenges during the early national and antebellum eras, most notably, the powerful persistence of racism and southern slavery, the possibility of forced removal, and the repeated denial of American citizenship. As a result, while they struggled to respond to the reality of their "defective" freedom, Black leaders often vehemently debated which tactics would bring true equality and liberation to their people.[3]

Despite these ideological conflicts, however, the story of New York City's Black leadership is not simply a saga of political feuding. Instead, it is a tale of the strivings and changes in political consciousness of a people who, against tremendous odds, remained determined to gain freedom, justice, and equality. Although they did not always agree on strategy, Black leaders actively sought to create unity and a sense of community as they fought to defy the limitations on their lives. Thus, this study explores the ways in which Black people dynamically confronted the transition from enslavement to emancipation in New York City during the early national and antebellum eras. In particular, it examines the internal battles and ideological struggles among members of the Black leadership over identity, political strategy, and their African heritage as they embarked on a mission to obtain freedom and equal citizenship. Ultimately, their journey represents a nascent Black Nationalism in nineteenth century America for it is a powerful story of community building, political organizing, racial advancement, and an indestructible desire to be truly free.

* * *

This book has benefited considerably from the blossoming of studies on Northern Black life that have emerged over the past several decades. Leon Litwack, Gary Nash, Julie Winch, James and Lois Horton, and Patrick Rael provided a tremendous service by opening a field of historical inquiry that had been severely neglected: Black culture, community, political activism, and identity in the early national and antebellum North. Their works have dramatically expanded our understanding of the free Black experience throughout the North, as well as in individual cities such as Philadelphia and Boston.[4] Patrick Rael's book, *Black Identity and Black Protest in the Antebellum North,* has been particularly useful in shaping the arguments in my study, because his conclusions have both supported and diverged from my own. We agree, for example, that the Black leadership's use of moral improvement was a "strategy for racial activism" rather than a "capitulation" to White standards of respectability. I also support his contention that scholars have not given sufficient attention to internal strategic disputes within the Black community and the serious obstacles that plagued their quest to achieve their goals.[5] My work seeks to build upon these notions by examining the complexity and the challenges of Black political activism in New York City. However, as chapters 1 and 2 of my study reveal, we differ about the influence of African culture on the Black leadership's political activism. Though Rael maintains that "black leaders' acculturation . . . deeply qualified their identification with Africa," I argue that Black activists drew upon their African heritage to mold and guide their political ideology.[6] Still I remain deeply grateful to the work of the scholars listed previously, because their skillful research and insightful analyses have created the context for my exploration of Black New York City.

Despite these scholars' significant contributions, however, until recently, there remained a paucity of monographs focusing specifically on the experience and political agitation of Black people in New York City during the early national and antebellum eras. Perhaps the most important exception was Shane White's book, *Somewhat More Independent,* which explored the end of slavery in New York City and the rise of the free Black community. Yet since his study ends in 1810, it does not investigate the issues of culture, identity, and political movements in the antebellum era.[7] Thus, it was not until the early 1990s that two monographs were published that exclusively interrogated conditions in antebellum Black New York: Rhoda Golden Freeman's *The Free Negro in New York City in the Era Be-*

fore the Civil War, and George E. Walker's *The Afro-American in New York City, 1827–1860.*

Because these studies had been originally written as dissertations decades before, Freeman and Walker must be credited for their valuable additions to our knowledge of Black New York City. Yet there were some important flaws in their analytical frameworks that caused them to reach some erroneous conclusions. Most significantly, because they both began their studies in 1827, they ignored the early development of community, identity, and political strategy among the leadership and its influence on the trajectory of political activism. This problem is augmented by their books' thematic, rather than chronological, organization; skipping between decades, they miss the importance of time as an interpretive method. Freeman, in particular, disregarded African cultural retentions, the development of self-help organizations and political institutions, intracommunity conflicts over the colonization question, the Colored Convention movement, and struggles for suffrage. As a result, she claimed that Black New Yorkers were "politically unorganized" and their connection to their African heritage had been entirely severed.[8] My research, on the contrary, reveals that Black people in early national New York City were a politically active community who remained deeply connected to African culture and laid the groundwork for political debate and agitation that lasted throughout the nineteenth century.

In the past several years, a few studies have begun to address the historiographical gaps Freeman and Walker created; most notably, Graham Hodges and Leslie Harris published insightful analyses of work, culture, and class in Black New York City from the colonial era through the Civil War. Where Hodges offered a comparison of Black life in rural New Jersey to the urban experience in New York City, Harris delivered a powerful illustration of the rise and fall of slavery and the resulting conditions among the Black working class. Harris, in particular, effectively grappled with the enduring legacy of slavery and the complex relationship between race and class.[9] Since the publication of her work, I have benefited greatly from her insights on Black New York City during this era. Yet, there remained a compelling need for a close examination of New York City's Black leadership and its role in community development and political activism. In response to this omission, Craig Wilder has recently studied the emergence of Black associations in New York City during the antebellum era. Indeed, Wilder has developed a fascinating exploration of Black conceptions of manhood and the relationship of Black organizations to the Protestant ethos and evangelical Christianity.[10] I, however, am interested in a different set of questions and have crafted this study to delve into the fundamental nature of Black political activism in New York City. Specifically, I seek to investigate the Black leadership's changing relationship to its African cultural heritage and the ideological battles among Black activists over questions of political strategy and racial identity as they responded to local, state, national, and international movements.

To fully grasp the form and function of Black political activism in New York, it is crucial to examine the connection between culture, identity, and Black Nationalism. Culture is especially relevant to understanding New York City's Black leadership because, during the early national era, its shared African heritage served as a basis for collective identity. The leaders recognized themselves as Africans or descendants of Africans and maintained strong ethereal and symbolic bonds to their homeland, which created a notion of community grounded in mutual responsibility and a commitment to racial advancement.[11] Building upon Sterling Stuckey's research, this study shows that African culture manifested among Black New Yorkers in a variety of ways throughout the nineteenth century including music, dance, burial traditions, the formation of Black organizations, public celebrations, and the development of Black political thought.[12] The influence of African culture was particularly significant because it provided a foundation of racial unity and political action. Indeed, it was Black New Yorkers' shared heritage that ultimately allowed early notions of Black Nationalism to emerge.

There has been extensive debate about the most appropriate definition of Black Nationalism, particularly in relation to the antebellum era.[13] My examination of Black activism in New York City has led me to embrace a combination of the analyses provided by Wilson Moses, Sterling Stuckey, and Craig Wilder. For Wilson Moses, a nation is "any group of people who view themselves as bound together by ties of kinship, history, and heritage, and who believe themselves to be distinct and separate from other groups by virtue of common beliefs, behaviors, and ways of thinking." In Stuckey's work, *The Ideological Origins of Black Nationalism,* he argues that Black Nationalism during this era was manifest in "a consciousness of a shared experience of oppression at the hands of white people, an awareness and approval of the persistence of group traits and preferences in spite of a violently anti-African larger society, a recognition of bonds and obligations between Africans everywhere, an irreducible conviction that Africans in America must take responsibility for liberating themselves." New York City's Black leaders certainly embraced these core principles of Black Nationalism, because they understood themselves to be a distinct race that shared a common heritage, history of oppression, and political destiny. Most importantly, they manifested these ideas in an enduring dedication to liberation and self-determination.[14]

Yet Craig Wilder has built upon these notions and applied them to the specific nature of political consciousness in New York City. Like Stuckey, he places Black Nationalism squarely within the structure of a Black cultural ethos that was centered on ideas of collectivity and a commitment to African peoples worldwide. However, Wilder also insightfully articulates the ways in which Black Nationalism operated as a political philosophy: "It neither dictated political strategies . . . nor precluded political goals. It even accommodated contradictory notions. . . . The best measure of antebellum nationalism was not how fully one sought to integrate or escape white America but how committed one was to the self-determination of Africans in the Diaspora."[15] Wilder's depiction of how Black Nationalism functioned is central to understanding identity and political activism in New York City's Black community, for, as we shall see, members of the leadership presented radically divergent and often conflicting strategies. Indeed, they regularly battled over which tactics would effectively liberate their people. Yet, ultimately, they remained united on the principles of self-determination and racial advancement in the United States and throughout the Diaspora.

In the early national era, Black New Yorkers infused their political activism with pride in their African heritage and drew upon their shared identity to advance the race. Unity, they believed, could be a bastion against the poverty, vilification, and discrimination facing them as a newly emancipated people in an urban environment. As a result, men and women formed benevolent and religious associations that emphasized mutual relief, community responsibility, and a powerful racial consciousness. In fact, this period witnessed a veritable flowering of Black organizations throughout New York City; the most enduring of which was the New York African Society for Mutual Relief, an independent Black male association whose membership formed the foundation of New York's leadership.[16] Founded by 1784, the African Society's early mission was to build a cohesive Black community. They structured their organization on African secret society arrangements, espoused a distinct commitment to racial advancement, and sponsored lively cultural celebrations. Indeed, this organization soon became a powerful Black institution that fortified the community and symbolized the potential that freedom promised. Perhaps most importantly, the African Society served as a model for other mutual relief, literary, and political associations that emerged in the nineteenth century, all of which served as tributes to their African heritage and their efforts to build a Black nation in America.

Despite their best intentions, activists found themselves in a troubling quandary. They quickly discovered that efforts to balance their African identity and passion for Black community building with a growing desire for freedom and equality in the United States created an ideological tension that plagued Black politics in New York City. This problem first came to light at the turn of the nineteenth century, as the expanding free Black population created tremendous resentment among White New Yorkers. It became particularly acute as Black organizations sought independence, began issuing demands for justice, and boldly displayed their freedom and African heritage in public celebrations. As Whites perceived such actions as threatening manifestations of Black progress, Black activists confronted a disturbing reality. Given their economic and political deprivation in American society, they recognized they would need White endorsement to gain equality. This realization caused some Black leaders to conclude that they might have to rely on moral improvement and patriotic appeals as a strategy to assuage White fear and achieve their goal of racial advancement. However, the rise of moral uplift as a Black political philosophy created a serious question for the Black leadership: Was it possible to claim both their African heritage and their right to American citizenship? As a result, beginning in 1808, Black leaders openly debated whether their connection to Africa might be irreconcilable with their mission to establish a community in the United States. Although Black activists struggled to merge these "warring ideals," diverging visions of the path to race uplift materialized and, by 1810, resulted in competing agendas.[17] Some leaders argued that members of the Black community should dedicate themselves to moral improvement and American citizenship, but others began to consider departing for more welcoming environments such as Africa, Haiti, or Canada.

In the early 1820s, discussions about identity, political strategy, and emigration heightened throughout the North and created intense disputes within the Black leadership.[18] As support for emigration increased, the conflict among Black activists focused on two crucial problems. First, there was persistent concern about the long-term ramifications of emigration; leaders understood it would require Black people to abandon their crusade for freedom and citizenship in the United States and leave their Southern brethren in bondage. Even more, however, at the core of the emigration debate was an equally vital issue: the relationship between emigration and identity. As Gary Nash pointed out among Philadelphians, freed people were faced with a perplexing identity crisis in the nineteenth century. Were they African, American, or a complex amalgamation of the two?

> Were these newly freed and dark-skinned people to regard themselves as Africans in America who might best return to the land of their ancestors, if that possibility presented itself? Were they Afro-Americans whose future rested where they had toiled most of their lives but whose cultural heritage was distinctly African? Or were they simply Americans with dark skin, who, in seeking places as free men and women, had to assimilate as quickly as possible to the cultural norms and social institutions of the dominant white society?[19]

As Nash suggests, the issue of identity was not just a personal choice; it was also profoundly political. For buried within this problem was a deeper question about how identity shaped the Black community's relationship to the United States. In many ways, the emigration movement, particularly to Africa or Haiti, embodied a Pan-African vision. One that not only rejected identification with America but also argued that free Blacks were part of an African community, and therefore, their ultimate destiny should be in a Black homeland.[20]

By the dawn of legal emancipation in 1827, debates over moral improvement, emigration, and expressions of African culture exploded as Black activists publicly clashed in their attempts to reconcile competing visions of American citizenship with their African heritage. In particular, as Black leaders grew concerned about White perceptions of their community, some denounced parades and other public displays of African culture, arguing that such actions were detrimental to their racial advancement. Yet the majority of the community opposed strict adherence to moral uplift and remained steadfastly committed to their traditions. As a result, at a time when Black New Yorkers should have been reveling in the joy of legal emancipation, they found themselves battling over whether moral improvement was necessary to force American society to deliver on its promise of justice, equality, and citizenship. To make matters worse, the debates over identity and emigration became particularly complicated with the rise of the White-dominated colonization movement.[21] In the end, as Blacks feared they would be involuntarily removed from the United States, they assumed a defensive posture. They decided to publicly denounce their African heritage and assert an American identity, a tactical move that had a lasting impact on the Black community.

Although there is a rhetorical connection between emigration and identity, we should not be too hasty in assuming that all Blacks who rejected repatriation entirely dismissed their African heritage. Their decision was partly based on identity, but there were also other concerns; in particular, emigration was tremendously perilous and the burgeoning nations of Haiti and Liberia were fraught with political turmoil. Even more, their choice to remain in the United States did not reflect an abandonment of African liberation; rather, it indicated a significant shift in political strategy. By the antebellum era, the widespread anxiety about the fate of those who still suffered in Southern slavery blossomed as Black leaders wondered: If they did not stay and fight for the enslaved, who would? Ultimately, the decision to continue the fight for abolition and citizenship illustrated a powerful transformation of their nationalistic effort. They elected to refocus their mission for racial advancement and self-determination onto their specific situation in the United States by creating a permanent, free, and equal Black community in their adopted home. The notion of Black Nationalism is especially appropriate here, because Black New Yorkers soon began to explore a variety of strategies to gain civil rights and uplift the community.

Indeed, Black organizations in the antebellum era made a decided move toward political action. The early Black associations were primarily concerned with benevolent and cultural activities, but in the 1830s and 1840s they experienced a profound ideological revolution. Across the North, intense political agitation emerged within the Black community as many became disillusioned with their unequal freedom. As the abolitionist movement moved into the center of political discourse, free Black New Yorkers were at the core of that struggle. Responding to specific issues such as Southern slavery and the protection of fugitives, Black leaders created political associations designed to destroy the institution of slavery. In coalition with White abolitionists, Black New Yorkers built national antislavery societies, established abolitionist newspapers, and bravely spoke out against the horrors of slavery in an effort to raise public consciousness and expunge slavery from America. Additionally, Black men and women in New York City across class lines committed themselves to "practical abolition"; as fugitives streamed into Northern cities, Black New Yorkers fought valiantly to guard and defend their brothers and sisters fleeing Southern bondage.[22]

Yet perhaps the most significant development was the Black leadership's commitment to forge a unified Black agenda. As racism and strategic disputes undermined efforts to maintain a strong biracial antislavery movement, Black New Yorkers sought to establish Black collective action on the regional and state levels. Between 1830 and 1864, Black activists throughout the North periodically gathered in Colored Conventions to identify effective tactics for defeating slavery, defending their rights in America, and gaining citizenship. Likewise, beginning in the late 1830s, Black New Yorkers held statewide gatherings and launched a struggle for unrestricted suffrage that lasted for over two decades. However, as this study reveals, the Colored Convention movement and the fight for voting rights highlighted two fundamental issues that stymied the quest for abolition and citizenship: continued ideological tensions within the leadership over strategy and the inability of moral improvement and patriotic appeals to stem the tide of American racism.

Still, the most compelling image that emanates from the story of Black New Yorkers is their indestructible dedication to gain freedom, justice, and equality in the United States. Although America remained tenaciously hostile to Black progress, Black activists refused to relinquish their fight for abolition, citizenship, and their right to claim space in this country. In no period was this more apparent than the 1850s, when Black leaders faced seemingly insurmountable odds such as the Fugitive Slave Act, persistent racial discrimination, the *Dred Scott* decision, the continuing power of slavery, and the denial of suffrage. Yet even surrounded by these painful obstacles, Black activists in New York City and throughout the North rallied their forces and forged a united front. By the early 1850s, Black leaders finally managed to foster the unity and collective agenda they had been seeking in previous decades. Even though Black solidarity, alone, was not enough to bring an immediate end to slavery and discrimination, their determination spoke volumes about their passionate desire to build a viable Black nation and force American society to live up to its principles.

As evidence of Black New Yorkers' enduring faith in the power of Black nation building, there is one particular story that illustrates how the issues of culture, community, and citizenship converged in a fascinating movement to carve out a permanent place in a hostile environment. In 1825, Black New Yorkers began a new endeavor; they expanded their real estate ventures into the sparsely populated center of Manhattan Island. From these original plots, a community called Seneca Village was born. The residents of Seneca Village were dedicated to constructing institutions and creating a lasting Black presence in New York City. Members of the African Society and the African Methodist Episcopal Church such as Andrew Williams, Epiphany Davis, and Samuel Hardenburgh were among the first Black people to purchase land in the area that became Seneca Village. Yet Blacks regardless of organizational affiliation demonstrated strong support for the establishment of this new community, and it grew steadily. By the 1840s, Seneca Village held many important Black institutions including three churches, two cemeteries, two schools, and numerous private residences.

However, Seneca Village was not simply a manifestation of economic self-determination or community building; it was also a strategic political maneuver. Because Black men in New York State could only obtain the franchise through property ownership, Seneca Village ultimately embodied their determination to gain political power.[23] In the end, this reality led to the painful destruction of Seneca Village in 1857 to create Central Park. Despite vehement Black protest, the community was erased from New York City and almost from historical memory. In the years before the Civil War, the loss of Seneca Village was symbolic of Black New Yorkers' lack of citizenship and the tremendous fear of Black power. Yet their activism continued, and Black leaders unceasingly progressed toward a vision of liberty and equality. Drawing upon their revolutionary spirit and determination to be truly free, Black New Yorkers unified their community and agitated for their rights.

The following chapters explore these themes of Black culture, identity, and political activism in New York City chronologically, beginning in 1784 and ending on the eve of the Civil War. The time frames for each chapter were carefully selected to reflect the most important moments in Black New York, highlighting events such as organizational formation, legal emancipation, and participation in national political movements. Chapter 1 begins in 1784 with the creation of the African Society and chronicles the emergence of the free Black community. Tracing the ramifications of the dramatic increase of freed people in New York City, this section explores how the burgeoning Black leadership combated the difficult transition from slavery by maintaining an ideological connection to its African heritage and establishing Black organizations and institutions. In particular, it examines early debates among Black activists over the merits of moral improvement and their African cultural legacy. This chapter concludes in 1809, with a discussion of the celebrations held in honor of the abolition of the slave trade and offers an analysis of how the community's shared African identity temporarily united them despite their strategic differences.

Chapter 2 opens in 1810, the year that marked the rise of emigrationist thought: a new strain of political consciousness among Black activists that responded to their unequal freedom by fostering early notions of Pan-Africanism and sparking movements to Africa and Haiti. As this chapter illustrates, the growing support for emigration raised critical questions about the Black community's political destiny. Should they unite with Africans in other parts of the diaspora and build a nation elsewhere, or should they remain in the United States and use moral appeals to force America to live up to its principles? Faced with this dilemma, the Black leadership's battle over moral uplift and African heritage, which had commenced the previous decade, soon morphed into a debate about identity and the future of Blacks in the United States. Ultimately, Black New Yorkers during this era decided to reject both moral improvement and early emigration movements, choosing, instead, to develop a nascent Black Nationalism, through the creation of more Black organizations dedicated to racial solidarity and benevolence. Black leaders would soon discover, however, that they would be forced to take a more definitive stand and finally determine whether they would stay in the United States and endorse moral improvement or flee from the land where their ancestors had worked, fought, bled, and died.

Chapter 3 focuses very specifically on the years from 1827 to 1829, a time of intense upheaval in the Black community. The year 1827 should have been a time of jubilant celebration for Black New Yorkers, because it was the year of their legal emancipation. Instead, however, it was an era of explosive debate, as the Black leadership became obsessed with creating an effective strategy for gaining all of the rights promised by this newfound freedom. In particular, faced with White opposition to the reality of Black emancipation, activists struggled to determine the "appropriate" manner in which to celebrate their emancipation day. As a result, many activists made an irreversible strategic decision. They began to denounce public demonstrations of their African heritage and, instead, embraced moral improvement in hopes that they could convince American society to extend equality and citizenship to the Black community. This ideological shift created tremendous conflict among Black New Yorkers, because many people were reluctant to relinquish their cultural legacy. However, the movement away from their African heritage and toward an American identity was sealed by the rise of the colonization movement. Fearful that they would be forcibly removed from the United States, Black activists concluded that the only way to battle slavery and gain citizenship was to assert themselves as Americans.

Chapter 4 begins in 1830 and illustrates how Black leaders grappled with the reality of their "defective" freedom. Although they had recently celebrated the end of chattel slavery, their challenges were only just beginning. Discrimination, the persistence of Southern slavery, and the denial of suffrage were only a few of the problems confronting them. Black New Yorkers soon realized that "freedom" was an illusory concept that seemed impossible to grasp. Thus, chapter 4 explores the decade of the 1830s as the Black community grew frustrated with the harsh conditions of post-emancipation life and temporarily revisited the possibility of emigration. Discussions about emigration and colonization found a voice during the first Black regional gatherings, the national Colored Conventions, which consumed New York leaders' attention in the early 1830s. These meetings marked a critical turning point in Black political ideology, because delegates ultimately resolved to reject emigration and recommit themselves to a Black Nationalist program that would improve conditions for their people in the United States. In so doing, however, Black leaders quickly discovered that they had dramatically different visions of how to gain their rights in America, as the conventions dissolved into passionate arguments about racial identity and moral improvement. Following the decline of the Colored Convention movement, Black New Yorkers returned to local organizing. Therefore, the remainder of chapter 4 chronicles their early involvement in the abolitionist cause and agitation for voting rights and White New Yorkers' virulent efforts to crush Black movements.

Chapter 5 opens in 1837 to provide context for the challenge of the 1840s, a time when Black leaders were faced with a national crisis in the abolitionist movement. Having finally settled the emigration question (at least for a while), Black New Yorkers committed themselves to gaining the elusive goals of true freedom and equality. However, conflicts over strategy emerged in 1837 that fractured the abolitionist movement and prevented activists from achieving their ultimate objectives. As the biracial antislavery coalition crumbled, Black activists focused their attention on establishing a unified Black political agenda. In the early portion of the decade, leaders throughout New York State agitated to obtain unrestricted access to suffrage. By 1843, they attempted to resuscitate the Colored Convention movement and create unity among Black leaders across the North. Yet chapter 5 reveals that, despite their dedication, internal strategic debates and American society's tenacious opposition to Black equality and citizenship thwarted their efforts.

In chapter 6, the pain and disappointment of the 1850s is measured against the strength and hope of the previous decades. In spite of the Black community's impressive organization and persistent activism, the 1850s steadily undermined its intensive labor. The Fugitive Slave Act, the lack of voting rights, and the resilience of American racism devastated Black New Yorkers. Fortunately, Black leaders were finally able to deliver on the promise of the Colored Convention movement and managed to establish cohesion among Northern Black activists. Even though they continued to agitate, their strategies achieved inadequate results and Black leaders found themselves trapped in a downward spiral. Although Black New Yorkers were able to make some headway in their burgeoning desegregation movement, public opinion was resolutely unchanged on the issues of slavery and suffrage. Faced with these problems and setbacks, some influential Blacks questioned the effectiveness of their strategies and again raised the perennial question of emigration. This time, the debate ripped the Black community apart as leaders resorted to desperate and frustrated outbursts. In the end, however, most Black New Yorkers elected to remain in the United States. Determined to gain equal citizenship in the country they had labored to build, Blacks in New York City continued their nationalistic movement to gain Black freedom and the rights of full citizenship.

Chapter 7 breaks from the chronology to focus on a Black community in New York City called Seneca Village, which existed from 1825 to 1857. This bastion of Black life and activism has barely been mentioned in the historiography, yet this new research on Seneca Village could transform our understanding of New York City's Black community. Seneca Village began as a small neighborhood in upper Manhattan but, with the commitment and leadership of its residents, it quickly blossomed into a symbol of hope for the entire Black population. Seneca Village ultimately embodied a powerful racial consciousness, the community's demand for political rights, and Black leaders' growing efforts to make a permanent home for their people in the United States. Yet chapter 7 concludes with the painful and violent destruction of Seneca Village and discusses the motivations of the politicians who created Central Park on that site in an attempt to annihilate Black institutions and autonomy. In many ways, it is appropriate to end this study with the story of Seneca Village because it was a microcosm of the Black experience in New York City. Seneca Village illustrated the Black community's hopes, strivings, and commitment to activism and longevity in a country that rejected them.

As the epilogue reveals, there is a deeper and more poignant moral to this story. Although Seneca Village was decimated and American society remained stubbornly resistant to the notion of Black freedom and equality, the Black community would not be silenced. Indeed, Black New Yorkers' continuing dedication to racial advancement was a powerful testament to the spirit of a people who were committed to move "onward forever," determined to create a life for themselves and their descendants in the United States.

AFRICAN OR AMERICAN?

CHAPTER 1

"Men and Women Who Would Be Free," 1784–1810

The success in introducing native Africans to the combined slave power of European nations was the beginning of untold woes. . . . In time, New York had its quota . . . [yet] in the progress of events, a few early manifested a determination to free themselves from the iron hand of the oppressor; hence very soon there was a large class of men and women "who would be free."
—John J. Zuille, 1892

. . . may the long wished for time soon arrive when slavery of every species shall be destroyed—when despotism and oppression shall forever cease—when the Africans shall be reinstated in their former joys . . . when the bursting acclamation of approbation shall resound from the tombs of our worthy departed ancestors; and all find protection under the fostering wing of Liberty.
—Henry Sipkins, 1809

Let it be our business to demonstrate to the conviction, even of the enemies of our freedom, that sobriety, honesty and industry, are among the distinguishing traits in our characters; that we know too well the value of liberty, ever to abuse her inestimable privileges; and that although the "Ethiopian cannot change his skin," yet his heart may, nevertheless, become an habitation for all the virtues which ever adorn the human character.
—Joseph Sidney, 1809

In 1784, the African Society of New York City held its first recorded meeting; a gathering where acclaimed Black poet, Jupiter Hammon, delivered a special lecture to the Black community.[1] Hammon's speech occurred at a critical time, when voluntary manumissions had created a small free Black population facing an uncertain future in the United States.[2] Educationally, economically, and politically deprived, the free Black community was in desperate need of counsel as it attempted to make the transition from slavery to freedom. Recognizing his tremendous responsibility to offer guidance, Hammon articulated a crucial message: "[T]hose negroes who have their liberty . . . all those of you, who follow bad courses, and who do not take care to get an honest living by your labour and industry, are doing more to prevent our being free, than anybody else."[3] Published a few years later, Jupiter Hammon's plea for moral improvement slowly developed into a philosophy for racial equality: the belief that Black people could secure an elevated status in American society by convincing Whites of their humanity, morality, and worthiness. Its proponents argued that Black people would eventually gain freedom and citizenship in American society *if* they behaved according to the prevailing notions of proper conduct.

Although Hammon's theory gained strength later in the nineteenth century, his was not the only voice to speak from within New York's Black community at the dawn of emancipation. On the contrary, Black New Yorkers were not entirely convinced that strict adherence to moral codes was the sole method to fortify and empower their community. Certainly, activists understood that appealing to Whites should be a critical component of their strategy, but, since many in their community identified as "Africans" or "descendants of Africa," visions for racial progress were also connected to their identity as African people.[4] As a testament to the enduring nature of African traditions, Black New Yorkers remained rooted in their cultural legacy through burial practices, dance, and public celebrations. Thus, Black activists carefully crafted a race uplift program that blended the tactical benefits of moral improvement with the power of their deep continuing connection to their African heritage. In particular, men such as Peter Williams Jr. and William Hamilton helped build independent Black organizations based on African secret society structures and infused them with concepts of moral uplift. Yet while most Black activists drew upon their African heritage to create a sense of community solidarity, the notion of moral improvement gradually increased in popularity. In fact, by 1809, a few leaders began to exclusively endorse moral uplift as the best path to racial advancement. As a result, the early national era witnessed the development of a continuum of Black political thought, ranging from moral uplift to celebrations of African heritage; a philosophical divide that ultimately formed the foundation of Black political debates throughout the nineteenth century.

* * *

Although the free Black population was still small in 1784, Black political strategies, culture, and community became increasingly important as the events of the late 1790s profoundly altered the face of freedom in New York State.[5] The turn of the century was a critical time for Black New Yorkers as the issue of emancipation burst onto the political scene. Enslaved people revealed the immorality of slavery and sparked the Northern antislavery movement by seeking their legal rights through the courts and becoming fugitives. The combined efforts of runaways and Black patriots to the American cause during the Revolutionary War inspired White reformers for, as enslaved Africans articulated their human rights and demanded freedom, government officials were forced to recognize the contradiction between revolutionary ideology and the practice of holding human beings in bondage.[6] Thus, White politicians and religious leaders across the North slowly brought abolition to the forefront of public discourse; by the end of the century, the problem of slavery could no longer be ignored.[7]

While antislavery thought took root in other parts of the North, however, the New York State Legislature was painfully slow in its response. In fact, in 1785, New York politicians defeated a measure that would have granted freedom to every Black person born "since the declaration of the independence of this State, and . . . all that may hereafter be born within the State."[8] As a result, it was not until 1799 that political reformers finally forced the issue of abolition and attained a limited victory with the passage of a Gradual Emancipation Act. The new law stated that children born after July 4, 1799, were free, but owed service to their owners until the age of twenty-five (for females) or twenty-eight (for males). Although this statute weakened slavery, it obviously did not abolish the system entirely. All enslaved Africans born before July 1799 were still consigned to a life of bondage, and even those born after 1799 toiled much of their productive years under a form of indentured servitude.[9]

This system of "freedom by degrees" was established to ensure that slaveholders would not suffer from the immediate loss of labor.[10] As historian Vivienne Kruger argued, "slavery was to be phased out in a way that would preserve the rights of property owners; current slaves would remain enslaved for life so that no slaveholder would lose his investment." In fact, the emancipation act rewarded slaveholders so extensively that the state gave them money to support enslaved children who were not old enough to work. As Arthur Zilversmit observed, New York state's programs were actually "thinly disguised schemes for compensated abolition."[11] Thus, the Gradual Emancipation Act was illusory in many respects because it did not actually "free" anyone; rather, the law protected individual property rights more than the right of humans to liberty. Although this new legislation promised freedom, actual liberation was a long time coming.

Despite the limitations of the Gradual Emancipation Act, there were some positive effects. Although Black people were still required to work under a cruel and unrelenting system of servitude, this law broke the cycle of inherited slave status. No longer were Black New Yorkers "born slaves," nor would parents pass down the horror of chattel slavery to their children. Changes for Black people were particularly striking in the city, where the need for slavery was already in rapid decline. Whether prompted by moral crisis or declining economic necessity, slaveholders in New York City began to manumit Black people before the required time. As a result, between 1800 and 1810, the free Black population skyrocketed to over 7,000 and slavery went into severe decline.[12]

The birth of emancipation was initially a cause for celebration among Black New Yorkers; however, they soon discovered that poverty, discrimination, and political inequality were overwhelming obstacles blocking their path to true freedom.[13] As these newly freed people faced this myriad of problems, they began to question what emancipation would truly mean for themselves and future generations. In response, a small cadre of Black leaders began to emerge, composed primarily of men such as Peter Williams Sr., John Teasman, and William Hamilton, who had the economic ability and political standing to address the problems of their community.[14] Yet because these early leaders were faced with the daunting task of easing the transition from slavery to emancipation, they struggled to identify a strategy that would unify and empower their community. Although Jupiter Hammon's moral uplift philosophy seemed to offer some hope for equality, Black activists were slow to embrace his program because it ignored the deep and abiding connection to their African heritage that influenced every facet of Black life during the early national era.

In New York City, there was a powerful legacy of African cultural traditions that manifested in a variety of ways including burial rites, ritual space, and public celebrations. Perhaps the most obvious examples were revealed to scholars in 1991, when an excavation inadvertently uncovered the African Burial Ground in lower Manhattan that had been in use from the 1650s until 1795. The "rediscovery" of this site exposed enduring cultural values that Black New Yorkers carried from their motherland, particularly the persistence of African spiritual beliefs in burial rituals. The fact that Blacks in the Americas observed traditional funerary practices is especially significant because it suggests that they remained linked to African cosmological interpretations of life and death. Burials and funerals were profoundly important because, according to many West African cultures, death is merely another phase in the life cycle. As Robert Farris Thompson explained, "the cemetery is not a final resting-place . . . but a door between two worlds, a 'threshold' marking the line between the two worlds, of the living and the dead." Tombs, therefore, represented a home for the continuation of the spirit.[15]

Researchers' findings supported the existence of African influence in New York City and alluded to the prevalence of an African worldview among Blacks, after they identified various artifacts in the burial sites. Scholars later reported, for example, that over 200 shells were recovered during the excavation. The director of the African Burial Ground Project, Michael Blakey, stated that items such as waist beads and cowrie shells placed in the coffins "were symbols of the passage in death across the sea and have been variously interpreted as a return to Africa or afterlife."[16] Robert Farris Thompson articulated this belief in more detail, arguing that in West African societies, shells operated as vessels to "enclose the soul's immortal presence." Once in the Americas, people of African descent expanded this notion into a distinct philosophy representing a return to Africa. As the African Burial Ground historian explained, "the shells stand for the sea. The sea brought us, the sea shall take us back. So the shells upon our graves stand for water, the means of glory and the land of demise."[17]

Perhaps the most compelling proof for the continuation of an African cosmology came when excavators exposed a grave with "brass tacks hammered into the coffin lid in an elaborate heart-shaped pattern." Although hearts were not uncommon icons in gravesites, African Burial Ground archaeologists believe that this unusually intricate pattern likely "had meanings for the mourners that were other than or in addition to those Europeans would have attributed to it." This symbol, scholars concluded, was either a West African representation of the soul or, more likely, the Akan symbol *Sankofa*. Sankofa's literal meaning is "go back and fetch it," but more specifically suggests that looking to the past will inform the future. In death, Black New Yorkers remembered that their African past was vitally important. Not just for the spirits of the deceased, but also for the living.[18]

Beyond cultural symbols, the method of burial was also worthy of note. Michael Blakey revealed that the bodies were "wrapped in linen shrouds with care and methodically positioned in well-built cedar or pine coffins." Likewise, the African Burial Ground's archaeology report indicated that "cloths for shrouds or winding sheets may have been considered, along with the coffin, a *sine qua non* for proper burial."[19] The Black community's use of shrouds was particularly telling because, although shrouding was common among Whites in England and the Americas, it also had strong roots in many parts of West Africa including Senegambia, Sierre Leone, Liberia, the Niger-Delta region, the Bight of Benin, and the Gold Coast.[20]

Equally revealing were observations by European contemporaries, who routinely monitored Black New Yorkers' use of the African Burial Ground. British colonists were well aware of the power and influence burial traditions held among African peoples and noted with interest the continuation of African funeral practices in New York City. Albeit with strong racial bias, Reverend John Sharpe described, in 1713, the "heathen rites" that were "performed at the grave by their countrymen."[21] Even as late as 1847, David Valentine recalled the African Burial Ground as a "desolate, unappropriated spot" where the Black community had retained its "native superstitions and burial customs, among which was that of burying by night, with various mummeries and outcries."[22]

Yet their fascination soon turned to fear, as British authorities became alerted to the fact that the African Burial Ground symbolically represented another resilient aspect of African cultural influence: the importance of ritual community space. Indeed, this site was important culturally, spiritually, and politically, because it was the one place where enslaved people could simultaneously perform traditional ceremonies and plot rebellions. Most notably, British officials concluded that enslaved Africans used the burial ground to plan an uprising that they carried out in 1712. By October 1722, the city council had apparently become so frightened about the potential connection between African cultural activities and resistance movements that it passed a series of laws restricting the ability of enslaved people to bury their ancestors according to African methods. Specifically, it banned night burials and large community gatherings in the African Burial Ground.[23] Worse, it tried to transform the site of resistance into one of horror. After another attempted uprising in 1741, city authorities elected to erect gallows adjacent to the African Burial Ground where they executed thirty accused conspirators. Thus, according to scholars Joyce Hansen and Gary McGowan, as Black New Yorkers "went about their daily business they lived with the constant reminders of those terror-filled days: The gallows on the Commons, the crowds of people witnessing the executions, and the screams of the condemned men as the fire consumed them, became a permanent part of their world—an indelible memory." For Black New Yorkers who visited the African Burial Ground after 1741, they were likely haunted by memories of the rebellions and the punishment enacted upon their brethren.[24]

Yet despite the ghastly events of 1741, it seems that the African Burial Ground retained its importance as ritual space for African cultural expressions. Indeed, it may even have been the site for Black community celebrations. If James Fenimore Cooper's description was accurate, a Pinkster festival was held on the Commons near the African Burial Ground in 1757.[25] As a few scholars, most notably Sterling Stuckey, have indicated, Pinkster was a critically important annual event because it contained strong African cultural elements. Although Pinkster had Dutch origins, Africans quickly seized the opportunity to infuse the celebration with rituals and cultural forms from their native land.[26] For example, James Fenimore Cooper claimed that a Pinkster festival was different from other public commemorations because its features were of "African origin." Even though he conceded that most Black New Yorkers were not African-born, Cooper argued, "the traditions and usages of their original country were so far preserved as to produce a marked difference between this festival and one of European origin." He further suggested that the "native Africans" were active in keeping traditional cultural practices alive for American-born Blacks. In particular, Cooper described Pinkster as being alive with music and dance that was "said to be a usage of their African progenitors." The power of ritual celebration in view of their ancestral burial site could not have been lost on the participants. Most importantly, as Terrence Epperson noted, "it indicates that the Burial Ground was used by New Yorkers of African descent for rituals other than burials."[27]

Despite the significance of the African Burial Ground, it was not the only location where free Blacks expressed their African heritage; in fact, Black New Yorkers routinely flaunted their cultural legacy through music and dance. Because Pinkster celebrations were not common in New York City by the 1790s, city marketplaces became ideal locations for both enslaved and free Black people to commune with each other and revisit traditional African dance forms. In Bear Market, established in 1771, and Catharine Market, built in 1786, folks from New Jersey, Long Island, and New York City gathered to socialize and "engage in a breakdown." Among the most famous dancers in regular attendance were a fellow named Francis (who apparently went by the name "Ned"), Bob Rowley ("Bobolink Bob"), and Jack.[28] The importance of African dance in New York City cannot be overestimated for, as many scholars have argued, dance was "the most durable of all cultural forms" brought from Africa to the Americas.[29] Dancing, therefore, was not simply sport or entertainment for Black New Yorkers; it was also a physical manifestation of their African heritage.

A close examination of marketplace dancing provides insight into the African cultural forms that were present. It appears that there was a considerable amount of improvisation in their performances, a key element that dance experts identify as a critical African retention that allows "freedom for individual expression."[30] In addition, one contemporary observer revealed that "their music or time was usually given by one of their party, which was done by beating their hands on the sides of their legs and the noise of the heel." This, again, was a distinctly African behavior that was used among people of African descent throughout the Americas. Such rhythmic activity, often known as patting Juba, was designed to substitute for a drum and "started as any kind of clapping with any dance to encourage another dancer." Even more, marketplace dancing in New York apparently became quite competitive and eventually involved Black dancers from New Jersey, Long Island, and Manhattan vying with each other for top honors. This practice also suggests an African root, as Eileen Southern and Josephine Wright argued that juba dancing in the United States was born out of the African *djouba,* which is a "competitive dance of skill."[31] Significantly, there were also African elements reflected in the dancers' physical appearance. The New Jersey dancers were known for "their suppleness and plaited forelocks tied up with tea-lead. The Long Islanders usually tied theirs up in a cue, with dried eel-skin."[32] As Sterling Stuckey revealed, these hairstyles represented a "centuries-old tradition in West Africa."[33]

In light of the continuing power of African culture in early national New York City, it is not surprising that Black leaders chose to instill political life with African traditions. Drawing upon the custom in many West African communities, Black New Yorkers organized themselves around secret societies. As scholars Carter G. Woodson and Michael Gomez revealed, the development of Black organizations was, itself, a manifestation of African culture because it reflected the transplantation of African secret societies into the New World context. Historian Carter G. Woodson argued that traditional African secret societies constituted the foundation of social and political structures and were maintained in the Americas in slightly modified styles: "The emphasis placed by the Negroes on secret societies in Africa has survived [in the United States] . . . to provide for the community certain facilities for social outlet which could not be otherwise afforded." Even though these organizations were not allowed to exist in the Americas in their original form, Woodson maintained that they conformed so closely to African configurations that Black associations "serve the Negroes in a way different from the manner in which similar organizations function among whites."[34]

Michael Gomez and Margaret Washington Creel expanded on this argument by further investigating the relationships between African secret societies and Black organizations. Like Woodson, Gomez observed that West African secret societies influenced specific Black associations, such as the Prince Hall Masonic order, concluding that Black freemasonry "is an institution derived from West Africa, and specifically Sierre Leonian, origins." Similarly, Washington Creel documented secret societies' influence on the Gullah of South Carolina, noting that "adaptive concepts of community (and aspects of spirituality) inherited from secret societies fused with Gullah interpretations of Christianity, becoming part of folk religion in the slave quarters." She further argued that the influence of secret societies infused Gullah spirituality with "a cultural and community building force and a means of instilling individual worth among bondspeople."[35]

In early national New York City, as in South Carolina, the tradition of African secret societies fostered a deep commitment to community building as a race uplift strategy. In particular, the Black leadership believed that the creation of autonomous Black political organizations and institutions could improve conditions for their people and establish a unified community ethic. As activist William Hamilton explained in 1809, racial advancement "depends much on our being united in social bodies."[36] He was apparently not alone in this conviction because, from their inceptions, Black organizations in New York City were part of a regional phenomenon. Across the North, emancipated Blacks created institutions and a community base as a way to combat the uncertainty of unequal freedom.[37] Although free Blacks in Rhode Island were the first to create an African Society, Black New Yorkers soon established similar associations to address the specific needs of their community.[38]

In fact, the most active and influential Black organization in New York City began a rich tradition of social and political activism when some committed Black men formed their own African Society. Following the tradition of societies in West Africa, most free Black organizations were shrouded in mystery and, as a result, little is known about their early activities. In the case of the African Society in New York City, even the official date of its formation is unknown. Although the African Society was obviously established by 1784, when members invited Jupiter Hammon to speak before the community, it may have been active even earlier. During enslavement, African Society members would have relied on community networks and covert gatherings to protect their organization. Secrecy within enslaved communities was central to their survival, an ethic they carried into emancipation. One later member, Walter K. Beekman, supported this fact in 1946: "How many secret meetings and conferences were held, the place and time of these meetings are questions that cannot be answered . . . for it must be remembered that there were positive restrictions against meeting in large numbers, and even in religious matters they were subjected to the spy system."[39] Apparently Black activists defied the official sanctions against public gatherings and met clandestinely, determined to work collectively to achieve their goals.

In its early years, the African Society illustrated its dedication to culture and community by focusing on one of the immediate concerns among its people: the acquisition and protection of burial ground. Beyond the cultural significance of Black funerary practices, the struggle over burial ground reflected the Black community's most basic human need, a need that was routinely ignored and disrespected. Even before the official formation of the African Society, burial rights had been an issue for Black New Yorkers. In 1788, it was discovered that medical students had been raiding cemeteries to acquire dead bodies for dissection and research. According to the *Daily Advertiser*, most Blacks were not "permitted to remain in the grave," instead, their remains were seized for medical experiments and then disposed "along the docks sewn up in bags."[40]

In response, members of the Black community submitted their grievances in the form of a petition that pleaded with the Common Council to intervene and stop the desecration of their burial sites. As they lamented,

> it hath lately been the constant practice of a number of young gentlemen in this City who call themselves Students of Physick [*sic*], to repair to the Burial Ground assigned for the use of your petitioners, and under the cover of the Night, and in the most wanton Sallies of Excess, to dig up the Bodies of the deceased friends and relatives of your Petitioners, carry them away, and without respect to Age or Sex, mangle their flesh out of a wanton Curiosity and then expose it to Beasts and Birds.

It is not clear whether the Common Council took any particular action regarding the Black community's complaint, because it was quickly overshadowed by a violent riot unleashed by White New Yorkers. When it was revealed that the medical students "had not only taken up the bodies of blacks and strangers, but those of some respectable persons," the White "respectable" citizens took to the streets and raged for three days until the militia successfully quelled the uprising. Because the White riot consumed the Common Council's attention, the Black New Yorkers' petition was likely ignored. Yet their commitment to the issue of burial rights persisted.[41]

In 1795, the African Society became involved in the fight for burial rights after the city terminated the use of the African Burial Ground. Initially, members tried to find their own solution and struggled to raise funds within the community to purchase land for a new burial site. However, poverty among newly freed people prevented them from procuring enough money to finance their efforts and they resorted again to petitioning, appealing to city officials to provide land on which to properly bury their ancestors. According to the minutes of the Common Council, they called themselves "free people of color" and had "lately associated under the name of the African Society for the laudable purposes of improving their morals, by promoting a spirit of brotherly Love and a strict Regard to the Laws of the State and also with Intent to procure a place for the erection of a Building for divine worship and the Interment of people of Colour." Six of the petitioners signed their names to the document, thus the Common Council considered Isaac Fortune, William Hutson, Abraham Dickenson, John Hall, James Parker, and Peter Francis to be the organization's leaders.[42]

The African Society's decision to use petitioning as a form of political agitation was deeply significant. Not only did this approach win the Common Council's approval, but it also reveals a great deal about the nature of Black activism during the early national era.[43] Petitioning was a strategy Black people throughout the North had used since the colonial period as a way to articulate political discontent.[44] The power of such an appeal lay in its ability to challenge the notion that Blacks were subhuman, by demonstrating their intellect and organizational skills, and in its powerful demand for equal rights, by entering their protest into the permanent record. In this case, the African Society's petition to the Common Council served multiple specific purposes. First, it asserted the petitioners' humanity and drew attention to their human and cultural need for proper burial of the ancestors; it demanded respect for Black people in death, if not in life. The document also forced the Common Council to recognize their benevolent community building efforts and consider the possibility that Black people could be contributing members to society. Finally, it suggested that the city should be responsible for providing restitution to the Black community.

Yet what is perhaps most important about the African Society's plea is what it tells us about Black political activism specifically in New York City. The petition's language exposed the Black leadership's changing ideology and the challenges activists faced as they struggled to gain justice and equality for their people.[45] In particular, it revealed that the African Society was beginning to strategically embrace aspects of moral uplift philosophy. Perhaps recognizing the efficacy of Jupiter Hammon's doctrine, the African Society members hoped to convince the Common Council that Black people could be worthy citizens; their words articulated a message of love, morality, and religious improvement and highlighted their desire to comply with the laws of the state. Yet the petition also contained powerful demonstrations of Black autonomy. Most notably, they stated that they wanted their own house of worship, separate from Whites, and affirmed their intent to associate and purchase property. Ultimately, however, for all their assertions of independence, African Society members still revealed their tenuous financial position by humbly requesting assistance from the city to acquire a burial ground for their community. In the final analysis, the African Society's petition exposed the complex position of free Blacks in early national New York. Although they yearned to be fully independent, economic and political constraints forced them to use a moral appeal to gain equal treatment.

Indeed, the African Society's perspectives embodied the Black leadership's political activism for the next two decades. Although economically disadvantaged, Black New Yorkers' desire for racial autonomy and equal justice continued to flourish and influenced many other areas of Black life including religious worship. In 1796, Black Methodists, including William Hamilton, Peter Williams Sr., William Miller, and James Varick, split from the White Methodists and established the African Methodist Church.[46] Frustrated by the "prejudice of caste [which] began to engender negro proscription," these church members demanded control over their religious lives and created their own institution. Although this move took place in the religious sphere, it was also deeply political. The division was not the result of doctrinal discord; rather, it was racism that ultimately drove Blacks out of the John St. Methodist Church. As scholar William Walls explained, "the growing conditions of slavery, humiliation, and persecution inspired a few . . . to move forward." Refusing to submit to continual racial indignities, Black Methodists protested against racial discrimination and asserted their freedom.[47]

For Black Methodists, independence meant the establishment of a self-sufficient institution. Their beginnings were humble, but entirely of their own creation. For several years, they held meetings in a house on Cross Street until they were able to purchase their own building. The new location had originally been a workshop for member William Miller's carpentry business, but the congregation converted the space into a religious home by building seats, a pulpit, and a gallery. Over the next few years, Abraham Thompson, June Scott, Thomas Miller, and William Miller held regular preaching and exhorting meetings, which were apparently quite successful because they quickly outgrew the original site. They eventually managed to raise enough money to buy a sizable plot of land on the corner of Church and Leonard streets, where they erected a new edifice to accommodate their congregation. In September 1800, Peter Williams Sr. laid the cornerstone for the first church built exclusively for the Black community in New York.[48] Shortly thereafter, on February 16, 1801, the state of New York officially recognized the African Methodists as an incorporated organization.[49]

In addition to economic and organizational independence, there were specific indications of Black Methodists' commitment to racial self-determination. Their articles of incorporation clearly stated that only "Africans or their descendants" could officially join the membership or be elected as church trustees. Likewise, they decided the church building was forever to be the property of "our African brethren and the descendants of the African race." These stipulations demonstrated the ways in which their identity as Africans served as a unifying force that fortified the institution. Beyond their official regulations, the African Methodists' boldness was critically important to this fledgling emancipated community because the congregation's actions inspired other Black religious denominations to establish their own independent organizations. Following the African Methodists, both the Episcopalians and the Baptists split from their White counterparts in

Peter Williams Sr. (Courtesy of the Emmet Collection; Miriam and
Ira D. Wallach Division of Art, Prints and Photographs; New York
Public Library; Astor, Lenox, and Tilden Foundations.)

1809. These groups also began modestly; neither had an adequate meetinghouse
and they were forced to wait several years before they obtained a legitimate church
and minister. Yet both institutions eventually became highly influential in the
Black community.[50]

Significantly, activists throughout the city were inspired by the African Society
and the African Methodists' courageous movement to establish autonomous Black
institutions. Most striking during this era was the rise of activism among women.
At first, Black women found avenues to make benevolent contributions through
participation in the churches. However, in 1802, they sought independence and
formed their own mutual relief society, the Female African Benevolent Association (FABA), which boasted over two hundred members.[51] Like the African
Society, this early self-help female organization reflected the signs of collectiv-

ity and race uplift through benevolence and institution building. Little else is known about FABA because, despite its impressive beginnings, the society soon fell victim to an insidious enemy that plagued most Black organizations during this era, namely, poverty. As the economic struggles among the African Society and the religious denominations attest, financial distress routinely prevented organizations from achieving the independence they desired. As Black activist William Hamilton noted in 1809, many early Black associations "perished and dwindled away" due to paltry resources in the Black community.[52] Without the time and resources necessary to cultivate lasting institutions, many mutual aid societies during this period did not survive; FABA was one of these ill-fated societies, destined to fold quickly.

Beyond benevolent associations, poverty also stymied the Black community's ability to gain full autonomy in the area of education. For newly emancipated Blacks, illiteracy was a lingering symbol of their enslavement and, thus, many activists believed that education offered a crucial path toward race uplift and equal opportunity. Although Black leaders believed that education would alleviate the substandard conditions under which their people labored, they found themselves with limited resources and initially had to rely upon benevolent Whites to provide institutional access to education. For this assistance, they turned to the New York Manumission Society (NYMS). Originally formed in 1785, the NYMS was composed of White politicians and merchants, such as John Jay, Rufus King, and Alexander Hamilton, who supported the goals of Black moral improvement, education, and gradual abolition. By 1787, the NYMS demonstrated its commitment to Black education by creating the first African Free School.[53]

Although the Black leadership was grateful for the educational opportunity the NYMS provided, they were also deeply troubled by the organization's policies. As many scholars have noted, despite its beneficial activities, the NYMS's strategies and motives were rather suspect.[54] Many of its members continued to hold slaves, and its public statements were often dominated by paternalistic rhetoric. In one of its early reports, the Manumission Society stated that they needed to "keep a watchful eye over the conduct of such Negroes as have been or may be liberated . . . to prevent them from running into immorality or sinking into idleness." Even their desire to create a school was connected to their belief that, through moral instruction, Blacks might be "kept from vicious courses and [become] qualified for usefulness in life." These sentiments reflected the Manumission Society's fear that, without their intervention, Black people would inevitably slip into crime and vice.[55] In the face of such opinions, Black activists became more determined to gain control over the educational system.

Black leaders began pressuring the NYMS to promote Black self-reliance and managed to win a minor victory; by 1799, Black activist John Teasman was elevated to the position of principal.[56] Although the Manumission Society paid him less than half the salary they gave his White predecessor, Teasman transformed the education of Black children in New York City and increased attendance by 30 percent in less than two years. Likewise, Teasman sought to further strengthen the Black community by educating adults in an African Evening School. As a testament to his belief in community building, Teasman introduced the Lancasterian method: an alternative system of education that encouraged older students to assist in instructing younger ones. This program reduced cost, reached more children, and, most importantly, taught these developing young Black students to work collectively.[57]

Despite Teasman's dedication, however, some Black activists were still not satisfied with the NYMS or the African Free School and thought that they should have complete control over their community's education. By 1803, Black leaders established three independent Black schools, two of which operated out of the African Zion Church. Little is known about these early schools; however, it is clear that these educational institutions, funded and operated by Black people, were part of the Black leadership's movement to control their own destiny. Yet education was a luxury that most Black families could not afford, and, like many Black organizations, these schools failed due to insufficient funds. Regardless of their financial struggles, however, Black activists were not discouraged, and other independent Black schools emerged throughout the nineteenth century.[58] Moreover, even in spite of their failure, the creation of Black institutions, such as FABA and Black independent schools, were crucial to Black New Yorkers' political development and reflected their commitment to autonomy and self-determination.

Fortunately for Black New Yorkers, there was an association that possessed the endurance that eluded other Black organizations. Just six months after the abolition of the slave trade, some original members of the African Society joined with other Black leaders to reform the organization. On June 6, 1808, nearly one hundred Black men gathered in the African schoolhouse on Rose Street to redesign the most prominent autonomous Black organization in New York City. Among the charter members were Peter Williams Jr., John Teasman, William Hamilton, Henry Sipkins, and Epiphany Davis. Their purpose, as they declared it, was to unite in an organization to combat the racism and oppression that plagued their lives and provide mutual aid and support to each other as necessary. In its early years, the African Society could only afford to give financial assistance to its own members. However, as the organization gained strength, members stressed a community ethic and became the most outspoken advocates for Black social and political rights in New York City.[59]

From the beginning, the African Society's founding members identified slavery and racism as the roots of their plight and declared their determination to break free from oppression. They decried the horrors that Europeans inflicted on Africans and Native Americans, remarking on the evils of the African slave trade and the process of enslavement. Yet they also espoused an enduring optimism; their organization's historical retrospective concluded with an inspiring image of Blacks who refused to succumb to oppression: "a few early manifested a determination to free themselves from the iron hand of the oppressor; hence very soon there was a large class of men and women 'who would be free.'" Indeed, the African Society was independent, self-sustaining, and functioned according to its own agenda. They institutionalized themselves and their intentions by passing a constitution, electing officers, and dubbing themselves the New York African Society for Mutual Relief. Still drawing upon the model of African secret societies, members at initiation were required to sign the organizational constitution and pledge to protect the secrets of the society.[60]

Yet even though they espoused racial pride and used African social arrangements, the African Society developed a complex political philosophy. As evidenced by their 1795 petition to the Common Council, the African Society sought to blend their belief in Black autonomy with a strategic appeal for moral uplift. Though they never abandoned the secret society structure or their passion for racial unity, African Society members established strict membership regulations that echoed Jupiter Hammon's advice. Emphasizing proper moral conduct as the key to racial progress, aspiring members had to apply in writing and have a current member vouch for their character. Such a rule, of course, demanded that applicants be literate, a requirement that many Black people could not meet. In addition, there was a substantial cost for joining the organization; the initiation fee was $100, with monthly dues of 25 cents. Obviously, in the early national era, these fees were considered quite high particularly for newly emancipated Blacks. More revealing, however, was an explicit section of the organization's constitution regarding moral conduct. Any member who drank, gambled, or engaged prostitutes would be expelled and forced to surrender his membership rights.[61]

Although these rules may have reflected elitism, they also revealed the leadership's urgent need for financial resources and an educated skilled membership base to sustain the organization. As the failure of other associations during this period demonstrated, Black societies needed to remain economically viable to survive. Certainly the African Society's policies seemed exclusionary, but they may have been necessary during the early tenuous years. It is significant to note that once the organization became more secure, the African Society reconsidered some of its earlier policies in an effort to reach more segments of the Black community; by 1838, they no longer required applicants to express their interest in writing and initiation fees were reduced to only $3. Yet their insistence on proper moral conduct remained firmly in place, which reflected the African Society's growing belief that moral improvement would transform the Black community and prove that Black men were worthy of American citizenship.[62]

Although their regulations may have deterred some Black folks from seeking membership, the African Society was extremely beneficial to New York City's Black activists.[63] Just as the African Methodists prompted the establishment of other Black denominations, the African Society inspired the creation of associa-

THE

CONSTITUTION

OF THE

NEW-YORK AFRICAN SOCIETY,

FOR

MUTUAL RELIEF.

What then am I who sorrow for myself?
In age, in infancy, from others aid
Is all our hope; to teach us to be kind,
That, Nature's first last lesson to mankind;
The selfish heart deserves the pain it feels.

Young's Night Thoughts.

PASSED JUNE 6, 1808.

New-York:

PRINTED FOR THE SOCIETY.

1808.

New York African Society for Mutual Relief Constitution. (Courtesy of the Collection of the New York Historical Society, Negative no. 77637d.)

tions such as the Wilberforce Philanthropic Society, which was active by 1809, as well as the Brooklyn African Woolman Benevolent Society founded in 1810. As Craig Wilder noted, the African Society was particularly influential in the formation of the Brooklyn association; the Brooklynites borrowed heavily from the African Society's constitution when drafting their own and likewise stressed mutual aid and moral improvement.[64]

More significantly, in spite of the African Society's increasing support of moral uplift, their influence was powerful and omnipresent in New York City's Black community. The success of the African Society and other Black organizations was likely sustained by their open expressions of African culture, which united the Black community despite their ideological and strategic differences. Although many working-class Blacks did not officially join associations like the African Society, they supported the activities that celebrated their African heritage. Perhaps aware of the power of African cultural expressions, Black societies highlighted their shared African identity as a way to unite the community. Not only did Black activists celebrate their cultural legacy by using traditional secret society structures, they also honored their motherland in many other ways including naming practices and community celebrations. Naming, in particular, represented the importance of a collective identity. Black leaders often chose to use the term "African" in their organizational names as has been demonstrated by the African Society, the Female African Benevolent Association, and the African Methodist Episcopal Church.[65] The Baptists and the Episcopalians also selected names that demonstrated their racial pride. The Episcopalians named their church after St. Philip because he was the first priest to convert African people, and the Baptists called themselves the Abyssinian Church to denote their African heritage. These demonstrations of African pride appealed to all free Blacks and helped solidify a common identity.[66]

Beyond the power of naming, community celebrations remained the most compelling demonstration of the leadership's efforts to draw upon their mutual African heritage to build a strong community. Beginning in 1808, activists ushered in a new form of public celebration that provided the opportunity for Black New Yorkers to mingle, socialize, consider their political condition, and reflect on their continuing connection to Africa. Because January 1, 1808 marked the official end of the international slave trade, the Black community routinely gathered between 1808 and 1815 to commemorate the end of the horrific trade in humans. As we shall see, these events created a sense of cohesion among New York City's Black residents because they proudly displayed African culture through music, dance, and parading.

Yet even though these public gatherings were designed to unite the community, the speeches delivered to commemorate the occasion revealed a growing ideological divide within the leadership. As Black activists struggled to identify the most effective race uplift strategy, some leaders began to question their attachment to their African past and wondered if they could reconcile it with growing appeals for moral improvement. As a result, a range of opinions began to emerge: would they choose moral uplift, their African heritage, or attempt to combine the two? The events of 1808 and 1809 are worthy of particular scrutiny because they reflect the Black leadership's struggle to merge multiple, and sometimes contradictory, political agendas.

The highlight of the 1808 festivities was Peter Williams Jr.'s address, which galvanized the Black community by celebrating the African homeland.[67] Williams's speech was carefully constructed and demonstrated his ability to combine notions of African pride and racial unity with moral uplift and personal responsibility. He opened by passionately regaling his audience with stories of precolonial Africa, the days before Europeans arrived on the shores of western Africa. He reminded his community that they shared a connection to Africa's glorious past and reminisced about how their ancestors lived peacefully prior to European contact. He spoke passionately about the arts, the emotions, and the spirit of community that had "rendered them a happy people." Yet, as Williams noted, the entrance of Europeans forever altered Africa and "the demon of indescribable misery has rioted, uncontrolled, on the fair fields of our ancestors."[68]

For Williams, however, reflecting on the past was not just about celebrating their heritage. He also thought that enslavement and the Middle Passage held important lessons for Black people. Williams eloquently bemoaned the destruction of Mother Africa and painted a painful illustration of the Middle Passage:

> Let your imagination carry you back to former days. Behold a vessel bearing our forefathers and brethren from the place of their nativity to a distant and inhospitable clime; behold their dejected countenances; their streaming eyes; their fettered limbs; hear them, with piercing cries, and pitiful moans, deploring their wretched fate. After their arrival in port, see them separated without regard to the ties of blood or friendship: husband from wife; parent from child; brother from sister; friend from friend. See the parting tear, rolling down their fallen cheeks: hear the parting sigh, die on their quivering lips.

Through his emotional re-creation of the Middle Passage, Williams made a crucial point about the need for racial solidarity. By focusing on the suffering of families and loved ones, he demonstrated how slavery had attacked the very essence of community. In addition, although Williams mostly blamed European greed for the slave trade, he cleverly balanced this picture with a reminder of the Black community's awesome responsibilities as children of Africa. He made a wrenching plea for unity, noting that dissension among African people had helped create their current plight. Williams indicted African traders for falling victim to the "bewitching and alluring wiles of the seducer" who promised "gaudy trifles" in exchange for human cargo. Due to an unholy alliance between Europeans and African traders, Williams lamented, Africa had become a shell of its former self.

He maintained hope, however, and believed that the solution to the plight of their homeland and the African diaspora was racial unity.[69]

Repeatedly referring to his people as "Africans" or "descendants of Africa," the theme of community solidarity dominated Williams's speech. Yet for Williams, true liberation required not just racial solidarity but also morality. Weaving in a political message about moral improvement, he warned his people that they must demonstrate their gratitude by proper conduct. Although this notion was somewhat reminiscent of Jupiter Hammon's perspective, Williams took a different approach and linked morality with their African heritage. He encouraged Black folks to live moral lives not just for themselves and their benefactors, but also to please their ancestors.

> Let us, therefore, by a steady and upright deportment, by a strict obedience and respect to the laws of the land, form an invulnerable bulwark against the shafts of malice. Thus, evincing to the world that our garments are unpolluted by the stains of ingratitude, we shall reap increasing advantages from the favors conferred; the spirits of our departed ancestors shall smile with complacency on the change of our state; and posterity shall exult in the pleasing remembrance.

Drawing a critical connection between morality and African spiritual beliefs, Williams hoped his audience would be inspired to accept moral uplift if they thought it would honor their African ancestors.[70]

This message was particularly significant because it demonstrated that, although Williams obviously saw the strategic value of moral improvement, he clearly remained grounded in African cultural values. In fact, his speech demonstrated an ongoing connection to Africa in two fundamental ways. First, his desire to please the ancestors reflected the West African belief that the ancestors continued to monitor the living even after they had crossed into the spirit world. In addition, Williams's closing remark evinced an early form of Pan-Africanism by recognizing that the destiny of all African people was interconnected. Brilliantly linking African redemption with the project of race uplift, Williams exclaimed, "may the time speedily commence, when Ethiopia shall stretch forth her hands; when the sun of liberty shall beam resplendent on the whole African race; and . . . promote the luxuriant growth of knowledge and virtue."[71] Ultimately, Williams's plan for the future blended morality and African heritage to create a vision of unity and empowerment for Africans throughout the Diaspora.

The following year, Black New Yorkers again commemorated the anniversary of the abolition of the slave trade. However, despite Peter Williams Jr.'s warning against disunity, they held three distinct celebrations. While William Hamilton spoke before the African Society, the African Zion Church selected Henry Sipkins as their orator, and Joseph Sidney addressed the Wilberforce Philanthropic Association. There has been some debate among scholars over the reasons why there were multiple celebrations in 1809. Leslie Harris argued that the division

was caused by political party affiliation, noting that Joseph Sidney was an ardent
supporter of the Federalist Party, and Mitch Kachun has suggested that the fight
was over the practice of parading.[72] Although parading and political affiliation
may have been factors, there were also tangible philosophical distinctions between
the leaders who spoke for the 1809 celebrations that were based on issues of African identity and moral improvement. The speeches delivered on that day gave
a hint of the growing ideological divide within the Black leadership, as William
Hamilton and Joseph Sidney presented radically different solutions to the plight
of their people.

When esteemed elder William Hamilton appeared before the African Society
in 1809, he delivered a bold message that ignored moral uplift and championed
early notions of Pan-Africanism and Black Nationalism.[73] For Hamilton, identity
was the critical issue and, like Peter Williams Jr., Hamilton argued for unity among
all African people regardless of their geographic location. He urged his people to
view themselves as Africans and encouraged them to embrace the term *African*
because "it makes no kind of difference whether the man is born in Africa, Asia,
Europe, or America, so long as he is proginized [*sic*] from African parents." Even
though Hamilton hoped their shared identity and heritage could unify African
people throughout the Diaspora, he also had a local vision for Black unity in the
United States. In particular, Hamilton used the African Society as a model to
illustrate how institution building could strengthen their community and provide hope for the future. He commended the African Society for its cohesion, its
dedication to race uplift, and the amelioration of poverty. Without community,
Hamilton argued, life is miserable and advancement is nearly impossible; however, with societies, Blacks have the potential to become joyful and prosperous.
For Hamilton, racial unity was the key to power, and he hoped that Black people
would use their common identity and heritage as a foundation for collective
political action.[74]

While William Hamilton issued courageous calls for African identity and racial
empowerment, the other speeches delivered on that day took decidedly different
approaches. Although Henry Sipkins opened his oration by glorifying precolonial
Africa, which he described as containing the "most blissful regions, productive
of all the necessaries and even luxuries of life," he quickly began to articulate a
more conservative moral uplift position than his predecessors had. In contrast
to Hamilton, who pushed for Black collective action, Sipkins reminded the community that they should forever be thankful to their White benefactors and prove
themselves to be worthy of freedom. Even more, echoing Jupiter Hammon, he
argued that his brethren should conduct themselves in an "upright and steady"
manner to demonstrate their gratitude for their newfound liberty. According
to Sipkins, this strategy would hasten the day when slavery would finally be
vanquished, "when despotism and oppression shall forever cease—when the
Africans shall be reinstated in their former joys."[75] Although Sipkins was careful

to properly acknowledge their common heritage, he had clearly begun to embrace moral improvement as the primary method for racial advancement.

Significantly, although Sipkins tried to reconcile African pride and moral uplift, Joseph Sidney's oration before the Wilberforce Philanthropic Association entirely ignored Africa.[76] In fact, it almost seemed that Sidney was ashamed of his race because he lamented the fact that "an Ethiopian can not change his skin." Yet, despite the mark of race, Sidney declared that Black people should make every effort to prove they were worthy humans. This statement was in stark contrast to the views of men such as William Hamilton, who argued that African heritage was a point of pride rather than an obstacle they must transcend. Equally striking is the fact that the majority of Sidney's speech focused on thanking benevolent Whites who had assisted in the cause of abolition, giving particular praise to the Federalist Party.[77] In the end, his primary message to the Black community was a harsh admonition; arguing that only through proper conduct could they "effectually put to silence every cavil, which may be offered against African emancipation, and eventually convert our enemies into friends." Epitomizing moral uplift thought during the early national era, Sidney's language reflected the belief that Blacks would eventually be treated as free and equal citizens if they demonstrated their worthiness.[78]

The speeches delivered in 1809 were exceedingly important, for they demonstrated a growing split within the Black leadership; a divide that shaped political debates among free Blacks for the remainder of the century. As they faced poverty, racism, and the denial of citizenship, Black leaders pondered which strategy would most effectively eradicate slavery and bring full citizenship. In particular, as evidenced by Peter Williams Jr., William Hamilton, and Joseph Sidney, they struggled over critical strategic questions: Would moral improvement actually provide the key to true liberation, and if so, could they find a way to combine their African cultural heritage with this philosophy? While Williams seemed to answer both questions in the affirmative, Hamilton and Sidney appeared to have concluded that these notions were incompatible and battled to advance their differing agendas.

In the midst of this political quandary, however, the events in 1809 offered a glimmer of hope because, at least temporarily, the Black community managed to unite despite their ideological differences. Although William Hamilton and Joseph Sidney characterized radically different ends of the political spectrum, the organizations they represented brought the community together by continuing a treasured cultural tradition. Reveling in their shared African heritage, the Wilberforce Philanthropic Association and the African Society held grand processions through the streets of New York. Black parades were especially important because, as Sterling Stuckey has suggested, they were reminiscent of Pinkster celebrations. As with Pinkster, parading proudly exhibited African culture and race pride. Eileen Southern and Josephine Wright concurred with Stuckey, arguing that processions incorporated African elements such as marching, drumming, singing in "the various languages of Africa," and displaying colors and banners. Likewise, Mitch Kachun noted that African cultural forms "had a significant impact on the style and content of their celebrations."[79] Indeed, in New York City, ritual celebration, music, and Black pride formed the foundation of Black parades and allowed the community to celebrate their unique cultural legacy.[80]

Yet parading for the Black community was far more than a flashy procession. On the contrary, it had developed into a common form of political and cultural expression. On July 5, 1800, the Black community claimed the day after American Independence Day as *Black* Independence Day and held a parade honoring the Gradual Emancipation Act with grand marshals, uniforms, banners, and music. In 1802, political consciousness was particularly evident in parading when Black sailors went on strike and marched with "drums beating and colors flying."[81] Thus, in 1809, Black New Yorkers continued the tradition by flaunting their freedom and African culture with two parades. Immediately following Joseph Sidney's oration, the Wilberforce Philanthropic Association marched in full regalia including badges, banners, and music. They took the streets of New York City, boldly parading down Leonard, Broadway, and Wall streets. Two Africans who had survived the slave trade held a place of honor alongside the deputy marshals. Celebrants appropriately called the procession a "Jubilee of Liberty." Likewise, preceding William Hamilton's address, the proud members of the African Society crowded into the African schoolhouse, formed a procession, and marched to the African Zion Church for the remainder of the program.[82]

The fact that the African Society paraded from one influential Black institution to another could not have been lost on the community or their enemies. Nor would they have missed the significance of the Wilberforce Philanthropic Association's courageous decision to strut through the heart of New York City's wealthiest White neighborhoods. Claiming the streets and marching in open defiance was a strong political act at a time when the humanity of Black people was still not widely acknowledged and when many of their people still languished in bondage. It allowed Black New Yorkers to seize public space and declare their right "to be" and exist as free and equal citizens. Leslie Harris recognized this phenomenon when she wrote that parades allowed Black people to "claim their rights to political, and sometimes economic equality."[83] Black parades, then, were important both culturally and politically; such activities allowed the Black community to simultaneously celebrate their African heritage and assert their rights as potential citizens.

Beyond their cultural and political significance, Black activists must have known that parades were a powerful way to unite the community. Flamboyant energetic processions would have appealed to Black folks across class lines because they presented an opportunity to publicly celebrate. As they were boisterous community events, parades allowed for free association and unbridled expression. Combined with distinctly African music, clothing, colors, and banners, parades must have been irresistible to the entire Black community. As Sterling Stuckey maintained, Black parades in New York City in the early nineteenth century created a Pan-African environment in which the entire community could honor their shared racial and cultural identity.[84] Ultimately, these celebrations held the Black community together and united them against the disappointments of unequal freedom and ideological differences among the leadership. At least for a brief moment.

* * *

Between 1784 and 1810, Black New Yorkers experienced both the joy of emancipation and the painful reality of unequal freedom. As they gradually escaped the confines of slavery, the nascent free Black community must have been filled with hope but they soon found themselves faced with racism and extreme poverty. In response, Black leaders struggled to find a strategy that would simultaneously unify and bring full equality to their people. At first, these activists drew upon the powerful legacy of their African cultural heritage to build a strong and lasting community. In particular, they developed autonomous Black organizations and institutions that allowed them to exercise independence and advocate on behalf of the race. Yet men such as Peter Williams Jr., Henry Sipkins, and Joseph Sidney quickly realized that the process of achieving true freedom and equality was much more complicated than they had envisioned. Just as Jupiter Hammon had predicted, it became apparent that the Black community would be repeatedly forced to prove their worthiness in order to gain their rights. As a result, moral uplift and republican rhetoric began to influence the leadership's language and behavior.

Initially it appeared that it might be possible to reconcile moral improvement and African culture, as the African Society and Peter Williams Jr. fought valiantly to merge these notions. However, by 1809, the speeches of William Hamilton and Joseph Sidney began to hint that, perhaps, these ideas were incompatible and a growing strategic divide surfaced within the leadership. Although the parades that concluded the 1809 festivities managed to momentarily supersede ideological differences, in the years that followed, the Black community's united front weakened as they were faced with persistent racism and questions about their future in the United States. Indeed, the political debates that emerged in 1809 persisted in subsequent decades as the Black leadership struggled to determine which tactics would achieve their goals of true freedom, justice, and equality. Ironically, the very cultural expressions that unified the community in the early national era would be hotly contested among Black New Yorkers, particularly after 1827, when many Black activists became desperate to gain inclusion into American society.

CHAPTER 2

"To Leave the House of Bondage,"
1810–1826

> According to the basis of the christian religion, we are bound to love
> God with all our soul, and our neighbor as ourselves; but this sacred
> injunction does not reach the heart of the oppressors of Africans: there
> is no flesh in their obdurate heart—it does not feel for man.
> —William Miller, 1810

> My brethren, the time is fast approaching when the iron hand of
> oppression must cease to tyrannize over injured innocence, and very
> different are the days that we see, from those that our ancestors did; yet
> I know that there are thousands of our enemies who had rather see us
> exterminated from off the earth, than partake of the blessings that they
> enjoy; but their malice shall not be gratified; they will, though, it blast
> their eyes, still see us in prosperity.
> —George Lawrence, 1813

> Go to that highly favored, and as yet only land, where the sons of
> Africa appear as a civilized, well ordered, and flourishing nation. Go,
> remembering that the happiness of millions of the present and future
> generations depends upon your prosperity, and that your prosperity
> depends much on yourselves.
> —Haytian Emigration Society Board of Managers, 1824

On January 1, 1810, Reverend William Miller, leader of the African Methodist Episcopal Church and African Society charter member, appeared before his
congregation to celebrate the anniversary of the abolition of the slave trade.[1] His
speech on that day was a defining moment for Black political philosophy as Miller
went a small but crucial step beyond anything his predecessors had previously offered. The subtle difference in Miller's oration was likely not immediately apparent
to most, because he followed the tradition established by Peter Williams Jr. and
William Hamilton of celebrating Africa's proud history: "That the inhabitants of
Africa are descended from the ancient inhabitants of Egypt, a people once famous
for science of every description, is a truth verified by a number of writers . . . the
first learned nation, was a nation of blacks." Yet the critical distinction appeared
when Miller maintained that, based on its glorious past, Africa was destined to

reclaim its former greatness and become a center of political power. As evidence, he offered the new colony of Sierre Leone, which he declared would eventually "blossom abundantly" and testified to the potential for African people to return to their motherland and create a free African nation.[2] Although Miller stopped short of issuing a call for emigration, himself, his words led to the development of a new political agenda, one that transformed the Black community's connection to its African heritage into a program for racial advancement. For as he raised the image of Africa's powerful destiny, Miller opened the door to the possibility of repatriation. It was, in fact, just shortly after Miller's speech that a few brave Black New Yorkers initiated an exodus from "their house of bondage."[3]

Reverend William Miller. (Courtesy of the Library Company of Philadelphia.)

Miller's address marked a turning point in Black political consciousness, and demonstrated that some activists were looking to their African origins for solutions as they became increasingly discouraged with their status in American society. Indeed, this move reflected the difficult times between 1810 and 1826 when the rapidly expanding free Black population in New York City faced a myriad of economic, social, and political challenges. In particular, racism and the enemies of freedom proved to be powerful foes as Black New Yorkers pressured American society to stay true to its rhetoric of freedom and equality for all. Black activists were quickly discovering that the dawn of freedom was not all that they had hoped for.

Even worse, Black leaders still found themselves confused over which strategy would improve conditions for their people and continued the debate that had begun the previous decade. Some activists, such as Joseph Sidney and Peter Williams Jr., initially remained hopeful that moral uplift would alleviate their community's plight, but soon Williams and others began to lose faith. Bolstered by speeches from William Miller and William Hamilton, Williams eventually expanded his early call for Pan-Africanism and encouraged his people to explore potential opportunities in Africa or Haiti. Support for repatriation surged during this era, resulting in a full-scale emigration movement. Ultimately, however, most Black activists were unwilling to exclusively endorse either emigration or moral uplift. Instead, as they had before, Black leaders struck a compromise and continued to implement a program of early Black Nationalism, which, grounded in an ideological connection to Africa, advocated for racial solidarity and institution building. In particular, they sponsored the formation of Black organizations, fostered a powerful community ethic, and even began to accumulate real estate; all of which symbolized Black determination to make a future in the United States, a country that their ancestors had labored to create.

* * *

A few years after William Miller's speech in 1810, there were already signs of reemergent ideological dissent within New York City's Black leadership. Despite Miller's urgings for activists to consider their potential role in Africa's political destiny, a group of Black New Yorkers called upon their people to demonstrate their allegiance to America. Their appeal was clearly a response to the political climate during the War of 1812. Faced with growing criticism from "detractors who believed that they sympathized with England," free Blacks became fearful of being labeled as traitors and felt compelled to declare their loyalty.[4] However as Black leaders scrambled to rescue their public image, they were faced with a unique dilemma. The United States rejected Black men as citizens and excluded them from participating in combat before they had the chance to prove themselves. As a result, members of the African Society and Wilberforce Philanthropic Association held a meeting in April 1814 to find an alternative way to show their patriotism. At that gathering, they passed a series of resolutions pledging their solidarity to the United States and their commitment to "maintain the rights of the land in which we dwell."[5]

Shortly thereafter, they delivered on their promise by printing an article in the *New York Evening Post* announcing, "the people of colour throughout the city and county of New York are requested to meet in the Park . . . [and] proceed in a body to assist in erecting the fortifications on Brooklyn Heights." Their plea was called a "Test of Patriotism" and suggested that because the Black community's loyalty was in question, the people should prove their American spirit by aiding the war effort. Beneath the call to action was a letter written by a "Citizen of Colour" (likely Peter Williams Jr.), who pleaded with the rest of the Black community to assist in the cause.[6] The tone of this message espoused traditional moral uplift rhetoric, arguing that it was "the duty of every coloured man, resident in this city, to volunteer" because the state of New York had passed an emancipation act. To show their gratitude for the abolition of slavery, he insisted, Blacks must defend the United States. "Our country is now in danger—our patriotism is now put to the test—we now have an opportunity of shewing [*sic*] that we are not ungrateful—that we are not traitors or enemies to our country; but are willing to exert ourselves, whenever or wherever our services are needed, for the protection of our beloved state." More importantly, the author implied that by doing their patriotic duty, Blacks could gain equal treatment, civil rights, and citizenship.[7] The Black community responded affirmatively to the call; led by African Society members Peter Williams Jr., Thomas L. Jennings, and John Teasman, thousands of Black New Yorkers flocked to Brooklyn and Harlem to assist in fortifying the city.[8] Two months later, after an act by the United States Congress permitting Black service in the army, Black New Yorkers formed two regiments and fought for the United States.[9]

Black participation during the War of 1812 signaled a temporary victory of moral uplift advocates and reflected the desperate hope that patriotism and military service would bring true freedom and equality to their people. However, not everyone in New York City's Black community was convinced that such a strategy would be successful.[10] Faced with the enduring nature of American racism, some activists concluded that they needed to explore a variety of methods to empower and uplift the race. Although no one in the Black leadership spoke publicly against the war effort, the slave trade commemorations held during that time reflected dissenting opinions over political strategy and reignited the growing divide within the community. As the speeches delivered between 1813 and 1815 illustrate, the spectrum of political thought that had emerged prior to 1809 expanded during this era and ranged from optimistic appeals for moral uplift to powerful endorsements of repatriation.

At the ideological center of this political spectrum was George Lawrence, the newest member of the African Society, who delivered the keynote address at the

slave trade memorial in 1813.[11] Electing not to fully endorse either moral uplift
or emigration, Lawrence sought a middle ground where he combined praise for
their African past, calls for racial unity, and a brief reminder of moral uplift's
strategic benefits. He opened by declaring his "sincere attachment to the interest
of Africa" and inspired his audience with images of their "mother country" prior
to the arrival of Europeans: "Africa! Thou was once free, and enjoyed all the blessings a land and people could. Once held up as the ornament of the world, on thy
golden shores strayed Liberty, Peace and Equality." Yet despite Lawrence's pride
in Africa's political legacy, he did not mention Sierre Leone or the possibility of
emigration; instead, he focused on developing a plan to improve conditions for
the Black community in the United States.[12]

George Lawrence was well aware of the challenges the free Black community
faced; in particular, he denounced the "enemies who had rather see us extermi-
nated from off the earth, than partake of the blessings they enjoy." Yet Lawrence
thought his people could remain in the United States and combat their conditions with racial solidarity, "let us be united, the glory of a people is union . . .
[and] Union is the foundation of liberty." More specifically, Lawrence argued for
the formation of Black organizations and praised existing associations for their
community building efforts. Their actions, Lawrence argued, had demonstrated
the humanity and ability of the Black race: "It has been said by your enemies that
your minds were not calculated to receive a sufficient store of knowledge to fit
you for beneficial or social societies; but your incorporation drowned that assertion in contempt; and now let shame cover their heads." Based on the success of
Black organizations, Lawrence was hopeful that racial unity could help end their
suffering and their people would find equality and justice. "The spring is come,
and the autumn nigh at hand, when the rich fruits of liberty shall be strewn on
the paths of every African, or descendant, and the olive hedge of peace encompass
them in from their enemies."[13] For Lawrence, it seems, the key to advancement
was not repatriation, but rather a brand of Black Nationalism that emphasized
racial solidarity in the United States.

It is important to note, however, that in spite of Lawrence's optimism, he worried that racial unity alone might not be sufficient to break free from the "iron
hand of oppression." To ensure victory in the battle for equality, Lawrence infused
his vision of Black Nationalism with an appeal for moral improvement. His concluding remarks encouraged members of the Black community to "cling closely
to the paths of virtue and morality" and let their "virtues shine conspicuously
before them." By combining racial solidarity with morality, Lawrence believed
Black people would "crush the power that still holds thousands of our brethren in
bondage" and hasten the day when "freedom and justice reign triumphant." In the
final analysis, although Lawrence celebrated their African past and advocated an
early form of Black Nationalism, he still believed that moral improvement could

be strategically useful as a weapon against slavery and a tool in their pursuit of equality and citizenship.[14]

Significantly, the notion of moral uplift held sway over many in the Black leadership, as evidenced the following year when the Black community heard a voice from one extreme end of the political spectrum. Perhaps no one more strongly championed morality than Joseph Sidney who, as he had in 1809, openly eschewed overt celebrations of Africa and calls for Black Nationalism. In fact, in a surprising twist, Sidney denounced Africa, arguing instead that Blacks should be thankful that they had been brought to the United States: "There are many of our countrymen dispersed through various parts of the United States, who have been enabled, by the spirit of Divine Grace, to love and fear their Creator, and to obey his bold commandments. Would this have been the case had we been born in Africa, the country of our forefathers? I believe it would not. Truly may it be said with respect to us, that, 'our lot hath been cast in pleasant places. . . .'" Close analysis of this excerpt explains his startling views; for Sidney, the price of slavery was apparently worth the everlasting salvation that Christianity offered. In addition, the remainder of his speech revealed his belief that Christian morality could hold the key to racial progress. In his mind, all human suffering, including slavery and racism, was caused by those who had veered from the path of Christian righteousness and, therefore, the solution to these problems was close adherence to religious principles.[15]

Indeed, Sidney believed that God was already rewarding Black people for their high moral conduct, given that it was only due to the "instrumentality of Jehovah" that "Africans were restored to the rights of man." Furthermore, Sidney felt confident that God was slowly destroying racism: "Our prospect daily brightens—the sons of African descent are no longer held in that contempt which was the lot of their forefathers—no, they are now considered as free men." Encouraged by the advancements that God had bestowed on the free Black community, Sidney urged his brethren to continue their commitment to morality. Only through this strategy, he believed, could Black people earn salvation, freedom, and racial equality: "Let us cease to do evil, and learn to do well, to be grateful to our friends, and forgiving to our enemies—Then may we expect that our God will grant us his blessing and . . . find us more united . . . and more esteemed and respected by our brethren of a different complexion."[16] Even though Sidney's perspective may have inspired hope and religious sentiment within the community, his depiction of the United States as a "pleasant place" did not reflect the reality of most emancipated Blacks in New York. In fact, given the resentment and disappointment most Black people felt about the system of slavery and their tenuous freedom, at least one man felt compelled to challenge his views.

In 1815, elder William Hamilton delivered a powerful rebuttal, arguing that his brethren should seriously question European and American standards of morality.

Scoffing at those Whites who with "bloated pride" believed that they had "superior souls," Hamilton proclaimed that if Whites were examples of superiority "may heaven in mercy always keep us inferior." In this clever turn of phrase, Hamilton castigated all those who had participated in and benefited from slavery because of the destruction and immorality that they had produced. Hamilton also cast doubt on the popular notion of White supremacy when he declared, "Some nations have painted their devil in the complexion of a White man. View the history of the slave trade and then answer the question, could they have made choice of a better likeness to have drawn from?"[17]

Yet it was apparently Joseph Sidney's negative portrayal of Africa that most disturbed Hamilton, because he dedicated the entire opening of his speech to celebrating Africa's past. Like William Miller had five years earlier, Hamilton painted an empowering image of Africa's illustrious history claiming that, "Africa has a long . . . and proud account to give of herself. She can boast of her antiquity, of her philosophers, her artists, her statesmen, her generals; of her curiosities, her magnificent cities, her stupendous buildings, and of her once widespread commerce." Furthermore, he concurred with Miller that Africa could be an influential political force in the future. Africa, Hamilton maintained, "being situated in the middle of the globe . . . would make a grand eligible situation for the seat of Authority." He was particularly hopeful about Africa's destiny because the slave trade, "that cursed viper that fed on Africa's vitals," had finally been destroyed. As a result, he believed that they were witnessing "the opening of a better day" and prophesized that their motherland would "ascend to the zenith of glory and aggrandizement." Ultimately, Hamilton hoped that Black New Yorkers would not just revel in their heritage, but also consider Africa's potential in the future. Combined with William Miller's suggestion that Africa would regain its former glory and serve as a homeland to free Blacks, Hamilton's ideas reflected a new race uplift strategy; one that eventually gave birth to emigrationist ideology in New York City.[18]

The Black leadership's speeches between 1810 and 1815 were deeply revealing; considered together, these orations embodied a critical political dispute over identity and Black people's place within American society. While George Lawrence and Joseph Sidney envisioned a hopeful future in the United States, William Miller and William Hamilton began to turn to Africa for answers regarding their community's destiny. Perhaps more than anything, the leadership's differing political perspectives demonstrated a range of responses to the same problem: a pervasive fear about whether emancipation would live up to its promise. The only remaining question was whether conditions would actually become severe enough to drive free Blacks from the United States. Black New Yorkers did not have to wait long for an answer. Following the War of 1812, newly emancipated people continued to converge on New York City where they hoped they would find better economic opportunities and their dreams of freedom would be realized.

However, as the free Black population reached over 12,000, many freed people found only poverty and inequality.[19] Compounding their economic struggles were inferior housing conditions and the denial of civil and political rights. Although the escape from slavery had seemed promising, the reality of "freedom" was not all they had imagined.[20] At the core of this multitude of problems, was a powerful, enduring negative force: the persistence of racism. As a result, the issue that prompted the most political action from New York's Black community was the continual vicious racial onslaught Whites unleashed against symbols of Black freedom.

Displeased with the growing number of free Black people and institutions, Whites mercilessly attacked Black establishments because they were the physical manifestations of Black autonomy; churches, in particular, were the most vulnerable. The largest of these, the African Methodist Church, was a central target for racial hostility and its congregants were continually harassed outside their building. After numerous assaults, trustee Isaac Fortune insisted upon police protection outside the church; in fact, in July 1810, Fortune paid the Common Council $20 to offset the cost of a watch house. Despite this effort, violence toward the African Church persisted. In 1815, a mysterious fire blazed through the church and the building was destroyed, leaving the community to rebuild.[21] Just six years later, in 1821, another suspicious fire decimated St. Philip's Episcopal Church. Members working inside discovered the blaze and, although everyone escaped, the wooden building was reduced to ashes. The "official" cause of the fire was reported as a defective flue, however the Common Council noted that an unidentified "unruly" man was restrained at the scene and taken into custody.[22] Black churches in New York City continued to be targeted by racist aggression during the nineteenth century, a problem that persisted in the United States well into the twentieth century.

Recognizing the importance of education in the project of race uplift, Whites also sabotaged the Black community's educational efforts. Although the African Free School managed to escape physical destruction, White New Yorkers in numerous neighborhoods circulated petitions demanding that the school be denied land in their area in order to prevent Black children from walking near their homes. Despite entreaties to the contrary, the African Free School was forced to postpone expansion until May 1813 when the Common Council finally granted land for the establishment of a new brick schoolhouse. Significantly, however, the Common Council was cognizant that many White New Yorkers opposed the notion of Black progress and pacified them by situating the school on Chamber Street in the midst of the predominately Black Fifth ward.[23]

Ironically, conditions in the Black community worsened after 1817 when the New York State Legislature announced that as of July 4, 1827, all Black New Yorkers would be legally free. This news must have been a cause for celebration in the Black community, but it also unleashed a backlash from those Whites who already resented the expanding free Black population. Racism in New York City soon became so virulent that Black institutions were constantly threatened by violence. In fact, any Black success during this period seemed to incite White rage. Most notably, the establishment of the African Grove Theater embodied how Black progress and initiative caused White fear and mob violence.

In the early 1820s, William Brown opened the African Grove in his backyard as a leisure and entertainment spot for the Black community. De facto segregation prevented Blacks from frequenting New York City's popular public gardens, and Brown apparently hoped to create such a resort for his people. The African Grove was described as a "tea garden" that served alcoholic beverages and provided lively entertainment. However, by the autumn of 1821, the African Grove moved because of noise complaints and became a full-fledged theater, with actors performing traditional Shakespeare as well as contemporary plays. Located in the heart of the Black community, it soon became a popular source of entertainment for Black folks where they could socialize and interact freely.[24] Despite the fact that the African Theater was only intended to serve a community function, some Whites increasingly viewed it as a statement of Black social and political equality. As with other Black organizations and institutions, once the African Theater established an enduring presence it represented a threat to Whites.

City newspapers, in 1821 and 1822, began using reports on the African Grove Theater as an opportunity to express their fears about the Black population and its growing social and political influence. The *Commercial Advertiser* noted, with concern, the increasing size of the Black community and questioned the morality of those who attended the African Theater. Even more telling, was the article's description of the African Theater as a threatening prospect because it was evidence that Blacks were trying to create something permanent.[25] Yet the most virulent attacks came from the *National Advocate's* editor, Mordecai Noah. He viewed, with distaste, the idea of Blacks as people who possessed the luxury to seek leisure and entertainment, and parodied their actions as pathetic attempts to mimic Whites:

> a garden has been opened somewhere back of the hospital called African Grove . . . at which the ebony lads and lasses could obtain ice cream, ice punch and hear music from the big drum and clarionet. . . . The gentleman, with his wool nicely combed, and his face shining through a coat of sweet oil, borrowed from the castors; cravat tight to suffocation, having the double faculty of widening the mouth and giving remarkable protuberance to the eyes . . . these black fashionables saunter up and down the garden, in all the pride of liberty and unconsciousness of want. In their address; salutations; familiar phrases; and compliments; their imitative faculties are best exhibited. . . . Thus they run the rounds of fashion; ape their masters and mistresses in every thing; talk of projected matches; reherse [sic] the news of the kitchen, and the follies of the day.

Although Whites may have found this behavior momentarily humorous, they increasingly perceived "the pride of liberty" among Blacks to be especially dangerous because of the political climate in 1821.[26]

Significantly, just as the African Theater was increasing in popularity, the New York State Legislature was debating the issue of suffrage. As the White community's concern about the extension of Black voting rights was heightened, so was its general awareness of Black activities. The African Theater symbolized, in many ways, the potential of Black social and political power. Even though the strivings of Black theatergoers were initially amusing, their behavior was quickly viewed as a frightening reversal of the social order. This perception was augmented by the fact that the African Theater segregated the seating at its performances, with the worst seats reserved for Whites. Upon receiving this news, Mordecai Noah sarcastically remarked: "The gentlemen of colour . . . have graciously made a partition at the back of their house, for the accommodation of the whites."[27] Such an arrangement would have represented, to the White community, an absurd and threatening demonstration of Black racial pride.

Though Mordecai Noah often used humor and sarcasm to articulate his ideas, he also resorted to open attacks. In one article, Noah used the African Theater as an example of how Black people were beginning to associate together and form a political alliance: "They [Blacks] now assemble in groups; and since they have crept in favour with the convention, they are determined to have balls and quadrille parties, establish forum, solicit a seat in the assembly . . . [and] outvote the whites." Such a statement reflected not only fears about Blacks having formal parties and engaging in other forms of social strivings, but also the possibility of Black voters. In another article on the same page, Noah expressed concern about the growing Black population and the suffrage more explicitly: "Our colored population increases daily . . . their votes in time will become formidible [sic] . . . and if they are organized and led by designing persons, they will give us great trouble."[28]

In addition to Noah's anxiety about the Black community's potential political advancement, he also resented its economic success. By 1822, the African Theater's owner, William Brown, opened a new location adjacent to the popular Park Theater. Trouble began when, according to historian Shane White, Brown purposely began "seeking out white patrons and aggressively enticing customers away from the most important theater in the city." Mordecai Noah criticized Brown's actions, arguing that "the sable managers, not satisfied with a small share of profit and a great portion of fame, [were] determined to rival the great Park Theater."[29] Ultimately, it was the combined fears about potential Black social, political, and economic power that finally sounded the death knell for this institution. In January 1822, the police raided the African Theater in the middle of a performance, arrested the actors, and ordered them to cease activity. However, the owners did not heed the warning and continued to hold gatherings. Not surprisingly, harassment persisted from both police and civilians; the culmination of these attacks occurred on August 10, 1822, when a White mob stormed the theater, destroyed most of the property, attacked the actors, and beat William Brown unmercifully. Brown responded to the riot by accusing the Park Theater managers of using the police to "quell his rivalry," yet his words had little effect. Although some of the rioters were arrested, the African Theater was besieged by White violence until 1829 when city officials closed it.[30]

As the story of the African Theater attests, many White New Yorkers objected to demonstrations of Black freedom. Most notably, beyond Black institutions, Whites resented the growing number of fugitives seeking refuge in New York. By the 1820s, New York City had become a haven for Blacks fleeing slavery, a place where they hoped they could find a safe and permanent home as free people. Entire families like the Trustys, who escaped slavery in Maryland, arrived in New York City seeking to blend into the community, find safety, and begin a new life. However, true security was often difficult to attain in nineteenth century New York City. Fugitive and legally free Blacks were constantly threatened by gangs of White men known as "blackbirders," who roamed the streets searching for Blacks to capture and return to a state of bondage. The situation in New York became so intense that the legislature passed an amendment to the Emancipation Act in 1817, which stated that anyone who would "seize and forcibly confine, or inveigle or kidnap, any negro, mulatto, mustee, or other person of color, with intent to carry him out of this state against his will" was subject to a considerable fine and hard labor.[31]

Yet despite the efforts of the New York State Legislature to stem the tide of kidnapping, both free and fugitive Black New Yorkers were in constant danger of reenslavement. During the summer of 1825, the Black community was warned about a notorious gang of blackbirders that routinely stole free Black children from the streets of Philadelphia. The men, known as the Johnson gang, lured children into an opportune location where they snatched them and sold them into slavery in the South.[32] Soon, similar incidents plagued New York City; "slave-nappers" targeted members of the Trusty family (by then known as the Garnets) shortly after their arrival in New York City. George Garnet jumped from his roof to escape, and his wife likewise managed to "elude their grasp." However, their daughter, Eliza, was not so fortunate; she was arrested and tried as a "fugitive from labor." Although Eliza was eventually exonerated, her suffering and the destruction of the family home drove her brother Henry "almost to madness." Henry purchased a knife and went in search of the kidnappers, "waiting and hoping for the assault of the men-hunters." Fearful for his life, his mother and friends found Henry and ferried him out of the city.[33]

Henry's actions were illustrative of an important principle; when a slave catcher seized a Black person, the community regularly rallied to the fugitive's defense.

In some cases, the result was a riot in which the disgruntled Black community voiced its resentment about the unjust treatment of fugitives and the system of slavery. The Black community's protests became so frequent, that one newspaper described how free Blacks had "set the city authorities at defiance" and "rule by open violence."[34] In June 1819 as a slave catcher attempted to return Thomas Harlett to his master in upstate New York, a group of about forty Black men gathered in protest. Escorted by a city marshal, the slave catcher then tried to seek refuge in City Hall. En route, the Black protesters fought with the slave catcher and tried to free Harlett. Although the efforts to rescue him failed, the Black community was learning to exercise its political voice; one it soon needed.[35]

Tension mounted outside City Hall, again, on September 19, 1826, as authorities determined the fate of an entire Black family who had escaped from Virginia. The family was headed by Ben Washington, a carpenter, and included his daughter, son-in-law, and three other women. As the case was being argued, a crowd gathered in the park outside City Hall. The magistrates complained about the assembly, because "the crowd uniformly insulted the officers who passed to and from the hall." Early in the afternoon, the police were sent to disperse the crowd but, later, the gathering of protesters had swelled to even greater numbers and blocked the exit. When the slaveholder, Mr. F. Alexander, emerged victorious, the Black crowd erupted into violence. As one newspaper reported, the audience "became outrageous and threatened to take the lives of those concerned." Although the police quickly restored order in the park, the riot spilled into nearby streets. One group chased a White man chanting, "kill him," while another group attacked the slave catcher's house. Ultimately, the police prevailed and arrested four men who were carrying "various weapons." Their sentences were considered harsh for the time, ranging from nine months in prison to three years of hard labor.[36]

The uprisings in 1819 and 1826 reminded White New Yorkers that Blacks would not passively accept oppression and injustice. Yet the uprisings were also important illustrations of the Black community's vulnerability. Continually threatened by the possibility of enslavement and unable to successfully protect fugitives, such riots were a revealing manifestation of Black political impotence. Indeed, some kidnapping victims had no advocate at all. One New York woman, in particular, learned painfully that "freedom" for Blacks was tenuous at best. Catherine Richardson was born in New York City to free Black parents who worked on a farm. As a child, she was bound out as a domestic servant and then sent to work for a Mr. Charles Johnson who made his living as a master mariner. After about a year and a half, Charles Johnson took her to Nassau, Bahamas, on one of his ships. Upon Catherine's arrival, Charles Johnson's sister, Elizabeth Yellowley, enslaved her. Johnson returned to New York City with an illegally obtained enslaved man and Catherine realized that she had been victimized by a cruel scheme.[37]

In 1811, Catherine Richardson brought her situation to the attention of the authorities in Nassau. While the attorney general reviewed her case, she was placed in the town jail. Her condition was apparently still unresolved in March 1812, since her plight was mentioned in the report of the African Institution of London, an organization dedicated to eradicating slavery. However, the directors of the African Institution did not appear to take any particular action on her behalf and she was never mentioned again in their reports. Catherine Richardson's experience reflected the danger and uncertainty of Black life in New York City during this era; although technically born free, she was kidnapped, enslaved, and her ultimate fate is unknown. For many free and fugitive Black New Yorkers, without protection or legal recourse, the threat of enslavement always loomed around the corner.

Plagued by violence, racism, injustice, poverty, and a tenuous social status, many Black New Yorkers realized that true freedom would remain elusive in the early nineteenth century. As a result, activists questioned their place in American society and wondered what the future would hold for them as free people. The concern over this issue reflected both their connection to Africa, and their doubts about whether Blacks, as a race, could achieve equality in the United States. As evidenced by the speeches of William Miller and William Hamilton, some Black leaders were unconvinced of the efficacy of moral uplift strategy and began to cast their vision outside the United States in hopes of finding a solution. As their frustration mounted, the issue of emigration gripped the Black community. Should they stay in the United States or, perhaps, emigrate to their homeland or another welcoming country? Support for emigration increased as news spread about the growing countries of Sierre Leone and Haiti, Black nations that represented their goal of racial autonomy and offered the citizenship that free Blacks so fervently desired.[38]

There is evidence that Black New Yorkers discussed emigration as early as 1792; however, the subject became particularly significant in 1812 with the increasing influence of Northern Black leader Paul Cuffe.[39] Cuffe, of African and Native American descent, was born in 1759 near New Bedford, Massachusetts. Early in life, he manifested a talent for sailing and navigation, which he ultimately made his life's work.[40] By 1808, Cuffe expressed considerable interest in the burgeoning country of Sierra Leone. Black people from Great Britain and Nova Scotia had settled this colony, including those from the United States who had fought with the British during the Revolutionary War. Following the abolition of the slave trade, Sierra Leone became known as a resettlement site for African peoples who had been stolen from their homeland during slavery.[41] Cuffe hoped to establish an official relationship with Sierra Leone for political, economic, and religious reasons, and on January 2, 1811, he set sail in his ship, the *Traveller,* from Philadelphia for Sierra Leone to determine how he could contribute to its success.[42]

Paul Cuffe and his Black crew arrived in Sierra Leone on March 1, 1811, and he remained there for over two months collecting information on the development and condition of the colony. He seemed encouraged by what he found but thought that Black settlers from the United States could contribute a great deal more. In

Captain Paul Cuffe. (Courtesy of the Photographs and Prints Division; Schomburg Center for Research in Black Culture; New York Public Library; Astor, Lenox, and Tilden Foundations.)

a letter to British abolitionist William Allen, Paul Cuffe wrote that an "endeavor should be kept open between Sierra Leone and America. . . . If this Channel can be kept open, I am in hopes that some sober families may find their way to Sierra Leone." In June 1811, Cuffe sailed for England where he hoped to meet with members of the African Institution of London, the philanthropic association that supported Sierre Leone. His primary purpose during that visit was to gain approval for the emigration of free Blacks from the United States into the colony. Cuffe was well received by leading members of the African Institution, including William Allen and William Wilberforce. After this meeting, Cuffe was motivated to go back to the United States and recruit more free Blacks to emigrate.[43]

However, Cuffe first made another three-month visit to Sierre Leone, where he continued his investigation and was careful to get an agreement from Sierre Leonian officials that settlers from the United States would receive full citizenship upon their arrival.[44] After gaining sufficient confirmation, Cuffe finally returned to the United States and arrived in New York City on May 13, 1812. The next day, he called a meeting of Black activists to discuss the issue of African emigration; present at the gathering were about twenty Blacks and a few White supporters. Apparently, the meeting was a success because the New York City African Institution was established and became active in the community. In June 1813, Cuffe noted that Blacks in New York, Philadelphia, Boston, and Baltimore had contacted him, expressing a desire to emigrate if "proper ways could be opened to go to Africa."[45]

Excited by the Black community's enthusiasm, Paul Cuffe wanted to return to Africa immediately, but his plans were put on hold because of the War of 1812. In January 1814, Cuffe wrote to the U.S. government requesting permission to resume his activities in Sierra Leone. Although his request was heard in Congress, it was narrowly defeated. He was forced to wait impatiently until the conclusion of the war before he could bring the first group of Black settlers to Sierra Leone. Soon after the cessation of war, on December 10, 1815, Paul Cuffe sailed for Africa with thirty-eight Black pioneers, two of whom were from New York City.[46]

Shortly after the initial exodus of Black settlers, the interest in emigration increased in New York. Among the converts was Peter Williams Jr., who became the leader of the New York City branch of the African Institution and wrote to Paul Cuffe about the "advantages which the African race . . . would enjoy on a return to their own soil."[47] Williams's support for emigration was telling because, just two years before, he had actively demonstrated his American patriotism during the War of 1812. Yet apparently disillusioned, Williams was now advocating for repatriation to Africa. Paul Cuffe returned to New York City several times in 1815 and 1816 to meet with Williams and his own sister, Freelove Slocum, who was also interested in the prospect of emigration.[48] Inspired by their dedication, Cuffe began to rely on Williams and the New York African Institution to dispense information and rally support for the cause of emigration. In June 1816, Cuffe wrote to Williams and asked for his assistance to spread the word in Philadelphia. Williams must have been successful in his task because Cuffe wrote later to thank him for his labor in creating an African Institution in Philadelphia: "At this time I am very happy to learn that thou art so well established in this African cause for the great good and improvement of that people. And also to find you have got the institution in Philadelphia willing to wear the yoke of Christian benevolence." Throughout 1815 and 1816, Paul Cuffe and Peter Williams Jr. encouraged skilled Blacks to settle in Sierre Leone and assist the community there.[49]

Yet, significantly, Cuffe and Williams's plans transcended the idea of transporting individuals to Africa; they also began to explore the possibility of developing a permanent commercial exchange between free Blacks in the United States and continental Africans. In 1816, Peter Williams Jr. suggested that Paul Cuffe should establish a shipping line to Africa to benefit both Blacks in the United States and the colony of Sierre Leone. Cuffe responded enthusiastically: "Esteemed friend Peter Williams Jr., In consequence of [what] thee mentioned that we the people of colour might establish a mercantile line of business from the United States to Africa, etc., should this still be your mind and you propose to carry it into effect this fall, we have no time to lose. After consulting thyself and friends, please to inform me your resolution." Based upon this letter, it would appear that a Pan-African trade might have been the original idea of Peter Williams Jr. and the members of the New York African Institution. Regardless, Cuffe apparently supported the notion and, in an effort to establish a successful relationship, encouraged correspondence between the African Institutions in the United States and the Friendly Society of Sierre Leone.[50]

In the year before his death, Paul Cuffe began to expand the emigration project beyond Africa. Although he never abandoned the idea of Black people repatriating to their homeland, Cuffe recognized the necessity of exploring all of their options, particularly because Sierre Leone was not independent from British control.[51] As a result, in December 1816, Cuffe wrote to Williams asking for his support for a voyage to Haiti, the first independent Black nation in the Western hemisphere. Cuffe urged Williams to "take a concern" in the trip to Haiti, but not to lose sight of "our African prospect." Although Cuffe commented regularly on his plan to explore possibilities in Haiti, he never made the journey. Before he got a chance to embark, he became seriously ill; even in sickness he continued to correspond about emigration, but on September 7, 1817, Paul Cuffe died. His death was a tremendous blow to the Black community, particularly those who were inspired by the notion of emigration.[52]

On October 21, 1817, the members of the New York African Institution gathered to commemorate the life and work of their departed friend Paul Cuffe. Peter Williams Jr. delivered a moving and eloquent tribute to Cuffe's unceasing dedication to the improvement of the Black community: "Capt. C was an advocate of African colonization. He wished to see that part of our nation, which are dispersed and kept in a state of bondage and degradation in christian countries, returning to the land of their ancestors." Williams was careful to remind the members of the African Institution that their obligation to emigration did not die with Cuffe. Rather, he argued, as a testament to Cuffe, they must continue with their important work.[53]

Perhaps prompted by the words and actions of Peter Williams Jr., the issue of emigration remained popular in New York City. Although Sierre Leone was increasingly viewed as a less desirable location (only twenty-seven Blacks had immigrated to Africa from New York City by 1820), Black New Yorkers began to refocus emigrationist thought on the new option produced by the successful revolution in Haiti.[54] Although Africa was still considered their homeland, free Blacks were particularly inspired by the possibility of Haiti because it represented the culmination of their strivings for political autonomy. As the only independent Black nation in the Americas, Haiti appeared to be the ultimate manifestation of what free Blacks hoped to achieve. During the revolution, enslaved people had thrown off their shackles and declared their right to self-determination. Their actions represented a model of racial solidarity and political autonomy that many free Blacks envied. As scholar Elizabeth Rauh Bethel explained, "Hayti stood as material New World evidence which challenged the ideology of Anglo-European world supremacy."[55] The existence of Haiti sent a message to the entire world that Black people were capable of asserting their humanity and worthy of gaining their freedom. As Blacks in New York gained their physical freedom, they longed for true autonomy and citizenship and Haiti seemed to offer these goals.

By 1818, Black New Yorkers had developed the Haytian Emigration Society of Coloured People with Peter Williams Jr. as the chairman. The notion of Haitian emigration attracted the most prominent members of the Black community including Peter Vogelsang, Boston Crummell, Samuel Cornish, Thomas L. Jennings, and James Varick.[56] It was also quite popular among leaders throughout the North including Bostonian Prince Saunders, who traveled to New York to garner support for the movement. Apparently the idea also had popular appeal beyond the leadership, because, on November 29, 1819, the Common Council received a petition from Edward Coggan, Samuel Griffith, and 105 other people of color asking for assistance so that they could immigrate to Haiti. Although the Common Council essentially ignored their request, the notion of Haitian emigration and Pan-Africanism soon received a boost from Haitian president Jean Pierre Boyer.[57]

In 1820, President Boyer successfully unified the Haitian republic under his rule and, in 1822, gained control over the entire island of Hispaniola. By the summer of 1824, President Boyer was increasingly enthusiastic for Blacks to come to his burgeoning country, because he sought solutions to Haiti's internal problems and hoped that a migration of Black Americans could bolster the economy. Boyer had started corresponding with benevolent Whites, such as British abolitionist Granville Sharp, as well as a member of the American Colonization Society (ACS), Loring Dewey, to discuss potential plans for Black emigration.[58] Yet because Dewey and the ACS were known for their racist views, and their desire to forcibly remove Blacks from the United States, Black New Yorkers were initially wary of supporting their emigration scheme. In fact, Samuel Cornish and Peter Williams Jr. attacked the White supporters of Haitian emigration during a meeting in June 1824, declaring their opposition to the ACS's anti-Black rhetoric.[59] However, Black leaders soon reversed their opinion, after they heard Boyer's message and emigration plans.

Boyer was able to win Black support by implementing two effective strategies. He articulated a political philosophy that resonated with Black leaders and created a plan that addressed their most fundamental needs. Although Boyer would later come under crushing criticism for his controversial policies and inept leadership, which eventually caused him to resign and flee Haiti in 1843, he earned widespread support among Blacks in the United States during the mid-1820s. His popularity rested, in part, on the fact that he espoused strong Pan-African leanings. For example, in one letter to Loring Dewey, he lamented the harsh and humiliating conditions that his fellow "descendants of the Africans" experienced in the United States: "You are not ignorant that there exist in the United States of America, several hundred thousand individuals of African blood, who on account of the dark hue of their complexions, are objects of all the prejudice and prepossession that can arise from difference of colour." Furthermore, he expressed a desire to assist his "brethren" in America who were struggling under racial oppression. As Boyer explained, he had a natural "sympathy" for those of "African blood" and yearned to give them refuge in Haiti: "My heart and my arms have been open to greet, in this land of true liberty, those men upon whom a fatal destiny rests in a manner so cruel."[60] For Black leaders in the United States, who were desperately seeking an asylum for their people, Boyer's Pan-African rhetoric would certainly have held tremendous appeal. Even more appealing, however, was President Boyer's special plan to encourage emigration.

In June 1824, Boyer dispatched a representative, Jonathas Granville, to New York to unveil his proposal for Haitian emigration. While there, Granville delivered four speeches on Boyer's behalf and, on June 16, 1824, President Boyer's plan was presented to a group of Black New Yorkers. The Haitian government agreed to pay part of any Black migrant's travel expenses, provide fertile land, tools, schooling, and, most importantly, full citizenship. Boyer declared, "Those who come, being children of Africa, shall be Haytiens as soon as they put their feet upon the soil of Hayti." Not surprisingly, the Haytien Emigration Society eagerly endorsed the plan and stated that they "highly approved" of Boyer's propositions. Shortly thereafter, inspired by President Boyer's words and promises, Peter Williams Jr. departed for Haiti to investigate the conditions on behalf of the community in New York City.[61]

Jean Pierre Boyer. (Courtesy of the Manuscripts, Archives, and Rare Books Division; Schomburg Center for Research in Black Culture; New York Public Library; Astor, Lenox, and Tilden Foundations.)

While in Haiti, Williams met with political officials to discuss the possibility of bringing more Black settlers. He must have returned with a positive report, because his visit ultimately led to an exodus from New York City. On August 30, 1824, a group of Black New Yorkers boarded the ship *De Witt Clinton* and went in search of true freedom, equality, opportunity, and citizenship. On this occasion, the board of managers for the Haytian Emigration Society of Coloured People prepared a special address offering advice to the emigrants. Peter Williams Jr. delivered the speech, which created a desirable image of Haiti as a place where Blacks could finally find what they had been seeking. "You are going to a good country, governed by good laws, where a dark complexion will be no disadvantage; where you will enjoy true freedom, and have as great advantages as any men in the world, to become independent and honourable, wise and good, respectable and happy. Should you not, under the ordinary blessings of Providence, become such, the fault will be your own, and your failure will discourage the great mass, whom you leave behind." As evidenced by this excerpt, Williams was quick to remind the emigrants that even though they were leaving the United States, they still had an obligation to their people who they left behind. Wishing them success, Williams exclaimed, "Go, remembering that the happiness of millions of the present and future generations, depends upon your prosperity, and that *your prosperity* depends much upon yourselves." After a brief reply thanking the board for its advice, the emigrants departed.[62]

Over the next few years, the Haitian government subsidized the transportation of over six thousand free Blacks from the Northern United States to Haiti and initial reports seemed favorable. Statements sent back to the United States spoke highly of the reception they received and indicated that the settlers were thriving in their new surroundings. However, the transplanted Black migrants soon found themselves confronting major problems. They were culturally distinct from their Haitian brethren in a number of important ways, and they particularly struggled with language barriers and religious differences. Most importantly, however, the process of land distribution quickly frustrated the colonists, and many suspected that they had been duped. Apprehensive that the government did not intend to deliver on its promise of land, they worried they would become permanent laborers rather than independent landowners. In the face of these problems and obstacles, many immigrants considered going back to the United States. In fact, in 1825, the secretary general of Haiti, Joseph Balthazar Inginac, stated that he believed nearly one-third of the original settlers had returned. New Yorkers were apparently among this group because, years later, Black activist James McCune Smith reported that Peter Williams Jr. had been compelled to return to Haiti and negotiate the release of their "disappointed, distressed, and dissatisfied brethren."[63]

Amidst growing disillusionment, there was another blow to the Haitian project. Perhaps partly in response to this reverse migration, Inginac announced in May 1825 that the government would no longer subsidize the cost of bringing free Blacks to the island. The government insisted that its decision was prompted by the immigrants' poor attitude and performance, but other political and financial considerations may have played a role. In particular, historian Chris Dixon argues convincingly that the refusal of the United States to unreservedly support the new Haitian government undermined relations between residents of the two countries. Ultimately, however, what was important to the free Black population in the United States is that the project of Haitian emigration appeared to be a failure by the end of the 1820s.[64]

Although emigration remained a popular topic throughout the nineteenth century, there was clearly not a consensus among the leadership that emigration was the best or only solution; a belief that was undoubtedly confirmed by the political struggles in Sierre Leone and Haiti. As a result, even though activists, such as Peter Williams Jr. and Samuel Cornish, endorsed emigration, they did not abandon the search for alternative remedies to their community's plight. As they weighed their options, most Black leaders determined that they were not yet ready to unconditionally embrace either emigration or Joseph Sidney's call for strict adherence to moral uplift. Instead, the majority of activists took the middle ground and adopted George Lawrence's vision of Black Nationalism. Despite the violent attacks that had been unleashed against their efforts, Black leaders were convinced, as Lawrence had urged in 1813, that strong, independent, Black organizations were the most effective weapons in the battle for racial advancement. Thus, Black leaders during this era sought to infuse their organizations and institutions with notions of racial solidarity, independence, and even expressions of African community ethics, hopeful that this strategy would unify the community and ultimately bring equality and justice.

The burgeoning movement for autonomy influenced every facet of Black life during this era but was considered the most complicated in the area of education. As in previous years, Black activists viewed education as a crucial component of racial advancement and, initially, Black activists were pleased with the African Free School's progress. In January 1815, the school moved to a new building designed to administer to more than two hundred students and, by 1820, it was already overcrowded as attendance soared past three hundred. Fortunately, by the end of 1820, they erected a two-story structure on Mulberry Street called African School No. 2, which serviced nearly five hundred children. In fact, there were many promising students being trained at the African Free School, including future activists and scholars such as Henry Highland Garnet, James McCune Smith, Charles Reason, Patrick Reason, and Alexander Crummell. By 1818, the school had a new library and an apprentice program that afforded students the opportunity to gain experience in skilled trades.[65]

Yet despite the school's growth, Black leaders faced a challenging obstacle; it was still controlled by the White-dominated Manumission Society, whose racism became shockingly apparent during two specific incidents. First, the Manumission Society fired respected Black activist, John Teasman, from his position as principal and replaced him with a White man, Charles Andrews.[66] To make matters worse, Andrews and the Manumission Society demonstrated decidedly paternalistic tendencies and insulted Black parents by attempting to instruct them in proper child rearing, morality, cleanliness, Christianity, and obedience.

New York African Free School, no. 2. (Courtesy of the General Research and Reference Division; Schomburg Center for Research in Black Culture; New York Public Library; Astor, Lenox, and Tilden Foundations.)

The ultimate transgression came in 1818, when the school's trustees delivered a condescending address suggesting that Black parents did not know how to raise their own children and that the Manumission Society should assume the role of parent.[67] The marked decline in attendance in the years that followed seemed to reflect the Black community's frustration with the Manumission Society's tactics and a desire for more influence over its children's education. The community elected, instead, to lend support to John Teasman who, since his dismissal, had opened his own school. Additionally, by 1812, there were at least three other Black operated schools in New York City.[68] These activities revealed not only the Black community's dedication to education, but also its commitment to developing autonomous institutions.

The fight for independence also influenced religious institutions during this period, because Black churches continued to be powerful strongholds and community centers in New York City.[69] The biggest development occurred among the Episcopalians who, after breaking from the Whites in 1809, established their own church with Peter Williams Jr. as their leader. Delayed by the economic depression during the War of 1812, the Episcopalians were finally able to lease three lots of land and construct a building named St. Philip's Church. Located in the heart of a Black neighborhood, the establishment of St. Philip's was truly a community effort. Black members performed all of the work on the church, and the women of the congregation raised money for the interior fixtures. St. Philip's Church was finally consecrated on July 3, 1819, and, although a suspicious fire destroyed St. Philip's in 1821, an improved edifice was erected by 1823. In a show of race solidarity, the Black Methodists contributed to St. Philips's fund in remembrance of the fire that had decimated their own church in 1815. The crowning moment for the Black Episcopalians during this era was the advancement of Peter Williams Jr. to the priesthood; in July 1826, he became the first Black Episcopal priest in the United States. For Blacks in New York City, particularly in light of his failed emigration schemes, Peter Williams Jr.'s success must have been a symbolic acknowledgment of their potential as a race.[70]

As evidenced by the racial solidarity between the African Methodists and Episcopalians, and the community's support for John Teasman, the movement for autonomy definitively embraced George Lawrence's call for racial unity and institution building. Nowhere was this commitment more apparent than in the formation and activities of Black benevolent associations.[71] The crown jewel of all Black organizations in this era was the African Society for Mutual Relief, which proved its dedication to racial unity, autonomy, and African cultural traditions in a variety of ways.[72] Institution building, in particular, was a critical part of the society's program, and the society demonstrated its commitment to success and longevity by drafting a petition seeking incorporation from the New York State Legislature. This was a particularly bold move by the African Society because, after all, slavery and discrimination still dominated most of the United States. The organization's historian later wrote that the African Society sought incorporation "before the manhood of its membership was acknowledged by the community at large." Yet incorporation was crucial to Black New Yorkers for a few key reasons. First, it symbolized their independence and was a powerful strike against the forces that sought to restrict and constrain their lives. It also offered tangible economic benefits, because it granted them the right to buy property and collect money as a corporation. Perhaps to the African Society's surprise, the state legislature had no objection to the "benevolent purpose" of the society and, on March 23, 1810, the hopes of the African Society were realized; it became the first Black mutual relief organization to be incorporated by the state.[73]

It is important to note that even after official endorsement from the state the African Society continued to flaunt its African heritage. Claiming March 23 as its new organizational anniversary, the African Society elected to memorialize the occasion "in an appropriate manner, to appear on the public streets with flying colors and a band of music." However, not surprisingly, racism and discrimination still plagued such demonstrations of African pride, and the African Society was warned not to proceed with its plans. One White "friend" reminded the society that although it was incorporated, it was still vulnerable to reprisals from enemies of the race: "Your society has a perfect right to every immunity which any other society has under its Act of Incorporation, and the city is bound by its obligations to preserve the peace, to protect and defend you; but such is the malignity of public prejudice that the authorities would be entirely powerless to protect you on the streets, and you would be torn in pieces by howling mobs." The African Society paraded regardless of the threats, declaring, "We will go though death stare us in the face." In so doing, the organizational historian reflected, the society "compelled the monster public prejudice to falter in its step . . . with the right secured to march through the public streets of the city at will, then and thereafter forever."[74]

Dr. James McCune Smith, a future member of the society, reported the events of that day and proudly stated: "In 1810, while New York was yet a slave state, a long array of colored men marched . . . in open day, bearing a banner inscribed with the portrait of a colored man and the words, 'Am I Not a Man and a Brother?'" Adding to the boldness of this behavior was society member Samuel Hardenburgh, who led the commemorative parade riding on horseback and carrying a drawn sword in his hand. This was a particularly shocking display of Black power at a time when slavery still dominated most of New York State. In an era when they should have been particularly fearful of White backlash, the members of the African Society flaunted their power and strength by marching in the streets in full regalia to celebrate the anniversary of its incorporation.[75]

Given the African Society's determination, it is not surprising that, on March 25, 1811, the proud members of the African Society paraded, again, to commemorate the first anniversary of its incorporation. For this special occasion, they selected elder and organizational vice-president, John Teasman, to address his fellow members. Foreshadowing George Lawrence's appeal, Teasman's commitment to racial solidarity was evident in his powerful denunciation of racism and his plea for Black unity. Although he began by expressing his gratitude for the incorporation of the African Society, he bemoaned the fact that the majority of Americans still viewed Blacks as subhuman: "notwithstanding all that you have done by the light of your daystar, still it is asserted that your genius is inferior." For Teasman, the solution to their oppression was education and the formation of Black associations. In particular, he believed that the African Society's example could "furnish a powerful argument" against slavery and racism. Ultimately, however, Teasman was most committed to the idea of Black unity. He urged his people to "be united as a band of brothers; be zealous in the noble cause in which you are embarked." For Teasman, unity and Black associations were the ultimate remedies for their plight and the plight of those still enslaved.[76]

Despite the African Society's strength at the 1811 celebration, one year later its members' belief in solidarity was put to the test. Without warning, their trusted treasurer, Daniel Berry, betrayed his brethren in the society and embezzled $500 from the organization. Immediately afterward, Berry disappeared from New York City and was never heard from again. This financial disaster almost destroyed the African Society; however, members refused to let the organization disintegrate. Member Peter Vogelsang reflected later: "At this momentous crisis, when all seemed lost—when we mutually accused each other with misplaced confidence; under this frown of fortune, the guardian angel of Africa was with us." The poignant image of the angel of Africa who watched over the efforts and strivings of the African Society was embodied in the society's enduring commitment to unity and autonomy. The membership rallied back and managed to raise enough funds to continue the society's activities. The members were careful, however, to elect as their new treasurer, a man described as "scrupulously careful and honest."[77]

The Daniel Berry fiasco divulged a few important facts about the African Society. First, Berry's disappearance revealed his own realization that he could not betray the society and remain part of New York's Black community. As has been demonstrated repeatedly in Black history, when a person betrays the community that person is literally and figuratively exiled. Indeed, years later, when another treasurer was similarly found to be short $1,100, he apparently fled and boarded a ship that "took him to distant parts." Second, the ability of the society to raise additional monies reflected the financial stature and determination of the members; although it was an arduous process, it was ultimately able to refinance the organization. Finally, as evidenced by Peter Vogelsang's comment, we see the members' commitment and unity; although such a tragedy could have divided and destroyed the organization, they were able to overcome obstacles and difficulties to rebuild their society. Even the devastating betrayal within the organization had not diminished their commitment to the community, nor their belief that racial solidarity was the answer to their plight.[78]

Within several years, the African Society had rebounded from its financial deficit and commenced its most enduring activity: the accumulation of real estate. On August 18, 1820, African Society members purchased a plot of land on which they constructed a meetinghouse. Members were quite pleased with its location for two revealing reasons. First, its position in the heart of the Black community allowed the building to become a community center for the entire Black population. In fact, they had apparently erected their lodge with the intention that it would also "accommodate other societies." Perhaps even more importantly, the African Society selected that site in hopes that, as the shipping industry expanded, the neighborhood would become "one of the most valuable locations in the city." However, as the organization's historian later reflected, "the change so confidently expected did not transpire, and the hope of our members never realized itself," as commerce expanded in the opposite direction. Regardless, the African Society members' planning and intentions demonstrated their dedication to community solidarity and economic autonomy. For many Blacks, their efforts must have been a symbolic representation of permanence and their hope that Black people could have a prosperous future in the United States.[79]

As evidenced by the African Society's social and economic endeavors, racial solidarity was the organization's motivating ideology. In fact, members routinely expressed their passionate belief in the power of unity during their anniversary celebrations. In 1815, Peter Vogelsang noted the problem of disunion in the Black community, lamenting that his people were plagued by the lack of "confidence in each other," an issue he believed exacerbated the "grievances under which we groan." Like fellow member George Lawrence, who spoke at the 1813 slave trade memorial, Vogelsang argued that the solution was for Black people to recognize "the importance of union" in their community. This strategy, he hoped, would "hasten the time . . . when slavery shall no more exist in these states; when every man in this republic whether European, Indian, or African, shall be eligible to citizenship, and enjoy the immunities of liberty and the rights of man."[80]

By 1823, members of the African Society had apparently crafted appeals for racial solidarity into a distinct philosophy, which one of its members articulated in honor of its thirteenth anniversary. Neither the text nor style of this address offers any clues regarding the speaker's identity; however, the anonymous author's message was deeply profound. The first step to unity, in his mind, was membership in a Black organization; such an affiliation necessitated the absence of selfish tendencies and forced people to recognize that they were responsible to a collective body. As he explained, membership in an association took the form of a "personal contract" that bound people to perform certain duties, "the neglect of which subjects the delinquent party to . . . public odium." More specifically, he offered a message consistent with African community ethics; he urged his brethren to view each other as a part of a family and remain conscious that one person, through his individual action, had the power to enhance the entire group.[81] These beliefs, he hoped, would easily translate into a political agenda in which activists recognized that they shared a common destiny with others in their community. In the case of the African Society, his vision was realized; this ideology inspired members to spread their philosophy to the rest of their brethren and develop other Black organizations.

As previously mentioned, the African Society had assisted in establishing the Wilberforce Philanthropic Association and the Brooklyn Woolman Association, but in 1825, the African Society supported yet another organization: the African Clarkson Association. As the African Society historian remarked later: "Our society after its incorporation, exerted a wide influence in the community. . . . In fact, it became so large that out of it sprang the Clarkson Society, the Wilberforce Society, the Union Society, the Woolman Society of Brooklyn, and our documents were taken as models for many others."[82] The African Clarkson Association did, indeed, echo the words of the African Society's preamble in its constitution, declaring, "having duly considered on the manifold vicissitudes of life, to which mankind are continually exposed; and actuated by a desire to improve our condition, [we] do form ourselves into an Association, for the benevolent purpose of raising funds, to be exclusively appropriated to aid and assist the widows and orphans of deceased members, and for improvement in literature." The African Clarkson Association also emulated the African Society by emphasizing racial solidarity and a strong community ethic. Not only was the organization financially accessible, initiation fees were more flexible and less costly, but the association demonstrated its commitment to community empowerment by focusing on the development of education and increasing literacy among its people.[83] Ultimately, like the African Society, the Clarkson Association's most important contribution was its existence as an autonomous Black organization designed to improve conditions for the race.

In addition to the African Clarkson Association, the African Society also continued to inspire the Wilberforce Philanthropic Association. Perhaps encouraged by the African Society's bravery at its anniversary celebrations, Wilberforce members honored their own success with an impressive procession in 1825. A foreign visitor, who documented the occasion, provided a fascinating and revealing account of the events:

> The coloured people of New York, belonging to this society, have a fund of their own, raised by weekly subscription, which is employed in assisting sick and unfortunate blacks. This fund, contained in a sky-blue box, was carried in the procession; the treasurer holding in his hand a large gilt key; the rest of the officers wore ribands [sic] of several colours, and badges like the officers of free masons; marshals with long staves walked outside of the procession. During a quarter of an hour, scarcely any but black faces were to be seen in Broadway.[84]

This description tells us a great deal about Black benevolent associations and the Black community in general during this period. Of particular note, is the place of honor that the organization's fund held in its commemoration; it indicates that, like the African Society, the Wilberforce Association placed significant importance on its ability to remain economically strong and independent. Yet perhaps the most important aspect of the Wilberforce Philanthropic Association's celebration was the mere fact that the members paraded at all. Such a public display, complete with marchers in full regalia, not only represented their connection to African culture but also reflected pride in themselves, their organization, their community, and their race.

Indeed, as in previous years, parades remained an important component in the struggle to forge a sense of community among Black New Yorkers. The visitor's statement that Broadway was completely overtaken by Black people suggests that the Wilberforce Association's procession was well attended by the entire community; very likely, Black New Yorkers remained supportive of these demonstrations of African culture and racial empowerment and enjoyed the opportunity for interaction. In fact, parades continued to be a critical way for Black New Yorkers to express racial pride and community solidarity at a variety of important community events. In both 1811 and 1814, the slave trade memorials commenced with impressive marches; in 1811, in particular, the African Society and the Wilberforce Philanthropic Association paraded "with music playing" along with "a number of citizens of colour, not belonging to either of the above societies, who felt a desire to honour the day by joining in the procession."[85] Even the Black patriots, who erected fortifications in Brooklyn during the War of 1812, marched to perform their work with a "delightful band of music and appropriate flags."[86]

Parades, therefore, were still not just ostentatious displays; they were opportunities to celebrate Black progress and crucial moments of racial solidarity when Blacks folks could unite together as a community. Furthermore, their actions sent a message about the permanence of free Blacks in the city and their commitment to unite against the odds. However, the Wilberforce Philanthropic Association's parade was important for one final reason; it was the last Black procession in New York City that was not the source of conflict and dissension in the community. As we shall see, by 1827, Black leaders became increasingly concerned about the Black community's image in American society and, as they became consumed by a desire to gain full citizenship, Black parades and other displays of African culture fell into disrepute.

* * *

For Black New Yorkers, the period between 1810 and 1826 caused a reconsideration of the meaning of "freedom" as emancipated Blacks found that their hopes and dreams were illusory. The violence, racism, discrimination, and poverty plaguing the community led some Blacks to despair, and their conflicting political perspectives reflected their frustration. Increasingly discontented with their status, a few activists began to "cast their minds to Africa" or to Haiti in search of the freedom, equality, and citizenship they so fervently desired.[87] The mere fact that free Blacks were considering emigration suggests that they were beginning to question their identity and their relationship to the United States. Men such as Paul Cuffe, Peter Williams Jr., and Jean Pierre Boyer saw themselves as part of a Pan-African community working toward the goal of racial progress, and their leadership inspired many Blacks to consider fleeing the United States to follow their dreams elsewhere.

In the end, however, only a few actually emigrated and the majority of Black New Yorkers elected to remain in the United States. For these courageous crusaders, the work of emancipation and equality was only just beginning. Among the Black leadership, racial solidarity and institution building continued to be the solutions; activists formed a series of Black organizations that assisted the community and created a sense of permanence and possibility in the United States.

Although unity and community building became crucial weapons in their fight against discrimination and injustice, the battle for total inclusion and equality intensified on July 4, 1827, the day that marked the ultimate day of emancipation for all Blacks in New York State. They soon discovered that the Black community would be faced with more obstacles as they continued their struggle to identify which strategy would gain equality and citizenship for their people.

CHAPTER 3

"Of What Use Are Processions?"
1827–1829

> Oh Liberty! . . . Thou hast loosened the hard bound fetters by which we
> were held; and by a voice sweet as the music of heaven, yet strong and
> powerful, reaching to the extreme boundaries of the state of New York,
> hath declared that we the people of colour, the sons of Afric, are free!
> —William Hamilton, 1827

> [Independence Day] is one [event] in which we are interested, and
> have cause to celebrate. . . . Indeed many of our forefathers laboured
> and shed their blood to produce it. . . . Why then should not the whole
> people, coloured and white, spend it as a day of rejoicing? . . . Can we
> not manifest the joy of our hearts and our gratitude to God, and our
> earthly benefactors without making a parade in the streets?
> —"R," 1827

> We wish to plead our own cause. Too long have others spoken for us.
> Too long has the publick [*sic*] been deceived by misrepresentations, in
> things, which concern us dearly. . . .
> —*Freedom's Journal*, 1827

On March 16, 1827, Black leaders unveiled a powerful new venue to articulate
their political voice, a newspaper they called *Freedom's Journal*. Plans for this
project had begun months prior, when a group of activists including William
Hamilton, Peter Williams Jr., Samuel Cornish, and John Russwurm met in the
home of African Society member Boston Crummell to craft a response to the
vicious attacks that local newspaper editors had launched against the Black community. At this meeting, they resolved to establish the first Black newspaper in
the United States and selected two well-educated and highly respected Black men,
Samuel Cornish and John Russwurm, to be its editors.[1] Because the inaugural
issue of *Freedom's Journal* appeared shortly before July 4, the official day of legal
emancipation in New York State, these activists were particularly hopeful that
the paper would be an effective tool to "vindicate our brethren" and "arrest the
progress of prejudice and shield [us] against consequent evils." Specifically, they
believed that *Freedom's Journal* could present an accurate view of their people
to combat the continual racist onslaught on their character; as they put it, "daily

slandered, we think that there ought to be some channel of communication between us and the public, through which a single voice may be heard, in defence
of Five Hundred Thousand Free People of Colour."[2]

Although concern over the Black community's image had one positive outcome,
the creation of *Freedom's Journal*, it also had significant consequences that revealed
deep divisions within the Black community over strategy. In particular, as Whites
grew increasingly fearful about the ramifications of emancipation, Black leaders
suspected that perhaps Jupiter Hammon had been right; they would have to win
the approval of American society in order to gain equality and citizenship. As a
result, many activists became consumed with the desire to appear "respectable"
and, in the months before legal emancipation, Black New Yorkers passionately
debated the question of how to "properly" celebrate their freedom. Most notably,
the leadership questioned the propriety of controversial demonstrations of African
culture and eschewed public processions. On the surface, Black New Yorkers appeared to be arguing over the tradition of parading, however buried within that
issue were complex questions about identity and the relationship of Black people
to the United States. Did they really see themselves as Americans? If so, did being
an American citizen require them to relinquish their connection to their African
heritage? Most importantly, would emancipation actually provide Black people
with the opportunity to be free and equal members of American society?

As Black activists pondered these questions, they were suddenly forced to take
a stand. As newly emancipated people flooded into the city from the countryside,
the enemies of emancipation galvanized their efforts to forcibly remove free Blacks
from the United States. In response to this growing colonization movement and
their concern about political conditions in Africa and Haiti, most leaders made a
crucial decision; they reflexively defended their right to American citizenship and,
in so doing, took a definitive step toward embracing moral uplift as a strategy to
obtain their goals. As they soon discovered, the debates over Emancipation Day
and colonization were deeply connected. Their ultimate move toward claiming
an American rather than an African identity marked a powerful turning point
and set the course for Black political action throughout the antebellum era.

* * *

On April 23, 1827, a "very large and respectable number of the People of Colour"
held a gathering in the African Society's meetinghouse to plan an appropriate
celebration honoring legal emancipation in New York State.[3] Led by William
Hamilton and William Miller, the group determined that the Black community
should commemorate July 4 as a "Jubilee of Emancipation from Domestic Slavery"
with an official address and prayers delivered from the various religious orders.
Although this program seemed like a conventional memorial for Black New
Yorkers, the committee, dominated by African Society members, took a rather
unorthodox position that threatened an important tradition in the communi-

ty.[4] Fearful that Whites would oppose a procession, the committee abandoned the practice of parading and declared that Black folks should "abstain from all processions in the public streets on that day." Committee members stated their decision was based on their desire to show proper "gratitude" for abolition, and, therefore, they urged their brethren to "do no act that may have the least tendency to disorder."[5]

This was a startling shift in philosophy for the African Society, which had a proud legacy of parading in honor of the organization's anniversary and had routinely organized large community celebrations. Even more, it seemed to be a dramatic change for William Hamilton and William Miller, who had publicly espoused Pan-Africanism and Black nation building beginning in 1809.[6] However, the political stakes were extremely high on the eve of emancipation, prompting activists to radically alter their strategy. Many Black leaders opposed parading on this occasion because it gave ammunition to White newspaper editors who were fanning the flames of violence and ill will by presenting negative views of the Black community. There were, indeed, a few journalists who were particularly well-known during this era for their unmerciful persecution of Blacks in their articles. Mordecai Noah, who had established quite a tradition of attacking of the Black community in the early 1820s, continued his crusade by openly accusing Blacks of being thieves and beggars. Likewise, John Jacob Flournoy, Southern proslavery propagandist, blanketed New York City with his assertions of Black "ignorance, brutal passions, lewdness, obscenity, animal appetites, viciousness, and illegitimacy."[7]

Aware of the public attention that emancipation brought on the Black community, the organizing committee likely wanted to prove that Black people could conduct themselves in an "appropriate" fashion. The committee astutely recognized that the Black community's image mattered, and that the status of Blacks in the United States ultimately depended on whether Whites believed that they were worthy of equality. In response, Black leaders chose to embrace moral uplift strategy and sought to provide an alternative image of their race. Hopeful that, through respectable behavior, they could advance the cause of abolition and gain citizenship, the organizing committee concluded that Emancipation Day should be commemorated in a solemn proper manner.

Yet while the organizing committee was carefully crafting a celebration that would serve its race uplift strategy, the vast majority of Black New Yorkers had a different agenda. Wanting to fully celebrate freedom in their distinct cultural and political style, another group formed its own planning commission to organize an alternative event.[8] On June 22, 1827, an announcement appeared in the pages of *Freedom's Journal,* declaring that there would be two separate emancipation celebrations in New York City; the first would occur on July 4, and honor their freedom in a "becoming manner," and the other, on July 5, would include a grand procession through the streets.[9]

"De grandest bobalition dat ever vus be!" This broadside depicts one example of the negative propaganda circulated in New York City in the months before legal emancipation. Not only did this broadside depict the Black community with unflattering images (an aminal and a devil), but it also mocked the decision to hold Black independence day on July 5. (Courtesy of the Collection of the New York Historical Society, Negative no. 77639d.)

The new group was clearly less concerned with winning popular approval, because its members created a celebration that challenged American society and flaunted their African heritage. Their critique of America was inherent in the decision to hold the celebration on July 5, a powerful political protest that flatly rejected the idea that July 4 could be a *Black* independence day. Black New Yorkers had been banned from July 4 celebrations in 1800, and they were well aware that the notions of freedom circulated during the Revolutionary War had not been uniformly applied to their people. This contradiction must have been glaringly apparent to the community and, particularly in light of Southern slavery, Black New Yorkers had to question if they could celebrate American independence with a clear conscience. Although the specific beliefs of the July 5 committee are not available, because *Freedom's Journal* declined to print its resolutions, the committee likely embraced the sentiments of Albany Blacks who "deem[ed] it proper to celebrate on the 5th," because "the 4th day of July is the day that the National

Independence of this country is recognized by the white citizens." Apparently, for many Black folks, a celebration on the fifth brought attention to their unique experience and more accurately reflected their reality as unequal residents in a hostile land.[10]

In addition to opposing July 4 as Blacks' independence day, the July 5 committee rejected the notion of a solemn commemoration. Reveling in their heritage, they remained committed to the tradition of parading because it allowed for ritual, ceremony, and the opportunity to socialize and interact freely. Ultimately, they must have recognized that to abandon parading would have been to abandon a crucial part of their cultural past and their ability to celebrate publicly as a Black community. As a result, although some in the leadership sought to emulate respectable behavior and gain White approval, the majority of Black New Yorkers wanted to claim the streets and honor their emancipation in a distinctly African fashion.

Even though a compromise was reached by having two commemorations, the movement to hold a procession disturbed members of the Black leadership, especially after another newspaper article reminded them about the power of their omnipresent enemies. Just one week before Emancipation Day, *Freedom's Journal* reprinted an editorial from Mordecai Noah that painted a grim picture of Black emancipation. Noah claimed that he doubted Blacks could become free and equal citizens because, "judging from the daily scenes exhibited in New York," Blacks would never be proved worthy of the "blessings of property, industry, peace and good behavior." In particular, he attacked the Black community for insisting upon a parade to celebrate "this Jubilee nonsense" and argued that all White New Yorkers should "fear excess, extravagance and riot of every sort" if the procession occurred. Even more, he sarcastically complained about the "fashionable participators in the 'rights of man,' who had the audacity to dispute our possession of Broadway, Bowery and Park!" After all, he concluded, such behavior would not be allowed in the South, and he could not understand "what results of any other than a pernicious nature can attend it here."[11]

In response, Black activists encouraged their community members to carefully consider the consequences of their actions. *Freedom's Journal*'s editors, John Russwurm and Samuel Cornish, renewed their objection to processions, stating, "We are no friends to public parades, and have long since entered our protest against them." Likewise, an anonymous author, known only as "R," denounced the July 5 celebration, maintaining that parades had little tangible value and did nothing to actually improve their status in society: "Of what use are processions? Do they make us richer, wiser, or better?" Even more, however, he urged his brethren to reflect upon the public perception that such displays created: "Have they not rather a tendency to injure us, by exciting prejudice, and making the public believe we ache for nothing so much as show?" Ultimately, the author claimed that they should abandon parades because their White benefactors "heartily disapprove of our making a street parade" and going forward would only "injure our reputation and interest as a people." He insisted that to properly show their gratitude for the end of slavery, Blacks must not march.[12]

What is most striking about R's letter, however, is that at the core of his remarks was a crucial perspective on identity. He suggested that free Blacks should view themselves as Americans and argued that the Fourth of July could unite Black and White people in a common celebration. Emphasizing that many Black men fought and died in the Revolutionary War, he insisted that all Americans, "coloured and white," should "spend it as a day of rejoicing." According to the author, if everyone acknowledged the Fourth of July as a shared day of freedom it would help Blacks and Whites see each other as equal American citizens. Significantly, R seemed to have the support of crucial segments of the Black community; following his letter, the African Society, Asbury Church, and Presbyterian Church printed a statement declaring their solidarity with the organizing committee and agreeing to celebrate on the fourth without a public procession.[13]

Despite appearances, however, the matter was not so easily resolved. On the contrary, Black New Yorkers remained hopelessly divided over their perspectives on "independence" day and the practice of parading; in fact, they still insisted upon holding separate and competing emancipation celebrations. Worse, the situation was far more complicated than it seemed because the true source of contention was not simply about the date and style of the commemoration but, rather, it centered on questions of identity and political strategy. Did they, as R had suggested, view themselves as true Americans? If so, what did being an American actually mean? Did embracing an American identity demand an endorsement of moral improvement and the renunciation of African traditions? Notably, the responses to these issues did not fall neatly along class lines or according to organizational affiliation; even those who had officially opposed parading remained deeply conflicted about their views on moral uplift and lingering connections to their African heritage. Ultimately, as the events on July 4 and 5 revealed, Black New Yorkers spent the days of emancipation engaged in a battle to reconcile these contradictory leanings.

The first signs of the ideological fissure among July 4 supporters came on the day of their respectable solemn commemoration. Tellingly, descriptions of the African Zion Church for the occasion reveal that even the decorations illustrated conflicting political philosophies on critical issues such as moral uplift, emigration, and national identity. Their endorsement of Black moral reform was apparent from the banners of the various Black societies, which adorned the church, inscribed with the words *unity, charity,* and *temperance.* Likewise, the portraits of White abolitionists, John Jay and Matthew Clarkson, hung on the walls in silent acknowledgment of their contribution to the abolition of slavery. Yet activists still included a bust of President Boyer of Haiti, which "filled our hearts with gratitude to heaven, for having placed a portion of our brethren, in a situation so favourable for developing their powers of body and mind, and evidencing to the world, that all men are equal by nature."[14] Even on the day when they were honoring their new status as free Americans, Black leaders recalled the notion of emigration and their tenuous position in the United States; they celebrated those who had sought a better life in Haiti and the hope of a free and independent Black nation.

Surrounded by this complex array of images, elder William Hamilton graced the pulpit and delivered an address honoring the abolition of slavery in New York State. As with the church decorations, his speech was a complicated amalgamation of the various ideas circulating in the Black community including African pride, gratitude to benevolent Whites, and moral uplift. Hamilton opened by reveling in the meaning of Emancipation Day, a moment that signified the liberation of African people. "This day we stand redeemed from a bitter thralldom. Of us it may be truly said, 'the last agony is o'er,' the Africans are restored! No more shall the accursed name of slave be attached to us—no more shall *negro* and *slave* be synonymous."[15] It is especially revealing that Hamilton chose to say the "*Africans* are restored," for his words reflected his perspective on the identity question. Unlike R, who made exclusive claims to an American identity, Hamilton impressed upon the audience that the privileges of freedom and equality were due to all humans, even those who asserted their African ancestry. To Hamilton, therefore, it was possible to be both a child of Africa and an American citizen; in fact, throughout his speech, he repeatedly referred to his audience as both the "sons of Afric" *and* as "citizens" of the United States. Hamilton's perspective was likely bolstered by his belief that Black people had finally won an ideological battle, a bloodless uprising in which Revolutionary War rhetoric was finally being applied to them. Emancipation, in Hamilton's view, entitled Blacks to equal citizenship, regardless of their African heritage, because legal emancipation signaled a "victory obtained by the principles of liberty . . . over prejudice, injustice and foul oppression."[16]

Although Hamilton commenced with a passionate introduction, asserting the rights of Africa's descendants to American citizenship, he clearly understood the political stakes on Emancipation Day. Aware that they were poised at a crucial moment in the battle for public opinion, Hamilton apparently recognized that Black civil rights would only be granted if they could demonstrate their worthiness. As a result, the majority of his speech dramatically departed from his oration in 1815 in which he had focused primarily on Pan-Africanism and Black Nationalism. Instead, he sought to redeem the image of his race by humbly offering thanks to the White benefactors and issuing a call for moral improvement. Obviously feeling compelled to demonstrate proper "gratitude," Hamilton honored the Manumission Society for its continuing support stating that its members had "laboured hard and incessantly in order to bring us from our degraded situation, and restore us to the rights of men. It has stood, a phalanx, firm and undaunted, amid the flames of prejudice, and the shafts of calumny."[17] Most surprising, however, was

the conclusion of Hamilton's speech. Rather than reiterating his previous suggestion that Africa might offer the key to his people's future, he acknowledged that
free Blacks would likely remain in the United States and the years immediately
following emancipation could determine the conditions for future generations.
Therefore, Hamilton made a crucial strategic decision: He elected to embrace
moral improvement as the best method for racial advancement.

For Hamilton, the success of moral uplift depended primarily on the youth
and the women; those he viewed as the potential and the moral barometer of
the race, respectively. He was particularly passionate about the young people,
because he knew that upon them "rest[ed] the high responsibility of redeeming
the character of our people." Because their honor and destiny were at stake, Hamilton chastised the younger generation for being "sunk into the deepest frivolity
and lethargy that any can be sunk" and urged the young people toward "the path
of virtue." In particular, he encouraged them to pursue education, because such
action would disabuse American society of the belief that "you are not capable
of the study of what may be called abstruse literature, and that you are deficient
in moral character." Ultimately, Hamilton hoped that young Black men would
realize appropriate moral conduct and educational enlightenment were their
duties to the Black community: "I look to you, and pray you, by all that proper
pride you feel in being men, that you show yourselves such, by performing acts
of worth equal with other men."[18]

As with the youth, Hamilton placed a great deal of responsibility on Black
women.[19] He castigated those women in the community who had forgotten their
purpose and encouraged them to reconsider the ramifications of their actions. "I
would have you discountenance that loud vocability of gabble, that too much char-
acterizes us in the street: I would look upon him, or her, that hailed me with too
loud, or vulgar accents, as one who had forgot what was due to female modesty."
Hamilton further suggested that if women refused to entertain the advances of
immoral men, men would be forced to alter their behavior. "It is for you to form
the manners of men. . . . If you give preference to men of understanding . . . they
will endeavour to make themselves suitable to your wishes." Thus, according to
Hamilton, if women and children transformed their behavior, the men would
likely follow. Yet it is important to note that Hamilton reflected a slightly more
progressive republicanism, for his speech concluded with a special plea for female
education: "Above all, endeavour to improve your own minds. I know that in the
ability to improve, you are more than a match for white females, in all proper
female education."[20]

In the final analysis, Hamilton's speech marked a critical shift in Black political
thought; though his previous orations had contained powerful celebrations of
Africa's past and its potential political destiny, his words in 1827 were influenced
by the significance of Emancipation Day and his concern about how free Blacks
were perceived by their critics. Like the rest of the Black leadership, Hamilton was

making a gradual turn toward moral uplift and republican appeals for citizenship. However, it quickly became clear that most Black New Yorkers had not unilaterally accepted the usefulness of moral uplift; for William Hamilton's speech marked the end of the July 4 emancipation activities, but not the festivities in honor of Black liberation.

The July 5 commemoration was a striking contrast to the preceding day; it was a boisterous, joyful celebration that flaunted both their freedom and their African heritage. Over two thousand marchers including newly freed Africans, several Brooklyn societies, and numerous musical groups flooded into the streets.[21] Even young children such as future activists Henry Highland Garnet and James Mc-Cune Smith "fell into the ranks" of the parade, which Smith later described as "a real full-souled, full-voiced shouting for joy, marching through the crowded streets, with feet jubilant to songs of freedom." African cultural influences figured prominently in this festival; Smith's depiction of jubilant feet moving to the rhythms of freedom was not the only reference to the power of African music on that day. The *New York American* also reported that there were five musical bands, whose performances demonstrated the "talent for music of the African race." Even more, Smith reflected that "Africa itself" was represented by "hundreds who had survived the middle passage" and recalled that Emancipation Day reflected a time when people "rejoiced in their nationality, and hesitated not to call each other 'Africans,' or 'descendants of Africa.'"[22]

Yet the most shocking part of the parade was not the exhibition of African culture but, rather, the identity of the participants. According to James McCune Smith, the African Society for Mutual Relief, the Wilberforce Philanthropic Association, and the African Clarkson Association all marched with their organizational colors and banners. In addition, he noted that the grand marshal was African Society member Samuel Hardenburgh, "a splendid-looking black man," who proudly rode on a white horse with a drawn sword in his hand and, accompanied by his official aides and the speaker of the day, marched through City Hall Park to salute the mayor before leading the procession down Broadway.[23] In violation of the official sanction, Hardenburgh and various members of the African Society had apparently assumed their conventional role and celebrated with their people. There is the possibility that as Smith was only fourteen years old in 1827, he confused the Emancipation Day parade with another Black community celebration. Yet considering the importance of this event, it seems unlikely. Even Smith reflected that Emancipation Day was so powerful that it was "never to be forgotten by young lads who . . . first felt themselves impelled along that grand procession of liberty."[24]

Assuming that the African Society and its affiliates participated in the July 5 procession, it appears that many Black leaders who still honored their African heritage and felt passion for freedom found the parade difficult to resist. Despite the opposition, those who ultimately participated in the march must have un-

derstood that the tradition of public celebrations served a critical political function. For as Black New Yorkers boldly claimed the streets, they demonstrated
a distinct racial consciousness and flaunted their status as free people. Perhaps
they hoped, as William Hamilton had suggested, that their African heritage and
racial identity would not preclude them from attaining equality and citizenship
in their adopted country. What they probably did not anticipate, however, was
that in the face of virulent White opposition, Hamilton's growing focus on moral
improvement would blossom into a full-fledged movement among the leadership.
Yet they would soon discover that the expansion of moral uplift strategy and the
subsequent calls for embracing an American identity would force them to make
a critical choice.

In the days following, it appeared that New Yorkers had accepted the inevitability of Black parading; even their opponents had to admit that the July 5 celebration was successful and above reproach. The *New York American,* for example,
reported that the marchers so were impressive that the "difference of colour was
forgotten."[25] More importantly, *Freedom's Journal* reflected on the July 5 festivities
and regretted the disharmony within the community over the event. Moved by the
banner entitled "unity" at the July 4 commemoration, the editors stated: "We are
brethren by the ties of blood and misfortunes, and we can perceive no sufficient
reasons, why matters of a trifling nature, should cause so much excitation and
division among us."[26]

Yet the discussion about Black parades and morality was not over. On July 13
and 20, Samuel Cornish and John Russwurm renewed the debate by dedicat-
ing significant portions of *Freedom's Journal* to an issue they thought had been
severely ignored: "the propriety of conduct." In veiled language, they questioned
the value of parading and other forms of public display, arguing that Black people
should avoid everything that "has the least tendency to bring our body still lower
in public estimation." Even more, they suggested that every action they chose,
even "mere trifles," should be subjected to a litmus test: "Are they becoming?
Do our true friends esteem us more highly for putting on such airs?" Although
Cornish and Russwurm believed it was wrong to tell their brethren "what should
or should not be done on particular days in the year," they remained shocked
that the community would spend so much time on the "frivolous amusements
of the hour" rather than on the issues that would "render us more respectable to
the world at large." Ultimately, they concluded that Black New Yorkers should
abandon all public processions because "no man of colour can be so foolish as
to persuade himself or others that they can have a favourable effect on the minds
of our friends."[27]

With this editorial, it became clear that opposition to parading had morphed
into an endorsement of moral improvement's potential to advance the race. Keenly
aware of their enemies, Cornish and Russwurm encouraged their brethren to
reform their behavior in hopes that their actions could transform public opinion.

Reverend Samuel Cornish. (Courtesy of the Collection of the New York Historical Society, Negative no. 74637.)

As they explained, "placed as we are in society, propriety of conduct never was more essential to any people than to us. . . . We wish not to hide the faults of our brethren—but to correct them—to render our whole body more respectable . . . to be a 'wall of fire' around them against the envenomed darts of pretended friends—to be champions in their defence against the attacks of open and manly foes." They seemed especially convinced that such a strategy would be successful because, in their estimation, any time a man lived according to "rules of propriety, economy and virtue," he would earn the respect and commendation of the "multitude" even in the "hour of adversity and trouble."[28]

Despite their urgings, Cornish and Russwurm did not immediately convince their brethren of the "impropriety" of parading because, by 1828, the advocates of July 5 celebrations seemed to have emerged victorious. Indeed, the tradition of Black public processions was a hard habit to break. For the first anniversary of the Abolition of Domestic Slavery, Blacks celebrated on July 5 with another grand procession. Although the event was apparently not hotly debated in the community, John Russwurm was typically cautious and issued his sincere hope that "everything will be done with the greatest decorum, leaving it out of the power of any set of men to speak disrespectfully of us." Even though some in the leadership obviously remained fearful about the community's public image, the rest of Black New York took to the streets. In keeping with tradition, Samuel Hardenburgh served as grand marshal and was followed by other members of the Black community, including all the Black benevolent societies of New York City and Brooklyn, who displayed banners and marched in time to musical bands. In 1828, Black New Yorkers learned from their previous disharmony and celebrated their emancipation as a united community.[29] Even John Russwurm depicted the 1828 celebration in a highly positive fashion: "We are proud to say, that notwithstanding the great crowd assembled on the occasion every thing passed off without the least riot or confusion."[30]

However, one week later, Russwurm renewed his attack on public displays, issuing a biting indictment of Blacks in Brooklyn for holding another parade. Although they had participated in New York City's celebration, Black Brooklynites resolved to have a march in the streets of their own neighborhood and, according to contemporary accounts, the procession was massive extending over a half mile. Russwurm reprimanded Brooklyn residents for reflecting poor taste and bringing out the "lower orders of society." He was particularly frustrated by the behavior of women, because he had received reports about "the insolence of certain Coloured females, and of the debasing excesses committed on that ever memorable day." Concerned about the frivolity and perceived lack of morality that allegedly accompanied the Brooklyn march, Russwurm urged his brethren to consider their actions more seriously: "Has any man yet been held in estimation on account of his *fine dress*? is it mark of *prudence* to put all our earnings upon our backs? and finally, from this imprudence, to be *unprovided* with the *food*, and *clothing*, and *fuel* during the chilling blasts of winter?" Perhaps recognizing the inevitability of parading, he reaffirmed his desire to celebrate in a "rational manner" and encouraged Blacks in the region to have one united celebration that would "be a *finale* for one year at least."[31]

John Russwurm's words were ultimately prophetic; the commemoration in

1828 was a "finale" of sorts. Although the July 5 supporters appeared to have won the ideological battle in 1827 and 1828, the advocates of moral uplift eventually won the war. In light of the tensions and passionate arguments over parading and immorality, emancipation celebrations in New York City did not persist into the 1830s and even Black organizations ceased parading for their anniversaries. Indeed, the last procession held in honor of the African Society's anniversary appeared in March 1829. In the end, parades fell into disrepute and emancipation commemorations disappeared altogether.[32]

The end of public festivals may have been due, in part, to Black New Yorkers' increasing disillusionment with emancipation because, as the years following 1827 demonstrated, the reality did not offer much to celebrate. Black New Yorkers found themselves in a state of "quasi-freedom" and, ironically, conditions were the worst for the masses of Black people, those who had insisted upon a grand celebration marking their freedom.[33] Yet it is clear that parades also vanished because of pressure from moral uplift advocates, as the postemancipation era witnessed Black leaders' increasing efforts to use moral improvement to reform their brethren and, hopefully, gain citizenship. Ultimately, however, the Black leadership's endorsement of moral uplift and renunciation of African cultural expressions had lasting ramifications. For although Black benevolent associations continued to function throughout the nineteenth century, their public image among Black New Yorkers faded as their celebrations, which had united the community, vanished.

Discussions about moral improvement became particularly pronounced following Emancipation Day, when newly freed people began flocking to urban centers; the Black population increased dramatically, from about 3,500 in 1800 to nearly 12,500 in 1827.[34] *Freedom's Journal* editors, John Russwurm and Samuel Cornish, were particularly disturbed by this migration and pleaded with freed Blacks not to seek opportunity in the crowded cities "where there is little for them to do, and where every thing is calculated to draw their uncultivated minds from the line of duty."[35] Clearly their concern partly stemmed from a desire to protect the freed people morally, because cities were considered breeding grounds for crime and sin. More importantly, however, they were aware that White New Yorkers shared these fears especially because New York City's newspapers routinely expressed doubt that newly freed Black migrants could become productive members of American society. The *New York Morning Chronicle* equated Blacks with poverty, disease, and crime and thought that emancipation would increase the evil in the city by "a ten-fold degree." Likewise, Mordecai Noah continued his attack on the Black community; arguing that "there are few subjects connected with the moral and political well being of the community, which are more fitted to excited feelings of anxiety and alarm, than the character of the negro population of this country." Even worse, he maintained that "the free negroes of this city are a nuisance incomparably greater than a million slaves."[36]

In response to these attacks, Black activists published letters in *Freedom's Journal* that angrily criticized Noah. One author, in particular, questioned White standards of morality on the grounds that, although there were some immoral members of the Black community, "such baseness of character and conduct . . . is confined to a very small portion of the people of colour; and we wish it were confined to a smaller portion of the whites." Another correspondent wrote that while many in the Black community "deeply regret the conduct of the vile . . . it is beyond their power to correct the evil."[37] However, others in the Black leadership apparently disagreed with this conclusion, because many activists began to dedicate themselves more fully to moral uplift in hopes that this strategy would alleviate racism and bring the rights of citizenship to their people. Samuel Cornish and John Russwurm, in particular, stressed their desire to improve the moral, social, and economic conditions in their community by affirming that their newspaper was dedicated to the "dissemination of useful knowledge among our brethren, [of] their moral and religious improvement" as an effective method for racial advancement. They also emphasized the importance of education, obtaining the suffrage, and remembering "rules of economy."[38] For Cornish, Russwurm, and increasing numbers of the Black leadership, proper moral conduct was becoming the primary way to improve their public image and thereby convince American society to end slavery and extend all the rights and privileges of citizenship.

In the two years following legal emancipation, Black activists focused much of their race uplift program on the issue of education. Perhaps recognizing the desperate need for literacy and skills among their people, particularly those who had just arrived from the countryside, Black leaders hoped they could transform the Black population into an educated, productive, respectable community that would prove the capacity of the race. John Russwurm, in particular, echoed William Hamilton's Emancipation Day appeal and stressed the importance of education for young people: "More general efforts should be made for the education of our rising youth, for it is upon them that all our hopes for the future respectability of our people are fixed." In that spirit, aware that the African Free School was not reaching as many children as possible, Black leaders resolved to review conditions in the Black community and ascertain why attendance rates were so low.[39] Significantly, the answer to this question created increasing activism among Black women; it soon became clear that children lacked appropriate attire and, for a solution to this problem, Black activists turned to the women.

On January 23, 1828, various "Females of Colour, Ministers of the different coloured Churches in this city, and Members of the Manumission Society," met to form the African Dorcas Association. According to the first article of its constitution, the African Dorcas Association's primary purpose was to provide clothing and other necessary items for poor students who could not afford their own. "Whereas, an unusual number of children belonging to the African Free Schools . . . absent themselves from school . . . [for] want of suitable clothing; WE, whose names are hereunto subscribed, do agree to form ourselves into an association for the purpose of procuring donations in clothing, &c. both for males and females of the said schools, to furnish them to such children as may need supply."[40] Cognizant that there would be some resistance to a female organization involved in education, Black ministers agreed to serve as a governing board to offer assistance and public legitimacy to the association by keeping the records, receiving donations, and setting the meetings. However, the women of the African Dorcas Association soon began to exercise more power over the organization's functioning; in February 1828, they held their first independent meeting during which they elected their own officers and board of managers. Significantly, many of the women who composed the organizational leadership were the wives, daughters, and sisters of African Society members and quickly became part of New York City's Black leadership.[41]

The African Dorcas Association revealed a great deal about the gender dynamics within New York's Black activist community. Certainly, it offered an indication that Black women had embraced moral uplift philosophy, because the association and its focus on children's education strongly conformed to White republican notions about the proper roles for women. It was a form of activism that reflected mothering and nurturing and was therefore not particularly threatening to the status quo. However, we should not be too hasty in assuming that the structure of political activism in the Black community reflected sexism, particularly because the African Dorcas Association's activities also reflected an African ethic in which people collectively contributed their skills to uplift the community. Because it had been determined that children were not attending school because they did not possess adequate clothing, Black women simply put their talents to work. It is important to recall that these activists saw themselves as part of a unified project and, although men and women performed different roles, everyone's contribution was seen as essential.[42]

Indeed, less than a month after its first meeting, the African Dorcas Association was already receiving praise for its endeavors. An editorial in *Freedom's Journal* stated, "Great good may reasonably be expected to result from the exertion of this laudable and novel institution." The article also provided a brief glimpse into their early activities; the women divided into sewing circles, which met every two weeks "to alter, mend, and make up clothing for the destitute boys and girls" and, in the meantime, they dedicated themselves to soliciting contributions. The newspaper admired the women for participating in "a purpose so praiseworthy" and encouraged others to support the effort. John Russwurm particularly appealed to Christian benevolence by evoking Biblical references: "Let many a poor and destitute child have cause to say 'I was naked and ye clothed me.'"[43]

Despite their excellent work, the advisory committee had perhaps foreseen that the women would come under public attack. By September 1828, *Freedom's Journal* surreptitiously spoke of antagonism toward the African Dorcas Association.

It is unclear precisely who their enemies were, or how the antipathy manifested itself, however the newspaper stated: "The Dorcas Society, in common with other institutions, has its enemies—this, as well as other considerations, should excite its members to renewed interest in the good work." This remark, of course, suggested that the African Dorcas Association's detractors also opposed the power and success of *all* Black institutions and educational efforts. In response, *Freedom's Journal* encouraged Blacks to support the African Dorcas Association's mission and denounced all those who would hinder the association's efforts. "Such as have the hardiness and meanness to persecute a society, so benevolent and good in its purposes and tendency, must eventually hide their heads in shame and disgrace."[44]

Regardless of the attacks against the African Dorcas Association, the organization flourished. By November, the women were again praised for their labor; an anonymous author, "Cato," wrote an article pleading with the New York community to assist the society's work for the children. "This society has already done much good; but requires aid from those who are able to bestow something to promote its humane object."[45] John Russwurm echoed the tribute, remarking on the association's "determination to perform every thing in their power to enable the poor children of our coloured brethren to attend their winter's school." By February 1829, the organization was able to report some successes; the women had managed to distribute 168 articles of clothing and clothe sixty-four boys and girls. As result, these underprivileged children were afforded the opportunity to pursue education and, hopefully, improve the future of the Black community.[46]

Yet despite the Black leadership's best efforts, Blacks continued to face bitter opposition from the enemies of emancipation. Clearly, the leadership's attempts to educate and reform the Black community were not sufficient to convince many Whites that Black people could be worthy citizens. The most threatening manifestation of this racism was in the form of a burgeoning colonization movement, which sought to relocate the free Black population to Africa. For this discussion, it is essential to understand the difference between emigration and colonization. *Emigration* was a movement that had been initiated by Black activists, such as Paul Cuffe and Peter Williams Jr., who thought that their people would never achieve full equality in the United States and therefore should seek freedom among their brethren elsewhere. *Colonization,* however, was an idea championed by White racists who did not want to interact with free Blacks on an equal basis and plotted to forcibly remove Blacks from the United States before they gained American citizenship and posed a real threat to Southern slavery. Although many Black New Yorkers had previously endorsed various emigration proposals, most were hostile to the colonization movement. Perhaps most poignantly, Blacks feared that they would be compelled to leave the land where their ancestors lived, struggled, fought, and died. Ultimately, the growing influence of colonization had unforeseen repercussions; as Black activists scrambled to defend their rights, they gradually distanced themselves from their African heritage and slowly embraced an American identity.

The rise of the colonization movement was marked by the formation of the American Colonization Society (ACS) on December 28, 1816. Even though the ACS was functioning by 1817, the organization did not gain much power or influence until the middle of the 1820s. At its inception, the ACS was composed of three dominant factions. One group, composed of wealthy slaveholders, hoped that the removal of free Blacks would increase the value of their slaves and discourage runaways. The second consisted of Northern racists, who feared that free Blacks would ultimately dominate the country's political, economic, and social system. Finally, there was a small minority of committed antislavery activists who were sympathetic to the problem of racism in American society and believed that colonization was appropriate restitution for the crime of slavery. By the 1820s, however, most antislavery activists had abandoned the organization; as a result, Southern slaveholders and Northern racists who were anxious to rid American society of its free Black population dominated the ACS. Together, they emphasized the worst aspects of the free Black community, describing them as "notoriously ignorant, degraded and miserable, mentally diseased, broken spirited, acted upon by no motive to honorable exertions, scarcely reached in their debasement by the heavenly light, the freedmen wander unsettled and unbefriended through our land, or sit indolent abject and sorrowful. . . ." Thus inspired by these negative images, the ACS secured territory on the coast of Africa in 1821, which they named Liberia, for their resettlement scheme.[47]

Within New York's Black community, there was increasing concern about the ACS's growing influence, not only because it represented the possibility of forced removal, but also because emigration had been deemed a failure following a flood of negative reports about conditions in Haiti and Liberia. Political turmoil had plagued the Haitian emigration scheme and caused Black leaders to temper their support of the plan, a move that increased by the late 1820s. Although *Freedom's Journal* celebrated the relocation of enslaved Virginians to Haiti in December 1827, by July 1828, they received a letter that "gave a gloomy picture of the affairs of that island, both political and commercial." Therefore, even though John Russwurm had praised President Jean Pierre Boyer in June 1827, describing Boyer as "a man of considerable intellect and great energy" who had successfully established a strong government, he began to openly criticize Boyer's policies. Russwurm noted, in particular, the reflections of an emigrant who bemoaned Boyer's taxation plans: "Ruin stares every body in the face . . . should this policy of the government be continued, we shall have to leave the Island." Perhaps most disappointing, however, was Boyer's decision to pay 150 million francs to France to secure Haitian independence, because his actions seemed to negate the armed struggle against slavery and caused major financial problems in the fledgling country. By 1829, John Russwurm revealed that endorsement of Haitian emigration had practically disappeared due to "unfavourable reports of those who have returned."[48]

There were also serious concerns within the Black leadership about Liberia. In particular, Black activists had doubts about the specific mode of governance in Liberia because the ACS controlled every aspect of the colony's functioning. As scholar Robert Johnson Jr. noted, the irony was that although they had gone to Africa "to escape White domination, [colonists] found themselves under the control of the same group of people they supposedly left in America." Even worse, they worried about political unrest and conflict in the new territory, especially after Black leaders heard news about unstable relations with indigenous Africans who resented the colony's existence. Tensions climaxed in 1822, when over eight hundred Africans attacked the settlers on November 8 and returned three weeks later with two thousand Africans for another battle. If these problems did not provide sufficient deterrents, Black New Yorkers were also receiving reports of the ghastly mortality rates among the colonists, often reaching 50 percent, which were the result of exposure to tropical diseases. Ultimately, death tolls soon revealed that "colonization was not merely a form of removal, but also of extermination."[49]

Black activists became so concerned by the possibility of forced removal to these troubled locations that they felt compelled to represent Black people's views on the colonization question in the pages of *Freedom's Journal*. As editors John Russwurm and Samuel Cornish explained: "We wish to plead our own cause. Too long have others spoken for us. Too long has the publick [sic] been deceived by misrepresentations, in things which concern us dearly." They further remarked that the paper was expedient at the time because "so many schemes are in action concerning our people."[50] These statements, of course, were veiled references to ACS's colonization schemes. Significantly, one day after the emancipation celebrations in 1827, a cogent anticolonization letter appeared in *Freedom's Journal*. It is particularly ironic that the letter coincided with Emancipation Day, because the author's words reflected the growing movement among free Blacks to remain in the United States and fight for their rights as American citizens.

Written by "A Coloured Baltimorean," the letter explained the reasons why Blacks could not, in good conscience, support colonization schemes. The author was later identified as William Watkins, a leader in Baltimore's Black community who became an ardent advocate of moral uplift. Distrustful of the ACS's slaveholding leadership, Watkins saw through its rhetoric and suspected that it wanted to remove the free Black population in order to strengthen slavery. He thought that it was especially suspicious that the ACS rejected Haitian emigration and the strengthening of an independent Black nation, but embraced a much more distant location. Recognizing that this effort might be part of a larger strategy to remove the free Black population's political influence, he questioned the ACS's motives: "Why this desire to be so remotely alienated from us? . . . is it not to get effectually and for ever rid of that heterogeneous, or supposed 'dangerous element in the general mass of free blacks', who, it is said, 'are a greater nuisance than even slaves themselves?'" Toward the end of the article, Watkins insightfully highlighted another glaring contradiction in the ACS's rhetoric. Though the ACS had argued that Blacks were morally and socially inferior, it simultaneously maintained that Blacks should "civilize" Africa. This conflicting logic suggested that the allegedly "immoral" free Black population should be responsible for uplifting and civilizing Africa. "They tell us that we, who are 'of all classes of the population of this country, the most vicious; who, being contaminated ourselves, extend our vices to all around us; to the slaves and to the Whites'; are to be the pioneers of this great work of regeneration and reform. Fine materials indeed to accomplish so glorious a work!" Thus exposing the ACS's faulty reasoning, William Watkins concluded with his affirmation that he would continue to advocate his beliefs as long as he "believed them [to be] right."[51]

Watkins's letter sparked a debate in the pages of *Freedom's Journal* that continued for the entire life of the paper, as the ACS's main spokesperson, John H. Kennedy of Philadelphia, bombarded the Black community with colonizationist propaganda.[52] Cleverly, Kennedy systematically addressed and sought to discredit the Black leadership's primary concerns. He began by arguing that the members of the ACS were not "knowingly hostile to African interests" and claimed that Blacks should consider Whites to be trustworthy until there was "evidence of the contrary." Next, Kennedy turned his attention to the issue of slavery. Aware that most free Black activists worried about what their absence from the United States would mean for those still in bondage, Kennedy insisted that free Blacks could actually help their brethren by leaving the country. The existence of free Blacks, Kennedy observed, was "a principle reason alleged for the rigours of slavery" because slaveholders were compelled to enact harsher regulations to prevent runaways. Yet Kennedy's most ingenious maneuver was his admission that American society was racist; through such a position, he hoped that Blacks would view him as an ally, an advocate who held their best interests at heart. He maintained that because free Blacks would never achieve equality in the United States, they should follow their friends in the ACS and gain true freedom elsewhere. By confirming the Black community's worst fear, that Blacks might never gain equality in the United States, Kennedy attempted to convince free Blacks that their best hopes for the future were in Liberia.[53] However, they were not so easily duped.

Despite Kennedy's ingenious attempts, a barrage of letters from throughout the Black community rejected his logic. Most importantly, the correspondence reflected a powerful endorsement of the notion that Black people could, and should, become equal American citizens. One author, calling himself "Investigator," boldly rejected colonization and argued that if Whites would simply extend equality to their Black brethren, the racial problems in the country would be solved. He further suggested that if colonizationists were true allies, they would "set the example" for positive interaction between the races. In his mind, this would have profound influence on "improving and ameliorating their condition." Demonstrating his belief that free Blacks should be incorporated into American society and extended their rights to full citizenship, Investigator concluded: "We wish to be treated according to our merits, and respected as virtuous citizens." Bishop Richard Allen of Philadelphia echoed this notion, arguing that Blacks should stay and fight for their rights because they had "tilled the ground and made fortunes for thousands. . . . This land which we have watered with our tears and our blood, is now our mother country and we are well satisfied to stay where wisdom abounds, and the gospel is free."[54] The messages from Investigator and Bishop Richard Allen are critically important, for they reflect the free Black leadership's new dominant view: the growing conviction that free Blacks should remain in the United States to agitate against slavery and claim their right to American citizenship.

It is important to note, however, that not all Black activists agreed on the issue of repatriation; differing positions on this issue eventually caused the failure of *Freedom's Journal*. At the newspaper's inception, John Russwurm and Samuel Cornish had been of like mind; they believed in the efficacy of moral uplift, but also had supported voluntary emigration to Haiti. However, the rising tide of racism pushed the men in opposite directions. Fearful of ACS's growing power, Cornish abandoned the notion of repatriation and clung desperately to his hope for moral uplift's potential. In fact, he increasingly used *Freedom's Journal* to speak out against colonization and, as an alternative, advocated Black settlement in rural areas.[55] However, as John Russwurm observed the persistence of American racism, he not only continued to support emigration, but also began to question if Black people would ever gain their rights in the United States. Although Russwurm initially kept his feelings out of the public realm, privately, their conflicting ideologies were doomed to collide. By September 1827, they parted ways; Cornish resigned from the paper, and Russwurm continued to edit *Freedom's Journal* on his own.[56]

Early in 1829, John Russwurm finally revealed his true opinion on colonization and publicly endorsed relocation to Liberia. Disappointed by what he viewed as the failure of moral uplift, he argued that the mark of race would always prevent Black people from achieving full equality. Indeed, the United States stubbornly remained a place where "the mere name of colour, blocks up every avenue . . . and from which it is impossible to rise, unless he can change the Ethiopian hue of his complexion." He further argued that regardless of wealth, education, or accomplishments, Black people were still considered inferior beings and "no opportunity will ever be afforded him to cultivate or call into action the talents with which an all-wise Creator may have endowed him." Most importantly, he firmly believed that Black people would never achieve citizenship in the United

States. As he bluntly concluded, "We consider it a mere waste of words to talk of ever enjoying citizenship in this country: it is utterly impossible in the nature of things . . ." For Russwurm, racism was an enduring force that nothing, not even moral improvement, could eradicate. "We are considered a distinct people, in the midst of millions around us and . . . at the end of a thousand years, we should

John Russwurm. (Courtesy of the Photographs and Prints Division; Schomburg Center for Research in Black Culture; New York Public Library; Astor, Lenox, and Tilden Foundations.)

be exactly in our present situation: a proscribed race, however unjustly—a degraded people, deprived of all the rights of freemen . . . prejudices . . . are not of our creating, and they are not in our power to remove." As a result, despite the colonizationists' severe racism, Russwurm argued that his people should depart for Liberia, where they could establish a "flourishing colony."[57] In the end, it was John Russwurm, the very man who had been one of moral uplift's most powerful advocates, who had lost hope.

Freedom's Journal's final issue appeared on March 28, 1829. As Russwurm turned toward colonization, Black New Yorkers withdrew support for the paper because they thought he had become a pawn of the White racists; as one scholar put it, "Russwurm and the Black community had reached an impasse in communication."[58] Russwurm's departing words were bitter, stating that he had been mistreated and misunderstood by his community. Calling his work a "thankless" job, he said that he was "not in the least astonished" that he had been "slandered by the villainous—that our name is byword among the more ignorant, for what less could we expect?" He claimed that despite his experiences, he was "unvanquished" and he believed that his talents would soon be "exerted under more favorable auspices, and upon minds more likely to appreciate its value."[59] With that departing shot, *Freedom's Journal* printed its last volume. By then Russwurm had resolved to leave for Liberia, and Peter Williams Jr. was reportedly the only person who assisted Russwurm in his relocation.[60] In fact, following his announcement about his plans to repatriate, the Black community expressed its displeasure in the form of a riot. Chanting "traitor" throughout the Five Points neighborhood, a group of Black folks hung an effigy of Russwurm in the square that they proceeded to pelt with rocks and set ablaze.[61] Through their actions, Black New Yorkers soundly rejected colonization and asserted their intention to remain in the United States; anyone who considered the alternative was apparently deemed a "traitor."

*   *   *

The year 1827 held monumental importance in the minds of free Black New Yorkers, because legal emancipation symbolized the coming to fruition of all their political and spiritual strivings. Yet the debates over parading and proper conduct quickly threatened to divide the community and revealed the complex political issues they were forced to contend with. Faced with vehement opposition from Whites, members of the Black leadership began to gravitate toward moral uplift as a strategy to gain White approval and, hopefully, equality and citizenship. Significantly, their endorsement of moral uplift brought moments of triumph; including the creation of *Freedom's Journal* and increasing activism among Black women. However, it also caused Black New Yorkers to grapple with a crucial conflict between their African heritage and White standards of respectability. Even more, it forced them to deeply ponder questions of strategy and identity.

By the eve of emancipation, most Black activists had resolved, as they had in previous decades, to take the middle ground; they tried to expand definitions of what it meant to be an American to include those who embraced their African heritage. They quickly discovered, however, that they would be required to take a more definitive stand.

As White support for the ACS intensified, the colonization movement forced Black activists into a defensive posture. Fearful of forced removal, the Black community began to publicly distance itself from Africa and espoused an American identity. In the final analysis, the debates over colonization and parading embodied larger ideological struggles over identity and citizenship; moreover, they marked a crucial shift in Black political thought that foreshadowed the ideological struggles that would haunt Black New Yorkers throughout the nineteenth century. For although most Black New Yorkers resolved to remain in their adopted country to agitate against slavery and gain their rights, they would soon discover that it would be a long and costly battle. As we shall see, arguments about emigration persisted, as did the profound debate over Black identity. Were free Blacks really just dark-skinned Americans, or were they displaced Africans? Within the answer to this complex question lay the Black community's destiny.

CHAPTER 4

"Our Own Native Land,"
1830–1839

> Brethren, what a bright prospect would there be before us in this land, had we no prejudices to contend against, after being made free. But alas! the freedom to which we have attained, is defective. Freedom and equality have been "put asunder." The rights of men are decided by the colour of their skin. . . .
> —Peter Williams Jr., 1830

> The time must come when the declaration of independence will be felt in the heart as well as uttered from the mouth, and when the rights of all shall be properly acknowledged and appreciated. God hasten that time. This is our home, and this our country.
> —Meeting of the People of Color, New York City, 1831

> . . . we will tell the white Americans that their country shall be our country—we will be governed by the same laws and worship at the same altar—where they live we will live, where they die there will we be buried, and our graves shall remain as monuments of our suffering and triumph, or of our failure and their disgrace.
> —Philip A. Bell, 1839

On July 4, 1830, exactly three years after Black New Yorkers commemorated their emancipation, Reverend Peter Williams Jr. assembled the Black community and asked them to consider leaving the United States. The significance of these events could not have been lost on the crowd; not only were they gathered to honor their new status as free Americans, but just months earlier the Black community had rioted against *Freedom's Journal* editor, John Russwurm, for abandoning the United States and repatriating to Africa. Yet Williams delivered a poignant message that must have resonated with his people. He reflected the disappointment of their "defective" freedom; despite legal emancipation, they were like "slaves in the midst of freemen" because the promise of justice and equality had still not been applied to them. Denied the basic rights of citizens and subjected to hostile exclusion, Williams insisted that July 4 was not a day to be celebrated because it "impress[ed] upon the minds of reflecting men of colour a deeper sense of the cruelty, injustice, and oppression of which they have been the victims." As a

Reverend Peter Williams Jr.
(Courtesy of the General
Research and Reference
Division; Schomburg Center
for Research in Black Culture;
New York Public Library;
Astor, Lenox, and Tilden
Foundations.)

result, he urged free Blacks to establish a refuge from persecution in case their "homes are made so uncomfortable that we cannot continue in them, or . . . we are driven from them."[1]

Because Williams had become a staunch emigrationist by 1812, he had always harbored a fear that the United States might eventually become uninhabitable for free Blacks; a belief that was certainly bolstered by the 1829 riot in Cincinnati, which had forced their Ohio brethren to flee to Canada.[2] Perhaps most painful for Williams was the realization that, in spite of their loyalty and patriotism, the free Black population was being pushed out of the country by evil forces in the form of the ACS. Therefore, Williams's pragmatic solution was for Black people to consider voluntary migration to a more welcoming country. "Will it not then be wise for us to provide ourselves with a convenient asylum in time? We have now a fair opportunity of doing so; but if we neglect it, it may be too late. . . . If it succeeds, ours will be the credit. If it succeeds not, ours will be the fault." According to Williams, Black New Yorkers should raise money and build a new community in Canada where, he believed, they could "rise to as prosperous and happy a condition as any people under the sun."[3]

Yet despite Williams's support for Canadian emigration, he still passionately asserted the free Black community's right to American citizenship. For Williams, emigration was a necessary escape hatch but he continued to agitate against forced removal and in favor of Black civil rights. In particular, he denounced the ACS and challenged Whites to "lay aside their prejudices" and embrace Black people as equal citizens. Furthermore, in response to the ACS's efforts, he articulated a surprising view of Africa; unlike his prior speeches, which had celebrated their motherland, Williams questioned the purpose of sending free Blacks to Africa because it was located "far from civilized society." As he put it, "What is there in the burning sun, the arid plains, and barbarous customs of Africa, that is so peculiarly favourable to our improvement?" Instead, Williams argued that free Blacks should be able to live as equal American citizens and bemoaned the fact that it was "nothing but prejudice" that "hinders our improvement here." He eloquently concluded, "We are natives of this country, we ask only to be treated as well as foreigners. . . . We cannot but doubt the motives of those persons who deny us these requests, and would send us to Africa to gain what they might give us at home."[4]

Williams's oration was deeply revealing, for his words illustrated a critical strategic contradiction Black leaders grappled with during the antebellum era. In the face of persistent racism, they felt compelled to consider emigration, but still they knew they had earned the right to stay in the United States as equal citizens and were outraged by the motives and strategies of the ACS. Yet as Black activists pursued the dual agenda of voluntary emigration and American citizenship, they began to wonder if they were sending a mixed message. Faced with this complex dilemma, Black leaders in the early 1830s began to organize regionally to determine whether emigration should remain a component of their race uplift program. In the resulting Colored Convention movement, Black leaders sought to settle a series of familiar, yet fundamental, questions. Did they believe American society would ever allow them to become equal citizens? If so, what tactics should the Black community use to gain its rights? Would their strategy require, as Peter Williams Jr. had indicated, a renunciation of their African homeland? Although it appeared that New Yorkers had settled these issues in the 1820s, it became clear that these questions were more difficult to answer than they had hoped; for while Black activists struggled against slavery, colonization, and voting restrictions, they faced frustrating internal battles over strategy and identity as well as powerful external opposition from the enemies of Black liberation.

* * *

Three days after Peter Williams Jr. delivered his historic address, a group of Black activists, including Peter Williams Jr., Thomas L. Jennings, Peter Vogelsang, Theodore Wright, and Benjamin Paul, formed the Wilberforce Colony Society to investigate the possibility of Canadian emigration. Shortly thereafter, they commenced their most influential activity; they issued a call for Northern Black leaders to craft a unified position on colonization and emigration, either to collectively remain or to leave. Among those to receive the appeal was Hezekiah Grice, a well-respected activist in Baltimore, who had been a long-time supporter of emigration.[5] Grice replied enthusiastically to the idea and sent a circular to his brethren throughout the North requesting their attendance at a convention to discuss the Black community's destiny.[6] In response, Grice received an urgent message from Bishop Richard Allen of Philadelphia. Apparently, Allen had seen the letter from New York activists endorsing the conference and was concerned that the New York contingency would gain the upper hand. Allen allegedly told Grice, "my dear child, we must take some action immediately, or else these New Yorkers will get ahead of us!" As a result, Allen and a group of local leaders immediately organized a national convention to be held in Philadelphia later that year.[7] These events ultimately served as the foundation for a series of meetings that brought Black leaders together from across the North for the first time in history; scholars would later refer to these gatherings as the National Colored Convention movement. However, a cloud of division hung over their endeavors from the beginning, because New Yorkers boycotted the first round of proceedings out of disgust for the Philadelphians' attempt to hijack the movement.[8]

On September 20, 1830, the first national Colored Convention assembled and, despite the fact that Peter Williams Jr. and other Black New Yorkers were absent, the delegates reinforced many of the views Williams had expressed during his July 4 speech. Reflecting the confusion and concern about the future of Black people in the United States, leaders felt compelled, as Williams had suggested, to establish their opinions on Canadian emigration and African colonization. Williams would likely have been pleased with the outcome because the attendees recognized the strategic benefit of having voluntary emigration as an option and passed a resolution indicating that Canada would be more receptive to Black people than the United States due to the language, climate, and availability of land. Most importantly, they noted it was a country where the government had "no invidious distinction of colour," and all people were "entitled to the rights, privileges, and immunities of other citizens." As a result, they determined to elect an agent who would select a plot of land where they would establish a permanent settlement. They also echoed Williams's firm rejection of African colonization and asserted themselves as Americans, declaring, "we, whose habits, manners, and customs are the same in common with other Americans" would never leave for the "afflicted country" of Liberia. Significantly, like Williams, their words became a critical part of the anticolonization struggle; as they moved decidedly toward establishing their rights as Americans, they simultaneously renounced their African heritage.[9]

New York activists reinforced this message on January 25, 1831, when they held a meeting in Boyer Lodge to repudiate African colonization and affirm their intentions to remain in the United States.[10] Alarmed by White acceptance of the ACS, Black leaders apparently felt moved to publicly declare their views on colonization as they missed the opportunity to do so as part of the Colored Convention. In their most important resolution, they rejected Africa as their homeland, stating, "we claim *this country, the place of our birth, and not Africa,* as our mother country, and all attempts to send us to Africa, we consider as gratuitous and uncalled for." Representatives of New York's Black community concluded their meeting with a moving and eloquent plea for liberty and freedom to be extended to their people. Renewing their belief that they would eventually obtain equal treatment, Black New Yorkers declared their right to citizenship drawing upon images of patriotism and birthright. "This is our home, and this our country. Beneath its sod lie the bones of our fathers: for it some of them fought, bled and died. Here we were born, and here we will die."[11]

Later that year Black activists from New York City, determined not to be excluded again, took their agenda to the second Colored Convention; among the delegates from New York were many familiar activists including William Hamilton, William Miller, and Henry Sipkins. The message that emanated from the 1831 meeting was quite similar to the prior gathering; attendees lamented the persistence of racism in the United States, reaffirmed their commitment to the Canadian plan, and continued to oppose the ACS. In their conventional address, delegates were saddened by the realization that "it is only when we look to our own native land, to the birthplace of our *fathers,* to the land for whose prosperity their blood and our sweat have been shed and cruelly extorted, that the Convention has had cause to hang its head and blush." Because of this merciless oppression, they urged the organizations dedicated to settlement in Canada to "persevere in their praiseworthy and philanthropic undertaking" firmly believing that "their labours will be crowned with success." They further reported that conditions for Blacks in Canada were daily improving, and they had begun to construct buildings and create a new life for themselves. Yet as they concluded, despite the fact that Canada remained an important alternative, they were determined to resist colonization in Africa. As they explained, "we would, in the most feeling manner, beg of [the ACS] to desist" because, even if racist persecution continued, "we would rather die at home."[12]

Black New Yorkers returned to their city with a renewed dedication to opposing the ACS in all its endeavors; in fact, the leadership nearly severed its relationship with its closest White allies, the Manumission Society, over the issue of African colonization. Although the Manumission Society had not taken a formal position on the issue, Charles C. Andrews, the headmaster of the African Free Schools, publicized his "decided colonizationist views" putting him at odds with the Black community.[13] Led by Colored Convention attendees Henry Sipkins and William Hamilton, New York City's Black leadership insisted upon Andrews's removal as headmaster and organized a boycott of the schools until he was fired and a Black man replaced him. By withholding their children from school, the families in the community sent a clear message to the Manumission Society that they would not support an institution that did not represent their interests. After "something of a struggle," the Manumission Society acquiesced to the Black community's demands; Charles Andrews was summarily dismissed and, in his place, a Black man, James Adams, was appointed. Through the exertion of public pressure and an effective boycott, the Black community successfully forced the Manumission Society to endorse the rejection of African colonization.[14]

Perhaps influenced by their struggle against Charles Andrews and the Manumission Society, Black New Yorkers came to the 1832 Colored Convention with a new perspective. Concerned about public perception, they worried that their endorsement of Canadian emigration was undermining their attempts to attain American citizenship by confusing Whites about their intentions. The issue came to a head as delegates considered a resolution that endorsed the resettlement scheme in Canada. Although the plan simply echoed the sentiments of previous conventions, there was apparently a rather heated debate over this issue. A large portion of the convention, including New Yorkers William Hamilton, Thomas L. Jennings, and Philip A. Bell, insisted that any support of Canadian emigration could be misconstrued and that the American public would assume they had "relinquished our claim to this being the land of our nativity."[15] Even the Canadian emigration committee members agreed and raised their own concerns about the ramifications of emigration on their enslaved sisters and brothers. The removal of free Blacks, they argued, would "weaken the situation of those who are left behind" because "the best and brightest prospect of the philanthropists who are laboring for our elevation in this country will be thwarted." Ultimately, the convention still voted to support the Canadian project in 1832, but the debates at this gathering prompted Black leaders to carefully consider the efficacy of their strategy.[16]

As a result, the 1833 Colored Convention witnessed a dramatic reversal of its race uplift program; delegates suddenly denounced the Canadian plan and dissolved the emigration committee. In a shocking turn, they decided to oppose the very purpose for which they had originally gathered. In the final report, the emigration committee simply stated, "there is not now, and probably never will be actual necessity for a large emigration of the present race of coloured people." Thus, they concluded that they would no longer recommend Canadian emigration and would not investigate the project any further. Certainly, they knew discrimination had not sufficiently subsided to warrant a complete abandonment of voluntary emigration, but Black leaders were concerned about the issues raised in 1832, namely, public perception and the antislavery movement. Therefore, delegates embraced the position of the New York leadership; they resolved that if they wanted to abolish slavery and attain American citizenship, they would have to stay in the United States and fight. As they stated in their convention address, their new focus would be to devise "plans for our mutual and common improvement in this, the land of our nativity." Thus ended the discussion of Canadian emigration within the Colored Convention movement; in 1834 and 1835, the subject did not appear at all. Instead, Black leaders continued their attack on African colonization and the ACS by creating a committee for the purpose of discouraging "the colonization of our people, anywhere beyond the limits of this CONTINENT."[17]

Although the Colored Convention attendees managed to agree on the colonization question, it was this move that, ironically, ended their gatherings. Once they decided to remain in the United States, it quickly became clear that leaders had vastly different perspectives about which race uplift strategies would effectively bring equality and citizenship. This problem eventually infected every aspect of the meetings between 1833 and 1835. The first signs of dissent within the convention came in 1833, when the Philadelphians unveiled their political agenda. For them, moral uplift was the best solution to achieve their goals because they believed, if it was successful, "every interest we aim to promote, every blessing we seek as men, or as citizens of this our beloved republic, must advance, must triumph." Guided by the Philadelphia delegation, the 1833 convention gave considerable attention to the issue of moral improvement. They focused especially on alcohol abuse, which they believed was "threatening a speedy death to every interest, whether social, civil, or religious." In response, delegates voted to create local temperance societies dedicated wholly to the challenge of abstinence and drafted an official report on the evils of alcohol that drew similarities between the production of rum and the perpetuation of slavery. They argued that "the RUM system, like that of *slavery*, is upheld by ignorance, avarice and incorrect views of duty" and, therefore, encouraged free Blacks to support temperance as strongly as any other reform program.[18]

The problem with the Philadelphians' strategy, however, was that the New Yorkers were not convinced that moral improvement and temperance were the most pressing challenges facing their people. Although they had obviously championed the benefits of moral reform in previous years, New Yorkers insisted that it was not the only issue; instead, they argued, abolition and anticolonization should consume Black activists' attention. After all, as Philip Bell explained later, it was their "sympathies for the slave" that had convinced free Blacks to remain in the United States, a country from which "while life lasts, in spite of the oppressor's wrongs, we will never be seduced or driven."[19] Because they pledged to stay and fight on behalf of the enslaved, New Yorkers thought abolition should be the dominant political issue. As a result, in 1834, when the Colored Convention was held in New York City and Black New Yorkers set the agenda, they gave only passing attention to the cause of moral reform and refocused on the cruel system "under which we labour from the effect of *American slavery* and *American prejudice*."[20]

The New Yorkers' focus on abolition and anticolonization only served to deepen the ideological divide between themselves and the Philadelphians. Although anticolonization had originally been an issue that united Black activists, in 1835 William Whipper, a wealthy Philadelphian, introduced a controversial resolution that revealed that leaders had dramatically divergent views about which tactics were necessary to effectively combat African colonization. The core of the conflict centered on the issue of naming because, as previously discussed, most free Blacks in the early nineteenth century used the term "African" in their organizational titles as a way of demonstrating their distinct identity and cultural pride. However as opposition to African colonization prompted Black activists to claim America as their homeland, some leaders pondered the ramifications of their naming tradition. In particular, men such as William Whipper argued that the answer to the racial problem was for Black people to completely assimilate into American society. Therefore, in his mind, they must break down the barriers of racial separation by removing racial designations and eradicating separate Black organizations and institutions. This belief led Whipper to propose that Black folks should "abandon the use of the word 'colored,' when either speaking or writing concerning themselves; and especially to remove the title of African from their institutions."[21] Although, according to the minutes of the convention, Whipper's motion passed unanimously after an "animated and interesting" debate, the New Yorkers ultimately did not comply with the plan.

On the contrary, Black New Yorkers remained reluctant to abandon the use of racial designations. It is true that they slowly relinquished the common use of "African" when referring to their race for, as African Society member James McCune Smith reflected, "it was in the after years, when they set up their just protest against the American Colonization Society and its principles that the term 'African' fell into disuse and finally discredit."[22] Likely, they were influenced by the movement, which began in the late 1820s, to distance themselves from explicit expressions of African culture. However, they were not yet ready to adopt Whipper's vision of complete assimilation into American society; instead, they chose a middle ground, which reflected their early commitment to Black Nationalism. Black New York activists ultimately resolved to embrace the term "colored"; a strategy they hoped would simultaneously assert their right to American citizenship, while still recognizing their position as a distinct group that shared mutual interests.[23] Notably, the vast majority of existing Black associations in New York City retained the use of "African" in their titles and even new organizations chose either "African" or "colored." Moreover, the leadership continued to create and support separate Black organizations and institutions long after the 1835 convention. They supported their decision so strongly that, in 1838, when Philadelphians continued to press the issue of removing racial distinctions, Samuel Cornish became enraged. He chastised the Philadelphians for "quarreling about trifles" and suggested that, given the virulent racism in American society, Black people should view being called "colored" instead of "Negro" as a "ray of Heavenly light."[24]

The debate over names was just one small part of a larger conflict between the Philadelphians and New Yorkers over strategy, a divide that became increasingly apparent as they struggled to maintain their regional alliance. The final nail in the convention's coffin came when the Philadelphians insisted that the improvement of their people, and of American society, depended upon moral uplift and convinced delegates to transform themselves into a new association, the American Moral Reform Society (AMRS).[25] Ultimately, the creation of AMRS sounded the death knell for the Colored Conventions in the 1830s; once it was established, the gatherings vanished. Even worse, the New Yorkers were nearly unanimously opposed to the decision to create AMRS; in fact, with the exception of Samuel Cornish, the New York delegation declined to join AMRS or participate in its functions.[26] Cornish was the lone New Yorker who continued to press the issue of moral uplift; he not only attended the AMRS conventions but also dedicated portions of his editorials in the Colored American newspaper to that issue.[27] Conversely, most Black New York activists boycotted the AMRS and directed their energies toward other issues such as abolition and obtaining the suffrage.

Although the formation of the AMRS led to the dissolution of Colored Conventions, in many ways the problems within the movement went beyond moral reform; unable to create a unified and consistent program of action, the conferences were plagued by disorganization and internal conflict.[28] In the final analysis, leaders in New York and Philadelphia were unwilling to surrender control and were therefore unable to form an effective coalition. Although the convention movement of the 1830s "failed," the gatherings represented crucial moments in the history of Black people in the United States. It was, after all, the first step toward regional cooperation, a bold move that reflected a significant shift in Black consciousness. One activist reflected nearly thirty years later, "at the present day, when colored conventions are almost as frequent as church meetings, it is difficult to estimate the bold and daring spirit which inaugurated the Colored Convention of 1830."[29] Moreover, the meetings allowed free Blacks to determine that they would stay in the United States and fight for citizenship and freedom. In the end, however, egos and internal division prevented this nationalistic effort from reaching its full potential.

As the New Yorkers withdrew from the Colored Convention movement, abolition consumed their political agenda. Indeed, the 1830s were a time of intense activism and potential as Black and White leaders began marshalling forces to eradicate slavery throughout the country.[30] During this time, Black New Yorkers worked consistently with a select group of White activists, such as William Lloyd Garrison, Arthur Tappan, and Lewis Tappan, who strengthened the movement by establishing a national antislavery organization, the American Anti-Slavery Society (AASS), in 1833. In addition, through the creation of antislavery newspapers such as the Liberator and the Emancipator, they began informing the public about the horrors of slavery. Black people not only supported these endeavors verbally and financially, but they considered the *Liberator* to be their paper. Although Garrison was the editor, the *Liberator* was founded largely with Black financing; in fact, several years after its creation, Garrison admitted that the paper owed its existence to the four hundred "colored subscribers" who were recruited by Black agents such as New Yorker Philip A. Bell.[31] Black New Yorkers clearly believed in the power of press because, in 1837, Bell, Samuel Cornish, and Charles B. Ray resuscitated the efforts their brethren had commenced in 1827 by establishing the *Colored American* newspaper.[32]

Black New Yorkers also found ways to contribute to the antislavery movement on the local level. In October 1833, White activist Arthur Tappan and his supporters began to plan a new organization, the New York Anti-Slavery Society (NYASS), a branch of the AASS that embraced a radical policy of immediate abolition and Black civil rights. At a time when most associations were still segregated based on race, the NYASS insisted that its organization should actively invite the participation of Black men. In its first annual report, the NYASS stated, "there is no way to destroy the prejudice which lies at the foundation of slavery, but to invite our colored brethren to a participation with us in all those happy and elevating institutions which are open to others." In keeping with this perspective, when the organization officially formed on December 4, 1833, the board of managers included Reverends Theodore S. Wright, Samuel Cornish, Christopher Rush, and Peter Williams Jr. Soon thereafter, other influential Black men in New York's community including Thomas Downing, the Reason brothers (Patrick and Charles), and Thomas L. Jennings joined them. Although they were a minority of the membership, the presence of Black activists in NYASS was crucial because they offered a level of experience and insight that gave the movement legitimacy and power in the Black community.[33]

Sadly, however, the increasing influence of the abolitionist movement was not lost on the enemies of Black freedom. Indeed, the growing agitation by Black activists against the system of slavery had powerful repercussions. As the abolitionist movement gained momentum, some White New Yorkers became increasingly anxious and unleashed a devastating backlash in the form of a violent race riot. Scholars have offered many explanations for this eruption of racial violence in New York. Linda Kerber argued that it was due to fear of racial amalgamation, and Paul Gilje maintained that it was the result of "concern over the development of a black subcommunity." Ultimately, it seems they were both right. Increasing political activism in the free Black community, the growth of Black institutions, and the threat of amalgamation, united to make the enemies of abolition uneasy and fearful. Thus, in July 1834, New York City convulsed with racial hostility and mob violence. Raging over the span of five days, the antiabolition riot of 1834 was one of the longest and most violent race riots in antebellum America.[34]

Although the 1834 riot targeted some White abolitionists, the vast majority of damage was inflicted upon the Black community. In fact, Linda Kerber noted that the attacks on Whites were merely a "sideshow" compared to what was taking place in the Black neighborhoods. At the mob's strongest point, with between seven thousand and eight thousand rioters, the crowd descended upon the Black regions of the city with a rage that prompted the *New York Evening Post* to report that "the fury of demons seems to have entered into the breasts of our misguided populace."[35] For days, they wreaked havoc on the community, destroying homes, stores, and churches, viciously driven to decimate the Black population. According to the *New York American,* for example, the home of African Society member Moses Blue was besieged, and a "missile" fired into the home of an unidentified Black woman leveled her to the ground. In addition, the paper noted that many Black-owned homes were "totally destroyed" by the mob. Historian Tyler Anbinder also indicated that Black institutions such as the African Society's meeting house, the African schoolhouse, the Abyssinian Baptist Church, and many successful businesses were singled out for excessive violence; an indication that "signs of African American economic independence clearly galled" the White mob.[36] Perhaps the most vehement rage was directed against St. Philip's Church and the home of its minister, Peter Williams Jr. For two hours, the horde devastated the church and his home without any intervention from the police or authorities. Apparently, Williams was a unique target because of a rumor that he had performed an interracial marriage ceremony. However, it is equally likely that Williams's well-known political perspectives and his work on behalf of liberation had singled him out for special hostility. Regardless of the reasons, the mob did demolish his home and his church.[37]

After several days of unabated violence, it was clear that the riot would not cease of its own volition. Because the police officers could no longer contain the violence on their own, city authorities finally summoned the militia. According to the *New York Evening Post,* the city had been "the prey of an infuriated mob" that could only be stopped by the "severest measures." If not, the editor predicted, "our government is at an end." In fact, the newspaper was in such strong support of military action that they declared the rioters should be "shot down like dogs."[38] Apparently, city officials were in agreement; they gave the arriving militia strict orders to shoot any rioters who appeared on the streets. Troops were placed throughout the city, particularly in the Black neighborhoods, and patrolled the streets all night. The militia maintained its watch until July 15, when it finally seemed that the mob would not resume its reign of terror.[39]

As if the preceding days of fury and destruction had not been enough, there was another unforeseen consequence for Black New Yorkers immediately following the 1834 riot. After the mob targeted St. Philip's Church, White Episcopal Bishop Benjamin T. Onderdonk became so concerned about the ramifications of the violence that he subsequently silenced the political voice of the church's leader Peter Williams Jr. According to Onderdonk, Williams must abandon all political activism because St. Philip's Church should be "found on the Christian side of meekness, order and self-sacrifice." As a result, Onderdonk demanded that Williams sever his relations with AASS and refrain from future public appearances or statements regarding abolition. Feeling compelled to obey his bishop, Peter Williams Jr. retired from the public eye. As Onderdonk requested, Williams made his actions public and published a letter in the city newspapers stating his intentions to resign from the AASS and abstain from political action.[40]

Williams's letter, which was also his final political statement, was a fascinating manifesto of his ideological perspectives. Using moral uplift rhetoric, he recalled his father's support of American independence during the Revolutionary War, an example that indoctrinated Williams with "an ardent love for the American government and made me feel . . . that it was my greatest glory to be an American." Bolstered by this belief, Williams reflected, he had labored to protect New York City during the War of 1812. "I entreated my brethren to help in the defence [*sic*] of the country, and went with them to the work."[41] Through this clever approach, Williams established Black men as war heroes and patriots; a critical strategy he hoped would advance their struggle for full citizenship. Indeed, even in spite of the riot, Williams never relinquished his hope that Black people would become American citizens. After all, he insisted, the language of the Declaration of Independence and the Bible guaranteed their human rights. Instead, he denounced the ACS and criticized its belief that "a colored man, however he may strive to make himself intelligent, virtuous and useful, can never enjoy the privileges of a citizen of the United States."[42]

Williams concluded his letter with the obligatory refutation of the AASS. He claimed that, although he had avidly supported efforts for education and moral uplift, he had never been an active member of the AASS. Even though his name had been included as part of the executive committee, Williams stated that he had declined the position and had only served in an advisory capacity. In closing, Williams declared, "in conformity to the advice of my Bishop, [I] publicly resign my station as a member of the Board of Managers of the Anti-Slavery Society." Perhaps as a final political commentary, Williams refused to make any overtly negative statement about AASS or its stated purpose. Thus ended Peter Williams Jr.'s public political career. After twenty-six years of service to New York City's Black community, one of its most articulate and dedicated spokesmen was permanently silenced.[43]

To add insult to injury, Peter Williams Jr.'s sacrifice was apparently not sufficient to quell the venomous racism that prompted the riot. On the following day, the *New York American* published a nasty retort from one Rinaldo Rinaldini, who challenged the authenticity of Williams's letter on the basis that a Black man did not possess the intelligence to draft such a document. Rinaldini railed against the *New York American*'s editor for having the audacity to publish Williams's letter, which he claimed had obviously been falsified. "How dare you!! In times of such excitement as these, fabricate and publish the letter of that nigger Williams, such an outrage upon truth and such a biting satire upon the American citizens as that is? A nigger write such a letter! Nonsense—they have no brains." Furthermore, he scoffed at the notion that Williams and his father had actually served the United States during the Revolutionary War and the War of 1812. Rinaldini concluded with a threat that, in retaliation for printing Williams's letter, the mob would attack the *New York American*'s office as they had Arthur Tappan's store.[44]

It is important to note, however, that in the face of such virulent and powerful racism, the Black community demonstrated its strength and resolve and did not passively accept this unprovoked attack on its members, homes, and institutions. Although they did not deign to respond to Rinaldini, they took action in other ways. In fact, Black agitation had commenced a few days before the violence erupted when African Society member Epiphany Davis wrote to the mayor prophesizing danger and pleading for protection. Obviously, the mayor ignored his warning but, once the riot began, free Blacks fought back. When rioters attempted to attack a Black barbershop, the owner "intrepidly kept possession of his premises, discharging a pistol three times at his assailants" until finally wounding a man in the crowd.[45] This brave man was apparently not alone because, years after the riot, the *Anglo-African* magazine praised esteemed leader William Hamilton for boldly wielding weapons against the mob. According to the article, an unidentified person encountered William Hamilton on the street in the midst of the carnage "loaded down with iron missiles." When asked where he was going, Hamilton apparently replied, "to die on my threshold!" This story revealed that Hamilton, and others, were willing to risk their lives to fight against the rioters and protect their family, property, and community.[46]

Perhaps the most powerful lesson that resulted from the 1834 riot was the determination illustrated by William Hamilton's bravery. Rather than passively endure injustice and abandon activism, Black New Yorkers remained undaunted. In fact, they became even more determined to fight slavery in all its insidious forms. Although, as we shall see in the following chapter, the antislavery movement soon faced internal dissent, Black New Yorkers in the early 1830s expanded their struggle against slavery by rededicating themselves to the cause of fugitives. Indeed, defending and protecting fugitives was uniquely important to Black New Yorkers because by the 1830s everyone, regardless of status or wealth, was in equal danger of illegal seizure on the city streets. Kidnapping had certainly been a problem throughout the early nineteenth century, but the cases of capture and enslavement flourished during this era as never before. As James McCune Smith reflected decades later, the 1830s were a time when "our free northern cities [were converted] into slave-hunting grounds; steady and persistent industry of the colored people was frequently interrupted, and at any moment they might be forced to fly and 'begin life anew.'" Although kidnapping plagued most Northern cities, New York was particularly susceptible to this problem and was known as a prime "slaveholder's hunting ground." One report even suggested that, per capita, more Black people were stolen in New York than on the West Coast of Africa. Frederick Douglass later confirmed this notion when he described New York as one of the best locations for "slave-hunting sport this side of Africa."[47] Likewise, activist William Johnson maintained that, because it was a popular shipping hub, New York City regularly operated as a "slave port" where slave catchers lured Black men onboard ships under the guise of hiring them as sailors or laborers and then sold them into Southern slavery.[48]

In response, Black leaders labored intensely to effectively harbor, protect, and defend fugitives and free Black folks alike. At first, evidence suggests that many Black activists worked clandestinely; for example, it appears that the African Society's lodge functioned as a safe house on the Underground Railroad. During a speech by a member in 1946, it was revealed that the African Society's lodge had a hidden passage that led to a secret chamber underneath the house. The area extended the entire length and width of the building, which was more than adequate space for effective concealment of fugitives. Particularly when one considers that the African Society's membership included men such as Charles Ray, a known conductor on the Underground Railroad, it seems likely that the African Society was involved in this secret activity.[49]

Despite the importance of covert agitation, however, activists soon recognized the need for a formal organization to raise public consciousness about the plight of fugitives. Indeed, organizing against kidnapping reflected a crucial first step among Black New Yorkers to move beyond benevolent associations to political organizations. In November 1835, a group of Black leaders, led by David Ruggles, formed the New York Committee of Vigilance.[50] The association's purpose was to protect its brethren against the constant threat of enslavement because, as they explained, "any colored person within this State is liable to be arrested as a *fugitive from slavery* and put upon his defence to prove his freedom." In response, it resolved to identify and extinguish the "cruel practice of kidnapping men, women and children [which] is carried on in this city, and to aid such unfortunate persons as may be in danger of being *reduced to Slavery*."[51] The association's efforts to combat the problem of kidnapping took a variety of forms. David Ruggles became a correspondent to the *Emancipator* and *Colored American* newspapers, thereby allowing him to regularly print warnings and updates concerning kidnappings. In addition, throughout 1836, David Ruggles and other leaders such as Thomas Van Rensalaer held a series of meetings designed to bring public attention to the problem of kidnapping and raise funds to rescue wrongly convicted fugitives.

On one particular occasion, David Ruggles held a forum to inform the community about a disturbing potential danger: the growing power of the New York Kidnapping Club, a secret organization that used a variety of deceptive maneuvers to capture free and fugitive Blacks. Apparently, one of the club's most insidious strategies was to pose as abolitionists. After identifying Mr. Boudinot, the Kidnapping Club's leader, many in the gathering were stunned to discover that the man who they had believed was their "abolitionist friend" was actually a kidnapper. In addition, Ruggles revealed that certain city officials regularly conspired with slave catchers: most notably, Mr. Nash, the city marshal. Ruggles was particularly concerned about Nash's participation, because such institutional protection allowed the Kidnapping Club to harass Black people throughout the city at will and the victims would have little or no recourse.[52]

By highlighting the danger of enslavement in their city, Ruggles and his supporters hoped to involve the entire Black community in their cause. Apparently their strategy was successful, because Black folks throughout New York City aided their efforts. Although the vigilance committee did most of the organizing, the association was entirely funded by members of New York's Black community.[53] As David Ruggles explained, the committee conducted fund-raising through an "effective committee" consisting of one hundred men and women. The members of this subcommittee had a list of ten to twelve friends from whom they collected one penny each week. Many were able to give much more, in some cases 50 cents, but this clever method ensured that at least a thousand people gave one penny each week. By the end of a month, the organization would have raised more than $40. As Ruggles concluded, "it is in this way that the operations of the committee have hitherto been mostly sustained." According to Ruggles, free Blacks supported the Committee of Vigilance because, to them, it was "practical abolition"; they knew their money was going directly to the liberation of someone in their community. The vast majority of the funds went to purchase the freedom or support the legal defense of those who had been illegally enslaved, which allowed contributors to see the immediate results of their donation. Although the Black community was extremely impoverished, by the end of 1836 it had managed to rescue 335 people from being returned to bondage. Ruggles was encouraged by this fact, especially because it proved that the Black community had committed themselves to action. "The colored people were awake," he maintained, and he proudly stated that he had never seen the community so committed to any other cause.[54]

Despite its efforts, the Committee of Vigilance faced some serious obstacles from the enemies of Black freedom. In particular, the committee had difficulty securing meeting space that was owned by "friends" of the cause and large enough to accommodate its needs. J. W. Higgins wrote passionately on this subject in the *Emancipator* noting, "the difficulties which we meet at every step in obtaining a permanent place for our regular meeting, are discouraging and almost insurmountable; but as liberty is our motto and vigilance the watch-word, we yield not to discouragement."[55] Although the committee remained confident that its efforts would be rewarded, individual members were soon persecuted for their activities. In fact, David Ruggles became such a nuisance to the Kidnapping Club that the leaders attempted to permanently silence him. After Ruggles investigated slave ships docked in New York City, Nash and several other notorious slave catchers forced their way into Ruggles's home and assaulted him. After placing him in handcuffs, Nash dragged Ruggles to the police station where he intended to surrender him as a slave; apparently, the high constable had drafted a writ that entitled Nash to claim Ruggles as a fugitive. By the next morning, Mr. Boudinot arrived and took Ruggles to Bellevue Prison where he exclaimed, "we have got him now . . . we will learn him to punish us as kidnappers." Although Ruggles was subsequently released, his ordeal revealed the tenuous nature of "freedom" in New York City. Boudinot reinforced this realization, when he reminded Ruggles that he could "arrest and send any black to the South . . . no man, no woman, no child is safe."[56]

Although Ruggles had sufficient connections to secure his own safety, many captured Blacks did not have the same good fortune. Throughout the 1830s, there were many cases that consumed the public attention, yet it was nearly impossible to protect the Black community because the laws of the land allowed the persecution and reenslavement of fugitives. Perhaps the most famous case of the 1830s surrounded Abraham Goslee, formerly known as Jesse Collier, who was apprehended in August 1836. The Goslee case became something of a cause célèbre, in which numerous New Yorkers were called to testify on his behalf. Although his lawyers obtained evidence stating that he was the son of a free woman in Maryland, Goslee had inadvertently been trapped into a confession. The court was now faced with a crucial question over which evidence to consider. After a grueling and complex legal battle, Goslee was remanded into custody and enslaved. The Black community was outraged and, in response, David Ruggles condemned the American judicial system, claiming that the courts had declared, "color is the badge and evidence of slavery, and that the colored citizen is therefore not a citizen."[57] In many ways, the Goslee case was the *Dred Scott* case of the 1830s, a definitive statement that free Blacks had no tangible rights.

Despite their frustrated struggle against slavery and kidnapping, Black New Yorkers remained defiantly committed to their cause. Even Black women became more actively involved in the abolitionist movement. Although never as outspoken as women in other regions, Black female New Yorkers found new and creative ways to make a contribution. Most notably, in September 1834, Henrietta Ray, Sarah Ennals, Sarah Elston, and Elizabeth Jennings, the female relatives of prominent Black leaders, established a Ladies Literary Society.[58] Their decision to form such an organization was particularly bold at a time when the education of women was still controversial, yet they must have embraced the sentiments of NYASS that "every measure for the thorough and proper education of colored females is a blow aimed directly at slavery." Soon, the society took even more concrete action. In September 1837, in honor of its third anniversary, the women were moved by the inspiring words of Elizabeth Jennings who urged them to "awake and slumber no more—arise, put on your armor, ye daughters of America, and stand forth in the field of improvement." Heeding Jennings's call, the members of the Ladies Literary Society created an affiliation with the Anti-Slavery

Convention of American Women and began collecting money for the *Colored American* newspaper. In addition, in 1838, Black women from throughout the city held a fundraiser in which they displayed products created by a free economy to demonstrate the results of nonslave labor; they donated the proceeds to aid fugitive slaves.[59]

As Black women increased their activism in the antislavery struggle, so did Black New Yorkers throughout the community. Indeed, abolition was a movement by and for the people. Beyond the protection of fugitives, perhaps the most obvious demonstrations of Black community solidarity in favor of abolition were the strategic political decisions concerning public celebrations of independence. Black New Yorkers had abandoned Black Emancipation Day and public processions by 1829, but they had apparently elected to celebrate American independence on the Fourth of July. However, in the mid-1830s, Black New Yorkers agreed to cease honoring Independence Day while slavery continued in the United States. As Henry Highland Garnet explained later, Black New Yorkers passed a resolution committing themselves "never to unite in the slightest in commemorating this day, until the last vestige of slavery was removed from the United States."[60]

Furthermore, Black New Yorkers sent a powerful political message by substituting an alternative independence commemoration: the abolition of slavery in the British West Indies. On the third anniversary of this momentous edict, a crowd of 3,500 New Yorkers held a grand celebration. Immediately afterward, the *Colored American* newspaper reflected: "We wish all the South could have been there. Could such have been the case, we verily believe, the next rising sun would have ushered in the Jubilee morning; and TWO MILLIONS of bleeding slaves, would have stood forth, disenthralled and redeemed." The irony of British emancipation in light of the continuation of Southern slavery was certainly not lost on Black activists. The *Colored American*'s editor Charles Ray, for example, could not resist the opportunity to consider the consequences of American independence from England: "Had Republican America remained a colony of Great Britain, the first of August 1834 would have emancipated every slave, and made us a nation of Freemen."[61]

Even with the Black community's commitment to abolition, Charles Ray's poignant concluding remarks demonstrated a painful reality; Black folks were only marginally free, an island in the midst of a stormy sea. Despite their best efforts, Southern slavery grew stronger with each passing day and most White New Yorkers had not yet accepted the notion that Black men could be free and equal citizens. Particularly disappointing to many Black activists was the realization that racism remained a persistent problem, even among their White allies in the abolitionist movement. Samuel Cornish had been among the first to identify this issue in the pages of the *Colored American* in 1838, when he criticized White abolitionists for focusing exclusively on slavery and ignoring the problem of racial prejudice. Cornish called upon their White "friends" to tackle the issue of racism because, although he knew it would be a challenging task, he believed that it was "the duty the abolitionists owe to their colored brethren." After all, Cornish insisted, "the real battleground between liberty and slavery is prejudice against color."[62]

Although Samuel Cornish's plea went largely unanswered in the antislavery community, his words apparently reached the ears of his own brethren and struck a cord. Thus, as Peter Williams Jr. had prophesized in 1830, frustration caused some free Blacks to question their tactics. Moral improvement and biracial associations, in particular, took a serious beating when activist Peter Paul Simons challenged the efficacy of these strategies in a speech before the African Clarkson Association. For an event held on April 23, 1839, Simons had been asked to address his brother Clarksons on the benefits of benevolence and moral uplift. Although the topic was consistent with the Black leadership's political strategy, few were likely prepared for Simon's powerful indictment of moral uplift as a method for Black elevation. Simons opened with a bold declaration, insisting that the commitment to moral elevation "has made us a moral people, but no more." He was especially troubled by his perception that such tactics had reinforced notions of inferiority, arguing that "it has carried along with it blind submission" to those of "pale complexions." Furthermore, Simons worried that such negative self-perception led to conflict and distrust among Black people: "This moral elevation of our people is but a mere song, it is nothing but a conspicuous scarecrow designed expressly . . . to hinder our people from acting collectively for themselves. For as long as it continues, we will have a lack of confidence in one another, and if we suspect each other, how can we act together?"[63]

Though Simons's support for racial unity was not new, his open denunciation of moral and intellectual elevation at the expense of "physical and political elevation" would certainly have sent shockwaves through the leadership. Undoubtedly, his concluding remarks, which dramatically called for action and foreshadowed Henry Highland Garnet's 1843 Address to the Slaves, would have roused some Black activists and horrified others. "Is it possible that this foolish thought of moral elevation suffers us to remain inactive? If so, then remain inactive, and you but raise another generation of slaves, and your children's children to latest posterity will spend their lives in as bitter oppression as you do now today. . . . No, we must show ACTION! ACTION! Action! And we will be in truth an independent people."[64] There was startling silence in response to Simons's address, at least publicly. The *Colored American* issued a brief statement declaring that they would become a "miserable people" if they learned to "despise or ridicule moral and intellectual elevation" and further implied that Simons was jealous of those who sought to improve themselves.[65] Yet the comparative silence in response to Simons's remarks may be due, in part, to the fact that something in his message resonated among members of the Black leadership.[66]

In fact, many Black New Yorkers already embraced Simon's desire for "political elevation" and had begun organizing to pressure White Americans to expand their definition of citizenship and extend suffrage rights. According to the New York State Legislature's ruling in 1821, Black people had restricted access to the suffrage contingent upon property ownership worth at least $250. Given the poverty in the Black community, this stipulation seriously limited the number of Black men who were eligible to vote because, by 1835, only sixty-eight Black men were able to vote in New York City.[67] Denied basic voting rights, the political potency of the Black community was severely hindered and, thus, the acquisition of the suffrage became a critical crusade for justice. Activism against disfranchisement commenced in February 1837, when Black leaders drafted a petition arguing for their right to equal suffrage.[68] In their appeal, they declared that the state should extend "the right of voting to all male citizens of the State, on the same terms, *without distinctions of color.*" Despite the strength of their conviction and their ability to garner 620 signatures, the petition not only failed to pass the state legislature but was overwhelmingly defeated with only eleven affirmative votes.[69] Initially, however, Black New Yorkers were not daunted and committed themselves to mapping out more effective strategies; they drafted a revised document, which demanded the "abolition of an odious distinction" that denied them the full rights of citizenship. Armed with this new ideological weapon, they decided to send Philip Bell on a tour through other New York counties to obtain support for a statewide alliance and encourage their brethren to overwhelm the state legislature with their message.[70]

Despite their best efforts, however, little progress was made and Black activists grew irritated and impatient. In fact, at least one Black leader resorted to angry diatribes. In the *Colored American* newspaper, African Society member Peter Vogelsang publicly aired his grievance about the fact that native-born Black men were exempted from voting while foreign-born immigrants had full access to the political process. Based on their birthright, Vogelsang insisted, he and his brethren had a stronger right to the suffrage than European immigrants. In an open letter to his people, he lamented that "YOU, natives of the soil, and I, a thirty-five year resident . . . are deprived the privileges granted to European *paupers,* blacklegs, and burglars!"[71] Clearly there was a strong tone of nativism in his language, but it is important to recognize that Vogelsang was simply reflecting the feelings of despair and betrayal that plagued Black men who had demonstrated their worthiness and loyalty yet were systematically denied citizenship.

Shortly thereafter, in June 1838, more frustrated Black leaders convened to form a permanent organization, the New York Association for the Political Improvement of the People of Color, which focused solely on obtaining the suffrage. In its constitution, members declared that they would "acquire for the colored citizens of the state, equal political rights and privileges, as enjoyed and exercised by other citizens." Yet despite their new organization, activists saw few options beyond petitioning, and they relied upon well-worn strategies. Hopeful that it would eventually be successful in swaying the opinion of the state legislators, the association claimed that through the use of petitions and the "influence of the press" it would "enlighten the 'public sentiment,' which sanctions and tolerates such disfranchisement."[72] However, although the Political Improvement Association circulated petitions and gained Black support, it failed to win the endorsement of the state legislature. Instead, the Black community's attempts to gain citizenship were continually rebuffed—a pattern, as we shall see, that was repeated throughout the antebellum era. Both Blacks and Whites understood that because suffrage allowed full access to the political process, it was the ultimate symbol of power and equality. For Black New Yorkers, it was this knowledge that motivated their desire to gain this unrestricted right; for Whites, it was this knowledge that drove them to keep it from Blacks at all costs.

*   *   *

The 1830s were a time of dramatic change and upheaval in the Black community. Black New Yorkers commenced the decade with strong hopes about the promise of legal emancipation, but the reality of "freedom" was a painful disappointment. Plagued by poverty, discrimination, and racial violence, the vast majority of Black New Yorkers languished in American society. Perhaps more than any other issue, the rising power of the ACS reminded free Blacks of their tenuous existence in the United States and prompted two competing responses: voluntary emigration to Canada and renewed efforts to force American society to expand their vision of citizenship to include Black men. These conflicting agendas faced off during the Colored Convention movement as Black leaders hoped to create a united front and form a strategic consensus among their people. Certainly, the Colored Conventions were transformative and full of potential; in fact, in the first few years, they managed to unite on the issue of anticolonization and send a definitive statement to American society about their intentions to remain in the United States and agitate for freedom and equality. However, their efforts had lasting repercussions. Not only did they elect to publicly distance themselves from their African heritage, but dissension over strategy and ego-driven posturing also prevented the Colored Conventions from maintaining a unified agenda.

Following the failure of the Colored Conventions, Black leaders in New York City refocused on their local community and organized themselves around crucial issues such as abolition. Yet as the constant threat of kidnapping and the 1834 antiabolition riot proved, American society was not ready to address questions of slavery and equal rights for free Blacks. The 1834 attack displayed, in shocking clarity, the Black community's vulnerability and lack of equality and citizenship. Although Black activists remained committed to political action, they soon discovered that they would face increasing obstacles. For, ultimately, the fight for abolition and suffrage was not only about political power and citizenship; it was also a struggle for the very future of the Black race in America. In the following decade, Black New Yorkers continued their crusade for abolition, citizenship, and the creation of a Black nation. However, the trials of the 1830s were a mere foreshadowing of the 1840s. Indeed, as the following years demonstrated, Black activists' efforts to fight against slavery and disfranchisement would continue to be stymied by squabbles over strategy and persistent impediments to the notion of Black equality.

CHAPTER 5

"Unity Is the Condition of Success,"
1837–1849

> Be active! Let defeat give you courage! Freedom never was attained
> without very great exertions and sacrifices. . . . Let us be united in
> feelings, though we may differ in opinions.
> —Austin Stewart, 1841

> Show me a people that are politically oppressed, and I will show
> you a degraded community; or if enterprising and intelligent, an
> unconquerable and struggling one.
> —Henry Highland Garnet, 1841

> The necessity of renewed and united activity in our great cause now
> presses upon us with more than usual weight. Ceaseless vigilance,
> unswerving integrity, and earnest and hearty activity, are the chief
> reliance of the proscribed. . . . Without concerted action, our efforts will
> be useless and unavailing. Unity of effort is the condition of success.
> —New York State Colored Convention, 1841

On December 7, 1837, Black leaders in New York City held a large gathering to discuss the plight of an alleged fugitive, Henry Merscher, who had been illegally enslaved by city officials.[1] What began as a meeting about the persisting problem of kidnapping became a revealing moment in the abolitionist movement, as the group erupted into debate over a controversial resolution that challenged the AASS's belief in nonresistance. The conflict commenced when David Ruggles suggested a clause declaring that the society should no longer "recommend non-resistance to persons who are denied the protection of equitable law." Even though Ruggles insisted that such a stance was a reasonable response to "avaricious kidnappers," other Black activists were not convinced. In particular, Charles Ray and Theodore Wright claimed that the resolution violated "the spirit and tendency" of the AASS and worried about openly opposing one of William Lloyd Garrison's most treasured principles because Garrison was considered an important "friend of the race." Ruggles immediately rose in defense of his position, but a "long and protracted discussion" ensued and Black New Yorkers found themselves hopelessly divided over strategy. In fact, the measure was put to an inconclusive vote three times before the chairman finally decided to remove the contentious statement and conclude the meeting.[2]

The debate among Black New Yorkers over Garrisonian nonresistance was critically important, for it reflected a larger ideological mood between 1837 and 1840 in which abolitionists across racial lines were questioning Garrison's strategies. This controversy ultimately led to a break in the antislavery movement. Though the rise of William Lloyd Garrison and the AASS in 1831 had initially provided Black activists with hope and promise, within several years there was growing tension and internal dissent as political philosophies clashed. By 1837, it was clear that, although abolitionists were united in their desire to destroy slavery, individual leaders had drastically different ideas about the proper tactics to employ. As a result, the fragile antislavery coalition collapsed in 1840.

The dissolution of the antislavery alliance dramatically altered the course of political activism for New York City's Black leadership. Although historians Jane and William Pease argued that debates among White abolitionists were "irrelevant" to Black leaders, this chapter reveals that the division within the biracial coalition was profoundly important for two fundamental reasons.[3] First, it thrust Black leaders into the center of the conflict by forcing them to determine where they would place their allegiance. More significantly, however, the eventual split in the antislavery movement convinced Black activists that they must establish a sense of unity within their *own* community if they hoped to succeed in their crusade for abolition and suffrage. Having witnessed the devastating impact of disharmony among White abolitionists, Black leaders firmly believed that unity was the key to victory. Thus, as young vital leaders, such as Dr. James McCune Smith, Henry Highland Garnet, and Charles Ray, stepped to the forefront of the community, they embarked upon an all-consuming mission to forge a unified Black political agenda.[4]

Yet despite their passionate commitment to the vision of unity, Black New Yorkers quickly confronted internal strategic conflicts of their own. As the new generation of Black leaders commenced their fight for universal emancipation and equal citizenship, they found themselves (as their forefathers had) struggling to identify which strategies would most effectively attain their goals. Initially, they considered rekindling previous attempts to create regional Black alliances, hoping that cohesion among Black leaders might overshadow the conflict within the abolitionist movement. Yet many Black activists were wary of such an endeavor, because the Colored Convention movement in the 1830s had degenerated into frustrating infighting, and they remained doubtful about whether national coalitions could be successful. Instead, regional organizing was delayed until later in the decade, as Black New Yorkers first held a series of state conventions in a desperate attempt to gain unrestricted voting rights. They soon discovered, however, that the same ideological issues that had ripped the abolitionist movement apart also stymied Black state and regional conventions. Ultimately, the 1840s proved to be a decade of vehement debate with the Black leadership over political strategy. Yet in the end, out of the confusion, Black activists emerged with a renewed dedication to unify and fight for their own liberation as they saw fit.

* * *

By 1837, as the meeting of Black New Yorkers revealed, there was growing concern within the abolitionist community about the efficacy of William Lloyd Garrison's unique political philosophy.[5] Nonresistance was not the only issue creating conflict among antislavery activists. Although Garrison's dynamic personality and commitment to abolition had catapulted him to national prominence in 1831, there was widespread concern about many of his ideas primarily led by White New Yorkers Arthur and Lewis Tappan. The Tappan brothers' opposition to Garrison centered on two issues: anticlericalism and political participation. Strong advocates of Christian evangelism, the Tappans denounced Garrison's belief that churches "obstructed progress" toward abolition and argued that religious reform and abolition were intricately linked. In addition, they criticized Garrison's view that the American Constitution, and by extension the American political process, was proslavery. Instead, they maintained that engagement in the political system could be an effective method to create substantive change. Initially, the Tappans did not discuss their reservations about Garrison openly but, after clergymen criticized Garrison in the summer of 1837, the seeds of discord began to blossom. Although the Tappans remained publicly neutral, privately, Lewis Tappan worked to oust Garrisonian ideas from the AASS. As a result, the conflicts between factions in the AASS were exacerbated, and the ideological lines were more sharply drawn.[6]

By the time of the Massachusetts Abolition Society's convention in May 1839, tensions were ready to explode. During that meeting, a group of ministers and abolitionists attacked Garrison for his anticlericalism and for urging activists to abstain from voting. Although the Garrisonians temporarily managed to withstand this internal revolution, the debate led to a permanent break within the movement as the Tappan brothers began to seek support for their agenda. On May 15, 1839, Lewis Tappan wrote to fellow abolitionist Gerrit Smith and attacked Garrison in veiled terms stating that he believed "we have greatly erred in associating with ungodly men in the Anti-Slavery enterprise." Furthermore, Tappan supporters recommitted themselves to suffrage after Lewis Tappan inserted a message into the AASS annual report that argued abolitionists should use direct action and the vote to achieve their goals. He explained, "If the ballot-box be given up, the cause is given up with it." Most notably, Tappanites began working to establish a third political party, the Liberty Party, to promote the abolitionist cause. Recognizing that their differences could not be ignored, activists on both sides scrambled to prepare themselves for the AASS convention to be held in New York City in May 1840.[7]

Indeed the 1840 convention turned into a showdown, where the Tappan faction attempted to wrest control of the national organization and eliminate Garrison's influence. In fact, the Tappanites opened the events with a rather bold statement, the absence of Arthur Tappan who resigned from the executive committee and boycotted the gathering. Yet his brother Lewis remained and was ready to fight for the future of the organization. Although the issues of nonresistance, clericalism, and political participation created considerable debate, the fragile coalition was not broken until Garrison presented a motion to appoint a woman, Abby Kelley, to the business committee. As the *Colored American* reported, her nomination raised the "vexed woman question," and threw the gathering into turmoil. After a vehement argument, the motion to allow female leadership passed, but only by a narrow margin.[8]

Frustrated and outvoted, 123 delegates entered their protest into the official record on the grounds that including women was not a wise or beneficial act; the Tappans were part of this dissenting faction, as were most of the Black New Yorkers. Their position was based on a pervasive fear that, if women were allowed to participate, the issue of abolition would be obscured by women's rights. Yet, in truth, the Tappans' challenge to the AASS was about much more; it was in response to all of Garrison's strategies. As one Garrison biographer put it, "Lewis Tappan insisted that the woman question was merely the occasion, not the cause, of the breach. The real issue . . . was Garrison's desire to 'make an experiment upon the public' by foisting a host of radical issues on the society." Ultimately, the Tappanites decided to abandon the AASS and led over three hundred delegates out of the meeting.[9] The following day, they convened in an alternate location and established their own organization, the American and Foreign Anti-Slavery Society (AFASS). The AFASS never reached the pinnacle of activism they hoped for, and they soon found themselves struggling for support.[10] More importantly, however, the withdrawal of the Tappanites from the AASS destroyed all hopes for a unified abolitionist movement.

Although the schism that devastated the antislavery coalition began among White abolitionists, the conflict was profoundly important to Black leaders. Certainly, Black activists had a vested interest in intellectual and political issues being debated because, quite literally, the future of the abolitionist movement was at stake. Yet the resulting split among antislavery advocates had a particularly significant impact on Black New Yorkers because they were quickly forced into the impossible situation of choosing sides. Caught in the cross fire between opposing forces, they were asked to either abandon their long-standing friend, William Lloyd Garrison, or betray their local supporters, the Tappans.[11] Where would their allegiances ultimately lie?

This was not an easy question for Black New Yorkers to answer. At first, it appeared that they would give the Tappans and the AFASS their exclusive endorsement. As evidenced by their withdrawal from the AASS 1840 convention, many prominent Black activists in New York such as Christopher Rush, Samuel Cornish, Theodore Wright, Henry Highland Garnet, and J. W. C. Pennington, who had been ardent AASS activists, joined the Tappans and worked diligently within the AFASS to build the new organization into a viable institution. However, the situation was more complicated than it seemed. A few leaders, such as Thomas Van Rensalaer and William Powell, remained explicitly loyal to Garrison and urged the rest of the leadership to do the same.[12] Furthermore, despite their demonstrated support for the AFASS, Henry Highland Garnet and Charles Ray were apparently not prepared to completely relinquish their connections to Garrison and the AASS; a fact that became abundantly clear at a meeting convened shortly after the explosion at the AASS convention.[13]

Late in May 1840, Black New Yorkers gathered in the First Colored Presbyterian Church to discuss the upcoming World's Anti-Slavery Convention in London. The main question on their agenda was which delegates to support; should they endorse Garrison, or James Birney and Henry Stanton who were representing the Tappans and the newly formed AFASS? Not surprisingly, Thomas Van Rensalaer spoke enthusiastically on behalf of Garrison; arguing that the community should give him its exclusive endorsement. What is perhaps most revealing about this meeting is that Tappan supporters, Henry Highland Garnet and Charles Ray, sought to establish a middle ground. Rather than risk alienating any of their allies, Garnet and Ray suggested that they should agree to "approve of the American delegation, sent out by American Abolitionists" because such a move would obviously not privilege or deny any of the delegates. As Charles Ray explained, he thought it was in their best interest to "remain perfectly free" to affiliate themselves with anyone who acted on behalf of the abolitionist cause.[14]

The events of this gathering were critically important because it signaled the beginning of a new era in which Black activists insisted upon establishing their own agenda, one that placed the higher cause of abolition and racial advancement above all else. Unable to heal the rift in the biracial coalition, they reached an important and defining conclusion. They sought to avoid the squabbling among their White associates and began to forge an independent Black agenda. Ultimately, the divide between the Garrisonians and the Tappanites marked a crucial turning point for Black New Yorkers because it allowed them to renew the journey they had begun in 1827 with the founding of *Freedom's Journal*. They elected to "plead their own cause" and seek to unite Black leaders on the issues of abolition and suffrage. In their minds, because unity was not possible in the antislavery movement, it was crucial to establish a sense of cohesion among Black activists and launch collective Black action on the issues they thought most important to their racial improvement. They would soon discover, however, that independent Black action was equally susceptible to internal strategic conflict.

In June 1840, shortly after the ill-fated AASS convention, Black leaders considered resuscitating a national Black political alliance. Faced with the dissolution of a unified antislavery movement, yet cognizant that significant change was impossible without a national coalition, many Black leaders hoped that they could revitalize the struggle by reestablishing the defunct Colored Convention movement. However, their plans for independent Black action were fraught with conflict from the beginning, as they questioned the merits of such an endeavor. The discussion commenced in the pages of the *Colored American* newspaper, when "JWA" from Wilmington, Delaware, wrote a letter asserting that the conditions of the race could be dramatically improved by a Black national convention. Although he admitted that past gatherings had failed because leaders had not been connected to the needs of "the people," he maintained that this problem could easily be corrected by a meeting of the best minds in their community. Issuing a call for unity, he argued that their goals could only be reached by collective, rather than individual, action. As he explained, "it is associated effort that is producing the mightiest revolution in the moral, political, and religious world." He concluded, therefore, that Black people must not be a "mass of inert matter," but rather move quickly toward their goals.[15]

The following week another correspondent, "Amana," echoed JWA's comments, arguing that free Blacks needed a regional gathering to strengthen their communication and create a unified movement to improve the lives of their people. He eloquently declared that the Black community needed to wake up and take action on its own behalf. In this way, Black activists would be infused with "a new spirit" that would incite them to "unite, as one band of brethren, to put forth every exertion for our elevation." According to Amana, the first step in this process was to assemble in a national convention and have a mutual exchange regarding the issues affecting their people. Essentially, like many Black leaders, Amana maintained that Black people could not effectively transform their lives by working in isolation, but they must unite despite their differences. Apparently, Black leaders in Connecticut agreed with Amana, because they issued a call for a national convention to be held in September in New Haven.[16]

However, a few activists remained doubtful about the potential success of the New Haven meeting. Although they endorsed Black conventions in theory, they maintained that the plans suffered from poor organization. One correspondent, "Americanus," indicated that he was hesitant to endorse a convention because he thought that prior gatherings were disorganized and lacked a clear purpose. Instead, he suggested that, before a meeting commenced, leaders should create an agenda and be ready to take immediate action on a clearly established program: "Let the objects be fully marked out, and then they will meet to execute them, not merely to contemplate what ought to be done." Clearly frustrated by slow progress, Americanus wanted the convention to have obvious results or not bother meeting at all.[17] Likewise, Charles Ray, the editor of the *Colored American*, denounced the gathering, arguing that the goals were not sufficiently stated and the "objects specified are either too indefinite, or not of sufficient magnitude, or beyond our control." Ray also suggested that further consideration should be given to the agenda, rather than take hasty action. Though he was careful to declare his support for the idea of national Colored Conventions, he insisted that he was unable to approve this particular attempt.[18]

Other Black activists in New York City must have agreed with Charles Ray because, rather than lending support to the New Haven convention, they focused their energies away from a national Black gathering onto the possibility of a New York state meeting because the purpose of a state conference was more apparent and easy to define. Most importantly, they hoped it would be simple to reach a consensus and establish a foundation of unity. Most Black New Yorkers could agree upon the necessity of obtaining unrestricted access to the vote. Beginning in the late 1830s, many Black New Yorkers had concluded that slavery was not the only oppressive force hindering their advancement. On the contrary, faced with restrictions based on property qualifications, Black activists in New York State believed that the persistent denial of the suffrage was an equally significant demonstration of the continuing problem of racism, because it was the ultimate barrier to full citizenship. This issue had become particularly apparent by 1840, because New York City's Black population had reached its highest point in the antebellum era, numbering over sixteen thousand, but less than ninety Black men were eligible to vote.[19] Thus, rather than become consumed with the ideological split between their abolitionist allies or the disorganization among Northern Black leaders, Black New Yorkers resolved to continue the fight for justice on their own. However, in spite of their attempts to avoid political disputes, they soon discovered that they were not exempt from internal conflict.

Black activists in New York City had begun renewed efforts on behalf of universal male suffrage just shortly before the ill-fated AASS convention. On April 27, 1840, a meeting convened in Jamaica, Queens, during which Black leaders from Manhattan, Long Island, and the surrounding boroughs formed a coalition and drafted an official declaration on their status in American society. Led by Thomas Van Rensalaer, J. W. C. Pennington, and William Johnson, the convention demanded their right to citizenship and expressed outrage at their exclusion from public facilities, education, and political enfranchisement. At the conclusion of this gathering, they vowed that they would "exert [their] energies in the use of all rightful and reasonable means to correct the abuse to which we have referred." In June, a group of activists, led by Charles Ray and Charles Reason, delivered on their promise by issuing a call for a convention in Albany where Black men from throughout New York State, regardless of status or occupation, could gather and "consider their political condition."[20] Specifically, they argued that their primary disability was the "deprivation of the free exercise" of voting and that their disadvantaged political condition was the root of all their other problems: "We are convinced, fellow citizens, that not only our political, but our depressed condition in all other respects in the State, owes itself . . . to the fact that we are politically weak, not possessing unrestricted use of the elective franchise."[21]

The state convention announcement was posted in the Colored American for the next several weeks and drew considerable attention. However, not all the attention was positive. In late June, their White "friends" at the National Anti-Slavery Standard printed an editorial expressing strong reservations about a convention of colored people. Though they claimed to support political action, they were highly resentful about the exclusion of Whites and maintained that separate Black institutions were contrary to the goals of abolition and racial progress. Arguing that separate action incited prejudice, the newspaper's editor, Nathaniel Peabody Rogers, stated that he opposed "all exclusive action on the part of the colored people, except where the clearest necessity demanded it." He accused Black New Yorkers of being hasty and of failing to understand that their decision was damaging to their ultimate goal. In particular, the article claimed that Black leaders were "not sharpsighted enough to perceive, that every thing that tends to separate the colored people from the whites, aids in building up an impassable barrier to their progress."[22]

Reflecting his growing frustration with the influence of White paternalism on the movement, Charles Ray was incensed by the National Anti-Slavery Standard's interference. In fact, he used his position as editor of the Colored American to reprint NASS's statement followed by a blistering response in which he argued that the "clearest necessity" demanded that Black New Yorkers convene to discuss their political condition. According to Ray, "there is, there can be no 'clearer necessity' than to feel and experience daily the political disabilities we labor under." Although he claimed that he did not want to deny the "Anti-Slavery fraternity," Ray was convinced that American society would never view Black men as equals until "we show we feel it; until we prove that we can think and act like men." In closing, however, he offered a compromise; he conceded that they would not prevent Whites from attending, but that the convention call was specifically directed toward their Black brethren.[23]

Yet, apparently, Ray's attempt at reconciliation was not sufficient because criticism about the exclusive nature of the proposed gathering persisted. This time, however, it emanated from within the Black community. On July 27, 1840, Black leaders in New York City gathered at Philomathean Hall to discuss the upcoming state convention. Attendance at this meeting reflected the new generation of Black activists in the city, including James McCune Smith, Charles Ray, Patrick Reason, and Philip A. Bell.[24] Under Patrick Reason's leadership, the group planned to select delegates and pass resolutions supporting the need for political elevation. Yet the meeting suddenly dissolved into argument and dissension. John Peterson offered a motion that declared that, due to the overwhelming prejudice in American society, it was "contrary to reason" to believe that Black people could advance their cause through any separate action. Although Patrick Reason ruled that the

Reverend Charles B. Ray. (Courtesy of the General Research
and Reference Division; Schomburg Center for Research in
Black Culture; New York Public Library; Astor, Lenox, and
Tilden Foundations.)

resolution was out of order, Peterson refused to be silenced. In fact, for several
hours, Peterson and James McCune Smith tried to pass a series of motions opposing the state convention, but they were unable to gain adequate support. The
debates persisted until late that night when they were forced to adjourn without
any conclusive decisions.[25]

One week later, another meeting was held to resume preparations for the convention. However, immediately following the opening business, James McCune
Smith "rose in opposition" again and tried to persuade his brethren that separate
action would be a costly mistake. Smith's exact words were not recorded, but he
reportedly supported his position "in a masterly and eloquent speech" that was
answered by Charles Ray "in an able and argumentative manner." Smith was
apparently quite convincing, because he won James Hudson and Thomas Van
Rensalaer to his side. Most notably, Van Rensalaer wrote a letter to the *Colored*

American denouncing his previous support of the convention on the grounds that Smith had persuaded him that such an "exclusive" gathering would be "injurious to us as a people." Although Van Rensalaer said he would not "censure the motives of those who are still in favor of the convention," he officially withdrew his support of the meeting. Yet the majority of attendees were not swayed; in particular, Charles Ray, Philip Bell, and Thomas Downing reaffirmed their strong support for the convention. With the most influential leaders in the community so severely divided, the gathering was forced to adjourn a second time without reaching a consensus.[26]

The debates over the 1840 suffrage convention were quite revealing, for the conflict over the creation of separate Black movements and institutions signaled the reemergence of a confusing strategic question that had plagued activists during the Colored Conventions of the 1830s. Would they have to relinquish racial autonomy to achieve their goals of equality? Men such as James McCune Smith and Thomas Van Rensalaer clearly answered in the affirmative and maintained that they should denounce any form of separate Black action, a conviction that became increasingly clear after a letter from James McCune Smith appeared in the *Colored American*. Feeling compelled to clarify his position, Smith argued that, although he supported Black political action, he could not endorse *separate* action because it was damaging to their cause. According to Smith, "a movement based on the complexion of the skin, will end in riveting still more firmly the chains which bind us."[27]

Yet although Smith saw himself as part of a biracial community of activists who shared common principles, Charles Ray, Philip Bell, and their supporters viewed themselves as part of a Black nation; a nation within a nation that must assert itself separately and declare its humanity before any coalitions could effectively exist. Charles Ray explained, "As long as we attend the Conventions called by our white friends we will be looked upon as playing second fiddle to them. They will always form the majority of such Conventions, and the sentiments and opinions thus promulgated will go forth as the sentiments and opinions of white men."[28] His position was fortified by the schism among White abolitionists because, as long as the division persisted, Black activists would be forced to choose sides and potentially weaken the movement.

The issue was not settled until August 7, when a sense of urgency developed about nominating delegates to appear in Albany. With the convention less than two weeks away, Black New Yorkers knew they had to make a final decision regarding their participation. As chair of the meeting, Philip Bell refused any further debate and refocused their attention on choosing their representatives. Although they originally intended to send five delegates, there was such a tremendous response that they increased the number to twenty-five. Perhaps most shocking, was that James McCune Smith was nominated as a delegate despite his demonstrated reservations to the very notion of a Black convention. Initially he

Dr. James McCune Smith. (Courtesy of the Manuscripts, Archives, and Rare Books Division; Schomburg Center for Research in Black Culture; New York Public Library; Astor, Lenox, and Tilden Foundations.)

declined but, after further consideration, Smith agreed to respect the "wishes of the people" and attend the gathering. Yet although Smith graciously accepted the nomination, he obviously had not entirely altered his opinion because he insisted that his ally, James Hudson, should also be appointed as a representative. In the end, Smith must have been placated by the outcome of the convention because, as Charles Ray had promised, any supporter regardless of color or gender was allowed to observe the proceedings although only delegates had voting privileges. With this matter finally settled, Black leaders turned their attention to the upcoming convention and the struggle to obtain the suffrage.[29]

Despite the debates plaguing the movement in the days before the convention, the state meeting in 1840 was reportedly quite successful. Convened in August in Albany, Black men came from throughout the state to discuss the condition of their people and identify tactics for obtaining the suffrage. Just as they had hoped, the Albany Convention of 1840 was a powerful demonstration of Black independent action, and the attendees were inspired by the extraordinary representation from throughout the state. Editor Charles Ray later wrote in the *Colored American* that the delegates impressed him with the realization that "we are a more talented, a better educated, more improved and elevated people than we had any anticipation we were, and we have always been very sanguine that we were a noble people." The New York City delegation dominated the convention, with Charles Ray as the chairman and Theodore Wright, Charles Reason, Patrick Reason, and William Johnson holding influential positions.[30] The majority of the convention was occupied with passing resolutions; the most pivotal of which asserted the need for direct action on the issue of the suffrage and argued that the liberation of Black people depended entirely upon political enfranchisement. In particular, they urged Black men throughout the state to "make early and energetic efforts in behalf of the great cause" and declared that they would not rest until they had achieved their goal. "[We] will leave no peaceful and rational means untried to accomplish these ends."[31]

The most moving display was the address the delegates issued to their "Colored Fellow Citizens." Asserting their determination to remain in the United States and gain full citizenship, Black New Yorkers sought to rouse their brethren into action with a particularly forceful opening: "Hereditary bondsmen . . . who would be free, themselves must strike the blow!" Their statement proceeded to criticize those who refused to take a stand and reminded them that there were consequences for inaction. In their minds, the right to vote was the "lifeblood" of political existence, and without suffrage, they were deprived of their "living principle." Still these Black activists offered hope for a brighter future, maintaining that through unified action Black men could fundamentally alter their position in society: "Brethren, by united, vigorous, and judicious and manly effort, we can redeem ourselves." However, delegates warned that redemption could only happen if Black people were determined and took action.

> Colored men of New York! Are you willing that your people should longer constitute the proscribed class? Are you willing ever to be deprived of one of the dearest rights of freemen? Are you willing to remain quietly and inactively, political slaves? Are you willing to leave to your children no better public inheritance than to be among the disfranchised—the politically oppressed? O No! Let the opinion of all people, of all ages, in all circumstances, in all relations be fixed upon this matter. Aye, and when the pure incense of prayer goes up, let it bear the gentle burden—No!

In this moving appeal for agitation, delegates declared that the future of the race hinged upon access to the vote because their present status and the condition of their children depended upon immediate action. Therefore, they concluded, it was the obligation of all men to answer the call.[32]

Even though their address to the Black population was an unapologetic appeal to political action, their message to White New Yorkers was a carefully constructed display of republican ideology. Reverting to a traditional moral improvement strategy, they apparently hoped to persuade White voters and politicians to extend suffrage rights on the grounds that property qualifications were immoral and denied Black men their rights as American citizens. Indeed, the early portion of the essay focused on the undue suffering endured by Blacks due to disfranchisement: "The impartial and proscriptive non-suffrage act, has been to us hurtful in the extreme. . . . It has been the source of evil, unmitigated, unalleviated." The authors also highlighted birthright and the tradition of Black patriotism, arguing that Black men were among the first settlers in New York and had always been quick to offer military service in defense of the country when called upon. In short, they claimed, "We are Americans." Yet the most compelling portion of their address argued that their right to suffrage was ultimately not based on morality or on American identity, but rather, on their rights as human beings, "We base our claim upon the possession of those common and yet exalted faculties of manhood. WE ARE MEN . . . on the ground of our common humanity, do we claim equal and entire rights with the rest of our fellow citizens." In this poignant statement, the convention advanced their political strategy by insisting that their humanity alone should be sufficient justification for the extension of the franchise.[33]

Once they returned to New York City, the local delegates convened a meeting among their people at which they presented the resolutions and received a hearty endorsement. Several months later, they received more encouraging news in the form of a letter from Henry Highland Garnet that was published in the *Colored American*. Garnet had traveled to Albany to plead their case before the state legislature, and he returned with an inspiring report. He demonstrated the fruits of their efforts by stating that he had presented state legislators with thousands of signed petitions pleading for universal male suffrage: 1,700 of which had come from New York City. This, Garnet claimed, sent a clear message to lawmakers, and he assured the readers that "we may 'hope on still.'" Garnet further believed that success was imminent because he had met with several influential state representatives who had promised "favor in regard to the measure." However, Garnet must have suspected that the battle for suffrage would be prolonged, because he urged his readers not to despair if their work did not yield immediate results. He argued that if they were denied suffrage rights, they should simply continue their efforts: "If we do not succeed this year, if our petitions are thrown aside, when then? Are we to be discouraged? Are we to lie upon our oars, and suffer ourselves to be borne along by the onward tide that threatens to carry us down deep in the gulf of lifeless inactivity, and irrevocable degradation? No! the citizens of New York are 'made of sterner stuff . . .' gentlemen, 'we must stand.'" Although Garnet seemed rather hopeful in February 1841, the era of good feelings among Black New Yorkers did not last; when the meeting of the state legislature closed, Black men still did not have the unrestricted right to vote.[34]

Even worse, frustration among New York City activists increased in the following months as the division within their community over strategy reemerged. Although support for the delegates had been strong when they initially returned, it quickly became clear that they had dissenters in their midst. Black leaders Thomas Van Rensalaer and David Ruggles formed a new association, the American Reform Board of Disfranchised Commissioners (ARBDC), in direct opposition to the state convention movement. The organization obviously shared the larger vision of universal male suffrage, but it did not endorse the statewide movement. The source of their discontent was not entirely clear, but it may have stemmed from Van Rensalaer's previous objections to the exclusively Black (rather than biracial) nature of the convention movement's delegation. This explanation seems especially likely, because they used the term "American," rather than "African" or "colored," in their organization's title.

Yet neither the defeat in the legislature nor internal discord prevented most Black leaders from supporting another state colored convention. Perhaps inspired by Garnet's impassioned plea for persistence, they refused to be deterred. In fact, many prominent Black leaders in New York City signed an urgent message that appeared in the *Colored American* on July 17 and reflected continuing optimism: "Brethren, be not discouraged; such disappointments should only act as stimulus, to strengthen and invigorate our souls, and rouse us to a determination of persevering in the struggle by stronger and still more unanimous efforts, and by the talismanic influence of agitation!" Attached to this inspiring passage was a call for another suffrage convention to be held in Troy, New York, in August. Because *Colored American* editor, Charles Ray, endorsed this effort, it was repeated in the paper throughout the remainder of the month.[35]

Significantly, however, there was one additional challenge to the convention. Not surprisingly, the call for universal male suffrage caused some conflict over the role of Black women in the movement. Although most Black activists during this era did not openly advocate for women's suffrage, there was apparently some debate about whether women should be allowed to observe the convention. One delegate, William Johnson, argued that men should bring their wives as a statement of unity and solidarity. However, Charles Ray was adamantly opposed to such a notion. Ray maintained that female presence would cause the convention to become overcrowded and interfere with the important business at hand. Ray argued a man could "do more work abroad without his wife than with her." The discussion over this issue reflected the national debate among activists about the role of women in the movement for Black rights, which had plagued the abolitionist movement in 1840. Ultimately, as they had during the AASS convention, Black New Yorkers decided that the issues of women's rights and racial advancement should remain separate, a decision that reflected their decidedly cautious stance regarding women's rights.[36]

After this brief conflict over female participation, Black leaders descended upon Troy, New York, for their next state convention. On August 25, 1841, the delegation from New York City arrived at the gathering with forty-six representatives, which was nearly twice the number that had been sent the previous year. Under Henry Highland Garnet's leadership, the Troy meeting echoed many familiar sentiments from the previous meeting. In particular, the delegates declared that their mission was "to affect an equalization of the elective franchise . . . [and to] elevate the colored man to the dignity of a freeman and restore to him his birthright privileges." They also reaffirmed their conviction that petitions and appeals to patriotism were still the most effective methods for influencing public opinion. Indeed, as they weighed the question of strategy, delegates clung to the notion that politicians would grant Black people the suffrage if they could simply be persuaded to do so. As a result, they asserted themselves as true Americans worthy of full citizenship and urged state legislators to reconsider their position.[37]

There was, however, one important addition to the rhetoric emanating from the New York State suffrage movement. It was a message the Black leadership desperately needed to hear. Austin Stewart opened the convention with an inspiring address in which he reminded his brethren that unity, despite ideological differences, was the ultimate solution to their problems: "Let us be united in feelings, though we may differ in opinions." This, however, was a lesson that the leadership had not yet learned. In fact, tensions arose early in the gathering. When Charles Reason and Henry Highland Garnet were chosen to draft a public address, they quickly found themselves at odds.[38] Apparently Reason was disturbed by a specific passage, which stated that the property qualification was "no longer sufferable." Although the statement seemed relatively benign, Reason was concerned by the implication of Garnet's words; in his mind, the message too strongly suggested resistance. In response, Garnet, Ulysses Vidal, Alexander Crummell, and Charles Ray became enraged and a raucous debate ensued. In fact, the discussion lasted for the remainder of the night and was not resolved until the following morning when the convention elected to adopt the controversial passage. Furthermore, perhaps to Charles Reason's chagrin, the delegates passed another potentially inflammatory resolution, which declared that they would "agitate, agitate, agitate, until the odious disfranchising act is expunged from the statute books of the state." Significantly, they took this final vote by standing, which forced each delegate to signal his position to the entire convention.[39]

In the end, however, Charles Reason redeemed himself in the eyes of the convention. His address to Black New Yorkers was a powerful call to action,

Charles Reason. (Courtesy of the Manuscripts, Archives, and Rare Books Division; Schomburg Center for Research in Black Culture; New York Public Library; Astor, Lenox, and Tilden Foundations.)

specifically targeted at Black men who, he claimed, needed to stand up for their manhood and defend their families against injustice. There were also particularly strong words directed at Black ministers who, in his view, had not sufficiently used their influence and position to advance the cause of the race. He eloquently stated, "We call for the action of the whole people. There is no time for delay. Inactivity is suicidal. That we shall eventually triumph is certain; for our cause is a great and just cause." Perhaps most significantly, Reason's conclusion was a dramatic appeal for racial solidarity and reflected his realization that his brethren were right: "unity of effort is the condition of success." With those inspiring and hopeful words, the 1841 state convention came to a close and Black leaders returned to their communities armed with the convention's new motto: to march toward victory, "onward forever . . . until our object be accomplished."[40]

However, Black New Yorkers did not heed their own call for unity. In fact, following the 1841 Troy conference, division among activists in New York City became apparent. Just one month later, the ARBDC held a competing convention dominated by leading Black figures such as Thomas Van Rensalaer, Thomas L. Jennings, David Ruggles, Thomas Downing, and George Downing. Thomas Van Rensalaer and David Ruggles had routinely criticized the state conventions and hoped the ARBDC could be a more effective vehicle for change. Ruggles, in particular, employed rather militant language, demanding the immediate extension of citizenship rights: "We must remember that while our fellow countrymen of the south are slaves to individuals, we of the north are slaves to the community, and will be so until we rise and . ... ourselves strike for reform."[41]

Although its revolutionary rhetoric reflected a radical political stance among its membership, the ARBDC had only limited effectiveness. Without a specific strategy beyond petitioning, the ARBDC had nothing different to offer than the state conventions did. Worse, others in the Black leadership accused them of being elitist and exclusionary. Charles Ray openly attacked the ARBDC in the pages of the *Colored American,* calling its convention "a failure indeed." He further claimed that there were only eight to ten delegates for a "supposedly national convention" and depicted the attendees as being jealous and self-motivated. Although the Downings had tried to bridge the gap by attending both conventions, their efforts were apparently insufficient and, in the face of such opposition, the ARBDC vanished as quickly as they emerged without reaching their goals. However, the most damaging result was the inability of the leadership to resolve differences and achieve its goal of a unified movement.[42]

Internal conflict and dissension was apparently infectious, for it also pervaded renewed attempts at establishing a national Colored Convention in 1843. Although the New Yorkers had dismissed such an idea in 1840, they had evidently become convinced that a regional meeting was necessary to revitalize the movement for abolition and suffrage. Hoping to create a sense of national Black unity, New York leaders invited activists from several states to New York City in May 1843 to form an agenda for a national meeting.[43] However, the signs of division appeared early on, as Black leaders soon found themselves clashing over the same issues that had devastated the abolitionist movement. Glaringly absent from this gathering were representatives from Philadelphia, which reflected the Philadelphians' frustration about the New Yorkers' refusal to unreservedly support William Lloyd Garrison at the AASS convention in 1840.[44] As a result, although the Philadelphians initially supported the idea of a national convention in 1841 and 1842, they soundly rejected the New Yorkers' efforts in 1843 and boycotted the Colored Conventions for the entire decade of the 1840s.[45] Likewise, the Black Bostonians equally resented the New Yorkers' rejection of Garrison and remained suspicious of their motives. Although the Bostonians ultimately resolved not to abstain from the proceedings, scholar Howard Bell noted that they participated quite reluctantly.[46]

In spite of the Philadelphians' antipathy and the Bostonians' reservations, Black Northern leaders converged on Buffalo, New York, in August 1843 hopeful that they could overcome conflict and create a unified Black agenda. More specifically, they sought to establish a sense of solidarity that they thought had been severely lacking after the failure of the Colored Conventions in the 1830s. They passionately explained in their call for convention,

Since we have ceased to meet together in National Convention, we have become
ignorant of the moral and intellectual strength of our people. We have also been
deprived of the councils of our fathers, who have borne the burden and heat of
the day—the spirit of virtuous ambition and emulation has died in the bosoms
of the young men, and in a great degree we have become divided, and the bright
rising stars that once shone in our skies, have become partially obscured.[47]

Yet they soon discovered that overcoming political division would not be an easy
task. Even without the Philadelphians, the Colored Convention of 1843 ultimately
illustrated a quintessential Tappanite/Garrisonian split as delegates vehemently
debated questions of direct action and political participation.

Tensions first emerged following speeches delivered by Samuel Davis and
Henry Highland Garnet, both of whom strongly denounced Garrisonian nonresistance and urged their people to take bold action to fight slavery. Davis, in
particular, declared that they were witnessing a moment in history when Black
people had awakened to their condition, and were "determined no longer to
submit tamely and silently wear the galling yoke of oppression." He further argued, in a surprisingly revolutionary tone, that Black activists should use "every
means in our power" to destroy slavery and uplift their people. He concluded
by encouraging his brethren to assert themselves politically and demand their
rights, reminding them that nothing would change if they were not willing to
"rise up and assert our rightful claims."[48] Yet, despite its power, Davis's message
was completely overshadowed by Henry Highland Garnet's address to the slaves,
which was later considered to be the most articulate and militant manifesto on
the Black experience since David Walker's *Appeal.*

Drawing upon the language he initiated at the suffrage conventions, Garnet
argued that the time had come for Black people to liberate themselves: "Brethren,
the time has come when you must act for yourselves. It is an old and true saying
that, 'if hereditary bondsmen would be free, they must themselves strike the first
blow.'" In a startlingly bold declaration, Garnet also praised Denmark Vesey and
Nat Turner as "noble men" and depicted their revolutionary actions as inspira-
tional moments in the liberation of enslaved people. Yet his most controversial
statement came when he urged other enslaved people to follow these examples
and rise up against the system of slavery: "Let every slave throughout the land do
this, and the days of slavery are numbered . . . *rather die freemen than live to be
slaves.*" He closed by reminding enslaved people that they had an obligation to
resist because the voices of their ancestors were calling them to agitate, and they
had no other option: "Let your motto be Resistance! Resistance! RESISTANCE!
No oppressed people have ever secured their liberty without resistance."[49]

Not surprisingly, Garnet's legendary address created deep concern among
those who endorsed Garrisonian nonresistance. Although Garnet had prepared
the document at the request of the convention, after hearing his message, some
were concerned that his words were excessively contentious and revolutionary.

Reverend Henry Highland Garnet. (Courtesy of the Print
Collection; Miriam and Ira D. Wallach Division of Art, Prints,
and Photographs; New York Public Library; Astor, Lenox, and
Tilden Foundations.)

Charles Ray, in particular, suggested that before releasing the address to the
public, it should be referred to a committee and put through "a close and critical
examination" because he had identified "some points in it that might in print
appear objectionable." A frustrated Garnet immediately rose in defense of his
stance and spent an hour and a half carefully articulating the "merits" of his position. Specifically, after he "reviewed the abominable system of slavery, showed
its mighty workings, [and] its deeds of darkness and of death," Garnet concluded
that resistance was the only reasonable response. Garnet's fervent plea was apparently deeply moving, for the minutes of the convention reported that "the
whole Convention, full as it was, was literally infused with tears." Yet his appeal
was evidently not convincing enough, for objections persisted.[50]

Most notably, Frederick Douglass, who was a staunch Garrisonian and had
been recently admitted as a member of the AASS, thought that there was "too
much physical force" in the address and urged continued endorsement of moral

suasion. As he explained, he was in favor of "trying the moral means a little longer" and feared that Garnet's message "would lead to an insurrection." Although Garnet attempted to defend his position again, Douglass insisted that the address would certainly prompt an armed rebellion and maintained that the delegates were responsible to "avoid such a catastrophe." Obviously, in comparison to Douglass's belief that moral suasion would ultimately be successful, Garnet's message seemed too violent, too revolutionary, and too drastic. Reflecting the deep division among the delegates over strategy, debate over Garnet's address consumed the rest of that evening and most of the following day. Indeed, although Garnet's address ultimately failed to receive the endorsement of the convention, the vote revealed a severe rift within the leadership. In the end, only one vote determined the final decision to reject Garnet's message of direct resistance.[51]

Following the debate over the effectiveness of Garrisonian nonresistance, delegates must have hoped that the conflict between Frederick Douglass and Henry Highland Garnet was over. However, their wishes would go unfulfilled. Douglass and Garnet clashed over political strategy for a second time during the 1843 convention, again over one of William Lloyd Garrison's most cherished principles. This time, the two men collided on the question of whether Black political participation was necessary to advance the abolitionist cause. More specifically, Douglass objected to the convention's fifth proposed resolution, which declared, "it is the duty of every lover of liberty to vote the Liberty ticket so long as they are consistent with their principles." Douglass's frustration centered on two issues. First, as mentioned earlier, Garrison's archenemies, the Tappan brothers and Gerrit Smith, had created the Liberty Party. In addition, Douglass believed that the Liberty Party's very existence violated Garrison's assertion that true abolitionists should abstain from engaging in the American political system as long as the country upheld slavery. In stark contrast, Liberty Party supporters not only maintained that slavery could be abolished through political pressure, but its central tenets also suggested that a third party was necessary because mainstream political parties were controlled by proslavery factions.[52] As a result, Douglass and other Garrisonians denounced the resolution, claiming that they were "opposed to all parties," including the Liberty Party, because they "believed them verily and necessarily corrupt."[53]

The problem, however, was that Henry Highland Garnet had become a staunch supporter of the Liberty Party. Not only had he led the charge for suffrage rights in New York State, which indicated his belief that political participation was essential for racial advancement, but he had also become convinced that the Liberty Party could help bolster the abolitionist movement by forcing the issue onto the nation's political agenda. Thus, after Douglass launched an attack against the motion, Garnet countered by asserting that if there was any amendment to the resolution, it should only be designed to make the convention's endorsement of the Liberty Party "still stronger." Garnet was not alone in his convictions, for his fellow New Yorkers Theodore Wright and Charles Ray also spoke on behalf of the controversial resolution. Evidently, the vast majority of the attendees agreed with the New York City delegation because they passed the motion and declared their unreserved support of the Liberty Party in two additional resolutions later in the gathering. However, despite the fact that the convention concluded with expressions of joy and thanksgiving about the success of their endeavors, the spirit of conflict and dissension over Garrisonian philosophy left a taint on the delegates as they returned home. Indeed, the controversy over strategy and the Liberty Party had only just begun.[54]

Questions about the Liberty Party's efficacy persisted on the state level, when Black New Yorkers met again in 1844 to address the issue of suffrage. Up until that point, the Liberty Party had not been discussed at length during these gatherings because, although some of its leaders including Garnet, Theodore Wright, and Charles Ray agitated on behalf of the party, there had not been widespread support within the Black community. Perhaps Black activists shared Samuel Cornish's view that if the small number of eligible Black voters only voted for the Liberty Party or abolitionists, they would "place themselves in a position, little or nothing short of absolute disfranchisement." Alternatively, they may have endorsed James McCune Smith's critique that Liberty Party leaders, despite their commitment to abolition, ignored the plight of free Blacks. Regardless, because they were in the midst of a crucial election year, Black New Yorkers in 1844 apparently thought it was necessary to seriously consider whether to endorse the Liberty Party ticket.[55]

Perhaps to the Liberty Party's shock, however, even its supporters expressed extreme reservations about the organization's potential. In the midst of the convention proceedings, Theodore Wright and Charles Ray surprised the delegates by encouraging them not to exclusively support the Liberty Party; specifically, they claimed the suffrage conventions should not become a movement for one political party. Instead, they drafted a formal protest, which denounced the very resolutions from the 1843 national colored convention that they had supported the previous year. They advocated a middle ground, stating that it was wrong to oppose the Whig and Democratic parties, even though they were "proslavery parties" that had "positively refused" to advocate for Black rights. According to Wright and Ray, if the delegates assumed "an attitude hostile to two political parties," they would weaken their ability to pressure politicians for voting rights. Other New York City activists such as James McCune Smith, Jeremiah Powers, Ulysses Vidal, and William Powell were also apparently concerned about diluting Black political power, because they supported Theodore Wright and Charles Ray in their plea to choose their political affiliations strategically.[56]

However, Henry Highland Garnet was not so easily persuaded. In particular, Garnet stressed that the description of the Whigs and Democrats as proslavery was accurate and, therefore, should not be ignored. The debate over Wright and

Ray's proposed resolution lasted for an entire day, until the issue was finally put to a vote the following morning. Rejection of the resolution was overwhelming, and the convention ultimately upheld Garnet's perspective by "express[ing] sympathy with Liberty Party principles." This decision, however, had significant ramifications; members of the New York City delegation, including Ulysses Vidal, William Powell, and James McCune Smith, resigned from the convention in disgust, on the grounds that the "refusal to accept and record the Protest . . . was a denial of the rights of the people of New York." Significantly, this dissension may have caused an extended split among Black activists in New York State because there were no representatives from New York City at the next two state conventions held in 1845 and 1851.[57] In a larger sense, the conflict was even more damaging than activists may have realized because, due in part to this internal division, efforts to obtain the suffrage constantly failed.

Indeed the Black leadership's attempts at petitioning were routinely rebuffed by the state legislature, a painful reminder that most White New Yorkers stubbornly refused to consider the notion of unrestricted Black suffrage. The denial of suffrage was based largely on racism, as evidenced by the testimony of New York State representatives in 1846. During debates concerning Black suffrage in the legislature, John Hunt of New York City argued that he opposed such resolutions because did not want "negro masters to reign over us." Further, he maintained that "Negroes are aliens" and, because Black people were not truly American, they were not entitled to rights of American citizenship.[58] His comments revealed that politicians' decisions were based on a deep and abiding fear of free Black people and their potentially transformative effect on American politics. As William Seward, governor of New York and supporter of Black suffrage, noted in 1845, if Black people were extended the right to vote "their influence would be immediately felt . . . and their votes will be cast in favor of those who uphold the cause of human liberty."[59] Although Seward intended his words to convince legislators to extend universal male suffrage, they likely had the opposite effect. In fact, state leaders resisted Black voting rights because they saw the truth in Seward's words; Black people would likely vote as a united block and, therefore, would have the power to elect controversial leaders and enact radical legislation. Ultimately, it was this very concept that made many politicians and White citizens incredibly uneasy and, thus, faced with the possibility of tangible Black political power, White politicians were determined to keep the Black community politically impotent.

The final blow to Black New Yorkers' efforts to influence the political process came in 1848 when the Liberty Party, the organization they had pinned their hopes upon, splintered into warring factions. Perhaps even more disheartening was the fact that the source of the conflict centered on the question of how serious the party was about their commitment to abolition. Indeed one group (which ultimately formed the Free Soil Party) thought that advocating simply for nonextension of slavery was sufficient and wanted to expand its platform beyond abolition. On the other side were the radicals, who advocated immediate abolition and were willing to sideline every other issue in order to root out slavery wherever it existed. Following the split, they first renamed themselves the National Liberty League, then the National Liberty Party, and finally the Radical Abolition Party in 1855.[60] Although the National Liberty Party held a convention in 1848 and reaffirmed their commitment to immediate abolition and equal rights for all, the internal conflicts and impotency of third party politics were taking their toll. Even the conversion of James McCune Smith to the Liberty Party cause and the appearance of Henry Highland Garnet as one of the assembly's vice presidents, was not enough to convince large numbers of Black voters to take a risk on the struggling organization.[61] As the 1840s drew to a close, the Liberty Party floundered and Black activists became increasingly despondent as their efforts to gain unrestricted access to the vote were repeatedly denied.

Perhaps partly due to these setbacks, Black leaders returned to their original mission to unify their people on the regional level. Indeed, the conclusion of the 1840s offered a glimmer of hope for Black activists because they were finally able to forge a feeling of cohesion at the national Colored Conventions. Although the Philadelphians continued their boycott, two additional Colored Conventions were held in 1847 and 1848 that revealed dramatic shifts in Black political thought. The 1843 gathering had been plagued by conflict over Garrisonian principles; however, the later conventions had no such problems. Reflecting national trends, Black leaders such as Frederick Douglass distanced themselves from Garrisonian ideology and issued urgent calls for action and racial solidarity. In particular, by the 1848 convention, Douglass led a committee that issued a powerful statement revealing the failure of moral suasion. They declared, "We are yet the most oppressed people in the world. . . . Our backs are scarred by the lash, and our souls are yet dark under the pall of slavery. Our sisters are sold for purposes of pollution, and our brethren are sold in the market, with beasts of burden." As a result, Douglass shed his Garrisonian affiliation and joined the demands for resistance to oppression.[62]

Furthermore, delegates concluded that they must form a united front because, regardless of their status, Black people shared a common destiny: "We are one people—one in general complexion, one in a common degradation, one in popular estimation. As one rises, all must rise, and as one falls all must fall." Ultimately, they recognized that Black people were interconnected and, in order to progress, delegates believed they must articulate a brand of Black Nationalism and move forward as a unified people. This transformative ideology was echoed in a startling decision unveiled in a resolution regarding the role of women, which proclaimed that, based on their belief "in the equality of the sexes," they would "invite females hereafter to take part in our deliberations."[63] Even though their decision signaled a crucial victory for Black women, its most important legacy was that it demonstrated Black activists were moving toward reconciliation. As former supporters of Garrisonian moral suasion embraced direct action, Black New Yorkers, who had previously supported the conservative policies toward women, acquiesced to the demand for women's participation; activists finally found a common ground. Perhaps Black leaders had finally realized that even if they had enemies all around, they must begin by defeating the enemy within.

* * *

The years between 1837 and 1849 proved to be a time of massive political activity among Black New Yorkers. As a new generation of leaders emerged ready to fight for independence and justice, the Black community witnessed a flowering of activism. Despite their commitment, however, Black leaders faced conflict and tension over strategy. Although Black activists had hoped to avoid the battles between their White allies and form a united agenda on abolition and suffrage, this vision proved to be more difficult to attain than they had imagined. The deep rift among White abolitionists had lasting repercussions for Black activists, as they scrambled to keep the movement intact. In particular, ideological divisions wreaked havoc on the Colored Convention movement as continuing conflict between the Garrisonians and the Tappanites prevented a unified coalition of Black leaders.

Suffragists in New York State were also victims of infighting; although the attainment of voting rights was an issue that unified Black leaders regardless of their position on the Garrison/Tappan split, they were still deeply divided over strategy. Activists such as Charles Ray, Thomas Van Rensalaer, David Ruggles, James McCune Smith, and Charles Reason agreed on the need for Black male suffrage; however, they continued to disagree about the most appropriate method for obtaining the elusive right to vote. To make matters worse, the New York State Legislature remained steadfastly opposed to the notion of unrestricted suffrage. Fearful of free Blacks and the potential of Black social and political power, politicians worked ferociously to protect the status quo. Ultimately, due to White opposition and conflict over strategy, Black New Yorkers' quest for unrestricted suffrage was a sad tale of unrequited strivings that would not achieve success until the post–Civil War era.

Yet despite devastating setbacks, Black activists would not be deterred. In the face of conflict and controversy, they never gave up on citizenship and their hope for a brighter future. Most significantly, by the conclusion of the decade, Black activists finally achieved their goal of unity. Only one question remained: Would unity be enough to gain freedom and equality? This was, indeed, a compelling question. As we shall see, the 1850s unleashed a horrifying reign of oppression against Black New Yorkers: one that put their unity and political determination to the test.

CHAPTER 6

"A Heavy and Cruel Hand
Has Been Laid upon Us,"
1850–1861

> By birth we are American citizens; by the principles of the Declaration
> of Independence, we are American citizens; within the meaning of the
> United States Constitution, we are American citizens; by the facts of
> history, we are American citizens; by the hardships and trials endured;
> by the courage and fidelity displayed by our ancestors in defending
> the liberties and in achieving the independence of our land, we are
> American citizens.
> —The Colored Convention, 1853

> A heavy and cruel hand has been laid upon us. As a people, we feel
> ourselves to be not only deeply injured, but grossly misunderstood. . . .
> The great mass of American citizens estimate us as being a characterless
> and purposeless people; and hence we hold up our heads, if at all,
> against the withering influence of a nation's scorn and contempt.
> —James McCune Smith, James P. Miller, and John J. Zuille, 1860

In March 1850, Black New Yorkers held a large community gathering in Shiloh
Presbyterian Church in response to growing fears about a particular piece of
legislation being debated in the halls of Congress: the Fugitive Slave Act. Deeply
concerned about the national government's attempts to compromise with the
Southern states over the system of slavery, Black New Yorkers were becoming convinced that "the enemies of the colored race . . . were threatening." To make matters worse, the Committee of Vigilance, the primary local organization dedicated
to the protection of fugitives, had disintegrated after its leader, David Ruggles,
was accused of financial impropriety and fell into poor health.[1] As a result, the
Black leadership had to resort to mass meetings to raise consciousness about
the plight of the fugitive. Black activists rallied their forces and passed a series of
ten resolutions, designed to declare their feelings about the national crisis and
the compelling need to take immediate action against slavery. In particular, they
declared that the admission of any slave state into the United States was a "surrender of the principle which the Constitution was established to protect" and
asserted that Black New Yorkers would not support any scheme for compromise

that did not "aim to effect" full abolition. To punctuate their point, Black activists called upon the members of Congress to "take from the nation the festering canker of slavery."[2]

However, despite the power and passion of the Black New Yorkers' resolutions, Congress did pass the Compromise of 1850, and the Fugitive Slave Act went into effect later that year. Unfortunately, the Fugitive Slave Act of 1850 was just the first in a series of devastating setbacks that plagued Black New Yorkers during the decade before the Civil War. In addition to the persistence of slavery, Black activists were continually disappointed by unrelenting racial discrimination, the denial of voting rights, and the passage of the *Dred Scott* decision, which confirmed their unequal status in the United States. Nearly thirty years after legal emancipation, Black New Yorkers still struggled at the bottom of American society, fighting to rise above their second-class status.

In response, leaders in the 1850s became increasingly organized and fought valiantly against racial discrimination and the persecution of fugitives. Their agitation did lead to some limited advancements; in particular, after extended legal battles, Black New Yorkers managed to desegregate public streetcars. Even more, they renewed efforts to build strong coalitions with other Black activists on the state and regional level to wage a war against the "twin prejudices" of slavery and racism. This time, Black leaders emerged triumphant in the sense that they overcame ideological disputes that had stymied their movement in previous decades and managed to build a unified Black coalition. However, these successes were not sufficient to counteract the overwhelming inequities the Black community faced. Racism became especially virulent during this era and, after the *Dred Scott* decision, it became apparent that total abolition and full citizenship would remain elusive dreams. Thus, as the decade ended, frustration drove some Black activists to reflect on their African heritage and reconsider emigration. In the end, however, although emigration debates nearly destroyed alliances within the Black leadership, most activists ultimately chose to remain in the United States and fight for the freedom and equality they so justly deserved.

* * *

Passed in September 1850, the Fugitive Slave Law turned the North into hunting grounds for slave catchers; according to the law's stipulations, any Black person could be seized on the streets and claimed as a fugitive. Indeed, Black rights were severely constrained by the legislation; alleged fugitives had no right to a jury trial, could not offer evidence on their own behalf, or vouch for the status of a captive. Only Whites were allowed to provide proof of a Black person's freedom, and, if none could be found, the authorities had the right to make the final decision. In addition, all Northerners were required to assist in the capture of an alleged fugitive or risk fines and potential imprisonment. Although there were some White activists who refused to comply with the decree, most New Yorkers were unwilling to compromise their own security to protect a Black person. Worse, there was a financial incentive for local officials to claim someone as a fugitive; they were paid $10 for identifying someone as an escaped slave and received only $5 for declaring someone free. Subject to the whims of city officials, Black New Yorkers lived in a state of "quasi-freedom" in which they could be unjustly identified as a fugitive and sent to Southern slavery.

The ramifications of the Fugitive Slave Act were glaring and immediately felt. Denied the protection of law and judicial due process, Black people, both fugitive and emancipated, knew they were in constant danger of enslavement. Within a few days after the passage of the Fugitive Slave Act, thousands of Black Northerners fled the United States and escaped into Canada seeking safety and refuge. As the situation became more desperate, Black New Yorkers joined the exodus; they uprooted their families and abandoned their communities out of fear for their survival. In the five years following the passage of the Fugitive Slave Law, the Black population in New York City declined by over two thousand and hit its lowest point since emancipation to less than twelve thousand; evidence, perhaps, that many Black folks must have decided to desert the state and search for a more hospitable destination.[3]

For those who remained, however, the Black response to the Fugitive Slave Act was swift and strong. Black New Yorkers, in particular, demonstrated their commitment to defending fugitives immediately after the Fugitive Slave Act was imposed, when the first of their brethren fell victim to the new law. On September 20, James Hamlet was seized from his job in New York City and identified as a slave belonging to a woman in Baltimore.[4] Although he was technically entitled to freedom, because his mother was a free woman, Hamlet was unable to testify on his own behalf and deemed to be a fugitive based on slave catchers' accusations. Hamlet was remanded into custody and taken back to Baltimore, where he was imprisoned in preparation for his impending sale into the Deep South.[5] The Black leaders in New York gave the Hamlet case considerable attention because they now realized that city authorities intended to comply with the law, and even legally free people such as James Hamlet could be enslaved with no hope of justice.

Immediately following James Hamlet's capture, the Committee of Thirteen, a new organization composed of the most prominent Black leaders in the community, called a meeting to urge Black people to "resist oppression" and "defend their liberties."[6] More than fifteen hundred Black New Yorkers responded to the cause and flocked to Zion Church, where activist William Powell opened with a powerful rejection of the new legislation and challenged his audience to defy the federal mandate. "This covenant with death and agreement with hell," Powell exclaimed, "must be trampled under foot, resisted, disobeyed, and violated at all hazards." Powell's revolutionary message so inspired the audience that they repeatedly broke into spontaneous cheers and chants. Following his impassioned oration, the group passed a series of resolutions in which it resolved to use any means necessary to "repel the agressor [*sic*] and defend our lives and liberties." Perhaps influenced by a statement Black New Yorkers issued the previous month, which had promised to meet slaveholders with "deep-stored and long-accumulated revenge in their hearts, and with death-dealing weapons in their hands," Committee of Thirteen member, Jeremiah Powers, not only supported the motions but concluded that the only reasonable response to the Fugitive Slave Act was the "bowie knife and the revolver."[7]

In the end, however, they took a more practical approach by raising $800, including a $100 contribution from Black activist, Isaac Hollenbeck, to purchase Hamlet out of bondage. Fortunately for Hamlet, there was enough money to free him, and he returned to New York City three days later. On October 5, 1850, there was a massive celebration in City Hall Park to honor the emancipation of James Hamlet; nearly five thousand New Yorkers thronged in the park to welcome home their stolen son. Several Black leaders, including William Powell and Charles Ray, addressed the audience, "depicting the unjust and cruel privations to which the people of color are subjected in this boasted land of liberty." As the men spoke, Hamlet stood before the crowd as "tears ran down his cheeks." Following the festivities, Hamlet was carried through the streets on the shoulders of his people and delivered back to his home.[8]

Although James Hamlet's story had a happy ending, not all captured fugitives had the same good fortune. Just two months later, Henry Long was taken from the streets of New York, submitted in the city court as an escaped slave, and returned to bondage. Again the Black community rallied to his defense at a meeting sponsored by the Committee of Thirteen; however the community's financial plight prevented it from donating enough funds to rescue him. Unlike Hamlet, Long was reenslaved and sent to the South, where he was auctioned in Georgia for the price of $750.[9] Similarly, several years later, Black New Yorkers tried to free Stephen Pembroke and his two sons, who had escaped from slavery in Maryland and were captured in New York City. Black activists became consumed with this case because Stephen Pembroke's brother, Reverend J. W. C. Pennington, was a well-respected leader in the community.[10] Following the announcement that the Pembrokes had been seized, a meeting was held in Shiloh Church, and, within a month, the community raised over $1,000 to purchase Stephen Pembroke's freedom. However, this success was overshadowed by the fact that his sons, Robert and Jacob, had already been sold into the Deep South and reenslaved.[11]

The stories of Henry Long and the Pembroke brothers revealed a disturbing reality; although the Black community had initially been able to fight the Fugitive Slave Act by purchasing James Hamlet, its economic plight prevented it from using that method as a permanent strategy. Despite the leadership's commitment and fiery rhetoric, these cases revealed the fragile state of "freedom" for Black New Yorkers. Even more, it demonstrated that the leadership needed to find an effective solution to protect the community. In response, Black New Yorkers began to agitate covertly, working as conductors on the Underground Railroad to secure the safety of fugitives. By 1851, Albro and Mary Lyons had assumed control over the Colored Sailors Home, which they turned into a refuge for fugitives seeking temporary assistance. Originally founded by activist and African Society member William Powell in 1839, the Colored Sailors Home had initially committed itself to assisting destitute Black seamen.[12] Yet under the Lyons family's leadership, the home provided protection to over one thousand fugitives between 1851 and 1862. According to the Lyons's daughter, Maritcha, the home served as a brief resting area where fugitives could stop on their way to their final destination: "Father's connection with the underground railroad brought many strange faces to our house, for it was semi-public and persons could go in and out without attracting special attention. Under mother's vigilant eye, refugees were kept long enough to be fed and to have disguises changed and to be met by those prepared to speed them on in the journey toward the North Star." The Lyons family operated in defiance of the Fugitive Slave Law and, due to their diligent labor, saved numerous fugitives from the horrors of slavery.[13]

The dedication of committed activists slightly alleviated the nightmare of the Fugitive Slave Act, but the passage of the law sent a clear and disturbing message to the Black community; it reminded Blacks that their right to American citizenship would be continually denied. Indeed the lack of equality and citizenship plagued Black New Yorkers in nearly every facet of their lives, even in their daily activities. By the 1850s, the city's segregated streetcars had become a symbolic reminder of the Black community's second-class citizenship; the privately owned streetcar companies created policies that required Black people to ride in separate cars marked for their use. These regulations were not only discriminatory and morally offensive, but also inconvenient because the "colored" cars tended to run infrequently.

Yet, as in previous decades, Black activists were not dissuaded; they determined to assert their rights and obtain all the privileges due to equal citizens. As early as 1850, Black leaders frustrated by unequal treatment began to lodge complaints against the railway companies. In September 1850, after a young Black woman was ejected from a streetcar, activist Philip A. Bell issued a statement opposing racially based restrictions.[14] However, it was not until 1854 that Black New Yorkers focused their attention on the problem of segregated streetcars. In a foreshadowing of similar events in the South nearly a century later, the movement for desegregated public transportation in New York City began with the action of a few determined women.

On July 16, 1854, Elizabeth Jennings and her friend Sarah Adams began their regular journey to the Colored Congregational Church. As Elizabeth Jennings was an admired schoolteacher, and the daughter of esteemed Black activist Thomas L. Jennings, she was well-respected in her community.[15] However, on this particular

Sunday, Jennings was "brutally outraged and insulted" by a streetcar conductor, an incident that catapulted her into fame and sparked a movement. According to Elizabeth Jennings, she attempted to board a Third Avenue streetcar on her way to church as she did every week. Yet, on July 16, she and her companion, Sarah Adams, were refused entrance; the conductor told her that she must wait for the next car that was intended to accommodate Black passengers. Jennings insisted that she did not want to be detained and refused to leave. This action resulted in a conflict with the conductor, who tried to convince Jennings to get onto another car. However, she was adamant in her objection and asserted her claim to respectability and American birthright: "I told him that I was a respectable person, born and raised in New York . . . and that I had never been insulted before while going to church, and that he was a good for nothing impudent fellow for insulting decent persons while on their way to church."[16]

Not surprisingly, Elizabeth Jennings's strong attitude and bold personality were repugnant to the streetcar conductor. He dragged Jennings from the car violently; according to Jennings, she clung to the window ledge while the conductor and the driver both pulled her down. All the while, her friend Sarah Adams was also being dragged from the car screaming for them to release Jennings. Fearful about the brute force being used against Jennings, Adams repeatedly yelled, "don't kill her!" Apparently, Adams's warnings did little to influence them, because they were not satisfied until they had removed Jennings from the car. However, she was not so easily deterred; Jennings jumped back into the car and attempted to take her seat. Frustrated, the conductor finally brought her to a police officer. The policeman claimed that she was attempting to start a riot and, as Jennings explained, "drove me away like a dog."[17]

In response to Jennings's ordeal, the Black community organized a mass meeting to plan appropriate action. Jennings herself was unable to attend because she was "quite sore and stiff from the treatment [she] received from those monsters in human form." However, she prepared a statement that was read to the entire assembly. In addition, her father issued several appeals to elevate the consciousness of his people in which he argued that the specific experience of his daughter was "only secondary, in our view, to the rights of our people." Outraged by the events, the community passed a series of resolutions denouncing the conductor's actions and declaring "equal right to the accommodation of 'transit' in the cars." Further, the community appointed a committee of five to research the case and bring it before the proper legal authorities.[18]

As promised, Black activists raised the issue in the city's court, and, in 1855, Jennings's case was heard before a judge and jury. Perhaps to the Black community's surprise, the judge concluded that Black people had the same right to ride the streetcars as any other citizen and could not be excluded based on race. There was, however, dissent among the jury. Because the judge had already ruled in Jennings's favor, the jury was only left with the responsibility of assigning damages but, according to the *New York Daily Tribune,* there were some jurors who "maintained some peculiar notions as to colored people's rights." As a result, despite the fact that Elizabeth Jennings sought $500, she was only awarded $225.[19] Regardless, the decision was a crucial victory for Black New Yorkers; a court of law had determined that they had the same rights to ride public transportation as any other citizen. For many leaders, this must have appeared to be a positive gain in the struggle for citizenship.

However, Jennings's success was only momentary. The Black community soon discovered that American society would not always concede to judicial decisions; apparently, those among the jury who held "peculiar notions" about Black equality were not alone. Shortly after Elizabeth Jennings won her case, the Reverend J. W. C. Pennington spoke publicly about the Black community's victory and, in retrospect, his decision may have been a critical error. Following his sermon in May 1855, Pennington urged his congregation to celebrate the judicial decision and exercise the right to ride the streetcars unhindered. Armed with the law on their side, Pennington maintained, Black New Yorkers must seize their newly won right and assert their right to citizenship: "the colored people [should] show a bold front in this and other kindred matters of equal importance, so that the coming age might know the value of perseverance."[20] Although Pennington's words were inspiring, he may have misjudged the extreme opposition to racial equality that persisted in New York City. Indeed, just two weeks after the fateful court decision, Reverend Pennington discovered the limits of legal desegregation.

Perhaps due to his public assertion of Black rights, J. W. C. Pennington was forcibly removed from a streetcar operated by the Sixth Avenue Rail Company on May 24, 1855. On that particular day, Pennington boarded a streetcar headed for downtown New York City. However, he was promptly informed that the Sixth Avenue Company did not allow Black people to ride in their cars, except in those specifically designated for Black passengers. Pennington refused to comply, and he soon found himself embroiled in a conflict that was strikingly similar to the episode Elizabeth Jennings had endured. The driver and conductor attacked him and "ejected" him from the car, yet Pennington clung to the back of the streetcar and rode to the next step where he found a police officer. Like Jennings, Pennington did not receive much assistance from the policeman who "advised him to drop the matter." Pennington grew angry and continued to protest his treatment. Annoyed, the policeman arrested Pennington and brought him down to the city jail. Pennington was subsequently released; however, this incident was enough to convince him that the Black community's battle was not over. The following day, Pennington obtained legal counsel and decided to sue the company. Claiming that it was a "simple question of civil law," he forced the issue back into the courtroom.[21]

As they had the previous year, Black New Yorkers held a public meeting to garner support for the desegregation movement. This time, however, they formed an organization, the Legal Rights Association, which was designed to "secure to colored people their right to ride in public conveyances." Not surprisingly, Elizabeth Jennings's father, Thomas, served as the organization's president for the first several years. Perhaps inspired by Elizabeth Jennings's bravery, the women of the community also became publicly involved by forming an auxiliary to the association that raised money to fund lawsuits. Most notably, in February 1856, the female branch of the association held a fundraiser that was attended by over three hundred community members and included speeches, music, and "promenading," which consumed the crowd until dawn. Bolstered by the community's support, the Legal Rights Association held a special meeting in December 1856 to support Reverend Pennington before his case went to trial.[22]

However, an unfortunate occurrence took place just days before Pennington's court appearance that foreshadowed the treatment of Blacks that persisted in the years that followed. On December 16, 1856, Peter S. Porter, his wife, and four other Black women attempted to board the Eighth Avenue streetcar. Porter was an officer of the Legal Rights Association and it is possible that he was targeted for his political beliefs because, although Porter and his companions were allowed to ride for a few blocks, the conductor suddenly approached him and tried to force him from the car. When he resisted, Porter was beaten "most ferociously." His wife attempted to rescue him, and she was likewise assaulted. According to the *New York Daily Tribune*, she was taken by the neck and strangled. Although Mrs. Porter and her husband survived the attack, there was a fatality. Mrs. Porter was apparently pregnant at the time of the attack, and the Legal Rights Association later reported that, due to her injuries, "her child has since died." The events of December 16 cast a disturbing shadow over the Pennington case and reminded the Black community that Blacks were constantly in danger of physical reprisals if they asserted their right to citizenship.[23]

Three days later, Reverend Pennington's case was heard before the Superior Court. A series of eyewitnesses testified that Pennington was forcibly removed from the streetcar in a rather violent manner, and other Black activists shared their own stories of mistreatment on the streetcars. Renowned leader Henry Highland Garnet stated that, on many occasions, he had been "hindered in his business" when he was denied access to the streetcars. Likewise, Thomas Jennings reported that there were not enough cars to accommodate the large Black population, especially because Whites rode in the colored car whenever convenient. In the end, after three days of court proceedings, the judge and jury ruled against Pennington. In direct opposition to the Jennings case, the judge instructed the jury that the streetcar company had the right to regulate who was allowed to ride the cars. Faced with this information, the jury had no choice but to obey the judge and deny Pennington's rights. This decision was a devastating blow to Pennington and the entire Black community, because the victory they had claimed in the Jennings case was suddenly and dramatically reversed.[24]

Although they faced a frustrating setback, Black community members continued to agitate and lodge complaints against their unjust treatment. In February 1857, Dr. James McCune Smith attended an open meeting during which he expressed his resentment over the regulations monitoring their travel. As Henry Highland Garnet and Thomas Jennings had previously suggested, Smith argued that there were not enough streetcars allocated to the Black population. In addition, perhaps in a veiled attempt to remind White New Yorkers that he was an educated Black doctor, Smith complained that he was often prevented from administering to sick children because he was routinely denied entrance to the Sixth Avenue company cars. Yet the streetcar companies were obviously not swayed because, one year later, another conductor assaulted a Black man, John Hunter. Again the city authorities supported the conductor's actions; when Hunter attempted to defend himself, he was arrested and brought to the city jail.[25]

In the face of such insult and injury, Black New Yorkers might have lost hope but, fortunately, the New York State Supreme Court soon gave the Black community cause to celebrate. Peter Porter had brought a lawsuit following the attack on himself and his wife in 1856, and his case was appealed to the highest court in the state. In February 1858, Judge Rockwell finally proclaimed that "colored people have the same rights in public conveyances" as any other citizen. Elated by the ruling, the Legal Rights Association held a public celebration, which was attended by over 250 people, honoring the "wholesome decision." John Hunter, the victim of the attack a month earlier, was elected as chairman, and several prominent leaders delivered addresses. In addition, the female branch of the association organized "grand entertainment" complete with food, music, and "promenading." The victorious Peter Porter concluded the meeting by enthusiastically declaring that finally "the five cents of a colored man were as good as those of a white man."[26]

After a painful and protracted struggle, Black leaders successfully desegregated the streetcars; however, their victory turned out to be more symbolic than transformative. Perhaps no one knew this better than J. W. C. Pennington, who had suffered the consequences of a premature celebration. Indeed, in the midst of the community's jubilation, Pennington declared that although no one had the right to remove Black people from public transportation, the community should be prepared for the "bitterest opposition" from the conductors. Ultimately, his comments proved to be prophetic.[27] About seven months after the State Supreme Court decision, another Black man was attacked on the Sixth Avenue streetcar. Apparently, a White man raised an objection to riding with "niggers," and, thus, the conductor attempted to remove the Black man. The situation nearly turned into a riot when a large group of passengers began to chant, "let the man ride," and an opposing group tried to drown them out with their own objections. The conductor successfully removed the Black man from the car but by then, the situation had grown severe and nearly 150 people surrounded the car. The scene almost erupted into physical violence; however, officials managed to circumvent conflict by letting the man quietly reboard and ride home.[28] Although physical violence was avoided in this case, it served as a reminder to Black New Yorkers that judicial decisions were not powerful enough to curtail racism or guarantee citizenship.[29]

As Black New Yorkers agitated for citizenship and racial equality, their strivings were paralleled in Black communities throughout the North. Faced with desperate times, there was increasing urgency for Black leaders across the region to meet, consider their options, and create a plan of action. Although Black leaders had struggled to create a national movement in previous decades, they renewed their efforts in the 1850s with a strong determination to create unity among their people.[30] The marked decline in conditions for free Blacks must have prompted Philadelphians to put aside old disagreements and unite with their brethren across the country, because they joined other Black activists in concluding that "the time has now fully come when the free colored people from all parts of the United States, should meet together to confer and deliberate upon their present condition, and upon principles and measures important to their welfare, progress and general improvement." Thus, in July 1853, the Colored Convention movement officially recommenced in Rochester, New York. Perhaps most significantly, reflecting its dedication to racial solidarity, the city of Philadelphia sent delegates to the national convention for the first time in nearly twenty years and ushered in a new era of Black political activism: a powerful moment, when leaders proved that their commitment to the community was stronger than their petty, ego-driven conflicts.[31]

Indeed, the Colored Conventions in the 1850s demonstrated a strong sense of solidarity among the delegates, as well as a burning feeling of urgency about the plight of their people.[32] Recognizing the severity of their situation, attendees at the 1853 convention declared: "Under the whole heavens, there is not to be found a people which can show better cause for assembling in such a Convention than we." Black leaders were particularly concerned with the Fugitive Slave Act, which they described as the "most cruel, unconstitutional and scandalous outrage of modern times." In addition, they mentioned the discriminatory legislation that was designed to drive Black people from the United States and the lack of access to the vote. These problems, the delegates concluded, signaled the need for "union, cooperation and action" within the Black community.[33] At the next convention, in 1855, the Black leadership expressed similar concerns; in particular, the leaders maintained that they must act quickly to "counteract the debasing influence that holds us in our present anomalous condition in this our native country." Calling for immediate united action, the delegates in 1855 sought solutions such as education and obtaining their political and social rights. As the leaders explained, they had laid the groundwork but "the work commenced at the National Convention at Rochester in '53, demands now a vigorous prosecution."[34] They remained convinced that, through the creation of a national agenda and united action, the Black community was destined to achieve equality and justice.

Freed from the troublesome infighting that had plagued conventions in previous decades, the Colored Conventions in the 1850s focused the interrelated issues of slavery and discrimination. Lamenting the "gross and flagrant" violations against their people, Black leaders in 1853 were especially disturbed about their "fellow countrymen now in chains" as well as "the wily and vigorous efforts of the American Colonization Society to employ the arm of government to expel us from our native land." In addition, they bemoaned the "heavy and cruel hand" that held Black people at the bottom of American society and pledged to use all reasonable means to obtain freedom for their enslaved brethren and justice for the entire race. These concerns were repeated in 1855, as delegates wrote eloquently about the plight of the "down trodden slave" and their frustration about the denial of rights to free Blacks. They powerfully concluded that the oppression of one man equaled the oppression of all, and argued, "there can not be one white free-man while there remains one black slave in the Union."[35]

Yet even though Black leaders in the 1850s were united in spirit and agreed upon their common problems, they still grappled with the question of strategy and struggled to determine which tactics would be the most effective weapons in their battle against slavery and racism. Ultimately, the fundamental question remained: How to convince American society to abolish slavery and accept Black people as full citizens? Although most Black leaders during this era had abandoned Garrisonian moral suasion, some activists still hoped that they could liberate their people by creating a transformation in American consciousness.[36] In the end, lacking any other potential approaches, convention delegates found it impossible to avoid traditional republican pleas for justice. Although this approach had limited success in the past, leaders continued to use Revolutionary War rhetoric, particularly appeals to natural rights, in an effort to influence public opinion and assert their right to citizenship.

In 1853, delegates insisted that the Constitution and the principles of American society guaranteed all humans, including Black people, equal access to citizenship rights: "By birth, we are American citizens; by the principles of the Declaration of Independence, we are American citizens; within the meaning of the United States Constitution, we are American citizens." They also used typical displays of patriotism and stressed the commitment Black people had demonstrated on behalf of American society declaring, "by the courage and fidelity displayed by our ancestors in defending the liberties and in achieving the independence of our land, we are American citizens."[37] In 1855, convention attendees echoed this same strategy. Claiming to speak on behalf of 3 million enslaved people and 250,000 free Blacks, they strongly asserted their humanity and insisted that Americans must destroy slavery and prejudice. As they explained, because the Constitution guaranteed liberty to all people, and "no law has ever been enacted which reduced our brethren to slavery, we demand their immediate emancipation and restoration to the rights secured to every person under the Constitution."[38]

Although Black leaders were as articulate and convincing in the 1850s as they had been in all the previous decades, their words continued to fall on deaf ears. The strategy of prompting a moral conversion among the American people had the same limited effect that it always produced. What leaders failed to recognize was that attitudes only change when an individual has the willingness to undergo a transformation. The reality was that most White Americans were not prepared to recognize Black people's humanity or their rights to freedom and citizenship. Ultimately, the social, political, and economic foundation of American society depended too strongly upon slavery and oppression to allow a moral awakening.

While the Colored Convention floundered, searching for solutions, delegates began a movement to create a national Black organization. In 1853, they formed a committee, led by New Yorker James McCune Smith, to establish the National Council of the Colored People (NCCP) for the purpose of "improving the character, developing the intelligence, maintaining the rights, and organizing a Union of the Colored people of the Free States." The idea was to draw upon the methods that activists had employed on the local level in prior decades, the creation of mutual relief associations, and unite their efforts to form a power base of Black leaders across the North. More specifically, activists hoped to establish a permanent society that could draw upon the strength of conventions and sustain a movement beyond these gatherings. They proposed to meet every six months and form committees that would deliberate on various issues such as education, business, agriculture, and developing Black newspapers.[39]

Despite their high hopes and good intentions, NCCP was plagued by disorganization from its inception. Although they had resolved to meet in January 1854, members were forced to postpone the gathering on several occasions and finally convened in New York City in May.[40] Although there is no record of the proceedings at this meeting, leaders apparently arrived at the 1855 convention with little to show for their efforts. Even though delegates continued to have hope that NCCP, "when duly organized," would have promise for the future, the organization never fully developed. Unable to reproduce their local effectiveness on the national level, activists abandoned NCCP in 1855 only two years after it had commenced.[41]

The failure of NCCP reflected the Black community's larger problems in the 1850s. Faced with a tremendous backlash from American society, leaders were often too consumed with local struggles, such as the protection of fugitives in their communities or desegregation efforts, to sufficiently develop a national movement. In addition, it was obvious that convention delegates could not identify new or effective strategies to advance their cause, because American society remained stubbornly resistant to Black social or political strivings. These challenges may explain why there were no other Colored Conventions held in the 1850s. In fact, there was only one more gathering, held in 1864, before the Colored Conventions ceased to exist. Although the disappearance of the conventions reflected the severe circumstances within the Black community, it is important to note that the spirit of unity born out of the conventions in the 1850s did not die. In 1859, the *Anglo African* offered a special tribute to the Colored Conventions; it argued that if the conventions had continued, "the result would doubtless have been greater general progress among our people themselves, a more united front to meet past and coming exigencies, and a profounder hold upon the public attention, and a deeper respect on the part of our enemies than we now can boast of."[42]

In the end, however, despite the Colored Convention's appeals for equality and civil rights, the movement ceased without adequately addressing one of the most glaring problems facing many Black Northerners struggling for inclusion, namely, disfranchisement.[43] For Black New Yorkers, the denial of suffrage rights was the most blatant and painful reminder of their second-class citizenship. As in previous years, the right to vote still represented, for many Black leaders, the ultimate barrier to equality and full citizenship. Therefore, following the national Colored Conventions, Black leaders in New York State revitalized their efforts to obtain full and equal access to the vote. However, they soon discovered that the same problems that had plagued the Colored Conventions would be revisited on the suffrage movement.

Over the next several years, as they had in the 1840s, Black New Yorkers convened a series of state conventions. The first, held in September 1855 in Troy, New York, sought to implement a different strategy. Just as the Colored Conventions had attempted to establish a national association, NCCP, suffragists in New York created a statewide organization, the New York State Suffrage Association, which promised to give the legislature and "our fellow citizens generally no peace" until they had unrestricted suffrage rights.[44] Perhaps having learned from the failure of NCCP, however, New Yorkers bolstered their regional association with local auxiliaries. Upon their return from the 1855 gathering, Black leaders in New York City held a citywide meeting and formed the New York County League for Political Advancement. Late in 1855, its members pledged to "arouse the people of the State to a sense of their duty in the present political struggle."[45]

In 1856, Black activists delivered on their pledge and sought to begin their efforts by "arousing" their own people because it was a crucial election year. At the state convention held in Williamsburgh, Chairman Henry Highland Garnet addressed the delegates and expressed his frustration about apathy among his people. He argued that community members had been "seized with a spirit of do-nothing" because they did not see the purpose of voting. Convinced of their political impotence, many Black men had resigned themselves to the status of noncitizen. Worse, according to Garnet, were the Black men who owned enough property to qualify for the vote and did not exercise their rights. Acknowledging that there were "not many inducements" for Blacks to vote, Garnet still urged his people to participate in order to "promote the cause of Liberty." Inspired by his address, delegates remained hopeful that their efforts to gain the suffrage would ultimately be rewarded; they renewed their commitment to activism by passing a series of resolutions, calling for local groups to submit petitions to the state legislature.[46] Frustratingly, however, although these activists were clearly dedicated to the cause and claimed to speak on behalf of six thousand colored voters in the state, they had no other recourse than to resort to petitioning. As the 1856 elections concluded, their strategy received no positive response from the state leaders, and Black New Yorkers remained a largely disfranchised population.

Although they had little impact on politicians or the political process during the elections of 1856, activists resolved to continue their efforts. In 1857, another state convention met in New York City under the able leadership of James McCune Smith, Patrick Reason, Philip Bell, Henry Highland Garnet, Charles Ray, and Thomas Downing. However, by this time, even the "friends" of the Black community admitted that their strategies were becoming rather ineffective. The editor of the *New York Daily Tribune* wrote that although he supported suffrage rights for Black men, he thought that conventions and petitions were insufficient to sway public opinion. Recognizing that "a very large majority of our fellow citizens are averse to seeing the Right of Suffrage extended to Negroes," the editor argued that Black activists should concede a loss on this issue. In particular, he argued that Black conventions were becoming a colossal waste of time and energy and questioned the intelligence of the delegates because "none but the most stupid of their number can believe . . . they can hasten or promote their enfranchisement by holding Conventions." He concluded that Black farmers who dedicated themselves to improving their land were doing more for the cause of Black equality than "a hundred who are shouting and blowing at Conventions;" a realization so obvious that the editor believed, "only supereminent knavery or transcendent stupidity can affect not to see it."[47]

Certainly, the editor's language was harsh and condescending; however, the analysis was perhaps more accurate than Black leaders were willing to admit. Despite the community building and empowering aspects of conventions and petitioning, these methods were not particularly effective in bringing about real change. American society was obviously not ready to accept Black people as equal citizens, and no amount of moral persuasion was going to alter that perception. This reality was reinforced in 1857 with a devastating legal decision that clearly defined Black people, emancipated and enslaved, as noncitizens. In the well-known *Dred Scott v. Sandford* case, the Supreme Court ruled that Black people had no rights that a White person was "bound to respect." Moreover, the decision clearly argued that all Black people, as descendants of slaves, were not included in the founding fathers' definition of "citizen" in the Constitution. According to Supreme Court Justice Roger B. Taney, in the majority opinion, Black people had always been considered to be "a subordinate and inferior class of beings, who had been subjugated by the dominant race, and, whether emancipated or not, yet remained subject to their authority, and had no rights or privileges but such as those who held the power and the Government might choose to grant them."[48] For Black New Yorkers, the most damaging part of the decision was the realization that, even as emancipated people, their race precluded them from the rights of citizenship.

Although the *Dred Scott* decision severely damaged the movement for suffrage and citizenship, Black New Yorkers refused to surrender. In 1858, Black activists declared that the Supreme Court's decision was a "foul and infamous lie, which neither black men or white men are bound to respect."[49] This message emanated from yet another state suffrage convention, where Black leaders continued to create petitions appealing for citizenship; in fact, they held two more meetings in 1859 and 1860.[50] However, as the editor of the *New York Daily Tribune* predicted, these efforts had little effect on improving the status of Black people in New York. Indeed, the state legislature routinely ignored or rejected the Black leadership's eloquent pleas for justice. Thus, in a final attempt to influence the political process, Black activists began to coordinate the voters who already existed in their community. Henry Highland Garnet realized that there were nearly six thousand Black men eligible to vote in New York State, with nearly half of those centralized in the New York City area. He maintained that if those men could be organized, the Black community could exercise some degree of political power.[51] However, as in the previous decade, there was ongoing discussion about political strategy. In particular, activists wondered, which political party should eligible voters endorse?

By 1855, the Liberty Party had resuscitated its attempt at formal organizing. Renamed the Radical Abolition Party, the organization held its inaugural convention in Syracuse, New York, in June 1855, and hoped to gain the endorsement of Black voters. Perhaps the earliest example of the party's desire for Black support came when James McCune Smith was selected as chair of the convention. It was the first time in American history that a Black man chaired a national political convention.[52] Likewise, the party repeatedly considered Frederick Douglass for various offices; first, in 1854, it contemplated running him for Congress; then, in 1855, he was nominated for secretary of state for New York; and finally, in 1856, Douglass was among the potential candidates for vice president of the United States. Douglass was not the only Black member nominated for office, however, as James McCune Smith was the choice for secretary of state in 1857. In addition, the Radical Abolition Party pressed controversial issues that would have appealed to the Black community. The party endorsed the use of violent action in Kansas to prevent the extension of slavery (even giving John Brown money and weapons to support efforts there) and criticized the Free Soil Party for supporting the Fugitive Slave Act of 1850.[53]

Yet despite its best efforts, the Radical Abolition Party did not make major inroads with either the Black community or the American political system. In fact, most Black New Yorkers thought the party's chance for success was "remote to the point of fantasy." By late 1856, Douglass abandoned the organization, as did Henry Highland Garnet. Ultimately, although men such as James McCune Smith, Frederick Douglass, and Henry Highland Garnet believed in the Radical Abolition Party's philosophy and goals, they resolved not to encourage their brethren to throw away their precious votes on candidates who were doomed to fail; it was a luxury they could not afford. At the suffrage convention of 1858, Black New Yorkers determined that, although they did not support all aspects of the Republican Party, political expediency required them to focus on the "defeat and ruin" of the Democratic Party. Therefore, they must endorse the party most likely to obtain that goal. According to the final resolution, delegates admitted, "we are Radical Abolitionists, and shall ever remain so" but feared that supporting Radical Abolition Party candidates would "give aid and comfort to the enemy, by electing the Democratic candidates." As a result, they urged their brethren to "concentrate their strength upon the Republican ticket."[54] The 1858 convention reflected the complicated political quandary Black New Yorkers faced; in the devastating wake of the *Dred Scott* decision, they clearly wondered if they were selling their principles in hopes of defeating the dreaded Democratic Party. In the end, even though a Republican was ultimately elected governor of New York State, the cost was the loss of the radical abolitionist agenda.

By the election of 1860, the Radical Abolition Party was dead; Black New Yorkers were no closer to eliminating the restrictions on voting rights; and activists realized that they needed to take their fight for the suffrage to the national level. Frustrated by the unresponsive New York State Legislature, Black New Yorkers believed that, by supporting other Black activists throughout the United States, they could effectively influence the national political scene. Yet, again, they found themselves using the same strategy as the Colored Conventions, appeals to patriotism and morality. In particular, they endorsed publications by Black leader William C. Nell, which sought to prove that Black people were worthy of citizenship because of their contributions to American society. Nell's efforts had actually begun in 1855 when he published *The Colored Patriots of the American Revolution*, which was a powerful appeal to citizenship based upon Black patriotism. He explored Black men's contributions during times of American military conflict: those who had displayed their loyalty to the United States even though the country did not recognize their right to freedom and citizenship. Nell also highlighted key figures including New Yorker Peter Williams Jr., using him as an example of the Black population's potential.[55]

As evidenced by the *Dred Scott* decision, most Americans were not sufficiently persuaded by William C. Nell's efforts or any of the Black leadership's appeals. However Black activists did not surrender the strategy, apparently still hopeful that reminders of Black patriotism and loyalty would alter public opinion. In 1859, Nell published a short article in *Anglo-African* highlighting a few Black contributions to American military conflicts and arguing that the *Dred Scott* decision and the denial of suffrage rights ignored "many of the prominent and significant facts in the early history of their country." As he concluded, Black people loved their "native land" and had demonstrated their loyalty through their willingness to die to protect the United States.[56] In 1860, William C. Nell made one final attempt in his treatise entitled *Property Qualifications or No Property Qualifications,* in which he attacked arbitrary racial restrictions. Focusing specifically on New York State, Nell detailed the rhetoric emanating from the Free Suffrage Convention held in New York City on May 17, 1860, when delegates based their right to elective franchise on the Declaration of Independence and their rights as descendants of Black Revolutionary War patriots. In particular, he noted their argument that Black New Yorkers had always been willing to "stand shoulder to shoulder" with their fellow Americans and fight for freedom.[57]

Black New Yorkers followed William C. Nell's appeal with a final petition to the state legislature in 1860, requesting unrestricted access to the suffrage. In retrospect, after nearly twenty years of such efforts, this attempt seemed to be an exercise in futility. However, activists were apparently still hopeful. Drawing upon the language in the 1853 Colored Convention address, Dr. James McCune Smith, James Powell, and John J. Zuille pleaded with New York politicians, asking them to search their consciences and reconsider their positions. Specifically, they maintained that Black people were "deeply injured" and "grossly misunderstood" by most Americans. In a poignant lamentation they declared, "our white countrymen do not know us. They are strangers to our characters, ignorant of our capacity, oblivious to our history and progress, and are misinformed as to the principles and ideas that control and guide us, as a people." These activists clung desperately to the belief that if White Americans understood the Black community's contributions and potential, they would accept Black people as equal citizens and members of American society.[58]

Following this passionate appeal, activists did have a brief glimmer of hope that their strategy had finally been successful and the tide of public opinion was turning in their favor; however, their hope soon turned to despair. In 1860, politicians were finally convinced to consider their petitions and place a referendum supporting unrestricted suffrage before the citizens of the state. Perhaps at least some state Republicans were influenced by the fact that the Black leadership had rallied behind the Republican Party in the preceding years. Yet most New Yorkers obviously remained fearful of Black political power, because they adamantly refused to lift the restrictions. Indeed, during the general election of 1860, New York voters rejected universal male suffrage by a strong majority.[59] To make matters worse, nearly a decade would pass between the 1860 general election and the day when Black New Yorkers finally achieved the unrestricted right to vote.

Although White New Yorkers again considered legislation to lift racial restrictions in 1869, they still refused to alter their position. Ultimately, it was not until the passage of the Fifteenth Amendment in 1870 that the issue was finally settled and Black New Yorkers could call themselves citizens.

In the final analysis, Black New Yorkers' battle for citizenship mirrored many of the setbacks that stymied the community during the 1850s. Indeed, their struggles against the Fugitive Slave Act, segregation, slavery, and disfranchisement illuminated a reality that was too painful to face. Despite the Black leadership's best efforts, White America was unyielding in its denial of justice, equality, and full citizenship. As a result, in the midst of these problems, though some activists continued to have hope, the pain of their defective freedom caused other Black leaders to revisit the perennial emigration question. Denied equal citizenship and pushed to the margins of the socioeconomic system, Black activists likely wondered if they could hope for a brighter future in the United States. Thus, for the first time since the 1830s, Black New Yorkers reflected on their choice to assume an American identity and reconsidered the notion that William Hamilton and William Miller had proposed decades earlier; perhaps Africa held the key to their destiny.

As a few Black activists returned to the issue of their African heritage, they may have been startled to notice that members of the Black working class had never fully abandoned African cultural practices. Although New York City's Black leadership had openly denounced public expressions of African culture beginning in 1827, such activities had never fully disappeared among many Black New Yorkers. Well into the middle of the nineteenth century, Black dance halls kept the Black community's connection to African music and dance alive. In 1841, Edward Z. C. Judson (who wrote with a pseudonym) described a trip to "Pete's" dance hall, which was described as "one of the upper-ten of darkydom." Upon entering, Judson and his friend found "not less than two hundred negroes of every shade, from the light, mellow-cheeked quadroon, down to the coal-black" dancing, gambling, and socializing. However, what is most compelling about his description is the African influence on their dance moves. Judson explained that at a certain point, the general dancing ceased "for a 'juba dancer' was on the floor. He was a young mulatto, and to the liveliest tune which the band could play, he was 'laying it down,' in a dance, where every step in the hornpipe, fling, reel, etc . . . was brought in; double shuffles, heel and toe tappers, in-and-out winders, pigeon wings, heel-crackers; and then to close up, the richest step of all that ever was danced, the winding-blade was footed." This young man was apparently only one member of a group of juba dancers at Pete's who routinely appeared at the "most fashionable hops."[60]

In the following year, during a journey to the United States, Charles Dickens found the same Black-owned tavern, which he called "Almack's," operated by a "buxom, fat mulatto woman, with sparkling eyes, whose head is daintly ornamented with a handkerchief of many colors." Notably, many other women in the club also wore similar scarves on their heads imitating the style of African and Caribbean women. Dickens also revealed African elements in dancing, when he witnessed a "regular breakdown" with musicians playing passionately and stamping their feet to the rhythm of the tune while the dancers took to the floor. As during Judson's visit, one dancer soon commandeered the dance hall and gave a powerful rendition with many African influences: "Single shuffle, double shuffle, cut and cross-cut. Snapping his fingers, rolling his eyes, turning in his knees, presenting the backs of his legs in front, spinning about on his toes and heels like nothing but the man's fingers on the tambourine; dancing with two left

"Ober to Tilly's Quarters." Black tavern dancing in antebellum New York City. (Courtesy of the Picture Collection; Branch Libraries; New York Public Library; Astor, Lenox, and Tilden Foundations.)

legs, two right legs, two wooden legs, two wire legs, two spring legs—all sorts of legs and no legs. . . ." Judson and Dickens's descriptions reveal that African cultural elements were still strong in New York City's Black community well into the 1840s and that dancing and public celebrations still operated as tremendously powerful coping mechanisms and tools for bringing the community together.[61]

In addition to Black dance and tavern life, Black folks in 1855 (much to the chagrin of many Black leaders) revitalized efforts to keep Black culture alive through public processions. Indeed, the masses of Black New Yorkers apparently still longed for the opportunity to parade and revisited their tradition in honor of the twenty-first anniversary of West Indian emancipation. As in 1827, when commemorating New York state emancipation, the community members were divided over how and where to express their joy about freedom in the West Indies. Because there was no Black newspaper in New York City in the 1850s, there is less information about the cause for the split. However, the New York Times reported that the conflict was motivated by the fact that the "more jovial didn't want to go with 'the priests,' but went in for a procession, and a parade, and a picnic with hot things to eat, a dance, and a good time with no white folks around." Thus while NYASS hosted a biracial gathering, where William Lloyd Garrison was the featured speaker, nearly five thousand Black New Yorkers met on Staten Island to hear one of their own, Stephen Myers of Albany, speak on the hope for total emancipation in the United States.[62]

It is significant to note that African drumming, dancing, and parading were all critical aspects of the exclusively Black celebration. As the New York Times stated, "before 10 o'clock, the streets of the city were alive with drums. Even earlier, by an hour or two, the sidewalks gave evidence of a gathering of our colored brethren." Once they arrived at the picnic grounds, there were large amounts of food, and the people were "talking loudly, laughing louder, and generally having the best possible time of it." Following the festivities in the park, a number of the Black male organizations formed a grand procession that "paraded the village." Despite the fun and merriment, however, Stephen Myers carefully reminded his audience of the great purpose for which they were gathered. "We do not come here with flags and drums and trumpets for the mere purpose of enjoying ourselves," he cautioned, "but to celebrate one of the great events recorded in the history of the world—the liberation at one stroke of the clock of 800,000 of our fellow-beings."[63] Thus, it seems that the celebrants remained cognizant of their greater purpose and chose to commemorate the occasion in distinctly African style.

Even though such bold manifestations of African culture were still controversial among the Black leadership during the 1850s, certain activists began to ponder their relationship to their African heritage.[64] Indeed, a few Black leaders renewed discussions about the possibility of Black people leaving their country of birth and seeking opportunity elsewhere. As in previous decades, these discussions unleashed a firestorm of opposition from those leaders who insisted that the vision of American citizenship should never be relinquished. New Yorker Henry Highland Garnet revitalized the emigration question in January 1848, when he wrote to Frederick Douglass about the future of Black people in the United States. Frustrated by the slow progress in the areas of abolition and equal rights, Garnet told Douglass, "my mind of late has greatly changed in regard to the American Colonization scheme. I would rather see a man free in Liberia than a slave in the United States." Although this statement was not exactly a ringing endorsement of emigration, a year later, Garnet was clearer in his position. In the pages of the *North Star* newspaper, Garnet declared his support for emigration to any country that could provide freedom, equal rights, and citizenship to Black people. He maintained that they should not wait until they were "driven from home and all its pleasures" but rather leave of their own accord.[65]

Henry Highland Garnet's change in attitude may have been partly influenced by Liberian independence. As a newly independent Black nation, Liberia now held the same hope and possibility that Haiti had possessed early in the nineteenth century. Thus, Garnet believed that free Blacks from the United States could transform Liberia into a powerful home for their people. He explained, "I believe that the new Republic will succeed—and that its success will . . . create respect for our race throughout the civilized world . . . it is my firm and sober belief that Liberia will become the Empire State of Africa." Although Garnet did not completely abandon hope that Black people could gain citizenship in the United States, he understood that many in the community had doubts. Garnet urged all those who had lost faith in the United States to go immediately to Liberia, where they could do some positive work to benefit the race. Although he claimed he would continue to agitate in the United States, Garnet believed that Black people "ought to go anywhere, where we can better our condition."[66]

Although Henry Highland Garnet was becoming increasingly enthusiastic about emigration, many in the Black leadership did not support his ideas. In fact, opposition to emigration and colonization remained strong among New York's Black activists. In April 1849, the community had called a meeting at Shiloh Presbyterian Church in response to the ACS's growing popularity. Black New Yorkers met for two days, during which many prominent leaders spoke eloquently against colonization. Charles Ray used republican rhetoric and asserted that Black people had a long and proud history in the United States that they should fight to protect. Other respected members of the community quickly followed him, declaring that they were Americans, equal citizens, and men who were determined to remain and secure their rights. In 1850, activists reaffirmed their intentions in an open letter to the enslaved. Concerned about the ramifications of a mass exodus, most activists resolved to remain in the United States and fight for immediate and total abolition. In an effort to encourage enslaved people not to lose hope, they reassuringly wrote: "You are ever in our minds, our hearts, our prayers. Perhaps, you are fearing that the free colored people of the United States will suffer themselves to be carried away from you by the American Colonization Society. Fear it not. . . . The land of our enslaved brethren is our land, and death alone shall part us."[67]

Because many Black New Yorkers strongly objected to emigration, the few who were brave enough to express such controversial notions faced the wrath of the leadership. Early in 1851, when Lewis Putnam established the Liberian Agriculture and Emigration Society (LAES), he and his supporters were vilified as traitors to the race and as secret affiliates of the ACS. During the remainder of that year, a few Black activists actively worked to discredit Putnam especially after he collected money from Black people throughout New York City who were interested in immigrating to Liberia. Samuel Cornish, in particular, accused him of embezzling the funds, although no compelling evidence was presented against him. The attack on Putnam was especially shocking because just one year before he had proved his commitment to the Black cause, by agitating on behalf of Black suffrage and urging eligible Black people to vote.[68] Yet, as a result of his apparent change of heart regarding the future of Black people in the United States, other Black activists went on the offensive. In his own defense, Putnam published an article stating that LAES had no connection to the ACS; however, the Black leadership was not convinced.[69]

Indeed, Black leaders continued to organize against LAES, and, at a public meeting held in October 1851, they refused to even entertain a motion by emigrationists. Denied the opportunity to represent the cause of emigration, Lewis Putnam and his associates were forced to silently observe the attacks on their character and intentions. Cornish argued eloquently against Liberian emigration, stating that given the plethora of problems in Liberia, Black people had better hopes for a future in the United States. At the conclusion of the meeting, the group passed a series of resolutions denouncing colonization and the LAES. In particular, the group stated that it opposed colonization in any form, especially when advocated by "renegade colored men, made under the guise of an emigration society." The group also specifically identified Putnam as an enemy of the Black race, demanded that he "disconnect" himself from the New York community, and urged Black New Yorkers not to contribute to his organization. Despite these harsh assaults on the LAES, it seems that there was at least a little local support for Liberia; the *New York Daily Tribune* reported that thirty-six Black New Yorkers sailed for Africa just weeks after that fateful meeting.[70]

Although there was minimal support for Lewis Putnam and the LAES within the Black leadership, there was a more positive response from White politicians. This fact, likely only raised the Black leadership's suspicions. Just months after the community meeting opposing Liberian emigration, the governor of New York issued a public address that strongly endorsed colonization. In January 1852, Governor Hunt argued strongly in favor of colonizing Black people in Africa, because he believed it was in their best interest. Although he maintained that the history of slavery in the United States was "revolting," Hunt insisted that the best method to improve "their unfortunate condition" was to send them back to Africa. Using old ACS rationalizations, Hunt asserted that free Blacks created an impediment to the abolition of slavery, because the failings of freedom caused slaveholders to doubt the efficacy of emancipation. "The anomalous position of the free coloured population undoubtedly forms one of the most serious obstacles to the gradual liberation of the slaves. We cannot close our eyes to the fact that although the free people of colour enjoy a certain degree of liberty, they are commonly treated . . . as an inferior race, and deprived of the social and political rights without which freedom is but an empty name."[71] Significantly, Hunt's description of the disappointment of unequal freedom articulated many issues that Black leaders probably agreed with. However, Hunt's observations led him to a conclusion that the Black leadership had vehemently fought against for decades.

Arguing that Black people could never achieve full equality in the United States, Governor Hunt resolved that the Black race had no future in this country. Claiming to be concerned for their destiny as a people, Hunt concluded that, like Native Americans, Black people "cannot permanently co-exist on the same soil with the whites, and a separation is necessary to prevent their ultimate extinction." He also argued passionately about the potential for Liberia, a republic that he believed could become a productive new home for Black people. Hunt wrote extensively about the financial and natural resources there and maintained that it would eventually become a great nation. Ultimately, he believed that it was divinely intended for Black people to return to their homeland and, through an act of Providence, "the oppressed sons of Africa" would be returned to their "native soil" after enduring a long period of oppression and degradation. Convinced that Black people wanted to return to Africa, Hunt was satisfied that he was acting in the best interest of the Black population.[72]

The Black leadership was devastated by Governor Hunt's message. Less than two years before, activists such as George Downing and Philip Bell had encouraged eligible Black voters to support Hunt because he "is all he should be on matters affecting our interests."[73] However his actions in 1852 belied that notion and, within days of Hunt's address, the Committee of Thirteen issued a call to respond to the "unexpected blow" that had been leveled against the Black Community. Originally founded as an association to protect fugitive slaves, the Committee of Thirteen expanded its agenda and passionately defended Black people's right to remain in the United States. In January 1852, the Committee of Thirteen convened the Black community in Abyssinian Baptist Church to declare their opposition to colonization and assert their rights as American citizens. Not surprisingly, assertions of American identity and appeals to citizenship dominated the Black leadership's response. The meeting commenced with a prayer by J. W. C. Pennington, who subsequently "denounced the foul system of colonization" and argued that Black people should not have to go four thousand miles in order to be considered men. George Downing followed Pennington and eloquently argued that the destiny of the Black community was inextricably linked with the future of the United States. It was the duty of every Black man, Downing maintained, to fight for the victory of a "grand principle." The group then approved thirteen resolutions denouncing colonization and asserting Blacks' rights as American citizens. In particular, the committee described Governor Hunt's ideas as being both "unconstitutional and unchristian." The group concluded with a series of recommendations to the Black population, including the accumulation of real estate and continued agitation for the suffrage.[74]

Although the Black community passed resolutions at the beginning of the meeting, several leaders still made moving addresses to the group, expressing in detail their reasons for opposing colonization. Drawing upon traditional Black political thought, J. W. C. Pennington argued that Black people had a right to citizenship based upon their demonstrations of patriotism. Echoing one of the resolutions, Pennington maintained that Black men should not beg for citizenship because they were already American citizens. Not only had they been born in the United States, he pointed out, but their "sweat and tears" had liberated the country and built it into the nation it had become. Pennington also pulled on his audience members' heartstrings, reminding them that they should not betray their ancestors who had sacrificed for their future: "Many of them fought, and bled, and died for [America's] liberty. And should they now forsake their tombs and flee to an unknown land? No!" He closed with a lengthy description of Liberia in which he countered Governor Hunt's depiction, arguing that Liberia was not entirely independent, nor did it hold the resources and possibilities that the colonizationists claimed. Before the meeting adjourned, Samuel Cornish, Philip Bell, George Downing, and Charles Reason all rose and echoed this sentiment, vehemently renewing their objections to the activities of the LAES.[75]

Significantly, members of the Black leadership did not end their anticolonization struggle with community meetings; in fact, they were so opposed to Governor Hunt's message that they took their resolutions and concerns directly to the source. On January 20, James McCune Smith, George Downing, and Philip Bell led a delegation to meet with the governor. He apparently received them "respectfully and cordially" and they reported that the governor "desired to be regarded as a friend of our people." During the meeting, Black activists told the governor that they were determined to oppose colonization efforts and that they were disappointed by his actions because "the colored man certainly had sufficient to struggle against, without having the Governor of the State to thus rear himself against them." Governor Hunt, perhaps shocked by the courage and determination of the representatives, stated that he would reconsider his position and assured them that he was in favor of extending Black men the unrestricted right to vote. When they finally left the governor's office, the committee was satisfied that Hunt would not allocate any state funds to support the ACS.[76]

Philip A. Bell. (Courtesy of the Manuscripts, Archives, and Rare Books Division; Schomburg Center for Research in Black Culture; New York Public Library; Astor, Lenox, and Tilden Foundations.)

Following the victory against Governor Hunt and the LAES, New York's Black leadership continued to oppose repatriation on the national level. Most notably, the leadership refused to participate in the 1854 emigration convention held in Cleveland, Ohio. Led by Martin R. Delany, the purpose of the gathering was to form a commission to investigate various locations that might be favorable for the *voluntary* relocation of free Blacks. In fact, Delany and his supporters were especially careful to separate their support of emigration from the ACS's forced removal schemes. In their call for convention, they issued a sharp warning: "Colonizationists are advised, that no favors will be shown to them or their expatriating scheme, as we have no sympathy with the enemies of our race." Yet even though the conveners painstakingly distanced themselves from the ACS, New Yorkers were still not convinced of the convention's merits. Likely with the support his brethren in New York City, Frederick Douglass attacked the convention on the grounds that it was "opposed in spirit and purpose" to the cause of Black people in the United States. Instead, he urged free Blacks to seek to obtain property in the United States and establish permanent residence in this country. What is most telling about the Black leadership's perspective on emigration is that when the convention commenced, the New Yorkers were quite obviously absent.[77]

By the middle of the 1850s, it seemed that Black New Yorkers were united in their decision to remain in the United States and agitate for abolition and citizenship rights. Indeed, their opposition to both colonization and emigration persisted over the next few years. In 1855, for example, a group of activists resolved to finance two ships to assist in *returning* those who had immigrated to Africa and wanted to come back to the United States. This action suggested that Black New Yorkers not only refused to emigrate themselves, but were committed to bringing their people home to continue the struggle in America.[78]

However, despite the apparent strength of their convictions, the emigration debate was far from over. In 1858, Henry Highland Garnet revived the emigration movement and forced Black New Yorkers to reconsider their relationship to the United States. Garnet had spent several years as a missionary in Jamaica and was disappointed when he returned to New York City and witnessed the deplorable condition of his people. Although he had acquired a rather considerable following, due to his new position as the pastor of Shiloh Presbyterian Church, the community was ill-prepared for the political issue that Garnet was about to unleash.[79] Ultimately, his sudden outspoken support of emigration became a political issue that ripped apart the Black community and caused devastating conflicts with his closest friends.

Shortly after his return to New York City, Henry Highland Garnet created the African Civilization Society to spread religion and establish business relationships in Africa. In particular, the society was interested in exploring the possibility of cotton production in West Africa; they hoped this endeavor would provide competition for Southern cotton, and destroy the system of slavery. However, the controversial portion of its plans lay in the idea that free Blacks should migrate from the United States and assist in the development of Liberia. Yet Garnet insisted that this was strictly an emigrationist scheme and should be entirely voluntary. At a meeting in New York City held in August 1858, he declared, "Let those who wish to stay here, stay, and let those who have enterprise and wish to go, go and found a nation of which the colored American could be proud."[80] Although Garnet stressed that Black people should not be *required* to leave, the plan awakened the old fears of forced colonization that terrorized the Black community.

By July 1858, Garnet and the African Civilization Society were under attack by others in the Black leadership, just as Lewis Putnam had been seven years earlier. Leading the movement was George Downing, who had already made his opposition to colonization quite clear. As a member of the Committee of Thirteen, Downing had spoken extensively at the community meeting in 1852 and had caused a conflict at the Colored Convention of 1855 when he demanded that a letter supporting colonization should be burned on the convention floor.[81] Thus, when Henry Highland Garnet announced his new organization, the African Civilization Society, Downing was outraged. Both Downing and Frederick Douglass wrote extensively about Garnet's scheme in Douglass's nationally circulated newspaper, arguing that it should be dismissed as another plot to remove the free Black population from the United States. Asserting their identity as Americans and claiming that the African Civilization Society was another "deceptive" tool

George T. Downing. (Courtesy of the Photographs and Prints Division; Schomburg Center for Research in Black Culture; New York Public Library; Astor, Lenox, and Tilden Foundations.)

of the American Colonization Society, Downing and Douglass urged their people to ignore Garnet and his organization.[82]

George Downing also continued his attack against Henry Highland Garnet on the local level. In December 1858, Downing wrote a letter to the *New York Daily Tribune* in which he clearly outlined his objections. He argued that the African Civilization Society was "the same rabbit with another tail," meaning that it was simply another manifestation of the racist colonizationists. Downing further argued that Blacks needed to focus on moral improvement and uplift before they could consider going to another country: "The colored people of this country must develop an intelligent character, a character for independence, for self-reliance . . . before they can be anything more than they are here, or will be in Africa, or anywhere else." Although he had asserted a strong American identity in earlier speeches, Downing concluded his letter with a different appeal. In fact, his position could be perceived as a nationalist argument, because he maintained that he could not support an emigration scheme endorsed by Whites. Downing claimed that although he thought Black people should remain in the United States, he did not object to emigration as long as it was not part of a movement "projected, impelled, directed, [and] subsisted by whites."[83]

Garnet responded within days to clarify his beliefs. He defended the African Civilization Society, claiming that its supporters were all true antislavery men who were committed to destroying slavery and uplifting the race. Moreover, he argued, nearly one-half of the officers and directors were Black. He further maintained that his plan was primarily a commercial enterprise, and he did not intend for all free Black people to leave the United States. Garnet emphasized that his main concern was to convert Africans to the Christian faith and mentioned that there were Black ministers across the North who had given their support. According to Garnet, he wished to "show that colored men and women can be missionaries and discharge every function that white men and women perform in Africa." In conclusion, he hoped that the goals of Christian reform and free labor could be achieved by sending Black people to Africa to uplift their race.[84]

Regardless of his attempts to defend his actions, Henry Highland Garnet increasingly found himself under fire. In response, Garnet actively sought alliances within the Black leadership both regionally and locally. He appeared in Boston where he discovered only a mildly warm reception, because he had to convince many Black Bostonians that he was still an advocate for their best interest. Garnet also found some support in New York City, particularly from Peter Porter who had been active in the desegregation movements. In addition, J. W. C. Pennington, although he changed his position on the emigration question a few times, was also an occasional advocate for Garnet. However, in 1860, Pennington turned against Garnet and accused him of working to "secure the expulsion of the free people of color" in coalition with the Republican Party. This attack must have been particularly painful for Garnet, because the vast majority of New York's Black leadership echoed Pennington's position. By the middle of 1860, George Downing, James McCune Smith, Charles Ray, and Charles Reason were all strong critics of Garnet. Sadly, this conflict was more than a political or ideological split; it was also deeply personal. Garnet, Downing, Smith, and Reason were all childhood friends and had attended the African Free School together. Now, as adults, they were engaged in an ugly, public dispute over the future of the Black community in the United States.[85]

The conflict worsened in March 1860, when the African Civilization Society unveiled plans to send a group of fifty-seven Black people to Africa. This decision obviously touched a nerve, because, the following month, a public debate was held in Zion Church during which Henry Highland Garnet was asked to explain his plans and defend his character. There were apparently between 1,000 and 1,200 Black New Yorkers in attendance, with a surprising level of support for Garnet; according to the *New York Daily Tribune,* there was equal endorsement for both positions. With the group so obviously divided, it is not surprising that the gathering deteriorated into a horrible conflict. The first problem emerged when Henry Highland Garnet objected to the presentation of lengthy letters opposing colonization and complained that his position was not given equal time. Although the women in the audience were apparently in "unanimous" support of Garnet, the "ladies" were overruled. Frustrated, Garnet attempted to force Downing to yield the floor and the scene became rather rowdy: "The excitement rose to such a height that [Garnet] was surrounded by those opposed to him, whereupon his friends also came up and some violent demonstrations were made, accompanied by cries of 'Hustle him,' 'Garnet,' 'Downing,' 'Go in Garnet,' etc. A conference then ensued between Messrs Downing and Garnet, the row meanwhile being most uproarious." When order was finally imposed, George Downing read a series of resolutions denouncing the African Civilization Society that called the organization "an auxiliary to the 'Negro-Hating' Colonization Society" and accused its supporters of trying to ship Black people off to Africa against their will. Based on these allegations, he asked the community to "declare to the world our uncompromising condemnation of and opposition to [the African Civilization] society."[86]

As might be expected, Downing's resolutions resulted in another nasty conflict. When Garnet claimed that Downing had prejudiced the audience by reading the resolutions before he had been given a chance to speak, Downing called Garnet a "convicted liar." Garnet then lunged at Downing, and, although he managed to compose himself, the crowd erupted as disorder took over: "Cheers, hisses, groans, catcalls, and all sorts of disturbances ensued for at least half an hour." Unable to regain control of the meeting, it soon became clear that further discussion would be impossible. Reverend Gray finally turned out the lights and forced everyone out of the church. The debate apparently continued in the street for a short time, where "threats of physical violence were freely used" but the audience finally dissipated. The *New York Daily Tribune* later described the event: "Aping their Southern masters in Congress, our colored friends called each other very hard names, almost got into a fight, and were finally dispersed in darkness." Although the details of the meeting are rather entertaining, it is also important to note that, regardless of the personal conflicts, there was considerable interest in the Black community regarding the emigration question. Over one thousand Black New Yorkers attended the meeting and were apparently equally divided over this issue. Although Garnet seemed to have few supporters in the leadership, there were obviously some in the community who were willing to consider his perspectives.[87]

Immediately following that fateful meeting, Garnet expressed his anger over what he perceived as unwarranted persecution from his detractors. In the *Anglo-African* magazine, Garnet wrote about personal attacks from his former friends and launched criticisms of his own. Specifically, he stated that James McCune Smith had threatened him and he mocked the coalition between George Downing and Frederick Douglass, claiming "there is no escape from the combined power of the allies."[88] Even though Garnet was obviously disturbed by the events of 1860, he had only witnessed the beginning; indeed, the conflict was far from over.

Early in 1861, the federal government selected Henry Highland Garnet as the New York State agent of emigration. For James McCune Smith, this was the final straw; he could tolerate no more. Smith challenged Garnet to focus his energy on the condition of Black people in the United States instead of other countries throughout the world. According to Smith, he and Garnet had made a pledge twenty-five years earlier that they would devote their lives to uplift the Black race, fight for abolition, and gain the suffrage. Because they had not yet achieved their goals, Smith argued, Garnet was obligated to honor his agreement.[89] Perhaps wounded by prior conflicts, Garnet lashed back at James McCune Smith calling him a "skunk" and the exact "opposite" of a gentleman. Even worse, he accused Smith of trying to keep the Black race as an oppressed group of menial laborers in a country that did not want them.[90]

As a new decade dawned, Garnet continued to defy Smith and Downing's wishes and, instead, expanded his emigrationist efforts to include an endorsement of the revitalized movement for Haitian emigration. The revival of Haitian emigration plans had commenced in 1858 when a Northern Black activist, James Theodore Holly, had begun to champion the virtues of reconsidering the Haitian project. However, it was not until 1859 that the movement really took root. During that year, the Haitian government, led by President Fabre Geffrard, mimicked similar schemes from thirty years prior by agreeing to provide inducements and travel stipends to American Blacks willing to relocate to Haiti. Inspired by these efforts, Holly began to openly promote Haitian emigration in the pages of the *Anglo-African* magazine in late 1859. In particular, he argued that they were on the verge of an "auspicious era when an intelligent emigration of colored Americans may set toward those shores, with every prospect of ultimate success in the regeneration of that people, and the promotion of the cause of the descendants of Africa throughout the world." By the end of 1860, Henry Highland Garnet had been converted to the vision of Haitian emigration and became an agent for Holly's Haitian Emigration Bureau headquartered in Boston.[91]

Perhaps to no one's surprise, Garnet again faced severe reprisals from his colleagues in New York City. George Downing denounced the Haitian emigration scheme on the grounds that it was attempting to "create in the minds of the colored people the impression that they cannot be anything in this country."[92] Likewise, James McCune Smith issued a passionate plea, in the *Anglo-African* magazine, for Garnet to reconsider the ramifications of his decision. In particular, he pointed out that a similar plan had failed in the 1820s and there was no compelling reason why Black Americans should be "dumped on the shores of Hayti." Especially, in Smith's view, because Black people wanted to remain in the United States: "Our people want to stay, and will stay, at home; we are in for the fight, and will fight it out here." To bolster his argument he offered hope for the abolition and suffrage movements in the United States, stating that he believed "the goal is within our reach." Yet the most poignant part of his plea was the conclusion of his letter; he praised Garnet for his worthy labor on behalf of the Black population in the United States over the years and begged him to stay and finish the work for Black liberation. "Shake yourself free from these migrating phantasms, and join us with your might and main. You belong to us, and we want your whole soul."[93]

Despite the power of Smith's impassioned appeal for Garnet to abandon emigration, the Haitian project continued to move forward and even gained some shocking new converts. In the spring of 1861, Frederick Douglass agreed to accompany Theodore Holly on a mission to investigate conditions in Haiti. Although he had obviously been a staunch anti-emigrationist in previous years, Douglass had suddenly reversed his position and agreed that the United States was rapidly becoming inhospitable to the Black race. In the pages of his paper, Douglass declared that "the inducements offered to the colored man to remain here are few, feeble, and very uncertain." According to historian Floyd Miller, Douglass had grown despondent about the setbacks in the 1850s, particularly the *Dred Scott* decision, and had arrived at the painful conclusion that free Blacks might need to consider opportunities elsewhere. As a result, in March of 1861, Douglass admitted, "We can raise no objection to the present movement towards Hayti . . . We can no longer throw our little influence against a measure which may prove highly advantageous to many families, and of much service to the Haytian Republic." Douglass became so committed to the notion that he planned to visit Haiti the following month to help plan a potential exodus of voluntary migrants.[94]

Yet, in a powerful stroke of fate, Douglass never made the journey to Haiti; before they had a chance to embark, shots were fired at Fort Sumter and the

Civil War commenced. The outbreak of war prompted Douglass and many other Black leaders to relinquish their emigration schemes and refocus attention on the United States, in hopes that slavery might be vanquished and the battle for suffrage might eventually succeed. Even Henry Highland Garnet had a change of heart. Although shortly after the war began Garnet continued to raise money for African repatriation, and did not immediately abandon the Haitian project, he reunited with his childhood friends James McCune Smith and George Downing in 1862 and declared that the abolition of slavery must be the Black community's primary focus. Even more, by 1864, Garnet was actively recruiting Black soldiers to fight with the Union on behalf of the abolition of slavery.[95]

In the end, the debates over emigration were crucial because they highlighted the plight of the Black community at a critical crossroads. After more than a half century of agitation, Black New Yorkers still struggled with the same problems that had plagued their mothers and fathers. While they wanted to honor their ancestors and obtain their rights as American citizens, many Black people must have privately wondered if their commitment would be rewarded and their dreams eventually realized. Ultimately, however, the vast majority of Black folks resolved to remain in the United States. With the country on the verge of civil war, Black people soon became consumed with the fight for the liberation of their Southern brethren, and the subject of emigration was postponed. Most significantly, Black activists resolved that they would, as James McCune Smith had urged, remain in the United States and continue the fight for equality. And, as he had requested, they gave their "whole souls."[96]

* * *

Intense struggle and disappointment plagued Black New Yorkers during the 1850s. After two decades of passionate organizing and agitation, the Black leadership's goals remained elusive. Even after forging a sense of Black unity, abolition and equal justice remained distant dreams that seemed impossible to reach. The dawning of the 1850s was particularly devastating as politicians passed the Fugitive Slave Act, which strengthened slavery and threatened the safety of every "free" Black person in the country. Although Black New Yorkers rallied against the legislation and fought to protect their community, the law was a continual reminder of their tenuous freedom in the United States. Compounding the problem of fugitives was the repeated denial of voting rights, which left the Black community politically ineffectual and frustrated. Their unequal position was further confirmed by the passage of the *Dred Scott* decision, which guaranteed that Black people would not be considered American citizens.

Yet, miraculously, Black New Yorkers refused to surrender hope. Despite horrifying conditions and frustrating setbacks, Black leaders continued to agitate for justice and equal citizenship on both the local and regional levels. Activists were able to make minor advances against segregation in New York City and fought unceasingly to protect their people against the threat of reenslavement wrought by the Fugitive Slave Act. Black New Yorkers also revitalized their suffrage movement within the state and waged a powerful campaign to pressure the state legislature for unrestricted voting rights. Perhaps most significantly, Black leaders renewed the Colored Conventions. This movement was critically important because Northern activists finally managed to create a unified coalition and commence an attack against slavery and racial discrimination.

Regardless of the Black activists' strong united front, however, American society remained intolerant of notions of Black progress. In the area of desegregation, Black New Yorkers quickly discovered that their victories could only be obtained only after lengthy exhausting battles. Even those triumphs were usually short-lived or insufficient to make permanent changes in racial ideology. Even worse, the Colored Convention and the suffrage movements were stymied by their inability to identify an effective strategy beyond petitioning or issuing dramatic appeals to the moral conscience of American society. In response, Americans stubbornly refused to abolish slavery and extend the rights of full citizenship to their Black brethren.

As a result, not surprisingly, by late in the 1850s, a few Black activists revisited the possibility of repatriation or emigration. Frustrated and disappointed, leaders such as Henry Highland Garnet began to suspect that they might never reach their goals of freedom, justice, and equality. The debates over the future of Black people in the United States nearly tore the leadership asunder. Yet what emerged from these conflicts was the Black community's determination to stay in the United States and agitate for its rights. The community's bravery, in the face of violent opposition, was a testament to the spirit and will of a people who would not be silenced. It was this very determination that was embodied in the story of Seneca Village, a Black community in upper Manhattan, where Black New Yorkers struggled to create a sense of permanence in the United States.

CHAPTER 7

"The Story of Seneca Village,"
1825–1857

On a brisk autumn day in 1871, workers made a shocking discovery while plowing up the ground in New York City's newly established Central Park. As they labored to uproot trees near the Eighty-fifth street entrance, landscapers uncovered two coffins; one enclosed the body of a Black man. According to an article in the *New York Herald*, the unearthing of this burial ground was a mystery because no one remembered the existence of a cemetery in that area.[1] Apparently less than fifteen years after the residents of Seneca Village were driven off their land, their story had already been forgotten by most New Yorkers.[2] Indeed, even in light of this burial site, no mention was made of the thriving community whose ruins and cemeteries lay beneath the hallowed land, and most New Yorkers never realized that the creation of Central Park had robbed an entire community of its homes, churches, and burial grounds. Reflecting the silence surrounding the history of Black folks, the story of Seneca Village was effectively erased from the memory of New York City. Dismissed as a shantytown or ignored entirely, Seneca Village nearly disappeared from New York City's history.[3]

Though generally forgotten, Seneca Village was a crucial symbol to the Black community during the antebellum era. To these newly emancipated New Yorkers, Seneca Village reflected their commitment to building institutions in the United States, the attainment of political power, and all their hopes for the future. For Black New Yorkers, Seneca Village was much more than a thriving neighborhood; it was a symbol of the success their people could achieve and their potential destiny in the United States.[4] Beginning in 1825, residents labored for over thirty years to construct homes, gardens, churches, schools, and cemeteries in an effort to create a future for their children and to honor their ancestors. However the success of Seneca Village could not remain a secret forever, and at least a few White New Yorkers became disturbed and threatened by the notion of a strong autonomous Black community. Consistent with the White backlash during the 1850s, politicians commenced an attack against Seneca Village that ultimately decimated a community and the dreams of its residents. This chapter is the story of Seneca Village: the Black people who made it a home and the movement to destroy it that culminated in the creation of Central Park.

* * *

The tale of Seneca Village begins rather modestly, with a few small plots of land and a group of determined Black activists. Prior to the Civil War, most New York City residents lived below Forty-second Street in the expanding, yet overcrowded, urban milieu. The territory stretching north of the city was still mostly rural and unpopulated. Loyalists had owned much of that region prior to the Revolutionary War, but abandoned the land following British withdrawal. In the early national era, the few men who owned these large tracts of land used them primarily for agricultural purposes. However, in 1825, landowner John Whitehead made a crucial decision that created a new possibility for Black New Yorkers. Whitehead, who owned property between Eighty-fifth and Eighty-eighth Streets near Seventh Avenue, chose to parcel off his land and sell individual plots to interested buyers. Perhaps to Whitehead's surprise, an unexpected group of people began to purchase his estate. Attracted by inexpensive land and the opportunity to create a community, Black New Yorkers began to invest in upper Manhattan Island. Andrew Williams and Epiphany Davis purchased the first plots from the Whiteheads in September 1825; Williams selected three lots on September 27 for which he paid $125, and, on the same day, Davis purchased twelve lots for $578. Shortly thereafter, the African Methodist Episcopal (AME) Zion congregation chose six adjoining tracts. From this initial activity, the community of Seneca Village was born.[5]

It was no coincidence that Andrew Williams, Epiphany Davis, and the AME Zion Church purchased their land simultaneously. It seems that there was a united effort to secure this land, which reflected a strong coalition within the Black community and its desire to create a space for its members. Black communities in New York had traditionally centered around churches and, as Black people flocked northward, Seneca Village would be no exception. Because Williams and Davis were members of Zion Church, their actions were likely a concerted effort. However, the commitment to create Seneca Village was not strictly a religious movement. Since the dawn of emancipation, Black New Yorkers had worked within institutions, such as the African Society, to accumulate property and build a viable community. As Williams and Davis were also charter members of the African Society, within weeks of their investment in northern Manhattan, other African Society members such as Samuel Hardenburgh soon joined Williams and Davis. The African Society had evinced a strong interest in purchasing land since 1820, and its members were clearly continuing the traditional emphasis upon accumulating real estate to inspire the creation of a strong Black neighborhood.[6] As a result, the real estate ventures of the society did not end in lower Manhattan; African Society members, followed by an array of Black New Yorkers, slowly migrated northward to establish the community of Seneca Village.

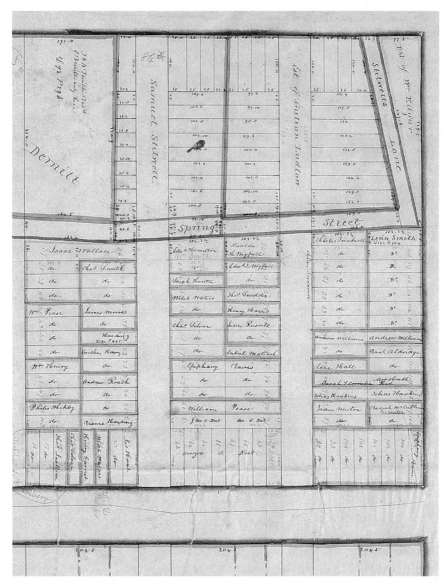

Map of Seneca Village in 1838 depicting the property owned by Andrew Williams, Epiphany Davis, William Pease, and George Root. Manhattan Square Benefit Map, 1838. (Courtesy of the Collection of the New York Historical Society, Negative no. 78801d.)

In less than fifteen years, as residents constructed homes, gardens, and barns, Seneca Village expanded considerably. The 1838 map of the community indicates a variety of property owners, ranging from those who owned several plots with grand homes to those who inhabited a single plot with a small cottage. For example, African Society member Epiphany Davis owned seventeen plots of land

and constructed two three-story homes on his property that must have been the envy of the community. Likewise, George Root controlled nine plots upon which he constructed several buildings; in addition to a barn, stable, and shed, Root built a two-story piazza that stretched the entire length of one tract. Andrew Williams only owned three plots, but he erected two buildings that were over two stories high. Despite these impressive displays, there were many properties that stood empty or only contained a small building city officials described as a "shack." William Pease was one such landowner; he purchased a single lot but was unable to afford the construction of an impressive building. Black female property owners Sarah and Cornelia Reed were in similar circumstances, they probably waited impatiently for the day when they would able to build on their land and permanently inhabit the burgeoning community of Seneca Village. William Pease and the Reeds represented a portion of the Black population who longed to be property owners but struggled against poverty. Their stories reflected the diversity within New York's Black community and the burning desire to create a unified Black neighborhood regardless of economic status.[7]

Although Seneca Village's popularity was steadily growing among Black New Yorkers, it is difficult to determine exactly how many people lived in the community. According to the 1855 census, there were 264 people living there; however, it is likely that the number was much higher. Many known Seneca Village landowners do not appear in the 1855 census, despite the fact that they had constructed homes and likely lived on their land. In addition, official reports indicated that there were over 300 homes in Seneca Village by 1857 and, given the predominance of large families in the antebellum era, it seems unlikely that there would be 300 homes and only 264 residents.[8] Further complicating the situation is the strong probability that Seneca Village was used as a haven for fugitive slaves during the antebellum era. As we shall see, many Seneca Village residents were connected to various political movements including the Underground Railroad and the protection of fugitives. Obviously, if the community became a refuge for fugitives, such residents would not appear in the census. Due to this combination of factors, the report on Seneca Village's population was probably skewed.

Regardless of the actual number of residents, Seneca Village blossomed into a flourishing community during the 1850s. The neighborhood stretched from Eighty-first Street to Eighty-ninth Street, between Seventh and Eighth avenues, and, in the upper region, there was extensive farmland with barns, stables, and several two-story homes. The property owned by long-time residents such as Andrew Williams, Epiphany Davis, and George Root continued to prosper, along with Henry Garnett (no apparent relation to activist Henry Highland Garnet) who owned two adjoining plots of land containing a barn, a stable, two sheds, and two houses. One of his homes was particularly impressive and towered three stories high with a basement and a porch.[9] Reflecting their desire to establish an independent self-sustaining community, many residents cultivated gardens to provide food for themselves and fellow community members. According to one newspaper report, Seneca Village contained numerous homes "of various degrees of excellence . . . a number of these have fine kitchen gardens, and some of the side-hill slopes are adorned with cabbage, and melon-patches, with hills of corn and cucumbers, and beds of beets, parsnips, and other garden delicacies."[10] Most striking, however, was the increasing number of affluent Black New Yorkers who invested in Seneca Village. George Webster and Charles Silvan, a Haitian immigrant, both owned property worth over $2,000, and O. P. McCollin and William Mathews controlled plots valued at $1,000. The fact that property values often exceeded the necessary amount to qualify for voting rights reinforced the image of Seneca Village as a community where Black folks were beginning to thrive despite the legacy of slavery.[11]

Although men such as Charles Silvan, George Root, and George Webster reflected the wealthiest component of Seneca Village, there were many regular folks who simply viewed the community as their home and labored to build something permanent. Families such as the Thompsons likely came to Seneca Village hoping to create a positive future for their children. Upon arriving in New York State in 1855, Richard and Mary Thompson purchased land in the community where their children, Alfred and Catherine, found respectable work as a cartman and a schoolteacher, respectively. Likewise, Solomon Hutchings, who was unable to afford his own land, rented a house in the neighborhood and brought his family to the community to seek opportunity. Eventually, he was employed as a common laborer and his daughter helped support the family as a domestic. Rare among the community residents were women such as Sarah Wilson, a single fifty-nine-year-old Black woman employed as a washerwoman, who managed to acquire a plot of land and construct a home worth $500. Wilson was even financially stable enough to adopt a young girl, Catherine Treadwell, and provide for her education.[12]

The examples of these struggling Seneca Villagers demonstrated that many Black folks were deeply inspired by this community's potential and flocked there in hopes of forging a better life. In many ways, their dreams were initially realized; although most Seneca Villagers' property was only worth about $500, this was still rather impressive for the antebellum era. Particularly compared to the experience of most Black New Yorkers who were crowded into attics and cellars in the Five Points district, Seneca Village must have seemed to be a veritable mecca and a symbol of what the Black community could eventually attain.

Thus Seneca Village residents were members of a burgeoning community, a neighborhood that demonstrated their hopes for a prosperous future as free people. Most notably, Seneca Village contained many institutions such as churches and schools: symbols of the Black community's longevity and fortitude. Continuing its tradition of independence and activism, the Zion Church established a branch in Seneca Village in the early years of the community's existence. Known after 1848 as the African Methodist Episcopal Zion Branch Militant, the Seneca

Village congregation worked tirelessly to develop a sense of permanence in its new home. By 1838, the congregation had raised enough money to construct a church. By 1853, there were over one hundred regular attendees with thirty permanent members. The congregants also carefully created a cemetery, where they could properly pay homage to their ancestors. In August 1853, the congregation held a ceremony to honor the placement of the cornerstone of its new church, a symbolic representation of the permanent structure it would eventually erect. The proceedings were officiated by elder Christopher Rush, who was superintendent of African churches and had participated in the famous 1796 move toward religious independence. Rush, himself, laid the cornerstone of the church; his presence signified the importance of the church not only to Seneca Village, but also to the entire Black New York community.[13]

Although the AME Zion Branch Militant may have been the largest and most influential church in Seneca Village, other religious institutions soon joined it. As early as 1840, there were reports of a church called African Union in New York City with a small presence in Seneca Village. African Union was apparently an "independent sect of Methodists" that was affiliated with a main body in Delaware. The New York City headquarters was located downtown near Fifteenth Street and, according to the *Colored American* newspaper, its one-hundred-member congregation was composed of a "plain and exemplary people." Although it may have been smaller than most Black churches in New York City, African Union managed to establish a branch in Seneca Village with a "small frame building." Under Reverend James Barney's leadership, African Union Church settled near the AME Zion church and offered religious salvation to the residents of Seneca Village.[14] African Union also followed AME Zion's example of creating a cemetery for the interment of its people. Although the records from AME Zion Branch Militant and African Union churches did not survive, these institutions were profoundly important to Black Seneca Villagers because they represented the continuation of the movement to build autonomous Black organizations and create a lasting legacy for the Black community.

Adjacent to the Zion and African Union churches was a third church called All Angels. Unlike Zion and African Union, All Angels was not a typical Black church because it did not have any official affiliation or connection with the Black community. In fact, it was under the leadership of a White minister, Thomas M. C. Peters, and affiliated with St. Michael's Protestant Episcopal Church. Furthermore, All Angels Church had a biracial and multiethnic congregation that included Black people, such as the Stairs and Riddles families, alongside Irish residents, such as Margaret McIntay and the Cassidy family. All Angels was certainly unique in its day, for most Black New Yorkers did not worship with Whites in the antebellum era. However, the existence of All Angels was a testament to a new social and political reality. By 1855, German and Irish immigrants had moved into New York City, and some found their way to the area surrounding Seneca Village. For

example, three Irish families, the Lanes, the Berrys, and the Foleys, moved near
Seneca Villagers Sarah Wilson and William Pease.[15] Although most European
immigrants remained in the area just south of Seneca Village, many joined All
Angels's congregation, which, by the 1850s, had a sizable wooden building that
was two stories high.[16] Most significantly, however, the arrival of these families in
the neighborhood illustrated a different kind of hope. Even though All Angels did
not reflect the efforts at Black autonomy evident elsewhere in the community, as
Black and White New Yorkers worshipped and were apparently buried together,
it offered the vision that the races could eventually coexist peacefully; a goal that
many Black activists longed for.

Black Seneca Villagers' dreams were also realized in their efforts to improve education among their people; by the 1850s, the community contained two schools.
Black activists in New York City gave considerable attention to the education
of their youth throughout the early national and antebellum eras, hopeful that
knowledge would be the key to racial uplift and community progress. This mission continued in Seneca Village partly as the result of the AME Zion Church,
which offered space in its basement for one of the schools.[17] In addition, there was
a branch of the African Free School although, by the 1850s, the school was under
the control of the public school system and was known as Colored School No. 3.
Yet under the leadership of seventeen-year-old Black Seneca Villager, Catherine
Thompson, Colored School No. 3 was an impressive institution because, despite
the fact that it was housed in an "old building," it was extremely "well attended."[18]
Although little else is known about these educational endeavors, they were clearly
an important demonstration of the Black community's continuing commitment
to the future of the race.

Despite the impressive institutions in Seneca Village, the neighborhood was
much more than a collection of residents, homes, churches, and schools. Considered separately, they were individual people or buildings, but together, they were
a community: a collective movement that symbolized the hope and possibility of
Black New Yorkers. Beyond its importance to the residents, Seneca Village represented and embodied a series of ideas: African pride and racial consciousness,
the creation of lasting Black institutions, and the potential attainment of political power. Seneca Village was home to a community of Black New Yorkers who
were truly "Africa's Children," those who recognized that they were descendants
of Africa and yet were determined to build a future for themselves in the United
States. Even though Seneca Village's mere existence gives tremendous insight into
the Black experience in New York City, it is crucial to try (as best we can) and
understand the *meaning* of Seneca Village because it may shed light on Black New
Yorkers' hopes, dreams, and political perspectives during the antebellum era.

Although most Black activists by the 1850s had ceased their public admiration
for Africa, their ideological connection to their homeland never fully disappeared.
Admittedly, many Black activists had grown so concerned with public perception

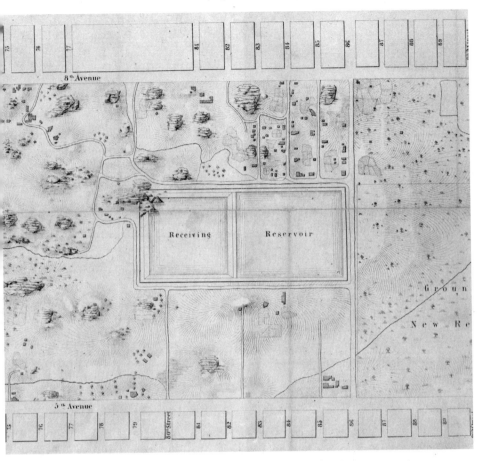

Map of Seneca Village in 1856, showing portions of the community and surrounding areas. Topographical Survey for the Grounds of Central Park. (Courtesy of the Collection of the New York Historical Society, Negative no. 67835.)

that they either avoided the subject of Africa or openly denounced their African identity hoping to convince White Americans that Black people could be true and loyal Americans. Nevertheless, there is evidence that Seneca Villagers remained attached to their African heritage and espoused a sense of racial consciousness. Indeed, individual residents maintained a connection to Africa and carried the memory of their people's history with them in various ways. In a powerful demonstration of the power of Black history and the community's desire to remember its past, Epiphany Davis's will contained a special stipulation for the future edification of his family. Written in 1843, the document demanded that, upon his death, his daughter Ann should receive a "picture called a section of a slave ship."[19] The now famous illustration depicted an image of the Middle Passage's

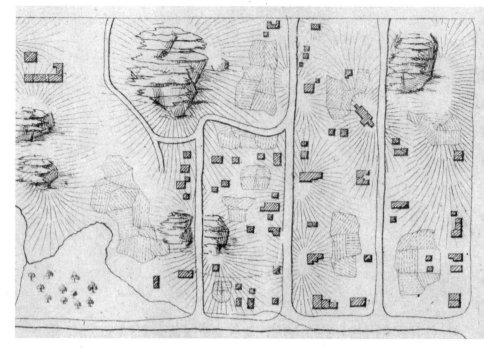

Enlarged image of the buildings in Seneca Village. (Courtesy of the Collection of the New York Historical Society, Negative no. 67835.)

horrors, showing how Africans were packed into floating torture chambers and reduced to chattel bondage in the Americas. Abolitionists had used this picture for years, to raise public consciousness about the need to abolish the ghastly slave trade and the system of slavery. Davis, however, hung this picture in his home as a constant reminder of the Black community's history and struggle. Moreover, he obviously recognized the importance of passing these memories and stories on to future generations so they would always remember that they were children of Africa, men and women who had endured slavery and risen to be free people.

Epiphany Davis was not the only member of the community who honored his African heritage. Samuel Hardenburgh, who rose to fame in Black New York for his perpetual appearance as the grand marshal in community parades, was among the earliest Seneca Village residents. As a member of the African Society, Hardenburgh had routinely reflected his connection to African culture by continuing the tradition of parading; he marched with the African Society on many occasions and in the famous Emancipation Day celebration in 1827. As previously discussed, Hardenburgh delighted Black New Yorkers by riding through the streets of New York, dressed in elaborate garb, flanked by various assistants, and carrying a drawn sword in his hand. Even after the Black leadership denounced parading, Hardenburgh insisted upon continuing the tradition, which indicated that he could not surrender his commitment to African celebrations. Hardenburgh must have carried his boldness and his connection to Africa with him to Seneca Village and, along with Epiphany Davis, influenced community members to remember and celebrate their African heritage.[20]

Even more than an enduring connection to Africa, however, Seneca Villagers demonstrated a distinct racial consciousness that acknowledged their unique identity as Black people in the United States. Their political and racial perspectives were particularly evident during the 1853 ceremony held to lay the cornerstone for the AME Zion Church. During the proceedings, Reverend Christopher Rush and Seneca Village residents buried several items within the cornerstone to save some meaningful items for future generations to unearth. Along with a hymnbook and copy of the discipline from the AME Zion faith, they included a text from the Epistle of Peter, chapter one, verse six.[21] Within this passage was a powerful testimony to the Black experience in the United States: "Wherein ye greatly rejoice, though now for a season . . . ye are in heaviness through manifold temptations."[22] This verse spoke of an abiding faith despite adversity; it reminded the Black congregants that even though they might be surrounded with the "heaviness" of racial oppression, they would always have reason to rejoice and receive salvation. Although this passage demonstrated the community's passionate belief in God, it also reflected a racial consciousness: an awareness of themselves as an oppressed people that would ultimately transcend their experience.

Indeed, though the Epistle of Peter suggested a spiritual transcendence that would rescue Black folks from their worldly pain, in a temporal sense, the community of Seneca Village provided a tangible escape from racial persecution. Faced with the ACS's repeated efforts to forcibly remove Black people from the United States, Seneca Village represented an independent autonomous Black community. Seneca Village was a permanent home that would serve as a beacon to the free Black community, symbolizing Blacks' right to remain in the United States and obtain the rights and equality they so justly deserved. Certainly, there must have been a level of pride among Seneca Villagers in the late 1840s and early 1850s, as they surveyed their community and saw the potential of their people and the future of the race. Especially placed in the context of Black activism in New York during the antebellum era, the establishment of Seneca Village was the most powerful example of the Black community's strivings to build a sense of stability for its people in spite of the hostile American environment. Although they were denied equal justice and the rights of citizenship, Black New Yorkers apparently believed that, through this community, they could assert their commitment to remain in the United States and win the battle for justice. Moreover, it reminded other Black people that their diligence would be rewarded and that, despite obstacles, they could rise to be free. In direct opposition to colonization schemes, Seneca Village gave Black New Yorkers hope for their future in the United States.

The existence of Seneca Village also offered protection from racial hostility in an even more concrete sense. Although the anti-abolition riot of 1834 had revealed the vulnerability of the Black community in New York City, and reminded the members of their tenuous freedom, Seneca Village was removed from the center of activity and contained a group of Black activists who were committed to protecting their people. In fact, it was Seneca Villager Epiphany Davis who wrote to the mayor days before the outbreak of violence, prophesizing danger and pleading for protection.[23] Obviously the mayor ignored his warning but once the 1834 race riot began to rage in lower Manhattan, the tiny community of Seneca Village remained safely out of harm's way. Perhaps the growth in the region by 1838 reflected an exodus of the riot victims who, bolstered by an increasing consciousness that Black New Yorkers needed to create an independent safe alternative to city life, sought a refuge from the devastating violence. Regardless, beyond potential race riots, Seneca Village offered safety for Black people fleeing another kind of persecution. Throughout the antebellum era, fugitive slaves flocked to the North seeking asylum and an end to the horrors of enslavement. Black activists in New York obviously had a tradition of protecting fugitives, and there is evidence that Seneca Village was used as a safe haven for those escaping slavery.

Located a few miles from New York City, Seneca Village was ideally situated away from the constant gaze of their enemies. City officials were unable to regularly patrol the community; therefore, it offered prime conditions for concealing fugitives. People could blend in easily and hide until it was safe to move them further out of danger. Beyond the practicality of location, we also know that individual residents of Seneca Village were active in efforts to assist fugitives. The African Society, which was influential in establishing Seneca Village, was reputed to be active in the Underground Railroad and apparently had a secret chamber in the basement of its meetinghouse for such purposes.[24] Through the African Society, Seneca Villagers were connected to men such as Charles Ray, James McCune Smith, John J. Zuille, and Albro Lyons, who were known conductors on the Underground Railroad. Moreover, in 1842, African Society member Albro Lyons moved into Seneca Village. Lyons had been particularly involved in the cause of fugitives because, as his daughter later reported, his operation of the Colored Sailors Home was a cover for harboring fugitives. He was also active in the movement to free alleged fugitive James Hamlet in 1850.[25] Because the nature of assisting fugitives necessitated complete secrecy, we may never know the full role of Seneca Village in the Underground Railroad. However, it is clear that the community had compelling links to the Underground Railroad and its setting provided the perfect opportunity to harbor fugitives and assist abolitionist efforts.

Yet Seneca Village's role in Black political activism did not end with its involvement in the abolitionist movement; on the contrary, its very existence bolstered the struggle for Black voting rights. Indeed, perhaps the most obvious benefit of Seneca Village was the potential it offered for political enfranchisement. According to the New York State Legislature's ruling in 1821, Black people had restricted

Albro Lyons. (Courtesy of the Photographs and Prints Division; Schomburg Center for Research in Black Culture; New York Public Library; Astor, Lenox, and Tilden Foundations.)

access to the suffrage contingent upon property ownership worth at least $250. Given these restrictions, land ownership was the key to political power and represented the only path to gaining political influence for the Black community. In fact, throughout the antebellum era, a few activists recommended the accumulation of property as a method to advance their cause. As evidenced by one of the resolutions that emerged from the 1840 New York State convention, Black leaders had concluded that because property ownership "secures to us the elective franchise, we do, therefore, strongly recommend to our people throughout the State to become possessors of the soil, inasmuch as that not only elevates them to the rights of freemen, but increases the political power in the State, in favor of our political and social elevation."[26]

Black New Yorkers echoed a similar sentiment at an anticolonization meeting in 1852. In one of the resolutions asserting the rights of Black people to remain in the United States, George Downing argued that they should "obtain real estate, and thus, if possible, be even more indissolubly linked with the soil." Recognizing the interconnected nature of property ownership and political power, Downing linked his real estate recommendation with a resolution declaring that the community should renew its efforts to gain the suffrage.[27] Downing was simply articulating a point that Seneca Villagers already knew. Property ownership gave Black male New Yorkers access to the vote; thus, Seneca Village offered the possibility of acquiring land and gaining access to the political rights they so fervently desired.

Unfortunately, Seneca Village's strengths were not lost on the Black community's enemies. A few White New Yorkers, who were concerned about the creation of Black institutions and the potential power of these newly freed people, apparently became determined to destroy this burgeoning community. Prompted by a disturbing combination of racism and greed, a group of White politicians including Mayor Fernando Wood plotted the destruction of Seneca Village and eventually succeeded. Unwilling to accept Black New Yorkers as free and equal citizens, Mayor Wood became consumed by a mission to decimate Seneca Village and replace the neighborhood with something more beneficial to his interests. The opportunity to destroy Seneca Village and simultaneously improve his financial holdings presented itself beginning in the late 1840s. To justify the destruction of Seneca Village, politicians must have realized they would need public support. But what issue could they find to inspire the residents of New York? The answer to that crucial question appeared thanks to the well-intentioned comments of Andrew Jackson Downing.

Downing, a staunch advocate of city parks, wrote extensively about the benefits of creating public space to improve the urban environment. As early as 1848, he published an article arguing that New York City would be the perfect home for a grand park that would be open to "every man, woman, and child in the city." Further, he maintained that such an establishment would promote "social freedom" by allowing interaction between various classes within the city.[28] Less than a year later, Downing advanced his proposition again, stating that New York City could potentially become the home to the "finest park" in the region.[29] As one contemporary observer later reflected, Downing's articles were the "actual beginning of the Central Park, the birth of the idea."[30] Although his motivations appeared to be pure, Downing's words served as the impetus behind a movement that eventually led to the destruction of Seneca Village.

Significantly, however, the early movements to establish a park in New York City did not immediately threaten the existence of Seneca Village. Convinced that a public garden would improve conditions in the city, Mayor Kingsland passed a resolution in July 1851 stating that the area known as Jones Woods near the East River would be transformed into a park for the enjoyment of the entire city.[31] Yet Mayor Kingsland came under instantaneous criticism from Andrew Downing. Though Downing supported the basic concepts of the initiative, he argued that the location was too small and the unfortunate selection was the result of the "narrow sighted frugality of the common council." Downing maintained that Jones Woods was not large enough to be anything other than a "child's playground" and suggested that the Common Council should consider the area above Thirty-ninth Street. This region, Downing argued, would have enough space to "have broad reaches of park and pleasure grounds, with a real feeling of the breadth and beauty of green fields, the perfume and freshness of nature."[32] There is no evidence that Downing knew anything of Seneca Village, but if he did, he apparently thought that the creation of a city park took precedence over the homes, churches, schools, and cemeteries that comprised Seneca Village's burgeoning Black community.

Following Downing's article, the Common Council reversed its position on developing Jones Woods into a city park and, on August 5, 1851, the council selected " the piece of ground lying between Fifth and Eighth Avenues, Fifty-Ninth and One Hundred Sixth Streets, for the purpose indicated over that known as Jones Woods." In a dramatic shift, the Common Council slated Seneca Village for destruction and determined to transform the area into a public garden. From the beginning, however, the decision was plagued by difficulty. First, the land in that region was considered to be undesirable for the creation of a park; one report, in particular, described the lands south of Seneca Village as "rocky" and "swampy." After further investigation, the Central Park Board of Commissioners determined that the region was "a pestilential spot, where rank vegetation and miasmatic odors taint every breath of air."[33] However the conditions of the land were not the only problem. By 1853, perhaps motivated out of a selfish desire to have the park located in their own neighborhood, many New York City residents opposed the creation of Central Park, arguing that Jones Woods was a more beneficial selection. As a result, thousands of New Yorkers signed a petition asking that the Common Council reconsider its decision and immediately recreate the park at Jones Woods. According to the petitioners, "the time to consummate this desirable object should be no longer delayed" and the council should act quickly to begin work on the property "so eligibly situated."[34]

However, the mayor ignored the hostile opposition, and the legislature passed an act to seize the land above Thirty-ninth Street including Seneca Village. Just three months after the AME Zion congregation laid the cornerstone to its new church, the Common Council appointed five commissioners to take the land and oversee the implementation of the plan to establish the park. Yet these plans were delayed. The power of the petitions forced an investigation of the movement against Central Park, and the Common Council had to temporarily suspend activity. Following an extensive review, a subcommittee passed a resolution to "destroy" the plans for the Central Park and return to the establishment of Jones Woods. Perhaps this was a time of hope for Seneca Villagers, because it appeared that their community would be spared. However, their dreams were quickly shattered with the stroke of a pen. In a stunning demonstration of mayoral power, the new city leader Fernando Wood vetoed the resolution and continued with the plans for Central Park.[35]

Mayor Wood's decision is crucial, because it suggests a possible conspiracy behind the creation of Central Park. Although the land was undesirable and public opinion favored Jones Woods, the mayor made a unilateral decision to continue with Central Park. What could have inspired him to reach such a conclusion? Apparently, there were significant political incentives prompting him to establish Central Park: the desire to raise property values in the surrounding area and to destroy Seneca Village. The first motivation is quite simple to understand; Mayor Wood owned property in a neighborhood adjoining Seneca Village and had a strong financial investment in the creation of Central Park. Cognizant that his property would dramatically increase following the establishment of the park, Wood was obviously an ardent advocate of its creation. His determination paid off because, once Seneca Village was eliminated, Mayor Fernando Wood's land value skyrocketed from a few hundred dollars to over $10,000.[36]

Yet the story of the creation of Central Park is not only about financial gain. On the contrary, both Mayor Fernando Wood and New York Senator James Beekman were committed to eradicating the free Black population from the North. Although Senator Beekman was initially in favor of the Jones Woods location because of his own financial self-interest (he owned land near Jones Woods), he would not have opposed the removal of Seneca Village because he was an ardent supporter of colonization and Black removal from the United States.[37] When Senator Munroe appeared on the congressional floor in 1852, he delivered a powerful address that revealed Beekman's support for the colonization movement: "The honorable Senator from the 5th (Mr. Beekman) has become deeply interested in the Colonization Society. He tells us his whole heart is in it." Senator Munroe concluded that the "direct effect" of the Colonization Society was the degradation of the Black community, the denial of social and political rights, the strengthening of the domestic slave trade, and the perpetuation of the system of slavery. Furthermore, he was convinced that supporters of colonization believed in the "incapacity, the unfitness of the colored man to our institutions." Thus, even though Senator Beekman was described as a "friend" to the Black community, it was clear that he harbored dangerous political perspectives regarding the future of the Black race in America.[38] As a result, although Beekman supported the Jones Woods location, he did not actively defend Seneca Village; instead, his colonizationist politics drove him to ignore a productive and successful Black community in the United States at his own financial expense.

If Beekman's colonizationist tendencies were not disturbing enough, Mayor Fernando Wood had an even more troubling record on racial matters. To begin, while a Congressman from 1841 to 1843, Wood routinely opposed the removal of property qualifications from Black voting. As a result, he must have found it particularly disconcerting that the vast majority of Seneca Villagers were able to gain voting rights through property ownership. Even more alarming, in 1857 (the same year as Seneca Village's final destruction), Wood strongly supported the *Dred Scott* decision that upheld notions of Black inferiority and stated that Black people could never be full citizens. In addition, Wood called for an end to antislavery agitation in Kansas and supported the extension of slavery into newly acquired U.S. territories. Wood was especially enraged by radicals in the Republican Party who supported Black rights and pushed to censure Republicans for attempting to secure equal suffrage for Black people. Specifically, he denounced Radical Republicans for promising "lazy, unfit blacks immediate suffrage, high pay and social superiority."[39]

Although many of Wood's most alarming racial views came to light *after* Seneca Village was demolished, they are important to chronicle because they illuminate deeply held racist beliefs that Wood carried with him as he decided Seneca Village's fate. By 1860, Fernando Wood's attack on Black people took an even more dramatic turn for the worse. Not only did he become a devout apologist for slavery, he also publicly insisted that abolitionists' commitment to Black freedom and equality were eroding American society. According to Wood, the only way to save the country was to "'extinguish the followers of the anti-slavery fiend stalking the country.'"[40] Further, he fueled fears that Black Republicans were advocating for a violent overthrow of slavery and prophesized that such a conflict would destroy the Black population. During a speech he delivered to Democratic Party members, Wood reinforced these notions of Black inferiority, stating that any successful armed rebellion would eventually lead to the "annihilation of the black race, which could not fend for itself."[41] One scholar, Ernest McKay, has argued that Wood's racial philosophy stemmed from an extended period of time he spent in Virginia, where he became accustomed to Southern ways. As McKay explained, "[Wood] saw nothing wrong with slavery. Neither the cruelty nor the immorality of the system troubled him."[42] Ultimately, Wood's racial politics influenced many of his political views and resulted in his extreme opposition to the Civil War.

Known as a "Peace Democrat," Wood was adamantly opposed to the possibility of war and fought to make all concessions to the South in order to keep it in the Union. One scholar wrote, "As mayor he had made it clear his sympathies lay with the seceding cotton states."[43] In fact, Wood publicly argued that most New Yorkers did not hold strong antislavery views because New York City's wealth relied upon "the continuance of slave labor and the prosperity of the slave master."[44] When it became apparent that compromise between the North and South was hopeless, Wood advocated for an extreme measure; he suggested that New York City should secede from the Union and become an entirely independent entity. On January 6, 1861, Wood appeared before the city Common Council and presented his radical plan. His argument was based on the notion that because the city of New York depended heavily on the Southern economy, the council must take action to protect the city's interests: "With our aggrieved brethren of the Slave States, we have friendly relations and a common sympathy. . . . While other portions of the our State have unfortunately been imbued with the fanatical spirit which actuates a portion of the people of New England, the city of New York has unfalteringly preserved the integrity of its principles of adherence to the compromises of the Constitution and the equal rights of the people of all the States." What is particularly striking about this excerpt is the way in which Wood openly sided with the view that the North was wrongly persecuting the South and that the rights of the individual states were being violated. He also suggested that New York City residents should continue to resist the "fanatical" abolitionist views of others in the region. As a result, Wood maintained that New York City must embrace a policy of separation in order to defend its financial holdings and political principles: "New York, as a *Free City,* may shed the only light and hope of a future reconstruction of our once blessed Confederacy."[45]

New York City ultimately remained in the Union; however, Wood did not temper his views during the war. He continued to oppose Republican efforts to increase the status of free Blacks or liberate anyone enslaved in the South. In particular, he objected to the 1862 Confiscation Act (widely considered as the predecessor of the Emancipation Proclamation) that provided freedom to all enslaved people in the Confederacy who took refuge behind Union lines and stated that Confederates who did not surrender within sixty days of the act's passage would be punished by having their slaves emancipated. Wood's view on confiscation is explained succinctly by his biographer:

> Confiscation had a logical extension, the divisive issue of ending slavery and its relationship to defining the status of freed blacks. . . . Based on racism, constitutional conservatism and his belief that freeing slaves foiled compromise, he fought against any alteration of the prewar South's social order. As a result, Wood did not accept the legitimacy of the 1862 Confiscation Act . . . [or] the Emancipation Proclamation, and vehemently opposed anything that might create black equality.[46]

Wood's political perspectives opposing Black equality became even more virulent during the war, after his brother became the publisher of the *New York Daily News.* The paper soon became the Wood brothers' mouthpiece. In June and July 1863, the paper regularly spewed racist propaganda against the war and the draft.

In fact, the Wood brothers were ultimately blamed for instigating the 1863 draft riots that decimated Black institutions and killed and tortured hundreds of Black people.[47]

Late in 1863, Fernando Wood was elected to the House of Representatives where he unilaterally opposed all legislation designed to advance the cause of Black people. He began by voting against the Thirteenth Amendment outlawing slavery because, as he argued on the floor of Congress, "'the Almighty has fixed the distinction of the races; the Almighty has made the black man inferior, and, sir, by no legislation, by no partisan success, by no military power, can you wipe out this distinction.'" He continued on his anti-Black rampage by voting against numerous other bills, including homesteads for emancipated Blacks and equal pay and treatment for Black troops. He even attempted to prevent Montana from becoming a state because it allowed Black voting. His final act of racial injustice was to deliver an "emotional speech" in defense of the Ku Klux Klan, arguing that it should not be prevented from its terror campaigns in the South.[48]

To say that Fernando Wood opposed Black advancement, voting rights, and equality would be an understatement of monumental significance, and there should be no doubt that his racist views influenced his desire to remove Seneca Village. As a result, in the ultimate act of racism and financial self-interest, Mayor Fernando Wood evoked the power of eminent domain and seized the land Seneca Village occupied. Initially passed in 1853, the decision became final in July 1855, and Seneca Village officially became the property of the city. According to the rule of eminent domain, the city had the right to deprive citizens of their land if it could be established that "the public good demands taking private property."[49] Yet in an effort to gain popular support, Central Park supporters still launched a propaganda campaign against Seneca Village to validate their actions. In its annual reports, the Central Park Board of Commissioners described Seneca Village in highly negative terms, arguing that "a suburb more filthy, squalid, and disgusting can hardly be imagined." The board further suggested that most residents were engaged in illegal activities and living in wretched conditions.[50] Historians of Central Park perpetuated these notions of Seneca Village and continued the myth that the community was simply a gathering of squatters and thieves.[51] However what the Board of Commissioners and future scholars failed to note, was that such descriptions were actually in reference to the "southern portion of the site" not the community of Seneca Village.[52] Seneca Village was, contrary to popular belief, a beautiful community composed primarily of families. Even one newspaper had to concede that the area occupied by Black people was a "pleasing" and "neat" settlement.[53]

Regardless of the reality of Seneca Village, the propaganda was enough to justify the seizure of the land and the removal of its occupants. By 1855, the Common Council began the process of destroying Seneca Village and ultimately assumed control of over 7,500 plots of land in upper Manhattan. There were delays along the way, because there was one stipulation to the law of eminent domain that allowed Seneca Villagers to remonstrate against their treatment. The city was bound to compensate landowners for the value of their land, but unfortunately for Seneca Villagers, the city was allowed to determine its own price for the land. This rule gave the city the upper hand, but Seneca Villagers had the right to protest the city's assessment.[54] In the initial appraisal, the city announced that it would pay just over $1 million for the land it had taken. This figure was clearly unfair, because the *New York Sun* newspaper had reported in 1851 that the land in that ward was valued at nearly $7 million.[55]

As a result, contrary to the popular notion that Seneca Villagers did not oppose their expulsion, the community organized and bombarded the Common Council with petitions appealing to the city government to reverse its decision.[56] Apparently, the petitioners fell into two general categories: those who did not want to surrender their property, and those who thought that they deserved more money for their property.[57] Andrew Williams, the original resident of Seneca Village, was among the petitioners who argued that the city was not paying a reasonable amount for his property because the city offered $2,335 and he knew that it was valued at over $4,000.[58] It is unknown what individual compromises the city eventually made with Andrew Williams or other Seneca Villagers, but the Common Council ultimately paid over $5 million for the entire ward above Forty-second Street.

Seneca Villagers were not sufficiently reimbursed for the loss of their property. Even if they had received a cash payment commensurate with the value of their land, how could money replace the community they had labored to build? For the residents, Seneca Village was a symbol of their sustained efforts to create a place for themselves and their people. To Black New Yorkers throughout the city, it was an icon of their creativity and the longevity of their social, economic, and political progress. Its destruction must have been devastating to the residents and the entire Black community. Yet, regardless of what the community meant to Black New Yorkers, Seneca Village was slated for destruction and residents were told to vacate the premises in February 1856.[59]

Significantly, however, despite the Common Council's proclamations, many Seneca Villagers stubbornly refused to leave. Apparently aware that their removal was the result of a conspiracy, some Black residents remained in their homes. According to the *New York Times*, the police had attempted to remove them but they had been unable to convince the residents to abandon their community: "The policeman find it difficult to persuade them out of the idea which has possessed their simple minds, that the sole object of the authorities in making the Park is to procure their expulsion from the homes which they occupy."[60] Although the city newspaper condescendingly accused the Seneca Villagers of having "simple minds," the residents were clearly far more astute than anyone guessed. Only through hindsight, can we now see that the Black community was correct; the decimation of Seneca Village was the result of a plot to undermine the potential of the Black population and satisfy men such as Fernando Wood.

Although Seneca Villagers had amazing insight, this gift was not enough to save their community. In August 1857, another announcement was released demanding that they abandon their homes immediately.[61] For those remaining few who did not comply, the police violently removed them in the following month. As the *New York Daily Tribune* reported nearly a decade later, the raid upon Seneca Village could "not be forgotten . . . many a brilliant and stirring fight was had during the campaign. But the supremacy of the law was upheld by the policeman's bludgeons."[62]

The final battle to save Seneca Village was long and bloody, but ultimately concluded in a devastating loss for the Black community. Despite their determination to remain and continue the project they had commenced, Seneca Villagers were ultimately forced from their community. One can only imagine the scene as these Black pioneers left their homes, schools, churches, and cemeteries, suddenly adrift without a community. For three decades, Seneca Village had served as a beacon of hope to free Blacks throughout the city, but, through an act of racism and greed, it was unjustly and violently extinguished.

"STILL MARCHING ON . . ."

When a colleague reviewed an early draft of this work he astutely noted that the opening passage of this book is inspiring and hopeful, but the closing scenes of this story are painful, disturbing, and devastating.[1] True, the 1850s proved to be a time of great disappointment and frustration for Black New Yorkers; the denial of suffrage, growing racial discrimination, challenges within the abolitionist movement, and the destruction of Seneca Village might have convinced activists that all hope was lost. Indeed, the mood on the eve of the Civil War hardly embodied the slogan "onward forever" that had been born out the struggle for unrestricted suffrage in the 1840s. Instead, the feeling was desperate as the recognition descended upon Black leaders that America's unrelenting racism and intolerance had stymied their best efforts.

Worse, although some Black New Yorkers had been hopeful that a Northern victory in the Civil War would result in the total abolition of slavery, they could not have imagined the horror that was about to be unleashed against them. Not only were Black men initially banned from enlisting in the Union army, but, in 1863, Northern opposition to the war and the imposition of the draft led to one of the bloodiest race riots in Northern history. The epicenter, of course, was the heart of New York City's Black community. Before the five-day reign of terror subsided, angry White mobs had lynched eleven Black men; tortured countless men, women, and children; torched Black homes and institutions; and chased hundreds of Black folks from the city.[2]

Yet despite the obstacles, frustrations, and impediments, we should not be too hasty to assume that the Black community was beaten. On the contrary, reflecting the tenacity that they had demonstrated for decades, New York's Black activists remained committed to the notion of "onward forever" and were convinced that their vision of freedom and full equality would eventually be realized. For, in the final analysis, the meaning of "onward forever" did not imply immediate success or victory. Rather it acknowledged the power of a protracted struggle, an ongoing commitment to persistently pursue their goals. Recall that the entire context to the notion of "onward forever" stated, "we are men, and men with a determined spirit to go on to victory; no favors, or frowns, or obstacles of any kind are to deter or awe us, until our object be gained . . . our motto, with all of us, should be 'onward and onward forever' . . . until our object be accomplished."[3] It is significant that these activists recognized that success would not be immediate, nor would the journey be free of conflict and setbacks. With full knowledge that their efforts would be fraught with challenges, Black New Yorkers still agreed that the struggle would continue until victory was theirs.

Perhaps the most powerful message of Black perseverance came on February 12, 1865, when one of New York's most prominent sons appeared before the House of Representatives and became the first person of African descent to address members of Congress. On that monumental occasion, Henry Highland Garnet delivered an impassioned sermon denouncing slavery and reflecting the hopes and dreams of his people on the dawn of national emancipation. Ironically, his childhood friend (and occasional nemesis) James McCune Smith later penned the introduction to this historic speech and, together, their words demonstrated a poignant and irrepressible spirit. Although deeply aware that their dreams would not be realized rapidly, they refused to relinquish the fight.

Dr. James McCune Smith, in his moving introduction to Garnet's address, reflected on his memories of Emancipation Day in New York City in 1827. Although he wrote eloquently of the joy, enthusiasm, jubilance, and pride in their African heritage on that day, Smith's most compelling message lay in his unwavering faith that Black people would ultimately triumph against their enemies. In his closing remarks about Emancipation Day, Smith described the young men who became consumed by the "grand procession of liberty": men who, even after the passage of time, remained unshaken in their commitment to freedom and equality despite any and all obstacles. As he poetically reflected, their procession toward freedom "through perils oft, and dangers oft, through the gloom of midnight, dark and seemingly hopeless, dark and seemingly rayless, but now, through God's blessing, opening up to the joyful light of day, is still *marching on*."[4]

As evidence of the Black community's unyielding struggle for justice and equality, Smith shared an impassioned reminiscence of the 1863 draft riots; a time when it seemed "the hand of every man was lifted against us." Smith noted that Black New Yorkers refused to relinquish hope even though the tried and true friends of the race had abandoned them: "Our professed friends, pale with affright, either gave up our cause as hopeless, or shudderingly shut their eyes . . . to avoid the coming shedding of blood." In their most dismal hour, there were men such as Henry Highland Garnet "who neither cowered nor flinched" but, instead, raised their voices like a "trumpet's call" and rushed into battle. Rather than succumb to defeat, the Black community galvanized its forces and redoubled its efforts. Even after the frightening outbreak of violence, Black New Yorkers still flaunted their support for the war they prayed would free their people and commenced a movement among Black men to "take up arms" on behalf of the Union. Indeed, as Smith recalled with pride, only seven months after the destructive pogrom, Black Union soldiers were celebrated in those same streets: "To have been mobbed, hunted down, beaten to death, hung to the lamp-posts or trees, burned, their dwellings sacked and destroyed, their orphan children turned homeless from their comfortable shelter which was destroyed by fire, and then, within a few months to be cheered along the same streets, are occurrences whose happening put ordinary miracles in the shade; the first, more hideous than hell, the last one which might be, and was, smiled on by heaven." For Smith, such triumphant moments convinced him that all hope was not lost and that victory could still follow devastating assaults.[5]

Similar concepts of endurance, perseverance, and resilience also surfaced in Henry Highland Garnet's eloquent address to Congress. Though his sermon primarily spoke of slavery's horrors, his closing remarks were particularly revealing about Black activists' continuing dedication to justice. Garnet boldly declared that demands for freedom and equality would not simply end with legal emancipation. Instead, he argued, the push for justice would only cease when inequality had been erased; racial discrimination had been removed; and all men had gained equal suffrage rights. For Garnet, true freedom would only be attained, "when emancipation shall be followed by enfranchisement . . . [when there is] no more trouble concerning the black man and his rights than there is in regard to other citizens . . . [and] when in every respect, he shall be equal before the law, and shall be left to make his own way in the social walks of life."[6] Thus, the abolition of slavery did not mean the end of the struggle. Garnet and other Black activists had seen the damage the evils of racism caused, and they remained committed to fight until the last remnants of oppression and injustice had been expunged from America. Perhaps most importantly, despite the challenges that lay ahead, it was a battle they were determined to win.

Garnet ended his remarks on that auspicious occasion with a plea, an echo of the slogan from the 1840s that adorns the preface to this book: "The nation has begun its exodus from worse than Egyptian bondage; and I beseech you that you say to the people, 'that they go forward.'"[7] These words merged beautifully with the message that emanated from the suffrage conventions. It was a call to action for Black folks to "go forward" and march "onward forever" until their goals were accomplished.

NOTES

Preface

The epigraph for the preface is from *Colored American*, September 4, 1841.

1. William Hamilton, "An Oration on the Abolition of the Slave Trade, Delivered in the Episcopal Asbury African Church, in Elizabeth St., New York, January 2, 1815. By William Hamilton, a Descendant of Africa" in *Early Negro Writing, 1760–1837*, ed. Dorothy Porter, (Baltimore: Black Classic Press, 1995), 392.

2. *Colored American*, December 19, 1840; Philip S. Foner and George E. Walker, *Proceedings of the Black State Conventions, 1840–1865* (Philadelphia: Temple University Press, 1979), 21–22.

3. Black activist Peter Williams Jr. used the term "defective" freedom during a speech in 1830. See: Peter Williams Jr., "A Discourse Delivered in St. Philip's Church, for the Benefit of the Coloured Community of Wilberforce in Upper Canada, on the Fourth of July, 1830," in *Early Negro Writing*, 296.

4. Leon Litwack, *North of Slavery: The Negro in the Free States, 1790–1860* (Chicago: University of Chicago Press, 1965); James Horton and Lois E. Horton, *Black Bostonians: Family Life and Community Struggle in the Antebellum North* (New York: Holmes and Meier Publishers, 1979); Gary Nash, *Forging Freedom: The Formation of Philadelphia's Black Community, 1720–1840* (Cambridge: Harvard University Press, 1988); Julie Winch, *Philadelphia's Black Elite: Activism, Accommodation, and the Struggle for Autonomy, 1787–1848* (Philadelphia: Temple University Press, 1988); James Horton and Lois E. Horton, *In Hope of Liberty: Culture, Community and Protest among Northern Free Blacks, 1700–1860* (New York: Oxford University Press, 1997); Patrick Joseph Rael, *Black Identity and Black Protest in the Antebellum North* (Chapel Hill: University of North Carolina Press, 2002).

5. Rael, *Black Identity and Black Protest*, 8–9, 119–20.

6. Ibid., 87.

7. Shane White, *Somewhat More Independent: The End of Slavery in New York City, 1770–1810* (Athens: University of Georgia Press, 1991). Although Shane White's article, "'It Was a Proud Day': African Americans, Festivals and Parades in the North, 1741–1834," included the antebellum era, there has still been a need for a full monograph that examines the Black community after legal emancipation. For his article, see *Journal of American History* 81, no. 1 (June 1983): 13–50.

8. Rhoda Golden Freeman, *The Free Negro in New York City in the Era Before the Civil War* (New York: Garland Publishing, 1994); George E. Walker, *The Afro-American in New York City, 1827–1860, Studies in African American History and Culture* (New York: Garland Publishing, 1993). These works were originally written as dissertations in 1966 and 1975, respectively. For Freeman's discussion on political consciousness and African culture, see R. Freeman, *The Free Negro in New York City*, xiv, 59.

9. Graham Russell Hodges, *Root and Branch: African Americans in New York and East Jersey, 1613–1863* (Chapel Hill: University of North Carolina Press, 1999); Leslie Maria Harris, *In the Shadow of Slavery: African Americans in New York City, 1626–1863* (Chicago: University of Chicago Press, 2003).

10. Craig Steven Wilder, *In the Company of Black Men: The African Influence on African American Culture in New York City* (New York: New York University Press, 2001).

11. This definition of community is drawn, in part, from Margaret Washington Creel's description of community in *"A Peculiar People": Slave Religion and Community-Culture among the Gullahs* (New York: New York University Press, 1988), 1–2.

12. Sterling Stuckey, *Slave Culture: Nationalist Theory and the Foundations of Black America* (New York: Oxford University Press, 1987). Stuckey opened the discussion about the influence of African culture in New York when he wrote, "as late as the 1820s, there were still thousands of African-born blacks in [New York] state, which guaranteed the presence of African values there, as elsewhere in the North" (ibid., 141).

13. For scholars who examine the early national and antebellum eras, a portion of the debate about the definition of Black Nationalism centers on the question of whether the establishment of an independent nation-state is a requirement for a movement to be considered nationalistic. Wilson Moses argues that early Black Nationalism's central tenet was "the creation of an autonomous black nation-state, with definite geographical boundaries—usually in Africa." I maintain, however, that although an independent country (such as Haiti or Liberia) was sometimes part of the Black Nationalist agenda in the antebellum era, there were also examples of nationalistic efforts that did not include such goals. Indeed, my research reveals that activists who elected not to emigrate used their sense of a common racial identity to build a "nation within a nation" in the United States. For more discussion on Black Nationalism, see Wilson Jeremiah Moses, ed., *Classical Black Nationalism: From the American Revolution to Marcus Garvey* (New York: New York University Press, 1996); Sterling Stuckey, *The Ideological Origins of Black Nationalism* (Boston: Beacon Press, 1972); E. U. Essien-Udom, *Black Nationalism: A Search for Identity in America* (Chicago: University of Chicago Press, 1962); John H. Bracey Jr., August Meier, and Elliott Rudwick, eds., *Free Blacks in America, 1800–1860* (Belmont, Calif.: Wadsworth Publishing Company, 1971).

14. Moses, *Classical Black Nationalism*, 2; Stuckey, *The Ideological Origins of Black Nationalism*, 6.

15. Wilder, *In the Company of Black Men*, 156.

16. Hereafter referred to as the African Society. This association flourished for over 160 years and did not die out until 1945. For more on the decline of the African Society, see ibid., 181–97. Although Craig Wilder argues that the African Society and the African Society for Mutual Relief were two distinct organizations, he admits that renowned historian Arthur Schomburg maintained that the African Society was the "parent" of the African Society for Mutual Relief. I concur with Schomburg and further suggest that the African Society for Mutual Relief was a reorganized and redesigned version of the original. For Wilder's argument, see ibid., 52.

17. There is, perhaps, a potential connection between Black New Yorkers' struggle to reconcile African identity with American citizenship and scholar W. E. B. Du Bois's concept of "double-consciousness." Although Du Bois was writing at the turn of the twentieth century, there is a compelling parallel between his description of Black identity in the postbellum South and the crisis free Black New Yorkers faced in the early nineteenth

century. Du Bois explained, "It is a peculiar sensation, this double-consciousness, this sense of always looking at one's self through the eyes of others, of measuring one's soul by the tape of a world that looks on in amused contempt and pity. One ever feels his two-ness—an American, a Negro; two thoughts, two reconciled strivings, two warring ideals in one dark body, whose dogged strength alone keeps it from being torn asunder." Throughout this study, as I chronicle debates within the Black leadership over culture, identity, and American citizenship, readers may see echoes of Du Bois's philosophy. However, I am hesitant to apply Du Bois's ideas too extensively in my work, because I do not want to extend the notion of double-consciousness beyond its original purpose. In my mind, Du Bois was articulating a particular experience in a specific historical moment. Yet perhaps future scholars will pick up where I have left off and examine these issues in more detail. For the complete context of Du Bois's discussion of double-consciousness, see W. E. B. Du Bois, *The Souls of Black Folk* (1903; repr., New York: Dover Publications, 1994), 1–3.

18. Although the first Black effort toward national organizing, the Colored Convention movement, was initially created to discuss the emigration question, few studies have adequately explored or understood the importance of emigration debates among Black leaders. Important exceptions to this historiographical gap include Howard Holman Bell, ed., *Minutes of the Proceedings of the National Negro Conventions, 1830–1864* (New York: Arno Press and the New York Times, 1969); Howard Holman Bell, ed., *A Survey of the Negro Convention Movement, 1830–1864* (New York: Arno Press and the New York Times, 1969); William Cheek and Aimee Lee Cheek, *John Mercer Langston and the Fight for Black Freedom, 1829–1865* (Urbana: University of Illinois Press, 1989); and Floyd J. Miller, *The Search for a Black Nationality: Black Emigration and Colonization, 1787–1863* (Urbana: University of Illinois Press, 1975). Still, none of these works explicitly examine Black New Yorkers and the issue of why New York activists often dramatically altered their views in different times. Floyd Miller, for example, wrote an excellent study on emigration, but focused primarily on movements in Boston, Rhode Island, and Philadelphia. In addition, those studies that focus on Black New York have argued that emigration was unilaterally rejected. In Rhoda Golden Freeman's second chapter entitled, "'This Country Our Only Home': Colonization Rejected," she argued that Blacks had no connection to Africa and refused to emigrate. Although Freeman mentions that some New Yorkers immigrated to Haiti, she provides no context for this movement and depicts it as an anomaly. R. Freeman, *The Free Negro in New York City*, 21–23. Similarly, George Walker documented Black opposition to colonization in the 1850s without mentioning the leadership's earlier commitment to the emigration movement. Walker, *The Afro-American in New York City*, 149–61. My work seeks to refute Freeman's and Walker's conclusions and contribute to Miller's study by exploring the specific nature of emigrationist thought in New York City.

19. Nash, *Forging Freedom*, 79.

20. For the purposes of this study, I use Wilson Moses's definition of Pan-Africanism: "the idea that Africans everywhere should work together for their mutual benefit and for the uplift of the mother continent." Moses, *Classical Black Nationalism*, 2.

21. As Floyd Miller indicated, it is crucial to carefully differentiate between colonization and emigration. Although colonization was largely dominated by Whites and focused on removing Black people from the United States, emigration was initiated by Blacks with the goal of gaining equality and citizenship elsewhere in the African diaspora. I have

attempted, throughout this work, to support and uphold this delineation between these movements. For more, see F. J. Miller, *The Search for a Black Nationality*, vii.

22. Black activist David Ruggles used the phrase "practical abolition" to describe the Black community's efforts to protect and defend fugitives in 1837. New York Committee of Vigilance, *First Annual Report*, 3.

23. The New York Constitution of 1777 guaranteed universal male suffrage and extended voting rights to the small free Black population. However, reflecting fears of Black political power, New York State passed a voting qualification law in 1821 that required free Blacks to reside in the state for three years and own $250 in property in order to vote. As a result, property ownership became the key to voting privileges and political enfranchisement. Walker, *The Afro-American in New York City*, 112–15.

Chapter 1: "Men and Women Who Would Be Free"

The epigraphs to chapter 1 are from John J. Zuille, *Historical Sketch of the New York African Society for Mutual Relief* (New York: n.p., 1892–1893), 4; Henry Sipkins, "An Oration on the Abolition of the Slave Trade; Delivered in the African Church; in the City of New York, January 2, 1809," in *Early Negro Writing*, 373; Joseph Sidney, "An Oration, Commemorative of the Abolition of the Slave Trade in the United States; Delivered Before the Wilberforce Philanthropic Association, in the City of New York, on the Second of January, 1809," in *Early Negro Writing*, 362.

1. Jupiter Hammon was the first published Black poet in the United States. Born on October 17, 1711, on the Lloyd Plantation in Long Island, New York, Hammon lived his entire life in bondage. Yet at the age of forty-nine, he wrote and published his first piece of literature. By the end of his life, he had published two essays, four poems, and a sermon. According to scholar Sondra O'Neale, there are several other essays and sermons by Jupiter Hammon that have never been located. For more on Jupiter Hammon, see Sondra A. O'Neale, *Jupiter Hammon and the Biblical Beginnings of African American Literature* (Metuchen, N.J.: Scarecrow Press, 1993).

2. In an effort to narrow the scope of this work, I will not focus on the conditions of slavery or the experiences of those held in bondage in New York City during the early national era. For an examination of slavery in New York City, see Edgar J. McManus, *A History of Slavery in New York* (Syracuse, N.Y.: Syracuse University Press, 1966); Shane White, *Somewhat More Independent*; L. M. Harris, *In the Shadow of Slavery*; Thelma Wills Foote, *Black and White Manhattan: The History of Racial Formation in Colonial New York City* (Oxford: Oxford University Press, 2004).

3. Jupiter Hammon, "An Address to the Negroes in the State of New York" in *Early Negro Writing*, 322–23. Craig Wilder also mentions this speech in his study. However, he is concerned with the religious nature of Hammon's speech, and I am interested in Hammon's message to the Black community members regarding their conduct as free people. See Wilder, *In the Company of Black Men*, 38, 64–69.

4. Peter Williams Jr., "An Oration on the Abolition of the Slave Trade, Delivered in the African Church in the City of New York, January 1, 1808," in *Early Negro Writing*, 345. James McCune Smith also noted, in retrospect, that people during this era had "rejoiced in their nationality, and hesitated not to call each other 'Africans,' or 'descendants of Africa.'" Henry Highland Garnet, *A Memorial Discourse Delivered in the Hall of the*

House of Representatives, Washington City, D.C., on Sabbath, February 12, 1865. With an Introduction by James McCune Smith, M.D.* (Philadelphia: J. M. Wilson, 1865), 24.

5. By 1790, there were only 1,036 free Black people in New York City, comprising about one-third of the overall Black population. L. M. Harris, *In the Shadow of Slavery,* 56.

6. L. M. Harris, *In the Shadow of Slavery,* 52; G. R. Hodges, *Root and Branch,* 141–46.

7. For more on Northern emancipation, see: Arthur Zilversmit, *The First Emancipation: The Abolition of Slavery in the North* (Chicago: University of Chicago Press, 1967); McManus, *History of Negro Slavery in New York,* 151–52; Samuel Sewall, *The Selling of Joseph* (Boston: n.p., 1700); Lawrence Towner, "The Sewall–Suffin Dialogue on Slavery," *William and Mary Quarterly* 21, no. 1 (January 1964): 40–52.

8. New York State Legislature, Assembly, *Journal of the Assembly, 1785,* 14; L. M. Harris, *In the Shadow of Slavery,* 56–61.

9. For a useful explanation of the 1799 Gradual Emancipation law, see Vivienne L. Kruger, "Born to Run: The Slave Family in Early New York, 1626–1827" (PhD diss., Columbia University, 1985), 820. For an excellent discussion of the complete process of emancipation in New York City, see L. M. Harris, *In the Shadow of Slavery,* 48–63, 70–71.

10. Gary Nash and Jean Soderlund used this term to describe the process of emancipation in Pennsylvania in *Freedom by Degrees: Emancipation in Pennsylvania and Its Aftermath* (London: Oxford University Press, 1991).

11. Kruger, "Born to Run," 820; Zilversmit, *First Emancipation,* 199.

12. Of the 8,916 Black people in New York City in 1810, only 1,446 remained enslaved. Between 1790 and 1810, the freed population grew astronomically from 1,036 to 7,470.

13. For an insightful discussion on the challenges facing Black New Yorkers during this era, see L. M. Harris, *In the Shadow of Slavery,* 72–120.

14. Many of those who comprised the Black leadership during this era had learned skills as enslaved people that they were able to translate into economic success as free people. As a result, most leaders were comparatively wealthy and, therefore, had the time and resources to commit to race uplift. For example, John Teasman, because of his education, found work as a teacher and principal. Apprenticeships likewise helped William Hamilton Sr. and Prince Loveridge, who became a skilled carpenter and a boot maker, respectively. Prior to gaining his freedom, Peter Williams Sr. worked for a tobacco manufacturer. Once free, Williams operated one of the most successful tobacco manufactories in New York City and achieved fame for being the first to use steam power to operate the machines. Similarly, Boston Crummell and Moses Blue drew upon their experiences to become the first Black oyster dealers in New York City. Zuille, *Historical Sketch,* 22; J. B. Wakeley, *Lost Chapters Recovered from the Early Years of American Methodism* (New York: Carlton & Porter, 1858), 431. Leslie Harris also mentions some of the African Society members' occupations, *In the Shadow of Slavery,* 120.

15. Robert Farris Thompson, *Flash of the Spirit: African and Afro-American Art and Philosophy* (New York: Random House, 1983), 132; Robert Farris Thompson and Joseph Cornet, *The Four Moments of the Sun: Kongo Art in Two Worlds* (New Haven, Conn.: Eastern Press, 1981), 27.

16. Spencer Harrington, "Bones and Bureaucrats: New York's Great Cemetery Imbroglio" in *Archaeological Ethics,* ed. Karen D. Vitelli (Walnut Creek, Calif.: AltaMira Press, 1996), 232.

17. R. F. Thompson, *Flash of the Spirit,* 135; Edna Greene Medford, ed., *The African Burial Ground: History Final Report,* The African Burial Ground Project, Howard University,

Washington, D.C., for the United States General Services Administration Northeast and Caribbean Region, November 2004, 184.

18. Michael L. Blakey, "The New York African Burial Ground Project: An Examination of Enslaved Lives, A Construction of Ancestral Ties," *Transforming Anthropology* 7: 53–58; Blakey, "The Study of New York's African Burial Ground: Biocultural and Engaged" in *African Roots/American Cultures: Africa in the Creation of the Americas,* ed. Sheila S. Walker (New York: Rowman and Littlefield Publishers, 2001), 222–31; Warren R. Perry, Jean Howson, and Barbara A. Bianco, eds., *New York African Burial Ground Archaeology Final Report,* prepared by Howard University, Washington, D.C., for the United States General Services Administration Northeastern and Caribbean Region, February 2006, vol. 1, 222, 274. For more information on the African cultural and spiritual presence in the burial ground, see Cheryl LaRoche, "Beads from the African Burial Ground, New York City: A Preliminary Assessment," *Beads: Journal of the Society of Bead Researchers* 6: 3–20; Jerome Handler, "A Prone Burial from a Plantation Slave Cemetery in Barbadoes, West Indies: Possible Evidence for an African-Type Witch or Other Negatively Viewed Person," *Historical Archaeology* 30: 76–86; Andrea Frohne, "Commemorating the African Burial Ground in New York City: Spirituality of Space in Contemporary Art Works," *Ijele: Art eJournal of the African World* 1, no. 1 (2000); E. Kofi Agorsah, "Archaeology and Resistance History in the Caribbean," *African Archaeological Review* 11 (1993): 175–95.

19. Blakey, "The New York African Burial Ground Project," 53; Perry, Howson, and Bianco, eds., *New York African Burial Ground Archaeology Final Report,* vol. 1, 294. The use of coffins seems to be the result of European influence, because scholars such as Christopher DeCorse have argued that coffin usage did not regularly appear in West Africa until after the 1870s. Christopher DeCorse, *An Archaeology of Elmina: Africans and Europeans on the Gold Coast* (Washington, D.C.: Smithsonian Institution Press, 2001), 100–101; Ross W. Jamieson, "Material Culture and Social Death: African-American Burial Practices," *Historical Archaeology* 29: 53; Agorsah, "Archaeology and Resistance History," 183. Although coffins were reserved for the wealthy in England until the late seventeenth century, English settlers in the Americas used coffins more regularly and perhaps influenced the Black community to use them as well. Yet it is striking that, according to the African Burial Ground's final archaeology report, over 91 percent of the deceased were buried in coffins. Perry, Howson, and Bianco, eds., *New York African Burial Ground Archaeology Final Report,* vol. 1, 250. For more on the use of coffins in England and the United States, see David Cressy, *Birth, Marriage, and Death: Ritual, Religion, and the Lifecycle in Tudor and Stuart England* (New York: Oxford University Press, 1997), 421–55; Ann Fairfax Withington, *Toward a More Perfect Union: Virtue and the Formation of American Republics* (New York: Oxford University Press, 1991), 92–143.

20. Joyce Hansen and Gary McGowan, *Breaking Ground, Breaking Silence: The Story of New York's African Burial Ground* (New York: Henry Holt and Company, 1998), 9, 13; Terrence W. Epperson, "The Politics of 'Race' and Cultural Identity at the African Burial Ground Excavations, New York City," *World Archaeological Bulletin* 7: 110–11. It should be noted that Epperson suggests shrouding was strictly a European Christian practice. For a detailed discussion on West African burial rites, see Medford, *African Burial Ground,* 175–79. For more on shrouding by Whites in England and the United States, see Cressy, *Birth, Marriage, and Death,* 429–35; Withington, *Toward a More Perfect Union,* 101–7. For shrouding in the Gold Coast, see Christopher DeCorse, "Culture, Contact, Continuity and Change on the Gold Coast, A.D. 1400–1900" *African Archaeological Review* 10 (1992): 163–96.

21. Epperson, "Politics of Race," 109–10; Terrence W. Epperson, "The Contested Commons: Archaeologies of Race, Repression, and Resistance in New York City," in *Historical Archaeologies of Capitalism,* ed. Mark P. Leone and Parker B. Potter Jr. (New York: Plenum Press, 1999), 82.

22. David T. Valentine, "History of Broadway," *Manual of the Common Council of New York* (New York: D. T. Valentine, 1865), 567; Jamieson, "Material Culture and Social Death," 47; Hansen and McGowan, *Breaking Ground,* 36–37; Sterling Stuckey, "African Spirituality and Cultural Practice in Colonial New York, 1700–1770," in *Inequality in Early America,* ed. Carla Pestana and Sharon Salinger (Hanover, N.H.: Dartmouth College Press, 1999), 181; Frohne, "Commemorating the African Burial Ground in New York City," 2–3.

23. New York City Common Council, *Minutes of the Common Council of the City of New York, 1784–1831* (New York: Published by the City of New York, 1917), iv, 88.

24. Hansen and McGowan, *Breaking Ground,* 52–53, 66, 70.

25. Epperson, "The Contested Commons," 94–96.

26. There has been a significant debate on the role and influence of African culture in Pinkster celebrations, primarily led by Sterling Stuckey and Shane White. My research has led me to support Stuckey's assessment of the strong African presence in Pinkster celebrations. Beyond Cooper's references to an African influence in Pinkster, Stuckey has compellingly argued that African music and dance shaped Pinkster celebrations. For example, Stuckey has written extensively about Pinkster in Albany where King Charley (who was originally from the Angola region) reigned over Pinkster and led the Toto dance accompanied by numerous other African cultural forms including drumming, music, language, song, and dance. Although less convinced of the extent of African influence, Patrick Rael agreed that although Pinkster began as a Dutch holiday, it soon became a "distinctly African American event." Rael, *Black Identity and Black Protest,* 57–58. For complete discussions on the African cultural influence in Pinkster, see Sterling Stuckey, *Going through the Storm: The Influence of African American Art in History* (New York: Oxford University Press, 1994), 53–80; Stuckey, "African Spirituality and Cultural Practice," 160–81.

27. James Fenimore Cooper, *Satanstoe, or the Littlepage Manuscripts: A Tale of the Colony* (1845; repr., New York: American Book Company, 1937), 60, 64–65; Epperson, "The Contested Commons," 82, 94–96.

28. Thomas F. De Voe, *The Market Book: A History of Public Markets of the City of New York* (New York: Augustus Kelley Publishers, 1970), 322, 344. "Breakdowns" were apparently a common dance form among enslaved Africans in the United States and were reported in Mississippi well into in the 1840s. Marshall Stearns and Jean Stearns, *Jazz Dance: The Story of American Vernacular Dance* (New York: Schirmer Books, 1968), 29. Sterling Stuckey, Leslie Harris, and Graham Hodges also mention dancing in these marketplaces. See Stuckey, "The Tambourine in Glory: African Culture and Melville's Art," in *The Cambridge Companion to Herman Melville,* ed. Robert S. Levine (New York: Cambridge University Press, 1998), 45–47; L. M. Harris, *In the Shadow of Slavery,* 69; G. R. Hodges, *Root and Branch,* 212–13. Stuckey also discusses the prevalence of marketplace dancing in Brooklyn in "African Spirituality and Cultural Practice," 164.

29. Stuckey, "African Spirituality and Cultural Practice," 163. For a complete discussion on the importance of dance as an African cultural retention, see Stearns and Stearns, *Jazz Dance,* 11–17, 25–32; Stuckey, *Going through the Storm,* 53–80; Stuckey, "The Tambourine in Glory," 37–64; Stuckey, "Christian Conversion and the Challenge of Dance" in *Choreo-*

graphing History, ed. Susan Leigh Foster (Bloomington: Indiana University Press, 1995), 54–66.

30. For a description of improvisation and African elements in African American vernacular dance, see Stearns and Stearns, *Jazz Dance,* 14–15.

31. Eileen Southern and Josephine Wright, *Images: Iconography of Music in African American Culture (1770s-1920s)* (New York: Garland Publishing, 2000), 26.

32. De Voe, *Market Book,* 344–45. There is also a possibility that the marketplaces served as a location for Black people to meet and secretly plot liberation strategies. One observer noted that a regular sight at the Oswego Market was an "ancient looking colored man" who went by the name "Coppie Gillie." Significantly, he was known to be "the last of that unfortunate company who were engaged in the Negro Plot of 1741-2." De Voe, *Market Book,* 335.

33. Stuckey, *Going through the Storm,* 70.

34. Carter G. Woodson, *The African Background Outlined, or Handbook for the Study of the Negro* (1936; repr., New York: Negro Universities Press, 1968), 169–70; Michael Gomez, *Exchanging Our Country Marks: The Transformation of African Identities in the Colonial and Antebellum South* (Chapel Hill: University of North Carolina Press, 1998), 94–102; Margaret Washington Creel, *"A Peculiar People,"* 2, 181–82.

35. Gomez, *Exchanging Our Country Marks,* 99–101; Washington Creel, *"A Peculiar People,"* 2, 52.

36. William Hamilton, "An Address to the New York African Society, for Mutual Relief, Delivered in the Universalist Church, January 2, 1809," in *Early Negro Writing,* 39.

37. The earliest information regarding a Black organization in the North was in Newport, Rhode Island, in 1780. Next was the African Society in New York City, and four years later, leaders in Philadelphia created the Free African Society for Mutual Assistance. Following in the footsteps of their brethren, Black Bostonians formed a mutual relief society in 1798 called the Sons of the African Society. It is not entirely clear when leaders in different cities began to work collectively, but free Blacks throughout the North were simultaneously organizing themselves as part of a race uplift strategy. For detailed information on each of these organizations, respectively, see Free African Union Society, *The Proceedings of the Free African Union Society and the African Benevolent Society, Newport Rhode Island, 1780-1824,* ed. William H. Robinson (Providence: The Urban League of Rhode Island, 1976); Winch, *Philadelphia's Black Elite;* Nash, *Forging Freedom;* Sons of the African Society, *Laws of the Sons of the African Society; Instituted at Boston, Anno Domini, 1798* (Boston: Printed for the Society, 1798); Wilder, *In the Company of Black Men,* 53.

38. Although there is scanty information regarding the earliest Black organizations in New York City, by 1792, newly freed Blacks had created at least two organizations: the Free African Society and the African Institution. It appears that between 1795 and 1808, the African Society attached the word "free" in front of its name. Perhaps this reflected the society's desire to emphasize its independence, new status, and right to citizenship as emancipated people. Regardless, the Free African Society and the African Institution were both benevolent organizations primarily dedicated to improving the conditions of the Black community. Peter Williams Jr. to Thomas Tucker, New York, June 10, 1816, Black Abolitionist Papers.

39. Walter N. Beekman, *Address by Walter N. Beekman, vice president, New York African Society for Mutual Relief* (Brooklyn: n.p., 1946), 2.

40. *New York Daily Advertiser,* February 16, 1788; Medford, *African Burial Ground,* 213.

41. De Voe, *Market Book,* 333; Epperson, "The Politics of 'Race,'" 112; Epperson, "The Contested Commons," 98–99.

42. New York City Common Council, *Minutes of the Common Council of the City of New York,* vol. 2 (New York: Published by the City of New York, 1917), 158–59. Graham Hodges also briefly mentions this petition in *Root and Branch,* 183. The allocation of burial ground to Africans is also mentioned in Spencer Harrington, "An African Cemetery in Manhattan," in *Eyewitness to Discovery: First-Person Accounts of More Than Fifty of the World's Greatest Archaeological Discoveries,* ed. Brian Fagan (New York: Oxford University Press, 1996), 326.

43. New York City Common Council, *Minutes of the Common Council of the City of New York,* vol. 2, 159. Although the Common Council granted their initial request and gave them sufficient funds to acquire the desired land located on Chrystie Street, the problem of adequate burial facilities persisted in the Black community well into the 1800s. In 1807, a group of White New Yorkers complained to city officials that Blacks were interring their dead in a vault inside the African Zion Church and the odor was becoming a public nuisance. Their decision to place their beloved deceased within the church reflects the importance Blacks placed upon protecting the spirits of their deceased community members. A Common Council committee investigated the issue and discovered that Blacks had run out of burial space in 1802 and had been interring approximately 150 persons in the vault annually. Thus, by the time of the protest against them, nearly 750 Blacks had been interred in the African Zion Church. Faced with the complaints of Whites, the Common Council granted additional land in Potter's Field one week later. New York City Common Council, *Minutes of the Common Council,* vol. 4, 522, 525.

44. For examples of early Black petitions, see Herbert Aptheker, ed., *A Documentary History of the Negro People in the United States: From the Colonial Times through the Civil War, vol. 1* (New York: Citadel Press, 1951), 1–16, 29–32, 39–45.

45. Many previous scholars dismissed the African Society as a "primitive" burial association and did not fully explore the larger significance of its political development. For examples of early depictions of the African Society as exclusively a burial society, see Leo H. Hirsch Jr., "The Negro and New York, 1783 to 1863," *Journal of Negro History* 16, no. 4 (October 1931): 439; John L. Rury, "Philanthropy, Self Help, and Social Control: The New York Manumission Society and Free Blacks, 1785–1810," *Phylon: The Atlanta University Review of Race and Culture* 46, no. 3 (1985): 238; Daniel Perlman, "Organizations of the Free Negro in New York City, 1800–1860," *Journal of Negro History* 56, no. 3 (July 1971): 181–97; Walker, *Afro-American in New York City,* 63–64; R. Freeman, *Free Negro in New York City,* 24–25; G. R. Hodges, *Root and Branch,* 199. Craig Wilder also notes this historiographical misinterpretation in *In the Company of Black Men,* 78.

46. Other leaders who participated in the initial split were George Collins, Francis Jacobs, William Brown, Abraham Thompson, June Scott, Samuel Pontier, and Thomas Miller. For more, see John Jamison Moore, *History of the African Methodist Episcopal Zion Church in America, Founded in 1796, in the City of New York* (York, Pa.: Teacher's Journal Office, 1884), 16; William J. Walls, *The African Methodist Episcopal Zion Church: Reality of the Black Church* (Charlotte, N.C.: A. M. E. Zion Publishing House, 1974). Craig Wilder also discusses the departure from the John St. Church in *In the Company of Black Men,*

44–49. According to Wilder, James Varick was born enslaved in 1768 near Newburgh, New York, and was brought to New York City by his master. During his time in New York City, Varick was trained as a shoemaker and converted to Methodism. Even while still enslaved, Varick served as the chaplain to the African Society for Mutual Relief. He finally gained his freedom on February 12, 1813, and later served as the pastor and bishop of Mother Zion Church. Wilder, *In the Company of Black Men*, 84–85.

47. J. J. Moore, *History of the African Methodist Episcopal Zion Church*, 15; Walls, *African Methodist Episcopal Zion Church*, 45; L. M. Harris, *In the Shadow of Slavery*, 84–85.

48. Peter Williams Sr. (1749–1823) was born into slavery on Beekman Street in New York City to George and Diana Williams, who had been enslaved in Africa and sold into bondage. Peter Williams Sr. was one of ten children born in the barn of his master, Mr. Boorite. As a young man, Williams married a free woman named Mary "Molly" Durham who was born in 1747 in the West Indies. Even after his marriage, Peter Williams Sr. was still enslaved and worked for a tobacconist, Mr. Aymar. Aymar taught Williams tobacco manufacturing, the trade that ultimately became his livelihood. During the Revolutionary War, Williams distinguished himself for service to the rebel cause; although he did not officially fight in the war, he saved the life of an American revolutionary by refusing to disclose his whereabouts. Even when threatened with death and offered gold in exchange for information, Williams protected Parson Chapman's safety. After the war, Williams's master, who was a loyalist, was forced to flee the country. For a while, Williams worked for another tobacconist, Mr. Milledollar, until he purchased his freedom. In 1783, Williams sold himself to the John St. Methodist Church as part of an arrangement to free himself; the church purchased Williams for £40 on June 10, 1783, and he agreed to pay the church back in installments. By November 4, 1785, Williams had fulfilled his obligation and was legally free. Shortly after obtaining his freedom, his son Peter Williams Jr. was born and, a few years later, Molly and Peter Sr. adopted a little girl named Mary. Peter Williams Sr. eventually opened his own tobacco manufactory located on Liberty Street. His business was extremely successful; he eventually owned his own house and store, as well as other property. In February 1823, Williams died at the age of seventy-four.

49. J. J. Moore, *History of the African Methodist Episcopal Zion Church*, 16–18; Walls, *African Methodist Episcopal Zion Church*, 48; Wakeley, *Lost Chapters*, 444; Jonathan Greenleaf, *A History of the Churches of All Denominations in the City of New York, from the First Settlement to the Year 1846* (New York: E. French, 1846), 321.

50. J. J. Moore, *History of the African Methodist Episcopal Zion Church*, 22–23; Walls, *African Methodist Episcopal Zion*, 50; Greenleaf, *History of the Churches*, 79–80, 240.

51. Peter Williams Jr. to Thomas Tucker, New York, June 10, 1816, Black Abolitionist Papers.

52. Hamilton, "An Address to the New York African Society," 39.

53. John L. Rury, "Education and Black Community Development in Antebellum New York City" (master's thesis, City University of New York, 1975), 5, 12; L. M. Harris, *In the Shadow of Slavery*, 64–65. The Manumission Society was formally called the New York Society for the Manumission of Slaves and Protection of Such of Them as Have Been or May Be Liberated. Significantly, this was the first organization to create a free school for children of any race.

54. Shane White developed a provocative critique of the Manumission Society, arguing that its members were not truly committed to abolition. Leslie Harris further maintained that the society hoped to manipulate the Black population into a permanent laboring

class. However, Arthur Zilversmit, Edgar McManus, and Rob Weston maintained that the society worked tirelessly to achieve the abolition of slavery using the method of gradualism. For more on the debate, see Zilversmit, *First Emancipation;* McManus, *History of Negro Slavery in New York;* L. M. Harris, *In the Shadow of Slavery,* 100–104; Rob Weston, "Alexander Hamilton and the Abolition of Slavery in New York," *Afro-Americans in New York Life and History* 18 (1994): 31–45.

55. New York Manumission Society Papers, vol. 4, 24, 87.

56. John Teasman was born enslaved in 1754 in New Jersey. Although nothing is known about his process of emancipation, he became active in education and Black rights upon his arrival in New York City. A charter member of the African Society for Mutual Relief, Teasman later became actively involved in Black Republican politics. Wilder, *In the Company of Black Men,* 125–26.

57. Robert J. Swan, "John Teasman: African American Educator and the Emergence of Community in Early Black New York City, 1787–1815," *Journal of the Early Republic* 12, no. 3 (1992): 335, 336, 338–39.

58. Ibid., 342; Rury, "Education and Black Community Development," 22.

59. Zuille, *Historical Sketch,* 49. The remaining members of the original African Society were William Hutson and James Parker. Surprisingly absent from the list was Isaac Fortune who had helped petition the Common Council for African American burial ground back in 1795. His name does not appear in any documents after the 1808 slave trade abolition commemoration, except in the Minutes of the Common Council requesting police protection in his neighborhood. New York City Common Council, *Minutes of the Common Council,* vol. 4, 309, 501. Craig Wilder and Robert Swan also discuss the founding of the African Society. Wilder, *In the Company of Black Men,* 83–84; Swan, "John Teasman," 346. For a full list of African Society members, see Zuille, *Historical Sketch,* 27–33.

60. Zuille, *Historical Sketch,* 4, 49, 55. The first officers selected were William Hamilton, president; Henry Sipkins, secretary; Adam Carman, assistant secretary; and Daniel Berry, treasurer.

61. Ibid., 52.

62. Although new financial and educational policies went into effect after 1838, the African Society continued to expel members for violations in moral conduct particularly if a member was found "spending his time in brothels, in gambling, or in tippling" (ibid., 3–4, 8, 11, 14).

63. For more on the Black working class's opinion of the Black middle class, see L. M. Harris, *In the Shadow of Slavery,* 174–76.

64. Craig Wilder offers a very useful chart that details the founding of various Black organizations during this period. Perhaps the only oversight is that he argues that the Wilberforce Philanthropic Association was not formed until 1812; however, existing speeches indicate that the organization had been established by 1809. Wilder, *In the Company of Black Men,* 74–76, 245.

65. Craig Wilder also notes the power of using the term "African" in organizational names. Ibid., 76.

66. On this point I disagree with Patrick Rael, who argued that the Black leadership's "cultural kinship with Africa based on institutional naming practices should not be overstated." He maintains that declining importation of people from the African continent mitigated the free Black community's connection to Africa, and Whites influenced their naming traditions. I believe that naming practices reflected a powerful African cultural

ethos and reflected the Black leadership's commitment to self-determination, autonomy, and their African heritage. For Rael's argument, see Rael, *Black Identity and Black Protest*, 87–89.

67. Peter Williams Jr. (1786–1840) was unique among his brethren, born a free man in New York City. His mother was a free woman from the West Indies and his father, a known activist in the Black community, had purchased his freedom about the time young Peter Jr. was born. As a child, Williams Jr. attended New York's African Free School and became an activist at a young age. In fact, he was only twenty-two when he was selected to give this address to honor the abolition of the slave trade. Peter Williams Jr. dedicated his life to the Black community and was particularly active on the issues of abolition and emigration. For more on Peter Williams Jr.'s political activism, see chapters 2, 3, and 4.

68. P. Williams, "An Oration on the Abolition of the Slave Trade," 346, 345. Shane White also briefly mentioned this celebration in an article published in 1994; however, he focuses on how the 1808 commemoration demonstrated Black people's willingness to celebrate freedom regardless of White people's opinion. Shane White, "'It Was A Proud Day,'" 38.

69. Ibid., 349–51.

70. Ibid., 352.

71. Ibid., 353. Graham Hodges also mentioned Peter Williams Jr.'s speech in *Root and Branch*, 188.

72. L. M. Harris, *In the Shadow of Slavery*, 90–92; Mitch Kachun, *Festivals of Freedom: Memory and Meaning in African American Emancipation Celebrations, 1808–1915* (Amherst: University of Massachusetts Press, 2003), 35–36. It is certainly possible that parading may have been a factor, because the Wilberforce Association declared, "every exertion has been made to fulfill the intentions of their constituents, to show their gratitude in the most public manner, for so great a blessing, and they cannot but lament that a division should exist, and indulge the flattering hope that all dissentions [*sic*] will cease." This passage does seem to suggest that the division in the community was connected to the question of how to properly "show their gratitude." Sidney, "An Oration, Commemorative of the Abolition of the Slave Trade," 363–64. However, there is a compelling contradiction in Kachun's explanation, because the Wilberforce Philanthropic Association *and* the African Society held parades on that day. If the fight was strictly about parading, then why did both organizations hold processions? Craig Wilder also mentions all three of these gatherings, although he does not speculate on the reasons for the division. Wilder, *In the Company of Black Men*, 92–96.

73. The early life of William Hamilton (1773–1836) remains something of mystery; he was even rumored to be the illegitimate son of the secretary of the treasury, Alexander Hamilton. Regardless, Hamilton soon gained training as a carpenter and spent most of his life as an activist. For more on William Hamilton, see chapters 2, 3, and 4. Hamilton died in New York City in 1836.

74. Hamilton, "An Address to the New York African Society," 35, 37, 40. Craig Wilder also includes a portion of this quote in *In the Company of Black Men*, 78.

75. Sipkins, "Oration on the Abolition of the Slave Trade," 367, 369, 371–73.

76. It may be more than coincidence that Joseph Sidney focused less upon Africa than did his predecessors. It seems significant that the Philanthropic Association named itself after William Wilberforce, a White abolitionist, rather than using "African" in its name. This decision may reflect a more conservative leaning among its membership, a possibility that is further strengthened by Sidney's other comments. Unfortunately, little else is

known about Joseph Sidney's life and his last public appearance seems to have occurred in 1814. For more, see chapter 2.

77. Sidney, "An Oration, Commemorative of the Abolition of the Slave Trade," 358–61. Most Manumission Society members and antislavery Whites affiliated themselves with the Federalist Party, a fact that most Black people recognized. L. M. Harris, *In the Shadow of Slavery*, 90–92. Additionally, as Edgar McManus argued, many Blacks supported the Federalist Party in an effort to thank White Federalists, such as John Jay, Alexander Hamilton, and Philip Schuyler, who had agitated against slavery. McManus, *History of Negro Slavery*, 186–87.

78. Sidney, "An Oration, Commemorative of the Abolition of the Slave Trade," 362.

79. Sterling Stuckey, *Slave Culture*, 142–44; Southern and Wright, *Images*, 28; Kachun, *Festivals of Freedom*, 22. Stuckey noted that these activities were found among African peoples throughout the West Indies and Canada as late as the 1850s. Shane White and Graham White also conceded that "northern blacks infused these events with their own cultural imperatives, creating something fresh." Shane White and Graham White, *Stylin': African American Expressive Culture from Its Beginnings to the Zoot Suit* (Ithaca, N.Y.: Cornell University Press, 1998), 101.

80. Stuckey, *Going through the Storm*, 55, 60–65, 74.

81. *New York Evening Post*, October 21, 1802; *New York Spectator*, October 23, 1802; Paul A. Gilje, *The Road to Mobocracy: Popular Disorder in New York City, 1763–1834* (Chapel Hill: University of North Carolina Press, 1987), 181–82; W. Jeffrey Bolster, *Black Jacks: African American Seamen in the Age of Sail* (Cambridge: Harvard University Press, 1997), 87–88.

82. Sidney, "An Oration, Commemorative of the Abolition of the Slave Trade," 363; Hamilton, "An Address to the New York African Society," 33.

83. L. M. Harris, *In the Shadow of Slavery*, 89. Leslie Harris, among others, focused on the political nature of parading and the ways in which parading demonstrated Black masculinity and assertions of political equality. Although I agree that parades were politically significant, I am equally interested in the cultural relevance of Black parades.

84. Stuckey, *Slave Culture*, 142.

Chapter 2: "To Leave the House of Bondage"

Epigraphs to chapter 2 are from Reverend William Miller, *A Sermon on the Abolition of the Slave Trade; Delivered in the African Church, New York, on the First of January, 1810* (New York: John C. Totten, 1810), 11; George Lawrence, "Oration on the Abolition of the Slave Trade, Delivered on the First Day of January, 1813, in the African Methodist Episcopal Church," 380; Haytian Emigration Society, *Address of the Board of Managers of the Haytian Emigration Society of Coloured People, to the Emigrants Intending to Sail to the Island of Hayti, in the Brig De Witt Clinton* (New York: Mahlon Day, 1824), 7.

1. There is little known about William Miller's life prior to his involvement in the establishment of the African Church. Despite his important role in New York City's Black community, the only other information about William Miller is a mention of his death in 1848. For more on his activism, see chapters 1, 3, 4, and the remainder of this chapter.

2. W. Miller, *Sermon on the Abolition of the Slave Trade*, 4, 6, 12.

3. Haytian Emigration Society, *Address of the Board of Managers*, 6.

4. Swan, "John Teasman," 353. The question of Black loyalty to the United States may have been a particularly touchy issue because many enslaved people sided with the British during the Revolutionary War in exchange for their freedom. In fact, an estimated ten thousand to twelve thousand Black people evacuated the United States with the British at the end of the Revolutionary War. This issue was particularly relevant in New York City, because the British occupied the city. As result, Black New Yorkers during the Revolutionary War chose sides strategically in an attempt to determine which group would best serve their interests. Thus, during the War of 1812, it was not clear if the Black community would ally with the British or with the United States. For more on Blacks in the Revolutionary War, see Sylvia R. Frey, *Water from the Rock: Black Resistance in a Revolutionary Age* (Princeton: Princeton University Press, 1991); G. R. Hodges, *Root and Branch,* 139–61.

5. *The Columbian,* April 25 and 26, 1814; Swan, "John Teasman," 353. For more on Black participation in the War of 1812, see Jack D. Foner, *Blacks and the Military in American History: A New Perspective* (New York: Praegen Publications, 1974); William C. Nell, *Property Qualifications or No Property Qualifications: A Few Facts From the Record of Patriotic Services of the Colored Men of New York During the Wars of 1776 and 1812* (New York: Thomas Hamilton and William Leonard, 1860).

6. Peter Williams Jr. was probably the author of this letter because he later remarked that during the War of 1812 he used "the humble services of my pen, my tongue, and my hands towards rearing fortifications to defend our shores against invasion. I entreated my brethren to help in the defence [*sic*] of the country, and went with them to the work." His own assertion that he used *pen* and tongue to encourage other Blacks to help supports the notion that he may have authored this plea. *New York Evening Post,* July 15, 1834; and *Commercial Advertiser,* July 15, 1834; William C. Nell, *The Colored Patriots of the American Revolution with Sketches of Several Distinguished Colored Persons to Which Is Added a Brief Survey of the Conditions and Prospects of Colored Americans* (1855; repr., New York: Arno Press, 1968), 323.

7. *New York Evening Post,* August 20, 1814; Shane White, "'We Dwell in Safety and Pursue Our Honest Callings': Free Blacks in New York City, 1783–1810," *Journal of American History* 75, no. 2 (1988): 445; Nell, *Property Qualifications or No Property Qualifications,* 10–11; Nell, *Colored Patriots,* 149; S. White, *Somewhat More Independent,* 105–6; L. M. Harris, *In the Shadow of Slavery,* 93. Shane White correctly argued that, although the British never attacked New York, the Black community's effort was an important "symbolic" demonstration of its patriotism.

8. Nell, *Property Qualifications or No Property Qualifications,* 10–11; Swan, "John Teasman," 354. Thomas L. Jennings (1791–1859) was born in New York City as a free man, and by 1821 he was making his living as a tailor. He soon became the first Black man in the United States to hold a patent, after he created an innovative dry cleaning process called "dry scouring." Throughout his life, Jennings used his fame and fortune in support of his race; he was a founder and trustee of the Abyssinian Baptist Church and later gave substantial sums of money to the abolitionist cause. He also became active on the issues of emigration, colonization, and suffrage. For more on his political activism, see chapters 3, 4, 5, and 6. Jennings died on February 11, 1859, in New York City.

9. J. Foner, *Blacks and the Military,* 23; L. M. Harris, *In the Shadow of Slavery,* 94.

10. The flaw in moral uplift was revealed following the war. Despite Blacks' intensive labor, their hopes for citizenship were disappointed. None felt this more strikingly than the Black men who had served in the military. Far from being treated as heroes, Black

veterans were denied military benefits; they were not extended the same pensions, land grants, or support for their widows and families that were given to White veterans until 1854. Nell, *Colored Patriots*, 153–54.

11. George Lawrence had only been inducted into the African Society eleven months earlier, on February 10, 1812.

12. Lawrence, "Oration on the Abolition of the Slave Trade," 375, 377.

13. Ibid., 378–80.

14. Ibid., 380–81.

15. Joseph Sidney, *An Oration Commemorative of the Abolition of the Slave Trade; Delivered in the African Asbury Church in the City of New York, on the First of January, 1814* (New York: J. S. Putney, 1814), 11.

16. Ibid., 6, 9, 12.

17. Hamilton, "An Oration on the Abolition of the Slave Trade," 395, 397–98, 396.

18. Ibid., 392–93, 398.

19. Encouraged by the Gradual Emancipation Act of 1799, many slaveholders in New York State manumitted Blacks before the 1827 deadline. During the first quarter of the century, the Black population nearly quadrupled, from 3,499 to 12,485. R. Freeman, *Free Negro in New York City,* app. A.

20. For more on the economic struggles in New York City's Black community, see Duke of Saxe-Weimar Eisenach Bernhard, *Travels Through North America During the Years 1825 and 1826* (Philadelphia: Carey, Lea, and Carey, 1828), i, 126–27; Kruger, "Born to Run"; Leonard H. Curry, *The Free Black in Urban America, 1800–1850: The Shadow of the Dream* (Chicago: University of Chicago Press, 1981); Kenneth Scherzer, *The Unbounded Community: Neighborhood Life and Social Structure in New York City, 1830–1875* (Durham, N.C.: Duke University Press, 1992); Bolster, *Black Jacks,* 32, 72, 159; A. J. Williams-Myers, "The Plight of African Americans in Ante-Bellum New York City," *Afro-Americans in New York Life and History* 22, no. 2 (July 1998): 52; G. R. Hodges, *Root and Branch,* 200–203. The most extensive work dealing with Black New York's working class is L. M. Harris, *In the Shadow of Slavery.*

21. New York City Common Council, *Minutes of the Common Council,* vol. 4, 389; vol. 5, 272, 278; vol. 6, 274; vol. 7, 729; vol. 9, 40; B. F. DeCosta, *Three Score and Ten: The Story of St. Phillip's Church of New York City. A Discourse Delivered in the New Church West 25th Street at Its Opening Sunday Morning, February 17, 1889* (New York: Printed for the Parish, 1889), 28.

22. DeCosta, *Three Score and Ten,* 25–26; *New York Spectator,* December 21, 1821; New York City Common Council, *Minutes of the Common Council,* vol. 12, 485.

23. New York City Common Council, *Minutes of the Common Council,* vol. 6, 23; vol. 7, 461–62. Perhaps because council members received regular reports on the school, they were more keenly aware of its benefits. In the Common Council's 1813 decision, city leaders stated that the African Free School should be allowed to construct new buildings: "It would seem unreasonable to drive such an Institution from among us merely because it may excite the complaints of a few. Besides it is a fact of common observation that there is not a better regulated or more orderly school in the Country than the one in question. And we believe, that religion and humanity demand of us sufficient patronage to perpetuate the establishment" (vol. 7, 461–62).

24. *Anglo-African,* January 1860; George A. Thompson Jr., *A Documentary History of the African Theatre* (Evanston, Ill.: Northwestern University Press, 1998), 4–5. Leslie Harris

also mentions the significance of the African Grove as independent Black recreation space. L. M. Harris, *In the Shadow of Slavery*, 78–79. For more on the African Grove Theater, see Shane White's study of this institution: *Stories of Freedom in Black New York* (Cambridge: Harvard University Press, 2002).

25. *Commercial Advertiser*, August 17, 1822.

26. *National Advocate*, August 3, 1821; G. A. Thompson, *Documentary History*, 20; S. White, *Stories of Freedom*, 74.

27. *National Advocate*, October 27, 1821; S. White, *Stories of Freedom*, 83.

28. *National Advocate*, September 25, 1821.

29. Ibid., January 9, 1822; S. White, *Stories of Freedom*, 83.

30. *New York Evening Post*, January 10, 1822; *Commercial Advertiser*, August 17, 1822; Gilje, *Road to Mobocracy*, 156–57; S. White, *Stories of Freedom*, 84–85.

31. Laws of New York State, 40th Session, March 31, 1817. This act was repealed in 1819, and reenacted with the addition of a due process clause. The issue of due process added a perfect judicial loophole, because it gave city authorities the power to determine if this stipulation had been adequately met. Essentially, despite the efforts to protect Blacks, the Black community was still at the mercy of city officials.

32. *Freedom's Journal*, June 8 and 22, 1827.

33. Garnet, *Memorial Discourse*, 18–20; Stuckey, *Slave Culture*, 138–40; R. Freeman, *Free Negro in New York City*, 46. Shortly after arriving in New York in 1825, the Trusty family changed its name to Garnet. The son, Henry, eventually became one of the leading Black activists of the nineteenth century. For more on Henry Highland Garnet, see chapters 4, 5, 6, and the epilogue.

34. *New York Evening Post*, September 21, 1826.

35. *The People v. John Dyos*, July 16, 1819, New York City Court of General Sessions, New York City Municipal Archives; Gilje, *Road to Mobocracy*, 150. Apparently, in New York City, Thomas Harlett was known by the last name "Jackson."

36. *New York Evening Post*, September 20–22, 1826.

37. African Institution, *Sixth Report of the Directors of the African Institution, Read at the Annual General Meeting on the 25th of March, 1812. To Which Are Added, an Appendix and List of Subscribers* (London: Ellerton and Henderson, 1812), 57–59.

38. There were various spellings of "Sierre" Leone; however, this appears to have been the most common.

39. In 1816, Peter Williams Jr. wrote a letter in which he stated that the New York African Institution, an organization devoted to emancipation and emigration, had been established in 1792. There are no other documented references to this organization until 1812, so it is unclear when Blacks became fully active regarding emigration. Peter Williams Jr. to Thomas Tucker, New York, June 10, 1816, Black Abolitionist Papers.

40. Peter Williams Jr., *A Discourse Delivered on the Death of Capt. Paul Cuffee, Before the New York African Institution, in the African Methodist Episcopal Zion Church, October 21, 1817* (New York: B. Young and Company, 1817), 6.

41. British abolitionist Granville Sharp spearheaded this movement, and the first African emigrants to Sierre Leone came from England in April 1787. The early years were extremely troubled and the project initially seemed doomed to failure. However, in 1791, a British commercial entity, the Sierre Leone Company, took charge of the colony. Slowly, settlers of African descent came from around the world to seek refuge in the fledgling

colony. By 1807, Sierre Leone was, again, on the brink of disaster but the British Parliament bailed it out. Eventually, philanthropists in London such as William Wilberforce, Zacharay Macaulay, and William Allen formed the African Institution to assist Sierre Leone. For more on this issue, see Sheldon H. Harris, *Paul Cuffe: Black America and the African Return* (New York: Simon and Schuster, 1972), 43–51; Graham Hodges, ed., *The Black Loyalist Directory: African Americans in Exile after the American Revolution* (New York: Garland Publishers, 1996).

 42. *Freedom's Journal*, March 16 and 23, 1827, and April 13, 1827. For excellent discussions on Paul Cuffe's life and times, see S. H. Harris, *Paul Cuffe;* Lamont D. Thomas, *Rise to Be a People: A Biography of Paul Cuffe* (Urbana: University of Illinois Press, 1986).

 43. Paul Cuffe to William Allen, April 24, 1811, Paul Cuffe Papers; African Institution, *Sixth Report of the African Institution*, 26–27; P. Williams, *Discourse Delivered on the Death of Paul Cuffe*, 10; S. H. Harris, *Paul Cuffe*, 80–81; Robert Johnson Jr., *Returning Home: A Century of African-American Repatriation* (Trenton, N.J.: Africa World Press, 2005), 26. For more on Paul Cuffe's assessment of Sierre Leone, see Paul Cuffe, *A Brief Account of the Settlement and Present Situation of the Colony of Sierra Leone, in Africa; as Communicated by Paul Cuffe. (A man of colour) To His Friend in New York: Also, an Explanation of the Object of His Visit, and Some Advice to the People of Colour in the United States. To Which is Subjoined, an Address to the People of Colour, From the Convention of Delegates From the Abolition Societies in the United States* (New York: Samuel Wood, 1812). See also Paul Cuffe to Thomas Wainer, July 11, 1811, Paul Cuffe Papers.

 44. R. Johnson, *Returning Home*, 28.

 45. Journal of Paul Cuffe, May 14, 1812; Paul Cuffe to the President, Senate and House of Representatives of the United States of America, June 1813, Paul Cuffe Papers; S. H. Harris, *Paul Cuffe*, 154–55. Some scholars, such as Craig Wilder, have argued that most Black New Yorkers did not seriously consider emigration. That, in fact, "Africa was not a destination, but a heritage." Certainly there was never a full-scale migration to Africa, but I believe my findings support the notion that (at least for some) Africa was both a destination and a heritage. For Wilder's argument, see *In the Company of Black Men*, 76–77.

 46. S. H. Harris, *Paul Cuffe*, 64, 187.

 47. Peter Williams Jr. to Paul Cuffe, August 2, 1816, Paul Cuffe Papers. Peter Williams Jr. has generally been depicted as an opponent of emigration; however, contrary to popular belief, he was one of its main proponents and was at the forefront of emigration movements to Africa, Haiti, and Canada. George Walker is one of the scholars who perpetuated the notion of Peter Williams Jr. as an anti-emigrationist. For more, see G. Walker, *Afro-American in New York City*, 150.

 48. Unlike every other member of her family, Freelove chose to keep the name of her father's former owner, Slocum. It is my contention that she intentionally retained the use of the name Slocum when she decided to come to New York City. John Slocum had manumitted her father and was a wealthy well-known Quaker. His son, Christopher Marshall Slocum, was a member of the New York Manumission Society, and Freelove likely used the Slocum name to gain respect in New York City and earn a position teaching in the New York African Free School. For more information on the Slocum family, see Charles Elihu Slocum, *A Short History of the Slocum, Slocumb, and Slocomb Families, 1637–1881* (Syracuse, N.Y.: Published by the author, 1882).

49. Paul Cuffe to Peter Williams Jr., June 14, 1816; Peter Williams Jr. to Paul Cuffe, March 22, 1817; Freelove Slocum to Paul Cuffe, December 9, 1816; and Paul Cuffe to Peter Williams Jr., August 30, 1816, Paul Cuffe Papers.

50. Paul Cuffe to Peter Williams Jr., August 30, 1816; Paul Cuffe to the Members of the Friendly Society, August 14, 1816; and Paul Cuffe to Peter Williams Jr., August 14, 1816, Paul Cuffe Papers; S. H. Harris, *Paul Cuffe*, 54–55.

51. R. Johnson, *Returning Home*, 43.

52. Paul Cuffe to Peter Williams Jr., December 1, 1816, Paul Cuffe Papers. In 1817, Paul Cuffe wrote to some of his regular correspondents discussing his intentions to sail to Santo Domingo. Paul Cuffe to Samuel J. Mills, January 6, 1817; Paul Cuffe to James Forten, January 23, 1817, Paul Cuffe Papers.

53. P. Williams, *Discourse Delivered on the Death of Capt. Paul Cuffe*, 15–16.

54. Information compiled from Tom W. Shick, *Emigrants to Liberia, 1820 to 1843: An Alphabetical Listing* (Newark: University of Delaware, 1971), 2–101. These emigrants, however, were not only destined for Sierre Leone; some were headed for the newly established American colony of Liberia. The country now known as Haiti was called by many different names during this period. As a result, the terms "Haiti," "Hayti," and "Santo Domingo" are used interchangeably in this section.

55. Elizabeth Rauh Bethel, "Images of Haiti: The Construction of an Afro-American Lieu de Memoire," *Callaloo* 15, no. 3 (Summer 1992): 828.

56. Like Peter Williams Jr., many of these men had demonstrated their patriotism to the United States during the War of 1812 and were now supporting emigration. The Haytian Emigration Society's Board of Directors were Samuel Cornish, Stephen Dutton, Benjamin Smith, Wright Seaman, Mark Jordan, Benjamin Paul, John B. Plet, William Deas, and Aaron Woods. Leaders who maintained membership in both the Haytian Emigration Society and the African Society were Adam Carman, Peter Vogelsang, George Collins, John Maranda, Thomas Sipkins, Boston Crummell, Thomas L. Jennings, Samuel Ennalls, Peter Bane, and James Varick.

57. New York City Common Council, *Minutes of the Common Council*, vol. 10, 636.

58. Charles Dixon, *African America and Haiti: Emigration and Black Nationalism in the Nineteenth Century* (Westport, Conn.: Greenwood Press, 2000), 35.

59. F. J. Miller, *Search for a Black Nationality*, 77–78.

60. Loring Daniel Dewey, *Correspondence Relative to the Emigration to Hayti of the Free People of Colour in the United States. Together With the Instructions to the Agent Sent Out by President Boyer* (New York: Mahlon Day, 1824), 7, 18.

61. Ibid., 8, 9–10, 30; John Edward Baur, "Mulatto Machiavelli, Jean Pierre Boyer, and the Haiti of His Day," *Journal of Negro History* 32, no. 3 (July 1947): 325; F. J. Miller, *Search for a Black Nationality*, 77; Dixon, African America and Haiti.

62. Haytian Emigration Society, *Address of the Board of Managers*, 3–8. Emphasis is theirs. The exact number of migrants who left in this group is yet to be determined. The final excerpt from Williams's speech is also quoted in F. J. Miller, *Search for a Black Nationality*, 79.

63. Dixon, *African America and Haiti*, 34, 40; F. J. Miller, *Search for a Black Nationality*, 80–81; Baur, "Mulatto Machiavelli," 326–27. For more on Peter Williams Jr.'s reverse migration efforts, see *Weekly Anglo-African*, January 12, 1861; F. J. Miller, *Search for a Black Nationality*, 108.

64. Dixon, *African America and Haiti*, 41–44. It is important to note that even after

the subsidies ceased, thousands more free Black Northerners emigrated to Haiti, and by 1828, the numbers reached thirteen thousand. Baur, "Mulatto Machiavelli," 326.

65. New York Manumission Society, *An Address to the Parents and Guardians of the Children Belonging to the New York African Free School by the Trustees of the Institutions* (New York: Samuel Wood and Sons, 1818), 21–23; Rury, "Education and Black Community Development," 28.

66. Historians Robert Swan and Leslie Harris noted that Teasman's dismissal from the school might have been due to his support of the African Society and its practice of parading. Swan, "John Teasman," 350; L. M. Harris, *In the Shadow of Slavery,* 103.

67. New York Manumission Society, *Address to the Parents,* 20–21.

68. Swan, "John Teasman," 351.

69. Although the AME Zion congregation had a strong and proud beginning, it suffered from some internal conflict during this period. In 1812, Abraham Thompson and June Scott left the AME Zion church, although Thompson quickly returned. In 1814, William Miller also left to establish the Asbury Church and Thomas Sipkins, who had been expelled from Zion for reasons that are not entirely clear, joined him. The exodus of leaders from Zion led to some contention; however, it did not threaten the overall support for Zion. For more, see Walls, *African Methodist Episcopal Zion Church,* 68.

70. *Commercial Advertiser,* October 21, 1820; DeCosta, *Three Score and Ten,* 20–21, 27–28; Shelton Bishop, "The History of St. Philip's Church in New York City," *Historical Magazine of the Protestant Episcopal Church* 15 (December 1946): 304. They elected a board of trustees, which included some African Society members: John Maranda, Lewis Francis, Samuel Class, William Tate, Thomas Zabriskie, John Bees, Andrew Rankins, John Kent, George Lawrence, and William Whitson.

71. In 1810, a new organization emerged, the African Marine Fund, which recognized that many Black sailors were impoverished or killed at sea and sought to provide for their relief. The African Marine Fund's constitution demonstrated a strong racial consciousness, stating that its desire to associate was based upon its concern for "the situation of our poor Africans and descendants of our mother country." Reflecting a true community ethic, the African Marine Fund was open to both males and females and had no age restrictions. Its primary goals were to provide schooling for poor children, ascertain the needs of the community, and to provide proper burials for its members. For more, see African Marine Fund, "Constitution of the African Marine Fund, for the Relief of the Distressed Orphans, and Poor Members of This Fund" in *Early Negro Writing,* 42–44.

72. Although Black men produced a series of associations, Black women were comparatively silent. Black organizations, according to African tradition, were gender segregated. If Black women's organizations existed, there is no remaining information about them. Among the men's organizations, the most notable new association was a branch of the Prince Hall Masonic Order. Sandy Lattion, James Varick, and William Miller established the Boyer Lodge in 1812 and named it after Haitian leader Jean Pierre Boyer. Masonry is a deeply secretive association and, therefore, little else is known about its development or structure. Walls, *African Methodist Episcopal Zion Church,* 90; Wilder, *In the Company of Black Men,* 74–76.

73. Zuille, *Historical Sketch,* 5; Peter Vogelsang, *An Address Delivered before the New York African Society for Mutual Relief in the African Zion Church, 23rd March, 1815, Being the Fifth Anniversary of Their Incorporation* (New York: Hardcastle and Pelsue, 1815), 6.

74. Zuille, *Historical Sketch,* 7. The report does not reveal the identity of this friend, but

it is likely that it was a member of the Manumission Society. The African Society renewed its incorporation every fifteen years until 1848 when New York State passed a general law protecting all of its rights and privileges as a corporation. Craig Wilder and Robert Swan also described this celebration. Wilder, *In the Company of Black Men*, 105; Swan, "John Teasman," 350.

75. Zuille, *Historical Sketch*, 7; *Frederick Douglass Paper*, January 26, 1855.

76. John Teasman, *An Address Delivered in the African Episcopal Church, on the 25th of March, 1811, before the New York African Society for Mutual Relief, Being the First Anniversary of Its Incorporation* (New York: J. Low, 1811), 4, 6, 7, 9, 11.

77. Zuille, *Historical Sketch*, 17; Vogelsang, *Address Delivered before the New York African Society for Mutual Relief*, 6–7. Craig Wilder also discusses the Berry incident; however, he argues that Berry was not publicly shamed. Yet Vogelsang did distinctly mention Berry in this 1815 speech and blamed him for almost causing the organization's property to be "sacrificed." For Wilder's discussion, see Craig Steven Wilder, "'The Guardian Angel of Africa': A Financial History of the New York African Society for Mutual Relief, 1808–1945," *Afro-Americans in New York Life and History* 26, no. 2 (July 2002): 69.

78. Zuille, *Historical Sketch*, 18. John Teasman, who died shortly after the Berry incident was resolved, played a key role in saving the African Society. Teasman had already served three years as vice president and was serving his second term as president when the tragedy occurred. According to Peter Vogelsang, Teasman conducted himself as an "honest, upright man" and guided the society past all the difficulties.

79. Zuille, *Historical Sketch*, 16. Craig Wilder also mentions the accumulation of this piece of property. Wilder, *In the Company of Black Men*, 105–6.

80. Vogelsang, *Address Delivered before the New York African Society for Mutual Relief*, 16.

81. *An Oration Delivered at the Fifteenth Annual Celebration of the New York African Society for Mutual Relief at the African Zion Church, the 24th of March, 1823. By a Member* (Brooklyn: G. L. Birch, 1823), 6–7.

82. Zuille, *Historical Sketch*, 15.

83. New York African Clarkson Association, *Constitution of the New-York African Clarkson Association* (New York: E. Conrad, 1825), 1, 4. There appears to be some dispute on this matter. Leslie Harris argues that Quaker women founded the organization in 1815, but the African Society's historical records insist that the Clarkson Association was the direct result of the society's influence. For Harris's argument, see *In the Shadow of Slavery*, 87.

84. Bernhard, *Travels through North America*, 127. Leslie Harris also includes a brief excerpt from this quote. L. M. Harris, *In the Shadow of Slavery*, 89.

85. Adam Carman, *An Oration Delivered at the Fourth Anniversary of the Abolition of the Slave Trade, in the Methodist Episcopal Church, in Second Street, New York, January 1, 1811. By Adam Carman* (New York: John C. Totten, 1811), 3; Sidney, *Oration Commemorative of the Abolition of the Slave Trade*, 16.

86. *New York Evening Post*, August 22, 1814; L. M. Harris, *In the Shadow of Slavery*, 93.

87. During a speech in 1810, African Society member Henry Johnson urged his audience to "cast the eye of the mind to Africa" and recall the days prior to European contact: a time when Africa was "free" and "happy." Henry Johnson, *An Oration on the Abolition of*

the Slave Trade, With an Introductory Address, by Adam Carman: Delivered in the African Church in New York. January 1, 1810 (New York: John C. Totten, 1810), 10.

Chapter 3: "Of What Use Are Processions?"

The epigraphs for chapter 3 are from William Hamilton, "An Oration Delivered in the African Zion Church, on the Fourth of July, 1827, in Commemoration of the Abolition of Domestic Slavery in this State," in *Early Negro Writing*, 97; *Freedom's Journal*, June 29, 1827; *Freedom's Journal*, March 16, 1827. A portion of this quote also appears in Timothy Patrick McCarthy, "'To Plead Our Own Cause': Black Print Culture and the Origins of American Abolitionism," in *Prophets of Protest: Reconsidering the History of American Abolitionism*, ed. Timothy Patrick McCarthy and John Stauffer (New York: The New Press, 2006), 115.

1. Samuel Cornish (1795–1858) was born to free parents in Sussex County, Delaware. In 1815, he moved to Philadelphia where John Gloucester, who founded the first Black Presbyterian Church, provided Cornish with education and training for the ministry. In 1818, Gloucester fell ill, and Cornish began preaching to his congregation every Sunday. In October 1819, Cornish was licensed to preach and spent six months working as a missionary among enslaved Africans in Maryland. The following year, he was sent to New York City to establish a mission in the heart of the one of the city's most impoverished Black neighborhoods. Within two years, Samuel Cornish was ordained as a minister and created the New Demeter Street Presbyterian Church. In 1824, Cornish married Jane Livingston, and they had four children: Sarah Matilda (1824–1846), William (1826), Samuel (1828–1838), and Jane Sophia Tappan (1833–1855). Only three of his children lived past infancy, and even the surviving children died young. His son drowned at the age of ten, and his daughters both died at the age of twenty-two. Likewise, his wife died in 1844. Despite the tragedies in his personal life, Samuel Cornish became one of the leading activists during the antebellum era. For more on Cornish's political activism, see chapters 4, 5, and 6. By 1855, Samuel Cornish was in declining health, and he moved to Brooklyn where he died in 1858.

John Russwurm (1799–1851) was born in Jamaica to an enslaved mother and a white merchant father. His father moved young John to Quebec when he was only eight years old; yet shortly thereafter they moved to Maine where his father married another woman. John Russwurm received his early education at the Hebron Academy and, in 1824, enrolled at Bowdoin College. When he graduated in 1826, Russwurm was among the first Black college graduates in the United States. He was even selected to deliver the commencement address, which was entitled "The Condition and Prospects of Haiti." The focus of his talk reflected Russwurm's political beliefs and foreshadowed his future commitment to emigration. For more on John Russwurm, see the remainder of this chapter.

2. *Freedom's Journal*, March 16, 1827. Capitalization is theirs. Albany activist Reverend Nathaniel Paul may also have been present at the planning meeting. For more on the formation of *Freedom's Journal*, see Bella Gross, "Freedom's Journal and the Rights of All," *Journal of Negro History* 17, no. 3 (July 1932): 242–43; Ralph Donald Carter, "Black American or African: The Response of New York City Blacks to African Colonization, 1817–1841" (PhD diss., Clark University, 1974), 135; Bernell Tripp, *Origins of the Black Press, New York, 1827–1847* (Northport, Ala.: Vision Press, 1992), 12–13; G. Walker, *Afro-American in New*

York City, 79; Wilder, *In the Company of Black Men,* 147–48; McCarthy, "'To Plead Our Own Cause.'"

3. It is important to note that, although slavery was technically terminated in 1827, some people were still held in bondage beyond that date in New York State. According to the stipulations of the gradual emancipation act, children born between 1799 and 1817 would be held in bondage until a certain age depending on their gender (twenty-eight for males and twenty-five for females); thus, a male born in 1816 would have been held in a form of slavery until 1844 and a female until 1841. This situation was rare in New York City, because such forms of servitude were less economically beneficial in urban areas. The other exception to the gradual emancipation act applied to enslaved Blacks from the South who were brought to live in the North; they could be forced to remain in slavery for six months after their arrival in New York State if their master so desired.

4. The rest of the organizing committee was composed entirely of African Society members including John Maranda, Thomas L. Jennings, Thomas Sipkins, John Robertson, Henry Scott, and Moses Blue.

5. *Freedom's Journal,* April 27, 1827, and June 29, 1827. Portions of this quote also appear in S. White, "'It Was a Proud Day,'" 39. A number of scholars mention the Emancipation Day debate, including Leslie Harris, who argues that it was evidence of a divide between the Black middle class and the rest of the Black community. I contend, however, that the debate revealed an even more complicated conflict that defied class boundaries. Because the Black leadership was not unified in its opinion of how emancipation should be "properly" celebrated, I suggest that the debate was about culture and strategic disputes over the most effective path to citizenship. L. M. Harris, *In the Shadow of Slavery,* 122–28. See also Kachun, *Festivals of Freedom,* 44–49. Patrick Rael also notes that there was a call to abstain from the procession, but does not comment on the fact that the parades went forward anyway. Rael, *Black Identity and Black Protest,* 65. Likewise, Shane White made note of the conflict, but does not offer an explanation for the ideological split. S. White, *Stories of Freedom,* 62–63.

6. Recall that, in 1810, the African Society had vociferously defended its right to march in spite of White opposition. For more on this, and the political perspectives of William Hamilton and William Miller, see chapter 2.

7. Carter, "Black American or African," 135; Gross, "Freedom's Journal and the Rights of All," 242.

8. Unfortunately, these activists did not leave any written evidence of their agenda or intentions and, therefore, the identity of the individual organizers is unknown.

9. *Freedom's Journal,* June 22, 1827.

10. Ibid., April 20, 1827. Graham Hodges and Leslie Harris also discussed the choice of July 5; Hodges argued that Black New Yorkers simply chose July 5 for reasons of safety and practicality, but Harris maintains that the decision simply reflected a carryover from 1800 when Black people were banned from celebrating on the fourth. G. R. Hodges, *Root and Branch,* 223; L. M. Harris, *In the Shadow of Slavery,* 123. I, however, do not believe that the matter is so simple. An examination of Black speeches and newspaper articles during this time reveals that Black New Yorkers were concerned both with the symbolic meaning of July fourth and with the conditions of their brethren who still languished in bondage. For them, celebrating "freedom" on American Independence day while so many of their people remained enslaved was a contradiction too glaring to ignore. Peter Williams Jr. made this point during his July 4 speech in 1830. For more, see chapter 4. In

addition, the conscious selection of July 5 sent a powerful statement at a time when, as Mitch Kachun suggested, "the most established model of politicized public celebrations was the Fourth of July." Kachun, *Festivals of Freedom*, 22.

11. *Freedom's Journal*, June 29, 1827. It is of particular note that Noah referred to the system of social control that slavery imposed in the South; the implication was that freedom was dangerous because the Black community could no longer be controlled.

12. Ibid. Although Russwurm and Cornish attacked Mordecai Noah's article, by defending the Black community members' right to "indulge" in parades "when they see proper," these two activists continued to believe that processions should be abandoned entirely.

13. Ibid.

14. Ibid., July 6, 1827.

15. Hamilton, "An Oration Delivered in the African Zion Church," 97. Italics are his. Also quoted in R. Freeman, *Free Negro in New York*, 4; G. Walker, *Afro-American in New York City*, 3.

16. Hamilton, "An Oration Delivered in the African Zion Church," 97.

17. Ibid., 98–100.

18. Ibid., 102–3.

19. In the early national era republican ideology viewed women as the moral conscience of society, and Hamilton apparently supported this notion. For more on republicanism and women, see Linda K. Kerber, *Women of the Republic: Intellect and Ideology in Revolutionary America* (New York: W. W. Norton and Company, 1986).

20. Hamilton, "An Oration Delivered in the African Zion Church," 104.

21. It is important to note that the marchers did not include women; in fact, James McCune Smith explicitly stated that while the men marched, the "sidewalks were crowded with the wives, daughters, sisters and mothers of the celebrants." It would be easy to assume that these comments revealed sexism within the Black community; men were allowed to publicly honor emancipation, while women passively observed. For, as William Hamilton suggested in his speech, women were responsible for moral uplift and maintaining a strong family and community base, but men, it would seem, were believed to have an exclusive right to public demonstrations and parades. However, this analysis may be too simplistic in relation to the Black community in New York City. Although women may not have marched in the July 5 parade, Black female organizations, such as the Daughters of Israel, did hold processions to celebrate their anniversaries. Because public demonstrations, such as parading, were not the exclusive domain of men, a glaring question still remains about why women did not march on Emancipation Day. There may not be an easy answer to this question, especially because July 5 supporters appeared less concerned with appeals to republicanism and respectability. It seems possible that after receiving threats of mob violence, Black male activists may have been worried about women's safety. This fear proved to be legitimate because some White coachmen and cartmen attempted to disrupt the parade. As a British visitor remarked, "the insulting behavior of many of the coachmen and carters was unblushingly displayed in their driving their vehicles so as to interrupt the progress and order of the process." Although the marchers escaped unscathed, their safety was not guaranteed, and women may have abstained from the procession for that reason. For James McCune's description, see Garnet, *Memorial Discourse*, 24; Stuckey, *Slave Culture*, 143–44. For the British visitor's remarks, see James Boardman, *America and the Americans: By a Citizen of the World* (London: Printed for Longman, Rees, Orme, Brown, Green, and Longman, 1833), 311. There is little surviving information about the

Daughters of Israel, which was apparently a Black women's mutual relief organization "whose immediate objects are to afford assistance to the sick and distressed—to feed the hungry and clothe the naked." It appears that it operated as a secret society complete with initiation procedures, organizational pledges, and colors. In one article, it was mentioned that members wore "white dress and cap and ribbon" to distinguish themselves. It is significant that the Daughters of Israel held parades to celebrate important occasions, because these activities demonstrate that Black women also claimed the streets publicly, in African style, to commemorate their accomplishments for the entire community to observe. *Freedom's Journal,* August 15, 1828.

22. Garnet, *Memorial Discourse,* 24; *New York American,* July 6, 1827; S. White, "It Was a Proud Day," 44. Smith's quote is also cited in Wilder, *In the Company of Black Men,* 78. A British visitor also noted that the "black and coloured population extremely well dressed, and wearing sashes and ribands, paraded the city in martial array with the accompaniments of bands of music, and colours." Boardman, *America and the Americans,* 310.

23. Garnet, *Memorial Discourse,* 24.

24. Ibid. Graham Hodges also used a portion of this quote, although he does not discuss the larger debates surrounding Emancipation Day. G. R. Hodges, *Root and Branch,* 224. Craig Wilder argues that such a parade reflected reinforced notions of masculinity but, likewise, neglects the larger conflict over parading. Wilder, *In the Company of Black Men,* 120–21.

25. *New York American,* July 6, 1827.

26. *Freedom's Journal,* July 6, 1827.

27. Ibid., July 13 and 20, 1827.

28. Ibid. A portion of this quote also appears in McCarthy, "'To Plead Our Own Cause,'" 122.

29. *Freedom's Journal,* May 9, 1828, and July 4 and 11, 1828; R. Freeman, *Free Negro in New York City,* 4; Rael, *Black Identity and Black Protest,* 60. Upon their arrival at the African Zion Church, Reverends William Miller and Christopher Rush performed religious services and John Peterson delivered the keynote address. However, there is no surviving text of the 1828 address.

30. *Freedom's Journal,* July 11, 1828.

31. Ibid., July 18, 1828. Italics are his. Portions of these quotes can also be found in S. White, "It Was a Proud Day," 40; S. White and G. White, *Stylin',* 103. Sandra Sandiford Young, "John Brown Russwurm's Dilemma: Citizenship or Emigration?" in *Prophets of Protest,* 103–5.

32. *Freedom's Journal,* March 28, 1829. According to James McCune Smith, the African Society ceased parading to honor its organizational anniversary in 1830. *Frederick Douglass Paper,* February 16, 1855. In fact, there was only one known parade in the 1830s, held to commemorate the anniversary of the African Clarkson Association. Significantly, the editor of the *Colored American* had to defend the conduct of Clarkson members after they were slandered in the *New York Times* following their procession. *Colored American,* April 29, 1837.

33. Scholar John Hope Franklin used this term to describe free Blacks in his work, *From Slavery to Freedom: A History of American Negroes* (New York: Alfred A. Knopf, 1948).

34. U.S. Census Office, *Return of the Whole Number of the Population* (Washington D.C.: n.p., 1811); *Journal of the Assembly of the State of New York,* 50th Session, Appendix C. For

more on the struggles of the Black working class during this era, see Williams-Myers, "Plight of African Americans"; L. M. Harris, *In the Shadow of Slavery.*

35. *Freedom's Journal,* June 22 and 29, 1827.

36. Ibid., August 17 and 24, 1827.

37. Ibid.

38. *Freedom's Journal,* March 16, 1827.

39. Ibid., March 16 and 28, 1829. There was another attempt toward Black independent education during this period, when activist Benjamin Hughes created an independent school in St. Philips Church. As with previous endeavors, however, his attempt struggled due to insufficient financial support, and Hughes eventually put his school under the control of the African Free School system.

40. Ibid., February 1, 1828.

41. Ibid., February 1 and 15, 1828. The advisory board consisted of William Miller, Christopher Rush, Samuel Todd, William Quinn, Peter Williams Jr., Benjamin Paul, and Samuel Cornish. The officers were chosen as follows: president, Mrs. Margaret Francis; secretary, Mrs. Margaretta Quinn; assistant secretary, Mrs. Henrietta Regulus; and treasurer, Mrs. Sarah Bane. In addition to the officers, the board of managers was composed of the following members: Elizabeth Lawrence, Nancy Scott, Mary Seaman, Maria Johnson, Harriet Stokely, Rebecca Matthews, Violet Jackson, Susan McLane, Esther Lambert, Harriet Woodruff, Maria Morris, Amelia Smith, Maria Degrasse, Esther Lane, Caroline Dennis, Mary Williams, and Diana Reynolds. Known relationships between these women and African Society members are as follows: Margaretta Quinn was the wife of William Quinn, Sarah Bane was the wife of Peter Bane, Elizabeth Lawrence was the wife of George Lawrence, Nancy Scott was the wife of Henry Scott, and Maria Degrasse was the daughter of George Degrasse. Mary Williams was Peter Williams Sr.'s daughter, and Peter Williams Jr.'s sister. Leslie Harris also mentions the formation of the Dorcas Association, although she seems to be most concerned with the active participation of men in the founding of the organization. She argues that Dorcas women were subject to the "explicit leadership of men." L. M. Harris, *In the Shadow of Slavery,* 179–80.

42. For an analysis of Black women's roles in Black communities, see Patricia Hill Collins, *Black Feminist Thought: Knowledge, Consciousness, and the Politics of Empowerment* (New York: Routledge, 1991).

43. *Freedom's Journal,* March 7, 1828.

44. Ibid., September 26, 1828.

45. It is possible that this author was Cato Alexander, an African Society member, who owned a successful hotel and tavern in downtown Manhattan. Shane White noted that Alexander was so well known in the city that "the designation 'Cato's' required no further explication if encountered, for instance, in a newspaper story." S. White, *Stories of Freedom,* 34.

46. *Freedom's Journal,* November 21, 1828, January 9, 1829, and February 7, 1829.

47. Carter, "Black American or African," 107, 109.

48. *Freedom's Journal,* December 21, 1827, July 11, 1828, February 14, 1829; Young, "John Brown Russwurm's Dilemma," 107. For discussion of Haiti's financial arrangements with France, see Baur, "Mulatto Machiavelli," 321–23. John Russwurm's quote in 1829 also appears in R. Johnson, *Returning Home,* 175.

49. R. Johnson, *Returning Home,* 45, 55, 128–29.

50. *Freedom's Journal,* March 16, 1827.

51. Ibid., July 6, 1827.

52. As examples, see Ibid., July 6, 1827; August 24 and 31, 1827; September 14, 21, and 28, 1827; October 5, 12, 19, and 26, 1827; November 2, 9, 16, 23, and 30, 1827; December 7, 14, 21, and 28, 1827; February 22 and 29, 1828; March 7, 1828; and July 18, 1828.

53. Ibid., September 21 and 28, 1827.

54. Ibid., October 5, 1827, and November 2, 1827. It should be noted that at least one letter probably confirmed the ACS's greatest fear. One Black correspondent, calling himself "Clarkson," maintained that the presence of the free population helped, rather than hindered, the enslaved, because that free Blacks could infuse enslaved people with "notions of liberty . . . [that] render them discontented, and dispose them to insurrection."

55. For an example of Cornish's newspaper advertisement, see Ibid., November 9, 1827.

56. For more on the collapse of *Freedom's Journal,* see Tripp, *Origins of the Black Press,* 19–22.

57. *Freedom's Journal,* January 9, 1829; February 14, 1829; March 7 and 14, 1829.

58. Carter, "Black American or African," 165.

59. *Freedom's Journal,* March 28, 1829; *New York Evening Post,* July 15, 1834. Just a few months after *Freedom's Journal* disintegrated, John Russwurm accepted a position as superintendent of schools in Liberia. He was well received in Africa; he edited a newspaper, the *Liberia Herald,* and became governor of the Maryland colony in Cape Palmas in 1836. He remained in that position until his death in 1851. Gross, "Freedom's Journal and the Rights of All," 280.

60. In 1834, Williams claimed that he had helped men such as John Russwurm and James Thompson immigrate to Liberia. *New York Evening Post,* July 15, 1834.

61. R. Johnson, *Returning Home,* 178. Sandra Sandiford Young and Timothy Patrick McCarthy also mention Russwurm's emigration to Liberia and the subsequent view among Black activists that Russwurm was a traitor to the Black community. Young, "John Brown Russwurm's Dilemma," 108–9; McCarthy, "'To Plead Our Own Cause,'" 131–32.

Chapter 4: "Our Own Native Land"

Epigraphs to chapter 4 are from Peter Williams Jr., "Discourse Delivered in St. Philip's Church," 296; "Resolutions of the People of Color, at a Meeting Held on the 25th of January, 1831. With an Address to the Citizens of New York, in Answer to Those of the New York Colonization Society" in *Early Negro Writing,* 285; *Emancipator,* January 17, 1839.

1. P. Williams, "Discourse Delivered in St. Philip's Church," 295, 297. Floyd Miller indicated that there was little discussion of emigration during the 1830s; however, this claim was not accurate for New Yorkers. In fact, emigration debates raged strongly throughout much of the decade. See F. J. Miller, *Search for a Black Nationality,* ix.

2. Although the events in Cincinnati occurred hundreds of miles away, the riot and its aftermath deeply influenced free Blacks across the North. In particular, many leaders feared that they might suffer a similar fate. Black Cincinnatians were first targeted by a referendum designed to force them out of Ohio, and, as the Black population expanded, Whites became increasingly fearful and attempted to expel Black people from the city. Before the Black community could respond, a bloody and horrifying pogrom was unleashed. Before the carnage subsided, two thousand Black people had fled the city and

sought refuge in Canada. Horton and Horton, *In Hope of Liberty,* 104. Recall that Peter Williams Jr. had a legacy of activism on the issue of emigration; he was a correspondent of Paul Cuffe, had been the president of the Haitian Emigration Society, and went to Haiti to meet with President Jean Pierre Boyer to discuss resettling free Black New Yorkers there. For more, see chapter 2.

3. P. Williams, "Discourse Delivered in St. Philip's Church," 297, 299, 300–301.

4. Ibid., 295, 296, 297.

5. Hezekiah Grice was indentured for most of his childhood, until he received a severe beating that prompted him to escape. By 1828, he became acquainted with abolitionist William Lloyd Garrison and determined to dedicate his life to the cause of his people. He was a strong supporter of emigration; in fact, his beliefs resulted in his withdrawal from the Colored Convention of 1832, the very institution he had created. Frustrated with his treatment by his colleagues and American society, Grice migrated to Haiti in 1832. By 1843, he was elected as director of public works and rose to considerable prominence. Although he left the United States, he returned frequently to consult with certain of his brethren including Thomas L. Jennings of New York City.

6. *Colored American,* October 7, 1837; *Anglo-African,* October 1859.

7. *Anglo-African,* October 1859; John W. Cromwell, "The Early Negro Convention Movement," in *The American Negro Academy Occasional Papers* (New York: Arno Press and the New York Times, 1969), 5. Apparently, African Society members Peter Williams Jr., Peter Vogelsang, and Thomas L. Jennings authored the letter from the New Yorkers.

8. There is still considerable confusion surrounding the actual origins of the Colored Conventions. Most contemporary scholars have maintained that Baltimore activist Hezekiah Grice was responsible for the initial call for the conference and have left the New Yorkers entirely out of the story. Yet there is another lesser-known version of the impetus behind the Colored Conventions published in the *Colored American* newspaper just a few years after the first group of conventions were held. Writing under the name, "Hamilton," the author asserted that he would reveal "the cause which first gave rise to the conventions." According to "Hamilton," the idea for the Colored Conventions was born within the Wilberforce Colony Society following the very gathering that opened this chapter, the July 4 commemoration held in 1830, where Peter Williams Jr. urged his people to consider emigration. *Colored American,* October 7, 1837. Howard Holman Bell confirms a version of this story in *Survey of the Negro Convention Movement,* 13–14. It is not clear who "Hamilton" actually was. The most likely candidate, William Hamilton, died in 1836 so, perhaps the author assumed this pseudonym in an effort to honor William Hamilton's contributions to the Colored Convention movement.

9. American Society of Free Persons of Colour, *Constitution of the American Society of Free Persons of Colour, for Improving Their Condition in the United States, for Purchasing Lands, and for the Establishment of a Settlement in Upper Canada, Also the Proceedings of the Convention, with Their Address to the Free Persons of Colour in the United States* (Philadelphia: J. W. Allen, 1831), 5, 10–11. For the list of delegates, see ibid., iv. Craig Wilder also discusses the role of New Yorkers in the discussion on emigration at the gatherings in the 1830s. Wilder, *In the Company of Black Men,* 161–63.

10. It should be noted that between 1830 and 1843, only thirteen Black people from the entire state of New York migrated to Liberia. This information is compiled from Shick, *Emigrants to Liberia.* Leslie Harris also briefly mentions this meeting. L. M. Harris, *In the Shadow of Slavery,* 141.

11. "Resolutions of the People of Color," 281–82, 284–85. Emphasis is theirs. Rhoda Golden Freeman mistakenly states that this gathering occurred in 1837, however, according to the published proceedings, it took place in 1831. R. Freeman, *Free Negro in New York City*, 25. Craig Wilder also discusses this quote and anticolonization. Wilder, *In the Company of Black Men*, 156–58.

12. H. H. Bell, ed., *Minutes and Proceedings of the National Negro Conventions 1830–1864* (New York: Arno Press and the New York Times, 1969), 12, 4, 15. Emphasis is theirs.

13. Garnet, *Memorial Discourse*, 23–24. Leslie Harris points out that the Black community's outrage over Andrews was also linked to an attack he committed on a Black student that "echoed the punishments of slaves." Apparently, a young male student addressed a Black visitor to the school by the title of "gentleman." Such behavior violated Andrews's belief that Black people were not full equals and should not be referred to as "ladies" and "gentlemen." As punishment for his actions, Andrews caned the young boy. For many Black parents, Andrews's caning episode was the final straw. L. M. Harris, *In the Shadow of Slavery*, 134–35; Wilder, *In the Company of Black Men*, 160.

14. Under James Adams, the African Free Schools resumed their regular functioning with enrollment reaching over one thousand students. *New York Manumission Society Papers*, vol. 8, 78–81; Rury, "Education and Black Community Development," 40.

15. Philip A. Bell (1808–1889) was born a freeman in New York City in the year of the abolition of the international slave trade. As a young boy, Bell attended the African Free Schools and eventually used his education to launch his career as a journalist and activist. He became politically involved with a range of issues including abolition, the protection of fugitives, anticolonization, and suffrage. For more on Bell's political activism in New York City, see the remainder of this chapter and chapters 5 and 6. Yet Bell is best known as a newspaper editor. While serving as a member of the African Society, Bell launched his own newspaper, the *Weekly Advocate*, in 1837. Fellow African Society members, Thomas L. Jennings and John J. Zuille, financed and printed the paper. Unfortunately, the *Weekly Advocate* quickly developed financial problems and Charles Ray assumed editorship of the paper. However, Bell rebounded and, between 1837 and 1842, Bell and Samuel Cornish coedited the *Colored American* newspaper. By the middle of the 1850s, Bell decided to migrate to San Francisco, California. Upon his arrival, Bell immediately made a place for himself in the Black community by becoming active in Black organizations and agitating on behalf of fugitives. Bell also brought his experience in the National Colored Conventions to assist in the creation of a series of Colored Citizens Conventions held in San Francisco and Sacramento between 1855 and 1857 and again in 1865. However, Bell was best known in the Bay Area for creating Black newspapers. Along with his colleague, Peter Anderson, Bell founded the *Pacific Appeal* in 1862, in San Francisco, which sought to be the voice of Black people in the West. However, by 1865, Bell and Anderson had a political feud that severed their relationship. Shortly thereafter, Bell started a rival newspaper, the *Elevator*, which served the Black community for two decades. After a lifetime as an activist and journalist, Philip Bell died in 1889.

16. *Minutes and Proceedings of the Second Annual Convention for the Improvement of the People of Colour in These United States, Held by Adjournments, in the City of Philadelphia, from the 4th to the 13th of June, Inclusive, 1832* (Philadelphia: Published by Order of the Convention, 1832), 8, 10, 17.

17. Significantly, delegates acknowledged that some people would still insist upon emigration, and, for those individuals, they still thought that Canada was preferable to Africa

or Haiti. *Minutes and Proceedings of the Third Annual Convention for the Improvement of the Free People of Colour in the United States, Held by Adjournments, in the City of Philadelphia, from the 3rd to the 13th of June, Inclusive, 1833* (New York: Published by Order of the Convention, 1833), 22–23, 31. Emphasis is theirs.

18. *Minutes and Proceedings of the Third Annual Convention,* 15, 17, 19. Emphasis is theirs.

19. *Emancipator,* January 17, 1839.

20. *Minutes and Proceedings of the Fourth Annual Convention, for the Improvement of the Free People of Colour, in the United States, Held by Adjournments in the Asbury Church, New York, from the 2d to the 12th of June, Inclusive* (New York: Published by Order of the Convention, 1834), 28.

21. *Minutes of the Fifth Annual Convention for the Improvement of the Free People of Colour in the United States, Held by Adjournments, in the Wesley Church, Philadelphia, from the First to the Fifth of June, Inclusive, 1835* (Philadelphia: Printed by William P. Gibbons, 1835), 14–15; Stuckey, *Slave Culture,* 204–5; Rael, *Black Identity and Black Protest,* 49–50, 108.

22. Garnet, *Memorial Discourse,* 24. Another indication that public demonstrations of African culture had become unpopular is that the Black leadership continued to denounce parades. At the 1834 Colored Convention, delegates passed a resolution agreeing to "discountenance and suppress" all processions, except those that were "necessary for internment of the dead." *Minutes and Proceedings of the Fourth Annual Convention,* 15. In 1840, the editor of the *Colored American* criticized his brethren in Newark for holding a procession in honor of West Indian Emancipation "with drum and fife." He claimed that such a demonstration was "deeply mortifying to the mass of our people" and hoped that "our people will cease celebrating events, interesting to us, by public processions." *Colored American,* August 15, 1840. He reiterated the plea in the following year, when he issued a plea for West Indian emancipation to be celebrated only with "special prayer and praise." *Colored American,* July 17, 1841.

23. *Colored American,* March 4, 1837; Rael, *Black Identity and Black Protest,* 102.

24. *Colored American,* March 15, 1838.

25. *Minutes of the Fifth Annual Convention,* 27, 28, 31.

26. Craig Wilder argues that Samuel Cornish was "Manhattan's delegate" to the AMRS convention. However, the evidence reveals that the New Yorkers were boycotting the AMRS, and Cornish was the only one who felt compelled to attend. Wilder, *In the Company of Black Men,* 79.

27. For examples of Cornish's commentary on the AMRS, see *Colored American,* March 4, 1837, and July 8, 1837.

28. New York's differing agenda compounded preexisting conflicts and caused the leaders to temporarily withdraw from efforts at regional cooperation. As previously mentioned, there was a historical tension between leaders in Philadelphia and New York City. Although New Yorkers attended in 1831, the tenuous relationship between New Yorkers and Philadelphians plagued the conventions on an annual basis. There was, for example, a constant effort on the part of New Yorkers to hold the convention in their city, rather than in Philadelphia. They attempted to pass such a resolution in 1832, but were unable to gain adequate support. Perhaps to ease regional competition, the 1834 convention was held in New York City but the gesture was not sufficient to mend the rift. In fact, the conflict between the two rival cities increased following the 1834 convention. The New York City

delegation accused the Philadelphians of embezzling funds from the convention treasury under the guise of travel expenses, an accusation that neither group took lightly. This issue was never sufficiently resolved, and it added to the animosity that already existed between the two groups. Although the New Yorkers attended the 1835 convention, the damage could not be repaired. *Minutes and Proceedings of the Second Annual Convention,* 21; *Minutes of the Fifth Annual Convention,* 29. Leslie Harris reached a similar conclusion, arguing that "such infighting led to the collapse of the convention movement." L. M. Harris, *In the Shadow of Slavery,* 185.

29. *Anglo-African,* October 1859.

30. David Walker's *Appeal to the Coloured Citizens of the World* in 1829 had raised national consciousness about slavery and the possibility of slave resistance, a possibility that became reality in 1831 with Nat Turner's rebellion. These events forced the problem of slavery before the American public, and Walker's untimely death ushered in a new group of abolitionist activists. Black New Yorkers stepped in to fill the void left by Walker and became part of the abolitionist leadership.

31. Charles H. Wesley, "The Negroes of New York in the Emancipation Movement," *Journal of Negro History* 24 (January 1939): 107–8.

32. Black activist David Ruggles also published a newspaper out of New York City in 1837, known as the *Mirror of Liberty.* However, due to his poor health, Ruggles was only able to print four issues over a period of three years. For more on the founding and challenges of Black newspapers during the antebellum era, see Armistead S. Pride and Clint C. Wilson II, *A History of the Black Press* (Washington, D.C.: Howard University Press, 1997), 3–63.

33. There were a few other antislavery organizations formed during this time including the United Anti-Slavery Society, which appears to have been largely composed of African Society members. Other associations were created as religious auxiliaries to churches such as the Roger Williams Anti-Slavery Society, which formed in March 1837 in connection with the Baptist Church. Black New Yorkers also formed antislavery associations among their youth such as the Young Men's Anti-Slavery Society and the Juvenile Anti-Slavery Society, which fell under the leadership of Reverend Theodore Wright in 1837. Little is known about these organizations, and neither had the longevity and influence of the NYASS. However, their creation reflects the strength of antislavery sentiments within the Black community. *Emancipator,* December 6, 1838; January 31, 1839; February 7, 1839; March 7 and 14, 1839; R. Freeman, *Free Negro in New York City,* 149, 156.

34. Gilje, *Road to Mobocracy,* 163; L. M. Harris, *In the Shadow of Slavery,* 197–201. For more on the amalgamation argument, see Linda K. Kerber, "Abolitionists and Amalgamators: The New York City Riots of 1834," *New York History* 48, no. 1 (January 1967): 28–39.

35. *New York Evening Post,* July 12, 1834.

36. *New York American,* July 12, 1834; Tyler Anbinder, *Five Points: The 19th Century New York City Neighborhood That Invented Tap Dance, Stole Elections, and Became the World's Most Notorious Slum* (New York: Plume, Penguin Putnam Books, 2001), 11–12. The article in the *New York American* mistakenly printed Moses Blue's name as "Moses Blew."

37. For more on the 1834 riot, see J. T. Headley, *The Great Riots of New York, 1712–1873* (Miami: Mnemosyne Publishing Co., 1969); Kerber, "Abolitionists and Amalgamators"; Leonard L. Richards, *"Gentlemen of Property and Standing": Anti-Abolition Mobs in Jacksonian America* (New York: Oxford University Press, 1970); Eugene Portlette Southall,

"Arthur Tappan and the Anti-Slavery Movement," *Journal of Negro History* 5, no. 2 (April 1930): 162–97; Anbinder, *Five Points*, 7–13. The riot is also given brief attention in Graham Hodges, *Root and Branch*, 227–28; Wilder, *In the Company of Black Men*, 143.

38. *New York Evening Post*, July 12, 1834.

39. Kerber, "Abolitionists and Amalgamators," 33.

40. The letter from Onderdonk first appeared in the *New York Evening Post* on July 14, 1834, and then in *New York American* and the *New York Spectator* on July 15, 1834. It was also reprinted in Carter G. Woodson, *The Mind of the Negro as Reflected in Letters Written during the Crisis, 1800–1860* (New York: Negro Universities Press, 1969), 629–630. Leslie Harris, Graham Hodges, and Craig Wilder also briefly mention the silencing of Williams, see L. M. Harris, *In the Shadow of Slavery*, 200; G. R. Hodges, *Root and Branch*, 239; Wilder, *In the Company of Black Men*, 144.

41. *New York Evening Post*, July 14, 1834.

42. Ibid.

43. Ibid. It should also be noted that there was some frustration in the Black community about Peter Williams Jr.'s decision. Alexander Crummell, while maintaining respect for Williams's labors on behalf of the race, thought that Williams's spirit had been broken. In a reply to Bishop Onderdonk, Crummell wrote that Williams was a "timid man" who "felt all his lifetime the extreme pressure of Episcopal power," because he had "lived in the dark and gloomy days of New York slavery . . . his soul was humbled and crushed beneath it." Wilson Jeremiah Moses, *Alexander Crummell: A Study of Civilization and Discontent* (New York: Oxford University Press, 1989), 24.

44. *New York American*, July 15, 1834.

45. In the *New York American* this man was referred to as "Davis," but the *New York Evening Post* reported the same story and called him "Marsh." Even more confusing, is that historian Tyler Anbinder identified this man as Thomas Mooney. Anbinder, *Five Points*, 11.

46. Mayor's Papers, 1834, New York Municipal Archives; *New York American*, July 12, 1834; *New York Evening Post*, July 12, 1834; *Anglo-African*, October 1859.

47. Garnet, *Memorial Discourse*, 26; Henry Louis Gates Jr., *Life and Times of Frederick Douglass* (New York: Library of America Series, 1994), 648; Marifrances Trivelli, "'I Knew a Ship from Stem to Stern': The Maritime World of Frederick Douglass," *The Log of Mystic Seaport* 46 (Spring 1995): 106.

48. At a meeting in May 1837, William Johnson claimed that there was a slave ship currently docked in the harbors of New York City preparing for its next voyage. Black activist David Ruggles later confirmed this report and added the story of the ship *Brillante*, which was allowed to dock in New York with enslaved Africans onboard, a blatant violation of the 1808 slave trade regulations. *Emancipator*, June 1, 1837; New York Committee of Vigilance, *First Annual Report*, 32, 33–46; C. Peter Ripley, ed., *The Black Abolitionist Papers: The United States, 1830–1846, vol. 3* (Chapel Hill: University of North Carolina Press, 1991), 168.

49. Beekman, *Address by Walter N. Beekman*, 6.

50. David Ruggles was born free in Norwich, Connecticut, in 1810. According to Craig Wilder, Ruggles arrived in New York City at the age of seventeen, where he became a grocer. Wilder, *In the Company of Black Men*, 135. By the 1830s, David Ruggles had achieved some notoriety in New York's Black community after writing an anticolonization manifesto that denounced ACS supporter Dr. David Reese and his schemes for Black removal.

Essentially, Ruggles maintained that it was only "cruel prejudice of caste" that prevented Blacks from enjoying all the benefits of freedom and, thus, there was no legitimate reason why Black people should be forcibly returned to Africa. He is best known for assisting Frederick Douglass during his escape from bondage. For more, see David Ruggles, *The Extinguisher Extinguished! Or David M. Reese, M.D., "Used up." Together with Some Remarks upon a Late Production Entitled "An Address on Slavery against Immediate Emancipation with a Plan of Their Being Gradually Emancipated and Colonized in Thirty-two Years," by Herman Howlett* (1834; repr., Wilmington, Del.: Scholarly Resources, Inc., 1970).

51. New York Committee of Vigilance, *First Annual Report*, 3. Emphasis is theirs. Other founders of the Committee of Vigilance included John T. Raymond, Robert Brown, William Johnston, George Barker, and J. W. Higgins. Craig Wilder also discusses the founding of the Vigilance Committee. Wilder, *In the Company of Black Men*, 165–66.

52. *Emancipator*, September 15, 1836, December 1, 1836, March 2, 1837, November 2, 1837. Harris also mentions the infamy of the Kidnapping Club. L. M. Harris, *In the Shadow of Slavery*, 208.

53. As Benjamin Quarles reported, among those who financially contributed to the abolitionist cause was "a colored woman who makes her subsistence by selling apples in the streets." Benjamin Quarles, *Black Abolitionists* (New York: Oxford University Press, 1969), 32, 75.

54. *Emancipator*, December 1, 1836; New York Committee of Vigilance, *First Annual Report*, 3, 13–14.

55. *Emancipator*, November 2, 1837. They noted, in particular, that they were able to find accommodations in the Broadway Tabernacle, but they were charged outrageously high rates and then relegated to the basement.

56. *Liberator*, August 6, 1836; *Emancipator*, October 6, 1836; *Weekly Advocate*, January 14, 1837.

57. New York Committee of Vigilance, *First Annual Report*, 29.

58. Henrietta Ray was the wife of Charles B. Ray, and Sarah Ennals and Sarah Elston were the daughters of African Society members Samuel Ennals and Alexander Elston. Both Thomas Jennings's wife and daughter were named "Elizabeth," so there has been some confusion about whether this Elizabeth Jennings was the wife or daughter of Thomas L. Jennings. However, it was likely his wife because, according to his daughter's death certificate, Elizabeth Jr. would have only been twelve in 1837.

59. *Colored American*, March 4, 1837, and September 23, 1837; *First Annual Report of the American Anti-Slavery Society*, 47. The Women's Anti-Slavery Convention had limited representation from Black women. Even when held in New York in 1837, evangelical White women proscribed Black women's participation.

60. *New York Times*, July 5, 1856. Although Blacks apparently abandoned this practice in the 1850s, their dedication in the 1830s reflected the power of the abolitionist cause among the entire Black community. In 1856, Henry Highland Garnet remarked that he wished Blacks were still supporting the agreement to boycott Independence Day.

61. *Colored American*, August 5, 1837; Rael, *Black Identity and Black Protest*, 60.

62. *Colored American*, June 9, 1838.

63. Ibid., June 1, 1839; L. M. Harris, *In the Shadow of Slavery*, 173; Rael, *Black Identity and Black Protest*, 157–58.

64. Ibid.

65. *Colored American*, June 8, 1839.

66. Simons was also not alone in his call for action against African colonization. On January 8, 1839, the Black community convened the "Great Anti-Colonization Meeting" during which participants described the notion as antirepublican, un-Christian, and "contrary to reason" and asserted the United States was the only logical home for free Blacks. Philip Bell concluded with his declaration that they must show the ACS that "we are freemen and we mean to be free." Additional opposition to the colonization issue appeared in the spring of 1840, when Samuel Cornish and Theodore S. Wright wrote a manifesto, *The Colonization Scheme Considered,* which unequivocally stated the Black community's rejection of colonization. After a powerful denunciation of the ACS and its motivations, Cornish and Wright concluded that the colony of Liberia was not stable or solvent enough to support or induce the migration of free Blacks. Therefore, they challenged the ACS to resolve their prejudice and treat Black people as equal citizens.

67. The small number of eligible Black voters stood in stark contrast to the over forty-three thousand voting Whites. *Constitution of the State of New York, Adopted in Convention, November 10, 1821. Hudson, New York,* 1822, 8; R. Freeman, *Free Negro in New York City,* 93.

68. Samuel Cornish, Thomas Downing, Thomas L. Jennings, Prince Loveridge, and Henry Sipkins led the meeting.

69. *Colored American,* March 11, 1837; R. Freeman, *Free Negro in New York City,* 95; G. Walker, *Afro-American in New York City,* 117.

70. *Colored American,* August 12, 1837; September 2, 1837; December 16, 1837; G. Walker, *Afro-American in New York City,* 119.

71. *Colored American,* March 15, 1838. Emphasis is his.

72. Ibid., June 16, 1838; G. Walker, *Afro-American in New York City,* 119.

Chapter 5: "Unity Is the Condition of Success"

Epigraphs to chapter 5 are from *Colored American,* September 11, 1841; ibid., February 2, 1841; ibid., September 4, 1841.

1. According to the *Colored American* newspaper, Henry Merscher had been "consigned to interminable bondage" by Judge Betts "without regard to the authority of the Writ De homine replegiando under which he was detained in the custody of the Sheriff, and without regard to the proof which Mr. M offered to adduce of his freedom." Ibid., December 9, 1837.

2. *Ibid;* Horton and Horton, *In Hope of Liberty,* 239.

3. For the Pease's argument, see William H. Pease and Jane H. Pease, *They Who Would Be Free: Blacks' Search for Freedom, 1830–1861* (New York: Atheneum, 1974), 75.

4. James McCune Smith (1813–1865) was born free in New York City to parents who had previously been emancipated. As a young boy, he was educated in the African Free Schools, where he established lifelong relationships with fellow students Henry Highland Garnet and George Downing who, likewise, also became important activists. As a child, Smith's intelligence singled him out for special recognition; in fact, at the age of eleven, he was selected by the African Free School teachers to prepare a speech in honor of a visit from Revolutionary War hero, General Lafayette. Even though he demonstrated a remarkable gift for science, Smith was denied admission to American medical schools because of race. Sorely disappointed, he soon received assistance from activist Peter Williams Jr., who arranged for Smith to enroll at the University of Glasgow in 1832. Smith spent the next five

years in Scotland earning three degrees: a B.A. (1835), a M.A. (1836), and a M.D. (1837). Immediately after completing his medical degree, Smith returned to his home in New York City where he opened a successful medical practice and two pharmacies. Smith soon became a powerful force in New York City's Black leadership; most notably, he joined the African Society and agitated for abolition and suffrage. For more on his political activism during the antebellum era, see the remainder of this chapter, chapter 6, and the epilogue. Beyond his political activism focusing on slavery, voting rights, and colonization, Smith became increasingly concerned with the plight of working class Blacks. During the 1840s, he worked diligently as the physician for the Colored Orphan Asylum and tried to raise consciousness among other Black activists about the economic issues in their community. In 1850, Smith helped establish a new organization to address the needs of Black workers, the American League of Colored Laborers, which advocated for education and training in mechanical skills as a method to improve conditions for their people. The following year, Dr. Smith prepared a rather elaborate statement on the socioeconomic status of the Black community. In particular, he outlined the economic problems plaguing their people that encouraged crime. Up until his death, Smith remained active in the Black community and often wrote for Frederick Douglass's newspaper under the pseudonym Communipaw. In 1861, he helped finance the creation of a Black newspaper, the *Anglo-African*, and was appointed as a professor of anthropology at Wilberforce College in 1863. A continuing heart problem prevented Smith from actually joining the faculty, a condition that eventually took his life in November 1865. His final major contribution was drafting the introduction to Henry Highland Garnet's address before Congress in February 1865.

Born in Falmouth, Massachusetts, Charles Ray (1807–1886) was first employed as a boot maker. At the age of twenty-three, he experienced a religious awakening and decided to pursue the ministry within the Methodist church. He was first educated at Wesleyan Academy in Massachusetts and then entered Wesleyan University in Connecticut, which offered training to Methodist teachers and preachers. Ray soon left Wesleyan, however, after enduring severe racism from his classmates. By 1833, he relocated to New York City, and the following year he married Henrietta Regulus who became the first president of the Ladies Literary Society. Sadly, Henrietta died in 1836. Charles Ray's first known political activity began in 1837, with his membership in the Young Men's Anti-Slavery Society. In 1839, he assumed the editorship of the *Colored American* newspaper and held this position until the paper folded in 1841. Four years later, in 1845, he established the Bethesda Congregational Church. During the 1840s, Ray agitated against slavery, on behalf of Black voting rights, and played a significant role in the Colored Convention movement. For more on his political activism, see the remainder of this chapter and chapter 6. In addition, Ray was a conductor on the Underground Railroad and was extremely dedicated to the cause of fugitives. In 1847, Ray joined the New York State Vigilance Committee, which was a biracial statewide organization founded by Quaker Isaac Hopper and dedicated to assisting and protecting fugitives. As one of his last activities, Charles Ray joined the New York Society for the Promotion of Education Among Colored Children in 1857 and issued a report on the declining quality of Black education.

Perhaps the best known of these men, Henry Highland Garnet (1815–1882), was born into slavery in Kent County, Maryland. His grandfather was said to be an African chieftain, and his father helped the family escape bondage when young Henry was only eight. Once they arrived in New York City, Henry enrolled at the African Free School where he became acquainted with many abolitionists and fellow students who influenced him throughout his life. After serving as a sailor and a farmer's apprentice, Garnet went to study at an academy in New Canaan, New Hampshire. Yet angry Whites soon caused Garnet to leave the academy, and he enrolled at the Oneida Institute in Whitesboro, New York. In 1840, he settled in Troy, New York, and two years later married Julia Williams. Throughout the 1840s and 1850s, Garnet rose to prominence as one of the leading Black activists of his time. For more on his activism during this antebellum period, see the remainder of this chapter, chapter 6, and the epilogue. During the Reconstruction era, Garnet continued to pressure the government for aid to newly freed Blacks and served with the Freedman's Bureau. In 1871, his wife Julia died and he married Sarah Thompson. In 1881, Garnet became the minister to Liberia where he died later that year.

5. For more on William Lloyd Garrison and his detractors, see Aileen S. Kraditor, *Means and Ends in American Abolitionism: Garrison and His Critics on Strategy and Tactics, 1834–1850* (New York: Pantheon Books, 1967).

6. Bertram Wyatt-Brown, *Lewis Tappan and the Evangelical War against Slavery* (1969; repr., Baton Rouge: Louisiana State University Press, 1997), 187–90; Quarles, *Black Abolitionists*, 42–43; Philip Foner, ed., *The Life and Writings of Frederick Douglass*, vol. 1 (New York: International Publishers, 1950), 40–41.

7. Lewis Tappan to Gerrit Smith, May 15, 1839, Gerrit Smith Papers, Syracuse University; *Sixth Annual Report of the Executive Committee of the American Anti-Slavery Society, with the Speeches Delivered at the Anniversary Meeting Held in the City of New York, on the 7th of May, 1839* (New York: Printed by William S. Dorr, 1839), 43–46; Wyatt-Brown, *Lewis Tappan*, 193–96; Henry Mayer, *All on Fire: William Lloyd Garrison and the Abolition of Slavery* (New York: St. Martin's Press, 1998), 256–58.

8. *Colored American*, May 23, 1840; Quarles, *Black Abolitionists*, 44–45; P. Foner, *Life and Writings of Frederick Douglass*, 43; Wyatt-Brown, *Lewis Tappan*, 197–98.

9. Wyatt-Brown, *Lewis Tappan*, 197–98; Mayer, *All on Fire*, 278–82. The Black New Yorkers who entered the protest were Patrick Reason, Thomas L. Jennings, and Thomas Downing.

10. Eventually, the AFASS reorganized itself into the American Missionary Association and became deeply involved in the famous *Amistad* case. It also turned its attention to the Liberty Party, which eventually gained some support from New York's Black leadership.

11. As Leslie Harris points out, Black New Yorkers also embraced the Tappans because they publicly denounced African colonization after Arthur Tappan visited the 1831 Colored Convention. L. M. Harris, *In the Shadow of Slavery*, 176.

12. *Colored American*, May 2, 1840; Pease and Pease, *They Who Would Be Free*, 79–80. Thomas Van Rensalaer's name is spelled differently in various documents. Sometimes it appears as "Renssalaer," "Rensallaer," or "Rensalear."

13. Another example of Black New Yorkers' divided loyalties came when Henry Highland Garnet found himself in a complicated situation. Although he was a member of the AFASS, he elected not to change the name of his juvenile society, the Garrison Literary and Benevolent Society, after intense public pressure. Quarles, *Black Abolitionists*, 105.

14. Charles B. Ray to James G. Birney and Henry B. Stanton, May 20, 1840, in *Black Abolitionist Papers*, vol. 3, 331–39; *Colored American*, May 23, 1840.

15. *Colored American*, June 13, 1840.

16. Ibid., June 20, 1840.

17. Ibid., June 6, 1840.

18. Ibid., July 25, 1840.

19. U.S. Census Office, *Sixth Census or Enumeration of the Inhabitants of the United States* (Washington, D.C.: Blair and Rives, 1841); R. Freeman, *Free Negro in New York City*, 93; G. Walker, *Afro-American in New York City*, 213–15.

20. Of particular note was the group's desire to draw representation from all its people regardless of status or wealth. The group asked "colored men in all sections of the State—men in all circumstances" to answer the call; the only requirement was that they must have a love of liberty and a desire for political and moral elevation. Careful not to alienate anyone in the community, the group elected to convene in August, a time when most farmers could leave their crops and tend to political business. The group called upon the farmer, the mechanic, the laborer and working man to leave their work for a brief moment and "be seen crowding the avenues that lead to the place of assemblage." *Colored American*, June 6, 1840.

21. *Colored American*, May 9, 1840; G. Walker, *Afro-American in New York City*, 120. Charles Ray, John J. Zuille, Theodore Wright, Charles Reason, and Timothy Seaman served on the organizing committee. In addition, William Johnson, Philip A. Bell, Henry Stoughtenburgh, Daniel Elston (likely Alexander Elston's son), Thomas Downing, Thomas Sidney, Frederick Olney, Patrick Reason, Z. S. Barbary, and Thomas Van Rensalaer signed the resolutions. There were also representatives from adjoining regions such as Brooklyn, Queens, Long Island, Albany, Tory, Geneva, Rochester, and Bath.

22. *National Anti-Slavery Standard*, June 18, 1840.

23. *Colored American*, June 27, 1840.

24. For biographical information on James McCune Smith and Charles Ray, see note 4, and for Philip A. Bell's biography, see chapter 4. Patrick Reason (1817–1857) was born in New York City to parents who had fled from Haiti following the Haitian Revolution. As a young boy, he attended the New York African Free School where his talent for art was quickly recognized. He was soon apprenticed to a White engraver who taught him the craft. At the age of thirteen, Reason received attention for designing the frontispiece to a book documenting the history of the African Free School. Little is known about Patrick's personal life; it is not clear whether he ever married or had children. Instead Patrick Reason made art and engravings his life's work, creating portraits of leading abolitionists during his career. Perhaps his most famous pieces were an engraving of the abolitionist symbol "Am I Not a Man and a Brother" in 1835, as well as his creation of a similar image entitled "Am I Not a Woman and a Sister." For more on Patrick Reason, and his brother Charles, see the remainder of this chapter and chapter 6.

25. *Colored American*, August 8, 1840.

26. Ibid., August 15, 1840. Scholar John Stauffer argued that McCune Smith was "skeptical of white abolitionists and their societies," but this meeting seems to indicate that, at least in 1840, Smith believed in importance of interracial coalitions. John Stauffer, *The Black Hearts of Men: Radical Abolitionists and the Transformation of Race* (Cambridge: Harvard University Press, 2000), 153.

27. *Colored American*, August 15, 1840.

28. Ibid., June 27, 1840.

29. Ibid., August 15 and 20, 1840. Thomas Van Rensalaer boycotted all the state conventions and worked to create an alternative organization.

30. There were also delegates present who lived in other areas of New York State, but had strong roots in New York City such as Henry Highland Garnet, Alexander Crummell, and John T. Raymond.

31. *Colored American,* August 29, 1840, and September 5, 1840.

32. Ibid., November 21, 1840.

33. Ibid., December 19, 1840; P. Foner and G. Walker, *Proceedings of the Black State Conventions,* 21–22. Emphasis is theirs.

34. *Colored American,* February 13, 1841. Emphasis is Garnet's.

35. Ibid., July 17, 24, and 31, 1841; G. Walker, *Afro-American in New York City,* 121. Henry Highland Garnet, Theodore S. Wright, Charles Ray, Charles Reason, Patrick Reason, Alexander Elston, John J. Zuille, William P. Johnson, Philip A. Bell, Daniel Elston, Ransom Wake, Thomas Hamilton, Prince Loveridge, and John Peterson each signed the call for convention.

36. *Colored American,* August 7, 1841.

37. Ibid., August 14, 21, and 28, 1841; *National Anti-Slavery Standard,* August 12, 1841.

38. Born to Haitian immigrant parents, Charles Reason (1818–1893) attended the African Free School and developed a talent for mathematics at a very young age. When he was only fourteen, Reason became an instructor at the school and used his salary to hire additional tutors. Reason later decided to pursue a future in the ministry, but he was denied entrance into the General Theological Seminary of the Protestant Episcopal Church based on his race. Disgusted, he left the church and enrolled at McGrawville College in upstate New York. Beyond his brother, Patrick (who became a famous artist and engraver), little is known about Charles Reason's private life, except that he was married and widowed three times and his third wife was named Clorice Esteve. Charles Reason became committed to the issues of abolition and suffrage during the 1840s; for more on his political activism, see the remainder of this chapter and chapter 6. For Charles Reason, the key to race uplift was Black education. He advocated for the creation of manual labor and industrial schools and helped form the American League of Colored Laborers, which focused on industrial education. In 1847, Reason and Charles Ray created the Society for the Promotion of Education among Colored Children, and Reason served as a school superintendent in 1848. In 1849, Reason became the first Black professor in the United States when he was hired at New York Central College in McGrawville, New York. Yet just three years later, Reason resigned to become principal of Philadelphia's Institute for Colored Youth. The following year, he represented Pennsylvania at the national Colored Convention. However, in 1855, Charles Reason returned to New York City, where he served as a teacher and school administrator. In 1873, he launched a successful crusade against the city's policy of segregated schools. One year after Charles Reason retired, he died in New York City in 1893.

39. *Colored American,* September 11, 1841.

40. Ibid., September 4 and 11, 1841.

41. *Liberator,* September 24, 1841; G. Walker, *Afro-American in New York City,* 125. Black Bostonian William C. Nell also lent his support to the ARBDC.

42. *National Anti-Slavery Standard,* September 23, 1841; *Colored American,* September 18, 1841.

43. Other than New York, they also had representation from Massachusetts, Connecticut, New Jersey, Pennsylvania, and Ohio.

44. Of course, the absence of the Philadelphians was also likely a testament to residual conflicts over strategy and ideology that had ended the conventions in the 1830s.

45. For more on the perspective of Philadelphians on this issue, see Winch, *Philadelphia's Black Elite,* 122–29.

46. For Bell's insight on the Bostonians, see *Survey of the Negro Convention Movement*, 71–72.

47. *Minutes of the National Convention of Colored Citizens: Held at Buffalo, on the 15th, 16th, 17th, 18th and 19th of August, 1843. For the Purpose of Considering Their Moral and Political Condition as American Citizens* (New York: Piercy and Reed, 1843), 3.

48. Ibid., 4, 5, 7.

49. Henry Highland Garnet, "An Address to the Slaves of the United States of America," in *Lift Every Voice: African American Oratory, 1787–1900*, ed. Philip S. Foner and Robert James Branham (Tuscaloosa: University of Alabama Press, 1998), 199, 201, 204, 205. Emphasis is his. Craig Wilder also discusses Garnet's speech. Wilder, *In the Company of Black Men*, 168–70.

50. *Minutes of the National Convention of Colored Citizens*, 13.

51. Ibid., 13–14, 18. After considerable discussion the subject was reopened and further debate ensued, but the address failed a second time by an even larger margin of 14 to 9. Ibid., 23–24; Bell, *Survey of the Negro Convention Movement*, 75.

52. *Liberator*, October 30, 1840, and November 6, 1840.

53. *Minutes of the National Convention of Colored Citizens*, 15.

54. Ibid., 15–16, 25–26.

55. *Liberator*, October 30, 1840, and November 6, 1840; *National Anti-Slavery Standard*, November 14, 1844.

56. P. Foner and G. Walker, *Proceedings of the Black State Conventions*, 32–33.

57. Ibid., 34–36. For notes on the conventions of 1845 and 1851, see ibid., 37–42, 54–78.

58. *Debates and Proceedings in the New York State Convention for the Revision of the Constitution* (Albany, 1846), 785; G. Walker, *Afro-American in New York City*, 126.

59. *Liberator*, July 18, 1845

60. Quarles, *Black Abolitionists*, 184–85; Wesley, "The Negroes of New York in the Emancipation Movement," 100. For more on the Liberty Party, see G. Walker, *Afro-American in New York City*, 136–41; Quarles, *Black Abolitionists*, 183–88.

61. *Proceedings of the National Liberty Convention, Held at Buffalo, New York, June 14th and 15th, 1848; Including the Resolutions and Addresses Adopted by That Body, and Speeches of Beriah Green and Gerrit Smith on That Occasion* (Utica, N.Y.: S. W. Green, 1848). For more on James McCune Smith's conversion to the Liberty Party, see Stauffer, *Black Hearts of Men*, 153–54.

62. *Report of the Proceedings of the Colored National Convention, Held at Cleveland, Ohio, on Wednesday, September 6, 1848* (Rochester, N.Y.: Printed by John Dick at the North Star Office, 1848), 18.

63. Ibid., 17–18.

Chapter 6: "A Heavy and Cruel Hand Has Been Laid upon Us"

Epigraphs for chapter 6 are from *Proceedings of the Colored National Convention, Held in Rochester, July 6th, 7th, and 8th, 1853* (Rochester: Printed at the office of Frederick Douglass's Paper, 1853), 11; Ibid., 16. This quote was also reprinted in another document published during the same period. See James McCune Smith, James P. Miller, and John J. Zuille, "The Suffrage Question" in *Documentary History of the Negro People*, vol. 1, 455;

1. In 1840, members of the Committee of Vigilance accused David Ruggles of embezzlement. Although Ruggles denied the claim, the conflict was well-publicized and weakened

the reputation of the organization. Unable to recover from the internal dissent, the committee began to collapse. The fate of the organization was sealed when David Ruggles's health failed and he left the city to seek treatment in 1842. *National Anti-Slavery Standard,* August 20, 1840; *Liberator,* September 29, 1847; Wesley, "Negroes of New York in the Emancipation Movement," 89.

2. *North Star,* April 5, 1850. Leading Black activists of the day, including Thomas Van Rensalaer, George Downing, Philip Bell, and John J. Zuille, attended the meeting.

3. New York State, Census for 1845 (Albany, New York: Carroll and Cook, 1846); U.S. Census Office, *The Seventh Census of the United States 1850* (Washington D.C.: Robert Armstrong, public printer, 1853); New York State, *Census for 1855* (Albany, N.Y.: C. Van Benthuysen, 1857). We will likely never know how many Black people fled New York City due to the passage of the Fugitive Slave Act, but thousands of free Blacks from throughout the North sought refuge in Canada during this period. For more on Black emigration to Canada, see Jane Rhodes, *Mary Ann Shadd Cary: The Black Press and Protest in the Nineteenth Century* (Bloomington: Indiana University Press, 1998).

4. In some documents, he is called George Hamlet, perhaps indicating that (like many fugitives) he changed his name. There was also one report stating that there was an attempt to rescue Hamlet before he was sent to jail, which, if true, suggested that the Black community was well-organized. According to the *New York Herald,* "when the fugitive was taken into custody, he gave a signal, upon which a large number of colored men congregated around him," but the police managed to disperse the potential rescuers. Samuel Rhoads, ed., *The Non-Slaveholder,* vol. 5 (Westport, Conn.: Negro Universities Press, 1970), 239. It should be noted, however, that the *New York Daily Tribune* denied this report, calling it "entirely false." *New York Daily Tribune,* October 2, 1850.

5. *National Anti-Slavery Standard,* October 10, 1850.

6. *New York Daily Tribune,* February 7 and 21, 1850. The entire membership was as follows: John J. Zuille (president), T. J. White and Philip A. Bell (secretaries), James McCune Smith (treasurer), William Burnett, Ezekial Dias, Thomas Downing, George Downing (Thomas Downing's son), Robert Hamilton, Junius Morel, Jeremiah Powers, J. T. Raymond, and William J. Wilson.

7. *The Fugitive Slave Bill: Its History and Unconstitutionality, With an Account of the Seizure and Enslavement of James Hamlet, and His Subsequent Restoration to Liberty* (New York: W. Harned, 1850), 31–32; P. Foner and G. Walker, eds., *Proceedings of the Black State Conventions,* 43–45; *North Star,* October 24, 1850; G. Walker, *Afro-American in New York City,* 174. Significantly, two-thirds of the audience was female despite the fact that men dominated the leadership of the meeting.

8. *New York Daily Tribune,* October 2, 1850; *Fugitive Slave Bill,* 5, 36; Quarles, *Black Abolitionists,* 198–99; R. Freeman, *Free Negro in New York City,* 62; G. Walker, *Afro-American in New York City,* 175–76; Wilder, *In the Company of Black Men,* 172.

9. *New York Daily Tribune,* December 24 and 30, 1850; R. Freeman, *Free Negro in New York City,* 62.

10. J. W. C. Pennington (1809–1871) was born into bondage in Hagerstown, Maryland, and trained as a blacksmith. He escaped from slavery in his twenties and lived in Pennsylvania and Hartford, Connecticut, before coming to New York City to serve as the minister at Shiloh Presbyterian Church. He held this position from 1847 to 1855. In 1849, he published his autobiography, *The Fugitive Blacksmith* (London: C. Gilpin, 1850), which revealed his status as a fugitive and caused him to flee to Europe. Two years later,

he received a divinity degree from Heidelberg University and officially purchased his freedom for $150. For more on Pennington's political activism, particularly his views on colonization, see the remainder of this chapter.

11. *New York Daily Tribune,* May 27, 1854; *Frederick Douglass Paper,* June 16, 1854; Stephen Pembroke, "I Set Out to Escape from Slavery," in *Lift Every Voice,* 273.

12. L. M. Harris, *In the Shadow of Slavery,* 238.

13. Dorothy Sterling, *We Are Your Sisters: Black Women in the Nineteenth Century* (New York: W. W. Norton & Company, 1984), 220–21.

14. *New York Daily Tribune,* September 7 and 16, 1850.

15. Elizabeth Jennings (1830?–1901) was born in New York, although there is some controversy surrounding the date of her birth. The U.S. census reports that she was born in 1830, but her death certificate indicates that she was born in 1826. In addition to having an activist father, her mother (also named Elizabeth) may have been a founding member of the New York Ladies Literary Society. Following the resolution of her desegregation case, Elizabeth Jennings withdrew from the public realm. She married Charles Graham sometime in the late 1850s, but tragedy struck her family during the 1860s. Amid the vicious 1863 Civil War draft riot in New York City, her young son Thomas apparently died due to convulsions. She and her husband braved the rioters and managed to get her son's body to Greenwood Cemetery in Brooklyn for a proper burial. Her husband died just a few years later, in 1867. Despite her personal crises, Jennings Graham remained committed to the Black community. In 1890, she berated her people for not financially supporting T. Thomas Fortune's newspaper and established a kindergarten in her own home in 1895. Elizabeth Jennings Graham died in 1901.

16. *New York Daily Tribune,* July 19, 1854.

17. Ibid.

18. Ibid.; *Pacific Appeal,* May 26, 1863; John H. Hewitt, "The Search for Elizabeth Jennings, Heroine of a Sunday Afternoon in New York City," *New York History* 62 (October 1990): 394.

19. *New York Daily Tribune,* February 23, 1856. Although the jury awarded $225, Judge Rockwell increased it by 10 percent and forced the company to pay court costs.

20. Ibid., May 8, 1855.

21. Ibid., May 25 and 26, 1855. This case was also briefly mentioned in R. Freeman, *Free Negro in New York City,* 24–25.

22. *New York Daily Tribune,* September 25, 1855; February 23, 1856; December 16, 1856.

23. Ibid., December 17, 1856.

24. Ibid., December 19 and 20, 1856.

25. Ibid., February 20, 1857; January 9, 1858.

26. Ibid., February 25, 1858.

27. Ibid.

28. *New York Daily Tribune,* September 25, 1858.

29. The Black leadership obviously remained concerned about the community's protection, because the Legal Rights Association met throughout the remainder of the decade. Ibid., February 24, 1859.

30. At the 1848 convention, delegates passed a resolution stating that the next convention would be held in either Detroit or Pittsburgh and would be held in 1850. For some unknown reason, they did not meet again until 1853 in Rochester, New York.

31. *Proceedings of the Colored National Convention, 1853,* 3. There were also some former New Yorkers present, who had moved to other regions and were now representing different states. For example, George Downing was a representative from Rhode Island, David Ruggles from Massachusetts, and Charles Reason from Pennsylvania. Significantly, Black New Yorkers also demonstrated a desire to put aside old petty rivalries when they agreed to let the 1855 convention meet in Philadelphia for the first time since 1835.

32. There was one critical challenge to the delegates' commitment to unity, when the first and only female delegate attended the convention in 1855. Although the 1848 convention had declared its support of women's rights and equality, there was a difference between theory and reality. Indeed, some Black leaders still clung to the old notion that Black rights and women's rights should remain separate. As a result, on the first day of the 1855 convention, when Charles Remond of Massachusetts made a motion that Mary Ann Shadd should be admitted as a delegate, the idea of her participation "gave rise to a spirited discussion." In some ways, it is ironic that Mary Ann Shadd would be a source of controversy at the Colored Convention because, in addition to the fact that she was the daughter of Abraham Shadd (one of the first and most active delegates at the Colored Conventions of the 1830s), she was a renowned activist, editor, and emigrationist. In the end, Shadd was allowed to attend as a delegate although the resolution passed by a narrow margin. The final vote was 38 to 23 with Frederick Douglass and William Watkins speaking in her favor, and Philip A. Bell, J. C. Wears, C. S. Hodges, Lewis Nelson, and J. C. Bowers arguing against her. Although the debate over female participation threatened the unity of the gathering, delegates were apparently able to overcome their differences of opinion and move forward as a united community. *Proceedings of the Colored National Convention Held in Franklin Hall, Sixth Street, below Arch, Philadelphia, October 16th, 17th, and 18th, 1855* (Salem, N.J.: Printed at the National Standard Office, 1855), 10.

33. *Proceedings of the Colored National Convention, 1853,* 3.

34. *Proceedings of the Colored National Convention, 1855,* 3, 5.

35. *Proceedings of the Colored National Convention, 1853,* 3, 4, 7, 10; *Proceedings of the Colored National Convention, 1855,* 33, 32.

36. As evidence of the Black leadership's movement away from William Lloyd Garrison and his political philosophy, Frederick Douglass and James McCune Smith denounced Garrison and the AASS in the pages of the *Frederick Douglass Paper* after Garrison claimed that colored people had "kept aloof from the Anti-Slavery movement." Smith was outraged by what he thought was a gross misrepresentation; he argued that Garrison owed much to the free Black population and even suggested that Garrison had taken his ideas for his publication, *Thoughts on African Colonization,* from his Black comrades. He concluded his statement by saying that Black men had been purposely excluded from the movement. Likewise, Douglass maintained that there was a feeling permeating the AASS, "telling the colored man that he cannot be at home in it." According to Douglass, members of the AASS "pitied" Black men and did not view them as equals. *Frederick Douglass Paper,* January 26, 1855; May 18, 1855.

37. *Proceedings of the Colored National Convention, 1853,* 11.

38. *Proceedings of the Colored National Convention, 1855,* 30–31.

39. *Proceedings of the Colored National Convention, 1853,* 18–19.

40. Apparently there was supposed to be another meeting in Cleveland, Ohio; however, they were forced to postpone it until July because of attendance problems. *Frederick Douglass Paper,* June 23, 1854.

41. *Proceedings of the Colored National Convention, 1855,* 15.

42. *Anglo-African,* October 1859.

43. There was only a brief discussion of the suffrage issue at the national Colored Convention in 1853, when delegates declared that they were "entitled to the right of elective franchise, in common with the white men of this country." Similar notions were echoed at the 1855 convention, when representatives protested that Black men had been "robbed" of their right to vote. *Proceedings of the Colored National Convention, 1853,* 40; *Proceedings of the Colored National Convention, 1855,* 30–31.

44. *New York Daily Tribune,* November 5, 1850; September 6, 1855; P. Foner and G. Walker, *Proceedings of the Black State Conventions,* 88–98. Philip A. Bell, Thomas L. Jennings, Charles Ray, James McCune Smith, J. J. Simons, and J. W. C. Pennington were among the representatives from New York City.

45. *New York Daily Tribune,* October 6, 1856; R. Freeman, *Free Negro in New York City,* 105.

46. *New York Daily Tribune,* September 24, 1856.

47. Ibid., September 22 and 26, 1857.

48. *Dred Scott v. John F. A. Sandford,* 1856.

49. P. Foner and G. Walker, *Proceedings of the Black State Conventions,* 99.

50. *Liberator,* October 1, 1858; *Anglo-African,* September 17, 1859; April 28, 1860.

51. *New York Daily Tribune,* September 24, 1856.

52. McCune Smith's selection may have been part of a concession strategy, because he had openly attacked the party earlier that year for not making room for Black men within the organization. *Frederick Douglass Paper,* December 15, 1854; January 4 and 19, 1855.

53. For more on the relationship between Black activists and the Radical Abolition Party, see Stauffer, *Black Hearts of Men,* 8–24.

54. *National Anti-Slavery Standard,* October 6, 1858; P. Foner and G. Walker, *Proceedings of the Black State Conventions,* 100; Quarles, *Black Abolitionists,* 188–89.

55. Nell, *Colored Patriots,* 322–23.

56. *Anglo-African,* January 1859.

57. Nell, *Property Qualifications or No Property Qualifications,* 3–4, 14.

58. J. McCune Smith et al., "Suffrage Question," 455.

59. Journal of the Assembly of the State of New York (1860), 737, 1129; Wesley, "Negroes of New York in the Emancipation Movement," 102.

60. Edward Z. C. Judson, *The Mysteries and Miseries of New York: A Story of Real Life by Ned Buntline* (New York: Berford and Company, 1848), part 1: 89, 91; part 2: 79, 82.

61. Charles Dickens, *American Notes for General Circulation,* 1942; reprinted with introduction and notes by Patricia Ingham, ed. (New York: Penguin Books, 2000), 101–2. Another visitor to the Five Points published his reflections in 1850, and offered a similar description of dance culture in the Black community. George G. Foster, *New York by Gas-Light: With Here and There a Streak of Sunshine* (New York: Dewitt and Davenport, 1850), 140–46.

62. *New York Times,* August 2, 1855.

63. Ibid.

64. Beyond the dance halls and occasional parade, the activities and gatherings that had previously helped Black New Yorkers cope with enslavement and unrelenting oppression in previous decades were beginning to wane in the 1850s. Catharine Market, which had served as a social haven for Black people seeking to interact and revel in African dance

forms since the 1790s, had fallen into neglect. In August 1859, a white New Yorker visited the marketplace searching for signs of the thriving cultural scene that had dominated that area for years. Instead, he found only "the last of the 'Long Island negroes,' some of which had for the last fifty years visited this market on Sunday mornings." When he asked the old woman where the others had gone, she replied that there were "'only about *four* who occasionally came—*the rest are all dead.*'" Disheartened by this sad scene, the author later reflected that he thought it was evidence of the American government's neglect and abuse of the Black population: "I felt that when Government made them free, Government should have removed some of the obstacles which interfered with the intellectual progress and the domestic comfort of the newly liberated African race—that they might . . . be a useful and respectable body of people." De Voe, *Market Book*, 369–70.

65. *North Star,* January 26, 1848; March 2, 1849; Quarles, *Black Abolitionists,* 216.

66. *North Star,* January 26, 1848; March 2, 1849; Quarles, *Black Abolitionists,* 216.

67. *National Anti-Slavery Standard,* May 3, 1849. In addition to the New Yorkers, there were also representatives, such as Charles Remond and Frederick Douglass, from other Northern cities. P. Foner and G. Walker, *Proceedings of the Black State Conventions,* 47.

68. *New York Daily Tribune,* November 5, 1850.

69. *New York Daily Tribune,* March 10, 1851; *Frederick Douglass Paper,* November 13, 1851; G. Walker, *Afro-American in New York City,* 155.

70. *New York Daily Tribune,* October 23, 1851.

71. *National Anti-Slavery Standard,* January 22, 1852.

72. Ibid.

73. *New York Daily Tribune,* November 5, 1850. George Downing (1819–1903) was born in New York City, the son of Black activist Thomas Downing. As a young boy, George attended the New York African Free School, and, by the late 1830s, he became part of the new young Black leadership in New York City. In November 1841, he married Serena Leanora de Grasse, the daughter of another New York activist George de Grasse. Downing's first known political participation revealed his dedication to unrestricted suffrage rights (see chapter 5). Later in the 1840s, Downing moved to Rhode Island and accumulated property including the Atlantic House, where the United States Naval Academy was located. He also built the Sea Girt Hotel, which was destroyed by fire in 1860. He was eventually considered one of the wealthiest Black men in the United States, and there is still a street in Newport, Rhode Island, named after him. Although Downing spent much of his adult life traveling between New York, Washington, D.C., and Newport, Downing remained particularly active in New York City politics on issues such as education, fugitives, and anticolonization. For more on his political activism in New York City, see the remainder of this chapter. From the late 1850s to mid-1860s, Downing led a series of desegregation movements including public schools in Rhode Island and streetcars on the Baltimore and Ohio Railroad. He even forced the U.S. Senate to open its gallery to Black people and protested curfews for Black people in Washington, D.C. In 1903, George Downing died in Newport, Rhode Island.

74. *Frederick Douglass Paper,* January 15, 1852; *National Anti-Slavery Standard,* January 22, 1852; G. Walker, *Afro-American in New York City,* 156–58.

75. *Frederick Douglass Paper,* January 15, 1852; *National Anti-Slavery Standard,* January 22, 1852; G. Walker, *Afro-American in New York City,* 156–58.

76. *Frederick Douglass Paper,* February 12, 1852.

77. *Arguments, Pro and Con, on the Call for a National Emigration Convention, to Be Held*

in Cleveland, Ohio, August 1854, by Frederick Douglass, W. J. Watkins, and J. M. Whitfield, with a Short Appendix of the Statistics of Canada West, West Indies, Central and South America (Detroit: Tribune Steam Presses, George E. Pomeroy and Co., 1854), 6–8.

78. P. Foner and G. Walker, *Proceedings of the Black State Conventions,* 90.

79. W. M. Brewer, "Henry Highland Garnet," *Journal of Negro History* 13, no. 1 (January 1928): 48.

80. *New York Daily Tribune,* August 11, 1858; R. Freeman, *Free Negro in New York City,* 33–34; G. Walker, *Afro-American in New York City,* 158–59; F. J. Miller, *Search for a Black Nationality,* 192.

81. *Proceedings of the Colored National Convention, 1855,* 28. Downing also denounced Harriet Beecher Stowe's *Uncle Tom's Cabin,* which had been used as a justification for colonization. American and Foreign Anti-Slavery Society, *13th Annual Report,* 109.

82. *Frederick Douglass Paper,* July 2, 1858; September 17, 1858; July 22, 1859; R. Freeman, *Free Negro in New York City,* 35.

83. *New York Daily Tribune,* December 8, 1858.

84. Ibid., December 10, 1858. For more on Garnet's political thought regarding emigration, see Stuckey, *Slave Culture,* 182–84.

85. *Anglo-African,* September 10, 1859; September 17, 1859; March 31, 1860. J. W. C. Pennington changed his mind about emigration numerous times over the years; in 1846, he had supported the notion of Jamaican emigration, but he denounced emigration at a public meeting in 1852. *Albany Patriot,* May 6, 1846; *Black Abolitionist Papers,* vol. 3, 474.

86. *New York Daily Tribune,* March 22, 1860; G. Walker, *Afro-American in New York City,* 159.

87. *New York Daily Tribune,* March 22, 1860; G. Walker, *Afro-American in New York City,* 159; R. Freeman, *Free Negro in New York City,* 36.

88. *Anglo-African,* April 7, 1860.

89. Ibid., January 6, 1861. Craig Wilder also documents a portion of the conflict between Garnet and McCune Smith over this issue. Wilder, *In the Company of Black Men,* 173–75.

90. Ibid., January 19, 1861; R. Freeman, *Free Negro in New York City,* 37.

91. *Anglo-African,* November 1859; F. J. Miller, *Search for a Black Nationality,* 108–9, 234–38.

92. Quoted in F. J. Miller, *Search for a Black Nationality,* 243.

93. *Weekly Anglo-African,* January 5 and 12, 1861. A portion of this quote also appears in Wilder, *In the Company of Black Men,* 174.

94. F. J. Miller, *Search for a Black Nationality,* 239–40.

95. Ibid., 262.

96. *Weekly Anglo-African,* January 12, 1861. Of course, reflecting the cyclical nature of Black history, the emigration question was only postponed. It re-emerged in the 1880s and also in the twentieth century, as the Black community continued to struggle with its relationship to the United States.

Chapter 7: "The Story of Seneca Village"

1. *New York Herald,* August 11, 1871.

2. There is significant confusion surrounding the community's name. The rector of St. Michaels Church maintained that the area was known as Seneca Village; however, there

is no other evidence that the community actually used that name. Other references to the region are "Yorkville" and the occasional derogatory mentions of "Nigger Village." If the community was in fact called Seneca Village, the most common question is why *Seneca*. We may never know the true answer to that query. Various scholars, who heard my presentations on this topic at academic conferences, initially suggested that the name was a reference to the Native Americans who originally inhabited that land, particularly because an old Native American trail passed nearby. However, we know that the Seneca did not live on Manhattan Island and had no significant connection to that region. There-fore, I have proposed that the name Seneca could refer to the Roman philosopher who wrote extensively about the rights of humans to freedom and liberty. Black New Yorkers who had been educated at the African Free Schools were trained in classic philosophy and would likely have been exposed to Seneca's ideas. Perhaps inspired by the ideal of liberty and equality, Black residents adopted the name Seneca to reflect their hope for their community's potential.

3. The truth about Seneca Village began to be revealed following a brief mention of the community in Roy Rosenzweig and Elizabeth Blackmar's study of Central Park, *The Park and the People: A History of Central Park* (Ithaca, N.Y.: Cornell University Press, 1992). Inspired by this citation, Cynthia Copeland at the New York Historical Society began to investigate the community and constructed an exhibit that became one of the most popular events at the New York Historical Society. Since then, other scholars of Black New York have mentioned Seneca Village briefly; however, there has still not been an extensive historical investigation of this important and influential neighborhood. For other discussions of Seneca Village, see Wilder, *In the Company of Black Men*, 101–2; L. M. Harris, *In the Shadow of Slavery*, 266–67.

4. Seneca Village was not the first effort by Black New Yorkers to establish an indepen-dent community in the state. In 1846, White abolitionist Gerrit Smith announced that he would donate 120,000 acres of land in upstate New York to three thousand Black New Yorkers. As a result, James McCune Smith suggested that Black people should abandon the city en masse and relocate back to the countryside. Because both Gerrit Smith and James McCune Smith argued that the problems of the Black community were unique to urban life, they maintained that Black folks could find prosperity in rural areas. This type of colonization scheme, they hoped, might not only provide financial opportunities, but would also allow Black men to gain voting rights through property ownership. Initially excited, Charles Ray and Theodore Wright also endorsed the plan especially after McCune Smith concocted a complex arrangement in which Black families throughout the city could establish a massive savings fund. McCune Smith and Ray were actively involved in recruiting settlers, and they were among the first recipients of the land along with Henry Highland Garnet. The first colonists named the community "Timbucto," which Garnet described as a "home and field of labor for colored men." However, the project was plagued with problems from the outset. First, the land was not particularly good for farming and the viable plots required start-up money to purchase tools and supplies. In addition, those who actually managed to resettle there were tricked by local White swindlers and driven off their land. At the community's height, only about twenty to thirty families had taken possession of the land and all eventually returned to New York City. Although Timbucto never fully took shape, it demonstrated both the desperation and the dedication of the Black leaders to improving conditions for their people. *New York Daily Tribune*, March 20, 1851; Stauffer, *Black Hearts of Men*, 139–45, 157–58.

5. New York City, Tax Records 1825, New York Municipal Archives.

6. Recall from chapter 2 of this study that, by August 1820, members of the African Society had recognized the need to have their own independent space in which they could gather and purchased a piece of property on which they constructed a meetinghouse. Zuille, *Historical Sketch*, 16.

7. Gardner A. Sage, Manhattan Square Benefit Map, 1838. According to this map, there were over two hundred plots of land in Seneca Village, although many of them had not yet been developed.

8. Board of Commissioners of Central Park, *Second Annual Report of the Board of Commissioners of the Central Park* (New York: William C. Bryant and Co., 1859), 60.

9. New York Common Council, *Central Park: Memorial of the Common Council of the City of New York to the Legislature Approved June 11th, 1853* (n.p, 1853). After considerable investigation, there does not appear to be any relationship between this Henry Garnett and the activist Henry Highland Garnet who has been discussed extensively in this study.

10. *New York Daily Tribune*, August 14, 1857.

11. Information compiled from the 1855 Census, New York County, 22nd Ward, 3rd District.

12. Ibid.

13. *New York Daily Tribune*, August 5, 1853.

14. *Colored American*, March 28, 1840.

15. 1855 Census, New York County, 22nd Ward, 3rd District.

16. All Angels Parish Church Records, 1849–1850.

17. *New York Daily Tribune*, August 5, 1853.

18. *Anglo-African*, July 1859. By 1856, perhaps aware of the impending doom, Black activists recommended that Colored School No. 3 should be combined with Colored School No. 4 in Harlem.

19. For Epiphany Davis's will, see the collection of wills in the city of New York, Liber no. 101, New York Municipal Archives.

20. For discussions of Samuel Hardenburgh's participation in Black parades, see chapters 2 and 3 of this study and Garnet, *Memorial Discourse*, 24; Stuckey, *Slave Culture*, 143–44; S. White, "'It Was a Proud Day,'" 44.

21. *New York Daily Tribune*, August 5, 1853.

22. 1 Peter 1:6 (King James Version).

23. Mayor's Papers, 1834, New York Municipal Archives.

24. Beekman, *Address by Walter N. Beekman*, 6.

25. Sterling, *We Are Your Sisters*, 220–21; *Fugitive Slave Bill*, 36. For more on the Hamlet case, see chapter 6.

26. P. Foner and G. Walker, *Proceedings of the Black State Conventions*, 10.

27. *Frederick Douglass Paper*, February 5, 1852.

28. Andrew Downing, "A Talk about Public Parks and Gardens," *Horticulturist, and Journal of Rural Art and Rural Taste* 3, no. 4 (October 1848): 155.

29. Andrew Downing, "Public Cemeteries and Public Gardens," *Horticulturist, and Journal of Rural Art and Rural Taste* 4, no. 1 (July 1849): 12.

30. Charles H. Haswell, *Reminiscences of an Octogenarian of the City of New York, 1816 to 1860* (New York: Harper and Brothers Publishers, 1897), 465. Roy Rosenzweig and Elizabeth Blackmar pointed out that William Cullen Bryant had also issued an appeal for a park in 1844, and therefore preceded Downing by five years. Rosenzweig and Blackmar, *Park and the People*, 15–17. However, it seems that Downing was used as the immediate impetus for creating a park.

31. Board of Commissioners of Central Park, *First Annual Report on the Improvement of the Central Park, New York* (New York: Charles Baker, Printer, 1857), 6; Rosenzweig and Blackmar, *Park and the People,* 18.

32. Andrew Downing, "The New York Park" *Horticulturist, and Journal of Rural Art and Rural Taste* 8 (August 1, 1851): 346–47.

33. Board of Commissioners of Central Park, *First Annual Report,* 6, 11–12.

34. James W. Beekman Papers, Jones Woods Petitions, New York City, 1853.

35. Board of Commissioners of Central Park, *First Annual Report,* 7–8; Rosenzweig and Blackmar, *Park and the People,* 56.

36. Fernando Wood's Tax Records, 1855–1860, Bureau of Old Records, New York City Municipal Archives. Significantly, a book published in 1913 also noted the dramatic rise in property values in 1858 and 1859 following the establishment of Central Park. Henry Collins Brown, *Old New York: Yesterday and Today* (New York: Privately printed for Valentine's Manual, 1922), 140–52.

37. James Beekman was one of the primary supporters of the Jones Woods location because he was a sizable property owner in that area, and he believed that his real estate value would increase dramatically. Rosenzweig and Blackmar, *Park and the People,* 21, 30–33, 51–53.

38. *Frederick Douglass Paper,* April 22, 1852.

39. Jerome Mushkat, *Fernando Wood: A Political Biography* (Kent, Ohio: Kent State University Press, 1990), 164, 170, 161. For more on the *Dred Scott* decision, see chapter 6.

40. Quoted in Mushkat, *Fernando Wood,* 100.

41. Fernando Wood, *Speech of Fernando Wood Delivered before the Meeting of the National Democratic Delegation to the Charleston Convention at Syracuse, February 7, 1860* (New York: n.p, 1860); Mushkat, *Fernando Wood,* 100.

42. Ernest A. McKay, *Civil War and New York City* (Syracuse, N.Y.: Syracuse University Press, 1991), 13.

43. James McCague, *The Second Rebellion: The Story of the New York City Draft Riots of 1863* (New York: Dial Press, 1968), 43.

44. McKay, *Civil War and New York City,* 14.

45. *New York Times,* January 8, 1861. Emphasis is his.

46. Mushkat, *Fernando Wood,* 143–44.

47. Ibid., 137–38. Historian Iver Bernstein also noted Wood was hailed as a hero by the mobs during the riot. Iver Bernstein, *The New York City Draft Riots: Their Significance for American Society and Politics in the Age of the Civil War* (New York: Oxford University Press, 1990), 26. It is also important to note that, later in 1863, Wood was honored by the New Jersey Democratic party and he joined in a toast celebrating the days when "Liberty wore white face, and America was not a negro." *New York Times,* November 25, 1863.

48. Mushkat, *Fernando Wood,* 153, 146, 185.

49. Board of Commissioners of Central Park, *First Annual Report,* 103. The policy of eminent domain was originally passed in 1807, and became the justification behind various "urban renewal" programs including an attempt to rid New York City of perceived "undesirables" in the famous Five Points region. For more on this effort, see Elizabeth Blackmar, *Manhattan for Rent, 1785–1850* (Ithaca, N.Y.: Cornell University Press, 1989), 175.

50. Board of Commissioners of Central Park, *Second Annual Report,* 60.

51. In 1967, the curator of Central Park argued that the area was a "discouraging sight" filled mostly with squatters' shacks and hog farms. Henry Hope Reed, *Central Park: A*

History and a Guide (New York: Clarkson N. Potter, 1967), 19–20. Even as recently as 1992, another scholar perpetuated this image of Seneca Village, writing that the area was occupied by five thousand or more "scavengers" who huddled in trenches and caves in a barren wasteland. Laurie Watters, *A Year in Central Park* (New York: Rizzoli, 1992), 15.

52. Board of Commissioners of Central Park, *Second Annual Report,* 60.

53. *New York Times,* July 9, 1856.

54. Board of Commissioners of Central Park, *First Annual Report,* 93.

55. *New York Sun,* July 12, 1851.

56. According to Elizabeth Blackmar and Roy Rosenzweig, the residents of Seneca Village accepted their fate and quietly relinquished their land. Rosenzweig and Blackmar, *Park and Its People,* 53.

57. Board of Commissioners of Central Park, *First Annual Report,* 105.

58. Andrew Williams's Affidavit of Petition, 1856, Bureau of Old Records, New York City Municipal Archives.

59. Board of Commissioners of Central Park, *First Annual Report,* 7.

60. *New York Times,* July 9, 1856.

61. *New York Daily Tribune,* August 27, 1857.

62. *New York Times,* August 17, 1866.

Epilogue

1. Thank you to John Brooke for this insight, which has allowed me to clarify my concluding remarks.

2. For more on the 1863 Draft Riots, see McCague, *Second Rebellion*; Bernstein, *New York City Draft Riots*; Adrian Cook, *The Armies of the Streets: The New York City Draft Riots of 1863* (Lexington: University Press of Kentucky, 1974); L. M. Harris, *In the Shadow of Slavery,* 279–87.

3. *Colored American,* September 4, 1841.

4. Garnet, *Memorial Discourse,* 25. Emphasis is his.

5. Ibid., 56–58.

6. Ibid., 86.

7. Ibid., 89. Significantly, Henry Highland Garnet presided over the 1841 convention when the speech was drafted using the term "onward forever."

BIBLIOGRAPHY

Primary Source Documents

MANUSCRIPT COLLECTIONS

African Free School Papers. New York Historical Society.
Alexander Crummell Papers. Schomburg Library.
All Angels Parish Church Records, 1849–1850.
Black Abolitionist Papers. Cornell University.
Frederick Law Olmsted Papers. New York Historical Society.
James W. Beekman Papers. New York Historical Society.
Mayor's Papers, 1834. New York Municipal Archives.
New York Manumission Society Papers. New York Historical Society.
Paul Cuffe Papers. New Bedford Public Library.
Seneca Village Exhibit and Archives. New York Historical Society.

NEWSPAPERS

African Repository. 1825.
Albany Patriot. 1844–1848.
Anglo-African. 1859–1860.
Colored American. 1837–1841.
The Columbian. 1809–1817.
Commercial Advertiser. 1797–1804; 1809–1860.
Emancipator. 1835–1840.
Frederick Douglass Paper. 1851–1860.
Freedom's Journal. 1827–1829.
Liberator. 1831–1860.
Mirror of Liberty. 1838–1840.
National Advocate. 1812–1829.
National Anti-Slavery Standard. 1840–1870.
New York American. 1821–1845.
New York Daily Advertiser. 1788–1790.
New York Daily Tribune. 1845–1860.
New York Enquirer. 1826.
New York Evening Post. 1801–1860. (Named the *Evening Post* from 1832 to 1860.)
New York Gazette and General Advertiser. 1790–1795.
New York Herald. 1840–1920.
New York Spectator. 1801–1802.
New York Sun. 1851.

New York Times. 1820–1860.
North Star. 1848–1850.
Pacific Appeal. 1863.
Rights of All. 1829.
Weekly Advocate. 1837.
Weekly Anglo-African. 1860–1861.
Zion's Watchman. 1836–1841.

PUBLIC DOCUMENTS

Censuses of the State of New York. 1825, 1835, 1845, 1855. New York State Secretary's Office, Albany, New York.

Censuses of the United States. 1800, 1810, 1820, 1830, 1840, 1850. United States Census Office, Washington, D.C.

Constitution of the State of New York, Adopted in Convention, November 10, 1821. Hudson, New York: n.p., 1822.

Debates and Proceedings in the New York State Convention for the Revision of the Constitution. Albany: n.p., 1846.

Minutes of the Common Council of the City of New York. 1784–1831. 19 volumes. New York Historical Society Archives, New York.

New York State. Board of Commissioners of the Central Park. Annual Reports on the Improvement of Central Park, New York, 1856–1858. New York: C. W. Baker, 1857–1859.

Sage, Gardner A. *Manhattan Square Benefit Map.* New York: n.p., 1838.

Selections from the Revised Statutes of the State of New York: Containing All the Laws of the State Relative to Slaves, and the Laws of the State Relative to the Offence of Kidnapping, Which Several Laws Commenced and Took Effect January 1, 1830. Together with Extracts from the Laws of the United States, Respecting Slaves. Published on behalf of the New York Manumission Society, by direction of the Standing Committee. New York: Vanderpool & Cole, 1830.

PRIMARY SOURCES

African Institution. *Sixth Report of the Directors of the African Institution, Read at the Annual General Meeting on the 25th of March, 1812. To Which Are Added, an Appendix and List of Subscribers.* London: Ellerton and Henderson, 1812.

Alexander, Archibald. *A History of Colonization on the Western Coast of Africa.* Philadelphia: William S. Martien, Printer, 1846.

American Society of Free Persons of Colour. *Constitution of the American Society of Free Persons of Colour, for Improving Their Condition in the United States; for Purchasing Lands; and for the Establishment of a Settlement in Upper Canada, Also the Proceedings of the Convention, with Their Address to the Free Persons of Colour in the United States.* Philadelphia: Printed by J. W. Allen, 1831.

Annual Report of the Interments in the City and County of New York for the Year 1842, with Remarks Thereon, and a Brief View of the Sanitary Condition of the City. Presented to the Common Council by John H. Griscom, M.D., City Inspector. New York: Printed by James Van Norden, 1843.

Anti-Slavery Convention of American Women. *An Address to Free Colored Americans. Issued by an Anti-Slavery Convention of American Women Held in the City of New York, by Adjournment from 9th to 12th May, 1837.* New York: W. S. Dorr, 1837.

Anti-Slavery Convention of American Women. *An Appeal to the Women of the Nominally Free States Issued by an Anti-Slavery Convention of American Women Held in the City of New York, by Adjournment from 9th to 12th May, 1837.* Boston: Isaac Knapp, 1838.

Arguments, Pro and Con, on the Call for a National Emigration Convention, to Be Held in Cleveland, Ohio, August 1854, by Frederick Douglass, W. J. Watkins, and J. M. Whitfield, with a Short Appendix of the Statistics of Canada West, West Indies, Central and South America. Detroit: Tribune Steam Presses, George E. Pomeroy and Co., 1854.

Auchincloss, Louis, ed. *The Hone and Strong Diaries of Old Manhattan.* New York: Abbeville Press, 1989.

Bannard, William. *A Discourse on the Moral Aspect and Destitution of the City of New York.* New York: Charles Scribner, 1851.

Barker, Peter. *Information for the Free People of Colour, Who Are Inclined to Emigrate to Hayti.* New York: Mahlon Day, 1824.

Barnard, William F. *Forty Years at the Five Points.* New York: n.p., 1893.

Belden, E. Porter. *New York: Past, Present and Future.* New York: G. P. Putnam, 1849.

Bell, Howard Holman, ed. *Minutes of the Proceedings of the National Negro Conventions, 1830–1864.* New York: Arno Press and the New York Times, 1969.

Bernhard, Duke of Saxe-Weimar Eisenach. *Travels through North America during the Years 1825 and 1826.* Philadelphia: Carey, Lea, and Carey, 1828.

Boardman, James. *America and the Americans: By a Citizen of the World.* London: Printed for Longman, Rees, Orme, Brown, Green, and Longman, 1833.

Brace, Charles Loring. *The Dangerous Classes of New York, and Twenty Years' Work Among Them.* New York: Wynkoop & Hallenbeck, 1872.

Brown, Henry Collins. *Old New York: Yesterday and Today.* New York: Privately printed for Valentine's Manual, 1922.

Carman, Adam. *An Oration Delivered at the Fourth Anniversary of the Abolition of the Slave Trade, in the Methodist Episcopal Church in Second Street, New York. January 1, 1811.* New York: John C. Totten, 1811.

Clarkson, Thomas. *History of the Rise, Progress and Accomplishment of the Abolition of the African Slave Trade by the British Parliament.* London: John W. Parker, 1839.

Cobb, Thomas. *An Inquiry into the Law of Negro Slavery in the United States of America.* 1858. Reprint, New York: Negro Universities Press, 1968.

Commissioners of the Almshouse, New York City. *Commissioners of the Almshouse vs. Alexander Whistelo, a Black Man; Being a Remarkable Case of Bastardy.* New York: Longworth, 1808.

Cooper, James Fenimore. *Satanstoe, or the Littlepage Manuscripts: A Tale of the Colony.* 1845. Reprint, New York: American Book Company, 1937.

Cornish, Samuel E., and Theodore S. Wright. *The Colonization Scheme Considered in Its Rejection by the Colored People—in Its Tendency to Uphold Caste—Its Unfitness for Christianizing and Civilizing the Aborigines of Africa, and for Putting a Stop to the African Slave Trade; in a Letter to the Hon. Theodore Freylinghuysen and the Hon. Benjamin F. Butler.* New York: Aaron Guest, 1840.

Cuffe, Paul. *A Brief Account of the Settlement and Present Situation of the Colony of Sierra Leone, in Africa; as Communicated by Paul Cuffe. (A Man of Colour) to His Friend in New York: Also, an Explanation of the Object of His Visit, and Some Advice to the People of Colour in the United States. To Which Is Subjoined, an Address to the People of Colour, from the Convention of Delegates from the Abolition Societies in the United States.* New York: Samuel Wood, 1812.

DeCosta, B. F. *Three Score and Ten: The Story of St. Phillip's Church of New York City. A Discourse Delivered in the New Church West 25th Street at Its Opening Sunday Morning, February 17, 1889*. New York: Printed for the Parish, 1889.

Delany, Martin. *The Condition, Elevation, Emigration, and Destiny of the Colored People of the United States, Politically Considered*. Philadelphia: Martin Delany, 1852.

De Voe, Thomas F. *The Market Book: A History of Public Markets of the City of New York*. New York: Augustus Kelley Publishers, 1970.

Dewey, Loring Daniel. *Correspondence Relative to the Emigration to Hayti of the Free People of Colour in the United States. Together with the Instructions to the Agent Sent Out by President Boyer*. New York: Mahlon Day, 1824.

Dickens, Charles. *American Notes for General Circulation*, 1842. Reprinted with introduction and notes by Patricia Ingham, ed. New York: Penguin Books, 2000.

Dickson, John. *Remarks of Mr. Dickson, of New York, on the Presentation of Several Petitions for the Abolition of Slavery and the Slave Trade in the District of Columbia: Delivered in the House of Representatives of the United States, February 2, 1835*. Washington, D.C.: Gales and Seaton, 1835.

Douglass, Frederick. *Life and Times of Frederick Douglass, Written by Himself*. 1892. Reprint, London: Collier-Macmillan, 1962.

Downing, Andrew. "The New York Park." *Horticulturist, and Journal of Rural Art and Rural Taste* 8 (August 1, 1851): 345–49.

———. "Public Cemeteries and Public Gardens." *Horticulturist, and Journal of Rural Art and Rural Taste* 4, no. 1 (July 1849): 9–12.

———. "A Talk about Public Parks and Gardens." *Horticulturist, and Journal of Rural Art and Rural Taste* 3, no. 4 (October 1848): 153–58.

Fitch, James D. *Report of the Resident Physician of the Colored Home*. New York: Commissioner of the Alms-House, 1846–1847, 1849–1852, 1860–1861. New York Historical Society Archives, New York.

Foster, George G. *New York by Gas-Light: With Here and There a Streak of Sunshine*. New York: Dewitt and Davenport, 1850.

Francis, John W. *Old New York: Or Reminiscences of the Past Sixty Years*. 1865. Reprint, New York: Benjamin Bloom, 1971.

Free African Union Society. *The Proceedings of the Free African Union Society and the African Benevolent Society, Newport Rhode Island, 1780–1824*. Edited by William H. Robinson. Providence: The Urban League of Rhode Island, 1976.

Freeman, Reverend F. *Africa's Redemption: The Solution of Our Country*. New York: Fanshaw, 1852.

The Fugitive Slave Bill: Its History and Unconstitutionality: With an Account of the Seizure and Enslavement of James Hamlet, and His Subsequent Restoration to Liberty. New York: W. Harned, 1850.

Garnet, Henry Highland. *A Memorial Discourse Delivered in the Hall of the House of Representatives, Washington City, D.C., on Sabbath, February 12, 1865. With an Introduction by James McCune Smith, M.D.* Philadelphia: J. M. Wilson, 1865.

Garrison, William Lloyd. *An Address Delivered at the Broadway Tabernacle, N.Y. August 1, 1838. By Request of the People of Color of That City, in Commemoration of the Complete Emancipation of 600,000 Slaves on That Day, in the British West Indies*. Boston: Isaac Knapp, 1838.

———. *An Address Delivered before the Free People of Color in Philadelphia, New York and Other Cities during the Month of June, 1831*. Boston: S. Foster, Printer, 1831.

———. *The Loyalty and Devotion of Colored Americans in the Revolution and War of 1812*. 1861. Reprinted in *The Negro Soldier: A Select Compilation*. New York: Negro Universities Press, 1970.

———. *Thoughts on African Colonization: Or an Impartial Exhibition of the Doctrines, Principles, and Purposes of the American Colonization Society, Together With the Resolutions, Addresses and Remonstrances of the Free People of Color*. Boston: Garrison & Knapp, 1832.

Greenleaf, Jonathan. *A History of the Churches of All Denominations in the City of New York, from the First Settlement to the Year 1846*. New York: E. French, 1846.

Griscom, John H. *The Sanitary Condition of the Laboring Population of New York. With Suggestions for Its Improvement. A Discourse (with Additions) Delivered on the 30th December, 1844, at the Repository of the American Institute*. New York: Harper & Brothers, 1845.

Hamilton, William Sr. *Address to the Fourth Annual Convention of the Free People of Color of the United States. Delivered at the Opening of Their Session in the City of New York, June 2, 1834*. New York: S. W. Benedict & Company, 1834.

Haytian Emigration Society. *Address of the Board of Managers of the Haytian Emigration Society of Coloured People, to the Emigrants Intending to Sail to the Island of Hayti, in the Brig De Witt Clinton*. New York: Mahlon Day, 1824.

Hodgkin, Thomas. *An Inquiry Into the Merits of the American Colonization Society: And a Reply to the Charges Brought Against It. With an Account of the British African Colonization Society*. London: J. & A. Arch, 1833.

Hopkins, Samuel. *A Dialogue Concerning the Slavery of the Africans; Shewing It to Be the Duty and Interest of the American States to Emancipate All Their African Slaves. With an Address to the Owners of Such Slaves. Dedicated to the Honourable Continental Congress. To Which is Prefixed, the Institution of the Society, in New York, for Promoting the Manumission of Slaves, and Protecting Such of Them as Have Been, or May Be, Liberated*. New York: Robert Hodge, Printer, 1785.

Jay, John. *An Address in Behalf of the Colored Orphan Asylum, Delivered at Their Seventh Anniversary, December 11, 1843*. New York: Mahlon Day and Company, 1844.

Johnson, Henry. *An Oration on the Abolition of the Slave Trade, with an Introductory Address, by Adam Carman: Delivered in the African Church in New York. January 1, 1810*. New York: John C. Totten, 1810.

Judson, Edward Z. C. *The Mysteries and Miseries of New York: A Story of Real Life by Ned Buntline*. New York: Berford and Company, 1848.

Krebs, John M. *The American Citizen. A Discourse on the Nature and Extent of Our Religious Subjection to the Government under Which We Live: Including an Inquiry into the Scriptural Authority of the Provision of the Constitution of the United States, Which Requires the Surrender of Fugitive Slaves. Delivered in the Rutgers Street Presbyterian Church, in the City of New York. December 12, 1850*. New York: C. Scribner, 1851.

Mar Quack, Martin. *A Brief Review of the First Annual Report of the American Anti-Slavery Society*. Boston: Calvin Knox, Printer, 1834.

Martin, Edward W. [James Dabney]. *Lights and Shadows of New York Life*. Philadelphia: National Publishing Company, 1872.

———. *The Secrets of the Great City: A Work Descriptive of the Virtues and the Vices, the Mysteries, Miseries and Crimes of New York City*. New York: Jones Brothers and Company, 1868.

Miller's New York as It Is: Or, Stranger's Guide-Book to the Cities of New York, Brooklyn and Adjacent Places. New York: J. Miller, Publisher, 1865.

Miller, Samuel. *A Discourse, Delivered April 12, 1797, at the Request of and before the New York Society for Promoting the Manumission of Slaves and Protecting Such of Them as Have Been or May Be Liberated. By Samuel Miller, A.M. One of the Ministers of the United Presbyterian Churches in the City of New York, and Member of Said Society.* New York: T. and J. Swords, Printers, 1797.

Miller, William. *A Sermon on the Abolition of the Slave Trade; Delivered in the African Church, New York, on the First of January, 1810.* New York: John C. Totten, 1810.

Minutes and Proceedings of the First Annual Convention of the People of Colour, Held by Adjournments, in the City of Philadelphia, from the Sixth to the Eleventh of June, Inclusive, 1831. Philadelphia: Published by Order of the Convention, 1831.

Minutes and Proceedings of the Fourth Annual Convention for the Improvement of the People of Colour, Held by Adjournments, in the Asbury Church, New York, from the 2d to the 12th of June, Inclusive, 1834. New York: Published by Order of the Convention, 1834.

Minutes and Proceedings of the Second Annual Convention for the Improvement of the People of Colour in These United States, Held by Adjournments, in the City of Philadelphia, from the 4th to the 13th of June, Inclusive, 1832. Philadelphia: Published by Order of the Convention, 1832.

Minutes and Proceedings of the Third Annual Convention for the Improvement of the Free People of Colour in the United States, Held by Adjournments, in the City of Philadelphia, from the 3d to the 13th of June, Inclusive, 1833. New York: Published by Order of the Convention, 1833.

Minutes of the Fifth Annual Convention for the Improvement of the Free People of Colour in the United States, Held by Adjournments, in the Wesley Church, Philadelphia, from the First to the Fifth of June, Inclusive, 1835. Philadelphia: Printed by William P. Gibbons, 1835.

Minutes of the National Convention of Colored Citizens: Held at Buffalo, on the 15th, 16th, 17th, 18th and 19th of August, 1843. For the Purpose of Considering Their Moral and Political Condition as American Citizens. New York: Piercy and Reed, Printers, 1843.

Moore, George Henry. *Historical Notes on the Employment of Negroes in the American Army of the Revolution.* 1861. Reprinted in *The Negro Soldier: A Select Compilation.* New York: Negro Universities Press, 1970.

Moore, John Jamison. *History of the African Methodist Episcopal Zion Church in America, Founded in 1796, in the City of New York.* York: Teacher's Journal Office, 1884.

Nell, William C. *The Colored Patriots of the American Revolution with Sketches of Several Distinguished Colored Persons to Which Is Added a Brief Survey of the Conditions and Prospects of Colored Americans.* 1855. Reprint, New York: Arno Press, 1968.

―――. *Property Qualifications or No Property Qualifications: A Few Facts from the Record of Patriotic Services of the Colored Men of New York during the Wars of 1776 and 1812.* New York: Thomas Hamilton and William Leonard, 1860.

Nesbit, William. *Four Months in Liberia or, African Colonization Exposed.* Pittsburgh: J. T. Shyrock, 1855.

New York African Clarkson Association. *A Call Upon the Church for Progressive Action, to Elevate the Colored American People.* n.p., 1848.

―――. *Constitution of the New-York African Clarkson Association.* New York: E. Conrad, 1825.

New York African Society for Mutual Relief. *Constitution of the New York African Society for Mutual Relief.* New York: Printed by Robert Sears, 1838.

New York [City] Committee on Fortifying the Harbor of New York. *Report of the Com-*

mittee of the Corporation on the Subject of Fortifying the Harbor of New York. New York: Southwick, 1807.

New York Common Council. *Central Park: Memorial of the Common Council of the City of New York to the Legislature Approved June 11th, 1853.* New York: n.p., 1853.

The New York Cries in Rhyme. 1836. Reprint, New York: Grosset and Dunlap, 1939.

New York Manumission Society. *An Address to the Parents and Guardians of the Children Belonging to the New York African Free School by the Trustees of the Institutions.* New York: Samuel Wood and Sons, 1818.

New York Society for Promoting the Manumission of Slaves. *Constitution of the New York Society for Promoting the Manumission of Slaves, and Protecting Such of Them as Have Been, or May Be, Liberated.* New York: Hopkins, Webb & Co, Printers, 1796.

The Old Brewery, and the New Mission House at the Five Points. By the Ladies of the Mission. New York: Stringer and Townsend, 1854.

Olmsted, Frederick Law. *Civilizing American Cities: A Selection of Frederick Law Olmsted's Writings on City Landscapes.* Edited by S. B. Sutton. Cambridge, Mass.: MIT Press, 1971.

———. *A Consideration of the Justifying Value of a Public Park. Prepared at the Request of the American Social Science Association and Read at Its Meeting in Saratoga, 1880.* Boston: Tolman & White, 1881.

———. *Creating Central Park, 1857–1861.* Edited by Charles E. Beveridge and David Schuyler. Baltimore, Md.: Johns Hopkins University Press, 1983.

———. *The Formative Years, 1822–1852.* Edited by Charles Capen McLaughlin and Charles E. Beveridge. Baltimore, Md.: Johns Hopkins University Press, 1977.

———. *Selected Letters of Frederick Law Olmsted.* Edited by Charles Capen McLaughlin. Cambridge, Mass.: McLaughlin, 1960.

An Oration Delivered at the Fifteenth Annual Celebration of the New York African Society for Mutual Relief at the African Zion Church, the 24th of March, 1823. By a Member. Brooklyn, N.Y.: Printed by G. L. Birch, 1823.

Parker, John P. *His Promised Land: The Autobiography of John P. Parker, Former Slave and Conductor on the Underground Railroad.* Edited by Stuart Seely Sprague. New York: W. W. Norton & Co, 1996.

Pennington, J. W. C. *The Coloured Population of the United States Have No Destiny Separate From That of the Nation of Which They Form an Integral Part.* Edinburgh: H. Armour, 1850.

———. *The Fugitive Blacksmith.* London: C. Gilpin, 1850.

———. *A Lecture Delivered before the Glasgow Young Men's Christian Association; and Also before the St. George's Biblical and Literary & Scientific Institute, London.* Edinburgh: H. Armour, 1850.

Philomathean Society of New York. *Constitution and By-Laws of the Philomathean Society of New York.* New York: City of New York University Press, 1835.

Phoenix Society of New York. *Address and Constitution of the Phoenix Society of New York and of the Auxiliary Ward Associations.* New York: n.p., 1833.

Proceedings of the Colored National Convention, Held in Franklin Hall, Sixth Street, below Arch, Philadelphia, October 16th, 17th, and 18th, 1855. Salem, N.J.: Printed at the National Standard Office, 1855.

Proceedings of the Colored National Convention, Held in Rochester, July 6th, 7th, and 8th, 1853. Rochester, N.Y.: Printed at the office of Frederick Douglass Paper, 1853.

Proceedings of the National Liberty Convention, Held at Buffalo, New York, June 14th and

15th, 1848; Including the Resolutions and Addresses Adopted by That Body, and Speeches of Beriah Green and Gerrit Smith on That Occasion. Utica, N.Y.: S. W. Green, 1848.

Pyne, Thomas. *A Sermon, Preached in the Chapel of St. Peter's Church, New York, on Thursday, the 10th of December, 1835, Being a Day Appointed by Authority as a Day of Public Thanksgiving.* New York: n.p., 1836.

Report of the Proceedings of the Colored National Convention, Held at Cleveland, Ohio, on Wednesday, September 6, 1848. Rochester, N.Y.: Printed by John Dick at the North Star Office, 1848.

Ripley, Dorothy. *An Account of Rose Butler, Aged Nineteen Years, Whose Execution I Attended in the Potter's Field, on the 9th of 7th Month, for Setting Fire to Her Mistress' Dwelling House.* New York: John C. Totten, 1819.

Ruggles, David. *An Antidote for a Poisonous Combination Recently Prepared by a "Citizen of New York," Alias Dr. Reese Entitled, "An Appeal to the Reason and Religion of American Christians etc. . . ."* New York: William Stuart, Publisher, 1838.

———. *The "Extinguisher" Extinguished! Or, David M. Reese, M.D., "Used up." Together with Some Remarks upon a Late Production Entitled "An Address on Slavery against Immediate Emancipation with a Plan of Their Being Gradually Emancipated and Colonized in Thirty-two Years. By Heman Howlett.* 1834. Reprint, Wilmington, Del.: Scholarly Resources, Inc., 1970.

Sampson, William. *Report of the Trial of James Johnson, a Black Man, on the 23d of October Last. Also, the Trial of John Sinclair, a German, Aged Seventy-Seven Years for the Murder of David Hill, on the Eighth Day of April Last.* New York: Southwick and Prism, 1811.

Sewall, Samuel. *A Dialogue Concerning the Slavery of Africans; Shewing It to Be the Duty and Interest of the American States to Emancipate All Their African Slavers. With an Address to the Owners of Such Slaves.* 1776. Reprint, New York: Arno Press, 1970.

———. *The Selling of Joseph.* Boston: n.p., 1700.

Slocum, Charles Elihu. *A Short History of the Slocum, Slocumb, and Slocomb Families, 1637–1881.* Syracuse, N.Y.: Published by the author, 1882.

Smith, Elihu Hubbard. *A Discourse, Delivered April 11, 1798 at the Request of and before the New York Society for Promoting the Manumission of Slaves, and Protecting Such of Them as Have Been, or May Be, Liberated. By E. H. Smith, a Member of the Society.* New York: T. & J. Swords, Printers, 1798.

Smith, James McCune. *The Destiny of the People of Color, a Lecture, Delivered before the Philomathean Society and Hamilton Lyceum.* New York: Published by request, 1843.

Sons of the African Society. *Laws of the Sons of the African Society; Instituted at Boston, Anno Domini, 1798.* Boston: Printed for the Society, 1798.

Stanford, John. *An Authentic Statement of the Case and Conduct of Rose Butler, Who Was Tried, Convicted, and Executed for the Crime of Arson. Reviewed and Approved by the Rev. John Stanford, M.A., Chaplain to the Public Institutions.* New York: Broderick and Ritter, 1819.

Sumner, Charles. *The Anti-Slavery Enterprise, Its Necessity, Practicability, and Dignity, with Glimpses at the Special Duties of the North: An Address before the People of New York at the Metropolitan Theatre, May 9, 1855.* Boston: Ticknor and Fields, 1855.

Tappan, Lewis. *The Life of Arthur Tappan.* 1871. Reprint, New York: Negro Universities Press, 1970.

Teasman, John. *An Address Delivered in the African Episcopal Church, on the 25th of March, 1811, before the New York African Society for Mutual Relief, Being the First Anniversary of Its Incorporation.* New York: J. Low, 1811.

Thompson, Mary W. *Sketches of the History, Character, and Dying Testimony of Beneficiaries of the Colored Home in the City of New York.* New York: John F. Trow, 1851.

United States Supreme Court. *Dred Scott v. John F. A. Sandford.* 60 U.S. 393, 19. How. 393, 15 L. Ed. 691. December term, 1856.

Vogelsang, Peter. *An Address Delivered before the New York African Society for Mutual Relief in the African Zion Church, 23rd March, 1815, Being the Fifth Anniversary of Their Incorporation.* New York: Hardcastle and Pelsue, 1815.

Wakeley, J. B. *Lost Chapters Recovered from the Early Years of American Methodism.* New York: Carlton & Porter, 1858.

Ward, Samuel R. *Autobiography of a Fugitive Negro.* New York: Arno Press, 1968.

White, Charles. *An Account of the Regular Gradation in Man and in Different Animals and Vegetables; and from the Former to the Latter.* London: C. Dilly, 1799.

Wilkes, Laura Eliza. *Missing Pages in American History, Revealing the Services of Negroes in the Early Wars of the United States of America, 1641–1815.* 1861. Reprint, New York: Negro Universities Press, 1970.

Williams, Peter Jr. *A Discourse Delivered on the Death of Capt. Paul Cuffee, before the New York African Institution, in the African Methodist Episcopal Zion Church, October 21, 1817.* New York: B. Young and Company, Printers, 1817.

Williams, Samuel. *Four Years in Liberia: A Sketch of the Life of the Rev. Samuel Williams. With Remarks on the Missions, Manners and Customs of the Natives of Western Africa. Together with an Answer to Nesbit's Book.* Philadelphia: King and Baird, Printers, 1857.

Wood, Fernando. *Speech of Fernando Wood Delivered before the Meeting of the National Democratic Delegation to the Charleston Convention at Syracuse, February 7, 1860.* New York: n.p., 1860.

Woodson, Carter G. *The Mind of the Negro as Reflected in Letters Written during the Crisis, 1800–1860.* Washington, D.C.: The Association for the Study of Negro Life and History, 1926.

Wright, Rev. Theodore Sedgewick, Charles B. Ray, and Dr. James McCune Smith. *An Address to the Three Thousand Colored Citizens of New York Who Are Owners of One Hundred and Twenty Thousand Acres of Land in the State of New York, Given to Them by Gerrit Smith, Esq. of Peterboro.* New York: n.p., 1846.

Yates, William. *Rights of Colored Men to Suffrage, Citizenship, and Trial by Jury: Being a Book of Facts, Arguments, and Authorities, Historical Notices and Sketches of Debates— With Notes.* Philadelphia: Merrihew and Gunn, 1838.

Zuille, John J. "Historical Sketch of the New York African Society for Mutual Relief." New York: n.p., compiled 1892–1893.

Secondary Sources

Agorsah, E. Kofi. "Archaeology and Resistance History in the Caribbean," *African Archaeological Review* 11 (1993): 175–95.

Anbinder, Tyler. *Five Points: The 19th Century New York City Neighborhood That Invented Tap Dance, Stole Elections, and Became the World's Most Notorious Slum.* New York: Plume, Penguin Putnam Books, Inc., 2001.

Andrews, Charles C. *The History of the New York African Free Schools.* New York: Negro Universities Press, 1969.

Aptheker, Herbert, ed. *A Documentary History of the Negro People in the United States: From the Colonial Times through the Civil War.* Vol. 1. New York: Citadel Press, 1951.

Baker Jr., Houston. *The Journey Back: Issues in Black Literature and Criticism.* Chicago: University of Chicago Press, 1980.

Bardolph, Richard. *The Negro Vanguard.* New York: Rinehart and Company, 1959.

Baur, John Edward. "Mulatto Machiavelli: Jean Pierre Boyer, and the Haiti of His Day." *Journal of Negro History* 32, no. 3 (July 1947): 307–53.

Beekman, Walter N. *Address by Walter N. Beekman, Vice President, New York African Society for Mutual Relief.* Brooklyn: n.p., 1946.

Bell, Howard Holman, ed. *A Survey of the Negro Convention Movement, 1830–1861.* New York: Arno Press and the New York Times, 1969.

Bernstein, Iver. *The New York City Draft Riots: Their Significance for American Society and Politics in the Age of the Civil War.* New York: Oxford University Press, 1990.

Bethel, Elizabeth Rauh. "Images of Haiti: The Construction of an Afro-American Lieu de Memoire," *Callaloo* 15, no. 3 (Summer 1992): 827–41.

———. *The Roots of African-American Identity: Memory and History in Antebellum Free Communities.* New York: St. Martin's Press, 1997.

Bishop, Shelton. "The History of St. Phillips' Church in New York City." *Historical Magazine of the Protestant Episcopal Church* 15 (December 1946): 298–317.

Black, Mary, ed. *Old New York in Early Photographs, 1853–1981.* New York: Dover Publications, 1973.

Blackmar, Elizabeth. *Manhattan for Rent, 1785–1850.* Ithaca, N.Y.: Cornell University Press, 1989.

Blakey, Michael L. "The New York African Burial Ground Project: An Examination of Enslaved Lives, a Construction of Ancestral Ties." *Transforming Anthropology* 7: 53–58.

———. "The Study of New York's African Burial Ground: Biocultural and Engaged," in *African Roots/American Cultures: Africa in the Creation of the Americas,* edited by Sheila S. Walker. New York: Rowman and Littlefield Publishers, 2001.

Blight, David. "In Search of Learning, Liberty and Self-Definition: James McCune Smith and the Ordeal of the Antebellum Black Intellectual." *Afro-Americans in New York Life and History* 9, no. 2 (July 1985): 7–25.

Blockson, Charles L. *Hippocrene Guide to the Underground Railroad.* New York: Hippocrene Books, 1994.

———. *The Underground Railroad.* New York: Prentice-Hall Press, 1987.

Bogger, Tommy L. *Free Blacks in Norfolk, Virginia, 1790–1860: The Darker Side of Freedom.* Charlottesville: University Press of Virginia, 1997.

Bolster, W. Jeffrey. *Black Jacks: African American Seamen in the Age of Sail.* Cambridge, Mass.: Harvard University Press, 1997.

Bolton, Reginald P. *Indian Life of Long Ago in the City of New York.* Port Washington, N.Y.: I. J. Friedman, 1971.

Bracey, John H. Jr., August Meier, and Elliott Rudwick, eds. *Blacks in the Abolitionist Movement.* Belmont, Calif.: Wadsworth Publishing Company, 1971.

———. *Free Blacks in America, 1800–1860.* Belmont, Calif.: Wadsworth Publishing Company, 1971.

Brawley, Benjamin. *Early Negro American Writers: Selections with Biographical and Critical Introductions.* Chapel Hill: University of North Carolina Press, 1935.

Brewer, William M. "Henry Highland Garnet." *Journal of Negro History* 13, no. 1 (January 1928): 36–52.

———. "John B. Russwurm." *Journal of Negro History* 13, no. 4 (October 1928): 413–22.

Bridges, Amy. *A City in the Republic: Antebellum New York and the Origins of Machine Politics.* New York: Cambridge University Press, 1984.

Brotz, Howard, ed. *African American Social and Political Thought, 1850–1920.* New Brunswick, N.J.: Transaction Publishers, 1992.

Brown, David E. "Underneath Central Park." *Metropolis* 16, no. 9 (May 1997): 43–50.

Brown, Delindus R. "Free Blacks' Rhetorical Impact on African Colonization: The Emergence of Rhetorical Exigence." *Journal of Black Studies* 9, no. 3 (March 1979): 251–65.

Brown, Henry Collins. *Book of Old New York.* New York: Privately printed, 1913.

Burke, Ronald K. "The Anti-Slavery Activities of Samuel Ringgold Ward in New York State." *Afro-Americans in New York Life and History* 2, no. 1 (1978): 17–28.

Carter, Ralph Donald. "Black American or African: The Response of New York City Blacks to African Colonization, 1817–1841." PhD diss., Clark University, 1974.

Cheek, William, and Aimee Lee Cheek. *John Mercer Langston and the Fight for Black Freedom, 1829–1865.* Urbana: University of Illinois Press, 1989.

Clarke, James Freeman. *Anti-Slavery Days: A Sketch of the Struggle Which Ended in the Abolition of Slavery in the United States.* New York: AMS Press, 1972.

Cohen, Patricia Cline. *The Murder of Helen Jewett: The Life and Death of a Prostitute in Nineteenth-Century New York.* New York: Vintage Books, 1998.

Collins, Patricia Hill. *Black Feminist Thought: Knowledge, Consciousness, and the Politics of Empowerment.* New York: Routledge, 1991.

Cook, Adrian. *The Armies of the Streets: The New York City Draft Riots of 1863.* Lexington: University Press of Kentucky, 1974.

Cox, Joseph Mason Andrew. *Great Black Men of Masonry, 1723–1982.* New York: Blue Diamond Press, 1982.

Cramer, Clayton E. *Black Demographic Data, 1790–1860: A Sourcebook.* Westport, Conn.: Greenwood Press, 1997.

Creel, Margaret Washington. *"A Peculiar People": Slave Religion and Community-Culture among the Gullahs.* New York: New York University Press, 1988.

Cressy, David. *Birth, Marriage, and Death: Ritual, Religion, and the Life-Cycle in Tudor and Stuart England.* New York: Oxford University Press, 1997.

Cromwell, John W. "The Early Negro Convention Movement." In *The American Negro Academy Occasional Papers.* New York: Arno Press and the New York Times, 1969.

———. *The Negro in American History: Men and Women Eminent in the Evolution of the American of African Descent.* New York: Johnson Reprint Corporation, 1968.

Curry, Leonard H. *The Free Black in Urban America, 1800–1850: The Shadow of the Dream.* Chicago: University of Chicago Press, 1981.

Curry, Richard Orr, ed. *The Abolitionists.* Hinsdale, Ill.: Dryden Press, 1973.

Cvornyek, Robert. "Financing the Dream: White Support and the African Civilization Society." *Afro-Americans in New York Life and History* 5, no. 1 (January 1981): 59–62.

Davis, Thomas J. *A Rumor of Revolt: The "Great Negro Plot" in Colonial New York.* New York: Free Press, 1985.

Decorse, Christopher. *An Archaeology of Elmina: Africans and Europeans on the Gold Coast.* Washington, D.C.: Smithsonian Institution Press, 2001.

———. "Culture, Contact, Continuity and Change on the Gold Coast, A.D. 1400–1900." *African Archaeological Review* 10 (1992): 163–96.

Dixon, Chris. *African America and Haiti: Emigration and Black Nationalism in the Nineteenth Century.* Westport, Conn.: Greenwood Press, 2000.

DuBois, W. E. B. *The Souls of Black Folk*. 1903. Reprint, New York: Dover Publications, 1994.

Dunbar, Alice Moore, ed. *Masterpieces of Negro Eloquence*. New York: The Bookery Publishing Company, 1914.

Eichholz, Alice, and James M. Rose. *Free Black Heads of Households in the New York State Federal Census, 1790–1830*. Vol. 14. Gale Genealogy and Local History Series. Detroit: Gale Research Company, 1981.

Epperson, Terrence W. "The Contested Commons: Archaeologies of Race, Repression, and Resistance in New York City." In *Historical Archaeologies of Capitalism,* edited by Mark P. Leone and Parker B. Potter Jr. New York: Plenum Press. 1999.

———. "The Politics of 'Race' and Cultural Identity at the African Burial Ground Excavations, New York City," *World Archaeological Bulletin* 7 (1996): 108–17.

Ernst, Robert. *Immigrant Life in New York City, 1825–1863*. New York: Octagon Books, 1979.

Essien-Udom, E. U. *Black Nationalism: A Search for Identity in America*. Chicago: University of Chicago Press, 1962.

Fabre, Genevieve, and Robert O'Meally, eds. *History and Memory in African-American Culture*. New York: Oxford University Press, 1994.

Fein, Albert, ed. *Landscape into Cityscape: Frederick Law Olmsted's Plans for a Greater New York City*. Ithaca, N.Y.: Cornell University Press, 1967.

Field, Phyllis F. *The Politics of Race in New York: The Struggle for Black Suffrage in the Civil War Era*. Ithaca, N.Y.: Cornell University Press, 1982.

———. "The Struggle for Black Suffrage in New York State, 1846–1869." PhD diss., Cornell University, 1975.

Filler, Louis. *Crusade against Slavery: Friends, Foes and Reforms, 1820–1860*. Algonac, Mich.: Reference Publications, 1986.

Fishel, Leslie H. Jr., and Benjamin Quarles, eds. *The Black American: A Documentary History*. Glenview, Ill.: Scott, Foresman and Company, 1970.

Foner, Jack D. *Blacks and the Military in American History: A New Perspective*. New York: Praegen Publications, 1974.

Foner, Philip S., ed. *The Life and Writings of Frederick Douglass*. New York: International Publishers, 1950.

Foner, Philip S., and Robert James Branham, eds. *Lift Every Voice: African American Oratory, 1787–1900*. Tuscaloosa: University of Alabama Press, 1998.

Foner, Philip S., and Ronald L. Lewis, eds. *The Black Worker to 1869*. Philadelphia: Temple University Press, 1978.

Foner, Philip S., and George E. Walker, eds. *Proceedings of the Black State Conventions, 1840–1865*. Philadelphia: Temple University Press, 1979.

Foote, Thelma Wills. *Black and White Manhattan: The History of Racial Formation in Colonial New York City*. Oxford: Oxford University Press, 2004.

———. "Black Life in Colonial Manhattan, 1664–1786." PhD diss., Harvard University, 1991.

Forbes, Ella. "African American Resistance to Colonization." *Journal of Black Studies* 21, no. 2 (December 1990): 210–23.

Foster, Charles I. "The Colonization of Free Negroes in Liberia, 1816–1835." *Journal of Negro History* 38 (January 1953): 41–66.

Fox, Dixon Ryan. "The Negro Vote in Old New York." *Political Science Quarterly* 32 (June 1917): 252–75.

Franklin, John Hope. *From Slavery to Freedom: A History of American Negroes*. New York: Alfred A. Knopf, 1948.

Franklin, V. P. *Black Self-Determination: A Cultural History of African-American Resistance*. Brooklyn, N.Y.: Lawrence Hill Books, 1984.

Freeman, Rhoda Golden. *The Free Negro in New York City in the Era before the Civil War*. New York: Garland Publishing, 1994.

Frey, Sylvia R. *Water from the Rock: Black Resistance in a Revolutionary Age*. Princeton: Princeton University Press, 1991.

Frohne, Andrea. "Commemorating the African Burial Ground in New York City: Spirituality of Space in Contemporary Art Works," *Ijele: Art eJournal of the African World* 1, no. 1 (2000). http://www.africaresource.com/ijele/vol1.1/frohne.html.

Fuller, Edmund. *Prudence Crandall: An Incident of Racism in Nineteenth-Century Connecticut*. Middletown, Conn.: Wesleyan University Press, 1971.

Gates, Henry Louis Jr. *Life and Times of Frederick Douglass*. New York: Library of America Series, 1994.

Gilfoyle, Timothy J. *City of Eros: New York City, Prostitution, and the Commercialization of Sex, 1790–1920*. New York: W. W. Norton and Company, 1992.

Gilje, Paul A. "Between Slavery and Freedom: New York African Americans in the Early Republic." *Reviews in American History* 20 (1992): 163–67.

———. *The Road to Mobocracy: Popular Disorder in New York City, 1763–1834*. Chapel Hill: University of North Carolina Press, 1987.

Gilje, Paul A., and William Penchak, eds. *New York in the Age of the Constitution, 1775–1800*. London: Associated University Presses, 1992.

Gilje, Paul A., and Howard B. Rock. "Sweep-O! Sweep-O!: African American Chimney Sweeps and Citizenship in the New Nation." *William and Mary Quarterly* 51, no. 3 (1994): 507–38.

Gilje, Paul A., and Howard B. Rock, eds. *Keepers of the Revolution: New Yorkers at Work in the Early Republic*. Ithaca, N.Y.: Cornell University Press, 1992.

Glaude, Eddie S. Jr. *Exodus!: Religion, Race and Nation in Early Nineteenth Century Black America*. Chicago: University of Chicago Press, 2000.

———. "The Language of Nation: Exodus Politics and the National Negro Movement, 1830–1843." PhD diss., Princeton University, 1997.

Gomez, Michael A. *Exchanging Our Country Marks: The Transformation of African Identities in the Colonial and Antebellum South*. Chapel Hill: University of North Carolina Press, 1998.

Goodheart, Lawrence B. "'The Chronicles of Kidnapping in New York': Resistance to the Fugitive Slave Law, 1834–1835." *Afro-Americans in New York Life and History* 8, no. 1 (January 1984): 7–16.

Gossett, Thomas F. *Race: The History of an Idea in America*. 1963. Reprint, New York: Oxford University Press, 1997.

Graff, M. M. *The Men Who Made Central Park*. New York: Greensward Foundation, 1982.

Gravely, William B. "The Dialectic of Double-Consciousness in Black American Freedom Celebrations, 1808–1863." *Journal of Negro History* 67 (Winter 1982): 302–17.

Gronowicz, Anthony. *Race and Class Politics in New York City before the Civil War.* Boston: Northeastern University Press, 1998.

Gross, Bella. "The First National Negro Convention." *Journal of Negro History* 31, no. 4 (October 1946): 435–43.

———. "Freedom's Journal and the Rights of All." *Journal of Negro History* 17, no. 3 (July 1932): 241–86.

Handler, Jerome. "A Prone Burial from a Plantation Slave Cemetery in Barbadoes, West Indies: Possible Evidence for an African-Type Witch or Other Negatively Viewed Person." *Historical Archaeology* 30 (1996): 76–86.

Hansen, Joyce, and Gary McGowan. *Breaking Ground, Breaking Silence: The Story of New York's African Burial Ground.* New York: Henry Holt and Company, 1998.

Harding, Vincent. *There Is a River: The Black Struggle for Freedom in America.* 1981. Reprint, New York: Vintage Books, 1983.

Harlow, Alvin F. *Old Bowery Days: The Chronicles of a Famous Street.* New York: D. Appleton and Company, 1931.

Harrington, Spencer. "An African Cemetery in Manhattan." In *Eyewitness to Discovery: First-Person Accounts of More Than Fifty of the World's Greatest Archaeological Discoveries,* edited by Brian Fagan. New York: Oxford University Press, 1996.

———. "Bones and Bureaucrats: New York's Great Cemetery Imbroglio." In *Archaeological Ethics,* edited by Karen D. Vitelli. Walnut Creek, Calif.: AltaMira Press, 1996.

Harris, Leslie Maria. "Creating the African American Working Class: Black and White Workers, Abolitionists and Reformers in New York City, 1785–1863." PhD diss., Stanford University, 1994.

———. *In the Shadow of Slavery: African Americans in New York City, 1626–1863.* Chicago: University of Chicago Press, 2003.

Harris, M. A. *A Negro History Tour of Manhattan.* New York: Greenwood Publishing Corporation, 1968.

Harris, Robert L. Jr. "Early Black Benevolent Societies, 1780–1830." *Massachusetts Review* 20, no. 3 (Autumn 1979): 603–25.

Harris, Sheldon H. *Paul Cuffe: Black America and the African Return.* New York: Simon and Schuster, 1972.

Haswell, Charles H. *Reminiscences of an Octogenarian of the City of New York, 1816–1860.* New York: Harper and Brothers Publishers, 1897.

Haynes, George Edmund. *The Negro at Work in New York City: A Study in Economic Progress.* New York: Arno Press and the New York Times, 1968.

Headley, J. T. *The Great Riots of New York, 1712–1873.* Miami, Fla.: Mnemosyne Publishing Co., 1969.

Herskovits, Melville. *The Myth of the Negro Past.* 1941. Reprint, Boston: Beacon Press: Boston, 1990.

Hewitt, John H. "Mr. Downing and His Oyster House: The Life and Good Works of an African-American Entrepreneur." *New York History* 74, no. 3 (July 1993): 228–52.

———. "New York's Black Episcopalians: In the Beginning, 1702–1722." *Afro-Americans in New York Life and History* 3, no. 1 (January 1979): 9–22.

———. "The Search for Elizabeth Jennings, Heroine of a Sunday Afternoon in New York City." *New York History* 62 (October 1990): 387–415.

———. "Unresting Waters: The Fight against Racism in New York's Episcopal Establishment, 1845–1853." *Afro-Americans in New York Life and History* 18, no. 1 (January 1994): 7–30.

Hickey, Donald R. "America's Response to the Slave Revolt in Haiti, 1791–1806." *Journal of the Early Republic* 2 (1982): 361–80.

Hill, Marilynn. *Their Sisters' Keepers: Prostitution in New York City, 1830–1870.* Berkeley: University of California Press, 1993.

Hinks, Peter P. *To Awaken My Afflicted Brethren: David Walker and the Problem of Antebellum Slave Resistance.* University Park: Pennsylvania State University Press, 1997.

Hirsch, Leo H. Jr. "The Negro and New York, 1783 to 1863." *Journal of Negro History* 16, no. 4 (October 1931): 382–473.

Hodges, George W. *Early Negro Church Life in New York.* New York: New York Public Library, 1945.

Hodges, Graham Russell, ed. *The Black Loyalist Directory: African Americans in Exile After the American Revolution.* New York: Garland Publishers, 1996.

———. *New York City Cartmen, 1667–1850.* New York: New York University Press, 1986.

———. *Root and Branch: African Americans in New York and East Jersey, 1613–1863.* Chapel Hill: University of North Carolina Press, 1999.

Holt, Michael F. *The Political Crisis of the 1850s.* New York: John Wiley & Sons, 1978.

Homberger, Eric. *The Historical Atlas of New York City: A Visual Celebration of Nearly 400 Years of New York City's History.* New York: Henry Holt and Company, 1994.

Horton, James, and Lois E. Horton. *Black Bostonians: Family Life and Community Struggle in the Antebellum North.* New York: Holmes and Meier Publishers, 1979.

———. *Free People of Color: Inside the African American Community.* Washington, D.C.: Smithsonian Institution Press, 1993.

———. *In Hope of Liberty: Culture, Community and Protest among Northern Free Blacks, 1700–1860.* New York: Oxford University Press, 1997.

Houseley, Kathleen. "'Yours for the Oppressed': The Life of Jehiel C. Beman." *Journal of Negro History* 77, no. 1 (1992): 17–29.

Hughes, Langston, Milton Meltzer, and C. Eric Lincoln. *A Pictorial History of Black Americans.* New York: Crown Publishers, 1956.

Jamieson, Ross W. "Material Culture and Social Death: African-American Burial Practices." *Historical Archaeology* 29, no. 4 (1992): 39–58.

Janvier, Thomas A. *In Old New York.* New York: Harper & Brothers Publishers, 1894.

Jentz, John B. "The Antislavery Constituency in Jacksonian New York City." *Civil War History* 27, no. 2 (1981): 101–22.

Johnson, Berman E. *The Dream Deferred: A Survey of Black America, 1840–1896.* Dubuque, Iowa: Kendall/Hunt Publishing Company, 1993.

Johnson, James Weldon. *Black Manhattan.* New York: Alfred A. Knopf, 1930.

Johnson, Robert Jr. *Returning Home: A Century of African-American Repatriation.* Trenton, N.J.: Africa World Press, 2005.

Johnson, Whittington B. *The Promising Years, 1750–1830: The Emergence of Black Labor and Business.* New York: Garland Publishing, 1993.

Johnston, Percy Edward, ed. *Afro American Philosophies: Selected Readings from Jupiter Hammon to Eugene C. Holmes.* Upper Montclair, N.J.: Montclair College Press, 1970.

Kachun, Mitch. *Festivals of Freedom: Memory and Meaning in African American Emancipation Celebrations, 1808–1915.* Amherst: University of Massachusetts Press, 2003.

Kaplan, Sidney, and Emma Nogrady Kaplan. *The Black Presence in the Era of the American Revolution.* Amherst: University of Massachusetts Press, 1989.

Katz, William Loren. *Black Legacy: A History of New York's African Americans.* New York: Atheneum Books for Young Readers, 1997.

Kerber, Linda K. "Abolitionists and Amalgamators: The New York City Race Riots of 1834." *New York History* 48, no. 1 (January 1967): 28–39.

———. *Women of the Republic: Intellect and Ideology in Revolutionary America.* New York: W. W. Norton and Company, 1986.

Kinshasa, Kwando Mbiassi. *Emigration vs. Assimilation: the Debate in the African American Press, 1827–1861.* Jefferson, N.C.: McFarland, 1988.

Kobrin, David. *The Black Minority in Early New York.* Albany, N.Y.: Office of State History, 1971.

Kraditor, Aileen S. *Means and Ends in American Abolitionism: Garrison and His Critics on Strategy and Tactics, 1834–1850.* New York: Pantheon Books, 1967.

Kruger, Vivienne L. "Born to Run: The Slave Family in Early New York, 1626–1827." PhD diss., Columbia University, 1985.

LaRoche, Cheryl. "Beads from the African Burial Ground, New York City: A Preliminary Assessment." *Beads: Journal of the Society of Bead Researchers* 6 (1994): 3–20.

Lewinson, Edwin R. *Black Politics in New York City.* New York: Twayne Publishers, 1974.

Lindsay, Arnett G. "The Economic Condition of the Negroes of New York Prior to 1861." *Journal of Negro History* 6, no. 1 (January 1921): 190–99.

Litwack, Leon F. *North of Slavery: The Negro in the Free States, 1790–1860.* Chicago: University of Chicago Press, 1965.

Loggins, Vernon. *The Negro Author: His Development in America to 1900.* Port Washington, N.Y.: Kennikat Press, 1964.

Mabee, Carleton. *Black Education in New York State: From Colonial to Modern Times.* Syracuse, N.Y.: Syracuse University Press, 1979.

Magubane, Bernard Makhosezwe. *The Ties That Bind: African American Consciousness of Africa.* Trenton, N.J.: Africa World Press, 1987.

Mayer, Henry. *All on Fire: William Lloyd Garrison and the Abolition of Slavery.* New York: St. Martin's Press, 1998.

McCague, James. *The Second Rebellion: The Story of the New York City Draft Riots of 1863.* New York: Dial Press, 1968.

McCarthy, Timothy Patrick, and John Stauffer, eds. *Prophets of Protest: Reconsidering the History of American Abolitionism.* New York: The New Press, 2006.

McKay, Ernest A. *The Civil War and New York City.* Syracuse, N.Y.: Syracuse University Press, 1991.

McKee, Samuel D. *Labor in Colonial New York, 1664–1776.* New York: I. J. Friedman, 1965.

McManus, Edgar J. *A History of Negro Slavery in New York.* Syracuse, N.Y.: Syracuse University Press, 1966.

Medford, Edna Greene, ed. *The African Burial Ground: History Final Report.* The African Burial Ground Project, Washington, D.C.: Howard University for the United States General Services Administration Northeast and Caribbean Region, November 2004.

Miller, Floyd J. *The Search for a Black Nationality: Black Emigration and Colonization, 1787–1863.* Urbana: University of Illinois Press, 1975.

Moses, Wilson Jeremiah. *Alexander Crummell: A Study of Civilization and Discontent.* New York: Oxford University Press, 1989.

———, ed. *Classical Black Nationalism: From the American Revolution to Marcus Garvey.* New York: New York University Press, 1996.

———. *Liberian Dreams: Back-to-Africa Narratives from the 1850s.* University Park: Pennsylvania State University Press, 1998.

———. *Wings of Ethiopia: Studies in African American Life and Letters.* Ames: Iowa State University Press, 1990.

Moss, Richard Shannon. *Slavery on Long Island: A Study in Local Institutional and Early African American Communal Life.* New York: Garland Publishing, 1993.

Mushkat, Jerome. *Fernando Wood: A Political Biography.* Kent, Ohio: Kent State University Press, 1990.

Nash, Gary B. *Forging Freedom: The Formation of Philadelphia's Black Community, 1720–1840.* Cambridge: Harvard University Press, 1988.

Nash, Gary B., and Jean R. Soderlund. *Freedom by Degrees: Emancipation in Pennsylvania and Its Aftermath.* New York: Oxford University Press, 1991.

Newman, Renee. "Pinkster and Slavery in Dutch New York." *Halve Maen* 66, no. 1 (1993): 1–5.

O'Neale, Sondra A. *Jupiter Hammon and the Biblical Beginnings of African American Literature.* Metuchen, N.J.: Scarecrow Press, 1993.

Osborn, Gardner. *The Streets of Old New York: An Historical Picture Book.* New York: Harper and Brothers, 1939.

Ottley, Roi. *Black Odyssey: The Story of the Negro in America.* New York: Charles Scribner's Sons, 1948.

Ottley, Roi, and William J. Weatherby, eds. *The Negro in New York: An Informal Social History.* New York: New York Public Library, 1967.

Over, William. "New York's African Grove Theatre: The Vicissitudes of the Black Actor." *Afro-Americans in New York Life and History* 3, no. 2 (July 1979): 7–13.

Ovington, Mary White. *Half a Man: The Status of the Negro in New York.* New York: Hill and Wang, 1969.

Pasternak, Martin B. *Rise Now and Fly to Arms: The Life of Henry Highland Garnet.* New York: Garland Publishing, 1995.

Payne, A. A. "The Negro in New York Prior to 1860." *Howard Review* 1 (June 1923): 1–64.

Payne, Daniel A. *History of the African Methodist Episcopal Church.* New York: Johnson Reprint Corporation, 1968.

Pease, William H., and Jane H. Pease. *Black Utopia: Negro Communal Experiments in America.* Madison: State Historical Society of Wisconsin, 1972.

———. *They Who Would Be Free: Blacks' Search for Freedom, 1830–1861.* New York: Atheneum, 1974.

Perlman, Daniel. "Organizations of the Free Negro in New York City, 1800–1860." *Journal of Negro History* 56, no. 3 (July 1971): 181–97.

Perry, Warren R., Jean Howson, and Barbara A. Bianco, eds. *New York African Burial Ground Archaeology Final Report. Vol. 1.* Washington D.C.: Howard University for the United States General Services Administration Northeastern and Caribbean Region, February 2006.

Phelan, Helene C. *And Why Not Every Man? An Account of Slavery, the Underground Railroad, and the Road to Freedom in New York's Southern Tier.* Interlaken, N.Y.: Heart of the Lakes, 1987.

Phillips, Christopher. *Freedom's Port: The African American Community of Baltimore, 1790–1860.* Urbana: University of Illinois Press, 1997.

Porter, Dorothy B. "David M. Ruggles, an Apostle of Human Rights." *Journal of Negro History* 28, no. 1 (January 1943): 23–50.

———. *Early Negro Writing, 1760–1837.* Baltimore: Black Classic Press, 1995.

———. "The Organized Educational Activities of Negro Literary Societies, 1828–1846." *Journal of Negro Education* 5, no. 4 (October 1936): 555–76.

Pride, Armistead S., and Clint C. Wilson II. *A History of the Black Press.* Washington, D.C.: Howard University Press, 1997.

Quarles, Benjamin. *Black Abolitionists.* New York: Oxford University Press, 1969.

———. *The Negro in the American Revolution.* Chapel Hill: University of North Carolina Press, 1996.

Rael, Patrick Joseph. *Black Identity and Black Protest in the Antebellum North.* Chapel Hill: University of North Carolina Press, 2002.

———. "The Lion's Painting: African American Thought in the Antebellum North." PhD diss., University of California at Berkeley, 1995.

Reed, Harry. *Platform for Change: The Foundations of the Northern Free Black Community, 1775–1865.* East Lansing: Michigan State University Press, 1994.

Reed, Henry Hope. *Central Park: A History and a Guide.* New York: Clarkson N. Potter, 1967.

Rhoads, Samuel, ed. *The Non-Slaveholder.* Westport, Conn.: Negro Universities Press, 1970.

Rhodes, Jane. *Mary Ann Shadd Cary: The Black Press and Protest in the Nineteenth Century.* Bloomington: Indiana University Press, 1998.

Richards, Leonard L. *"Gentlemen of Property and Standing:" Anti-Abolition Mobs in Jacksonian America.* New York: Oxford University Press, 1970.

Richards, Phillip M. "Nationalist Themes in the Preaching of Jupiter Hammon." *Early American Literature* 25, no. 2 (1990): 123–38.

Roediger, David R. *The Wages of Whiteness: Race and the Making of the American Working Class.* New York: Verso, 1991.

Roff, Sandra Shiock. "The Brooklyn African Woolman Society Rediscovered." *Afro-Americans in New York Life and History* 10, no. 2 (July 1986): 7–28.

Rosenzweig, Roy, and Elizabeth Blackmar. *The Park and the People: A History of Central Park.* Ithaca, N.Y.: Cornell University Press, 1992.

Rury, John L. "Education and Black Community Development in Ante-Bellum New York City." Master's thesis, City University of New York, 1975.

———. "The New York African Free School, 1827–1836: Conflict Over Community Control of Black Education." *Phylon* 44, no. 3 (September, 1983): 187–97.

———. "Philanthropy, Self Help, and Social Control: The New York Manumission Society and Free Blacks, 1785–1810." *Phylon: The Atlanta University Review of Race and Culture* 46, no. 3 (1985): 231–41.

Salwen, Peter. *Upper West Side Story: A History and Guide.* New York: Abbeville Press, 1989.

Samkutty, E. C. "The Promised Land in Afro-American Poetic Vision." *CLA Journal* 35, no. 4 (June 1992): 422–31.

Sante, Luc. *Low Life: Lures and Snares of Old New York.* New York: Farrar, Straus, and Giroux, 1991.

Schama, Simon. *Landscape and Memory.* New York: A. A. Knopf, 1995.

Scherzer, Kenneth. *The Unbounded Community: Neighborhood Life and Social Structure in New York City, 1830–1875.* Durham, N.C.: Duke University Press, 1992.

Schor, Joel. *Henry Highland Garnet: A Voice of Black Radicalism in the Nineteenth Century.* Westport, Conn.: Greenwood Press, 1977.

Scott, Anne Firor. "Most Invisible of All: Black Women's Voluntary Associations." *Journal of Southern History* 56, no. 1 (February 1990): 3–22.

Scruggs, Otey. "Two Black Patriarchs: Frederick Douglass and Alexander Crummell." *Afro-Americans in New York Life and History* 6, no. 1 (January 1982): 17–30.

Sheehan, Arthur, and Elizabeth Odell. *Pierre Toussaint: A Citizen of Old New York.* New York: P. J. Kennedy and Sons, 1955.

Shick, Tom W. *Behold the Promised Land: A History of Afro-American Settler Society in Nineteenth Century Liberia.* Baltimore, Md.: John Hopkins University Press, 1980.

———. *Emigrants to Liberia, 1820 to 1843: An Alphabetical Listing.* Newark: University of Delaware, 1971.

Siebert, Wilbur Henry. *The Underground Railroad from Slavery to Freedom.* 1898. Reprint, New York: Arno Press, 1968.

Simmons, Rev. William J. *Men of Mark: Eminent, Progressive and Rising.* 1887. Reprint, New York: Arno Press and the New York Times, 1968.

Smith, C. S., ed. *History of the African Methodist Episcopal Church.* New York: Johnson Reprint Corp., 1968.

Smith, James Wesley. *Sojourners in Search of Freedom: The Settlement of Liberia by Black Americans.* Lanham, Md.: University Press of America, 1987.

Smith, John David, ed. *The American Colonization Society and Emigration: Solutions to "The Negro Problem."* New York: Garland Publishers, 1993.

Smith-Rosenberg, Carroll. *Religion and the Rise of the American City: The New York City Mission Movement, 1812–1870.* Ithaca, N.Y.: Cornell University Press, 1971.

Southall, Eugene Portlette. "Arthur Tappan and the Anti-Slavery Movement." *Journal of Negro History* 15, no. 2 (April 1930): 162–97.

Southern, Eileen. "Music Practices in Black Churches of New York and Philadelphia, ca. 1800–1844." *Afro-Americans in New York Life and History* 4, no. 1 (January 1980): 61–78.

Southern, Eileen, and Josephine Wright. *Images: Iconography of Music in African American Culture (1770s–1920s).* New York: Garland Publishing, 2000.

Stansell, Christine. *City of Women: Sex and Class in New York, 1789–1860.* New York: Alfred A. Knopf, 1986.

Staudenraus, P. J. *The African Colonization Movement, 1816–1865.* New York: Columbia University Press, 1961.

Stauffer, John. *The Black Hearts of Men: Radical Abolitionists and the Transformation of Race.* Cambridge: Harvard University Press, 2000.

Stearns, Marshall, and Jean Stearns. *Jazz Dance: The Story of American Vernacular Dance.* New York: Schirmer Books, 1968.

Sterling, Dorothy, ed. *Speak Out in Thunder Tones: Letters and Other Writings by Black Northerners, 1787–1865.* New York: Doubleday & Company, 1973.

———. *We Are Your Sisters: Black Women in the Nineteenth Century.* New York: W. W. Norton & Company, 1984.

Stott, Richard Briggs. *Workers in the Metropolis.* Ithaca, N.Y.: Cornell University Press, 1990.

Streifford, David M. "The American Colonization Society: An Application of Republican Ideology to Early Antebellum Reform." *Journal of Southern History* 45, no. 2 (May 1979): 201–20.

Stuckey, Sterling. "African Spirituality and Cultural Practice in Colonial New York, 1700–1770." In *Inequality in Early America,* edited by Carla Pestana and Sharon Salinger. Hanover, N.H.: Dartmouth College Press, 1999.

———. "Christian Conversion and the Challenge of Dance." In *Choreographing History,* edited by Susan Leigh Foster. Bloomington: Indiana University Press. 1995.

———. *Going through the Storm: The Influence of African American Art in History.* New York: Oxford University Press. 1994.

———. *The Ideological Origins of Black Nationalism.* Boston: Beacon Press, 1972.

———. *Slave Culture: Nationalist Theory and the Foundations of Black America.* New York: Oxford University Press, 1987.

———. "The Tambourine in Glory: African Culture and Melville's Art." In *The Cambridge Companion to Herman Melville,* edited by Robert S. Levine. New York: Cambridge University Press, 1998.

Sutherland, Daniel E. *Americans and Their Servants: Domestic Service in the United States from 1800 to 1920.* Baton Rouge: Louisiana State University Press, 1981.

Swan, Robert J. "John Teasman: African American Educator and the Emergence of Community in Early Black New York City, 1787–1815." *Journal of the Early Republic* 12, no. 3 (1992): 331–56.

Tarry, Ellen. *The Other Toussaint: A Modern Biography of Pierre Toussaint, A Post-Revolutionary Black.* Boston: The Daughters of St. Paul, 1981.

Thomas, Lamont D. *Rise to Be a People: A Biography of Paul Cuffe.* Urbana: University of Illinois Press, 1986.

Thompson, George A. Jr. *A Documentary History of the African Theatre.* Evanston, Ill.: Northwestern University Press, 1998.

Thompson, Robert Farris. *Flash of the Spirit: African and Afro-American Art and Philosophy.* New York: Random House, 1983.

Thompson, Robert Farris, and Joseph Cornet. *The Four Moments of the Sun: Kongo Art in Two Worlds.* New Haven, Conn.: Eastern Press, 1981.

Todd, Charles Burr. *In Olde New York: Sketches of Old Times and Places in Both the State and the City.* New York: The Grafton Press Publishers, 1907.

Towner, Lawrence. "The Sewall–Suffin Dialogue on Slavery." *William and Mary Quarterly* 21, no. 1 (January 1964): 40–52.

Tripp, Bernell. *Origins of the Black Press, New York, 1827–1847.* Northport, Ala.: Vision Press, 1992.

Trivelli, Marifrances. "'I Knew a Ship from Stem to Stern': The Maritime World of Frederick Douglass." *Log of Mystic Seaport* 46 (Spring 1995): 98–110.

Turner, James, ed. *David Walker's Appeal to the Coloured Citizens of the World, but in Particular and Very Expressly, to Those of the United States of America.* New York: Black Classic Press, 1993.

Uya, Okon Edet, ed. *Black Brotherhood: Afro-Americans and Africa.* Lexington, Mass.: Heath, 1971.

Valentine, David T. "History of Broadway." In *Manual of the Common Council of New York.* New York: D. T. Valentine, 1865.

Walker, George E. *The Afro-American in New York City, 1827–1860.* Studies in African American History and Culture. New York: Garland Publishing, 1993.

Walls, William J. *The African Methodist Episcopal Zion Church: Reality of the Black Church.* Charlotte, N.C.: A. M. E. Zion Publishing House, 1974.

Washington, Margaret, ed. *Narrative of Sojourner Truth.* New York: Vintage Books, 1993.

Watters, Laurie A. *A Year in Central Park.* New York: Rizzoli, 1992.

Wegelin, Oscar. *Jupiter Hammon, American Negro Poet: Selections from His Writings and a Bibliography.* Freeport, N.Y.: Books for Libraries Press, 1970.

Wesley, Charles H. "The Negroes of New York in the Emancipation Movement." *Journal of Negro History* 24 (January 1939): 65–103.

———. *Negro Labor in the United States, 1850–1925.* New York: Vanguard Press, 1927.

———. "Negro Suffrage in the Period of Constitution-Making, 1787–1865." *Journal of Negro History* 32 (April 1947): 143–68.

———. "The Participation of Negroes in Anti-Slavery Political Parties." *Journal of Negro History* 29 (January 1944): 32–74.

Weston, Rob. "Alexander Hamilton and the Abolition of Slavery in New York." *Afro-Americans in New York Life and History* 18 (1994): 31–45.

Whitby, Gary L. "Horns of Dilemma: The Sun, Abolition, and the 1833–34 New York Riots." *Journalism Quarterly* 67, no. 2 (1990): 410–19.

White, Shane. "'It Was a Proud Day': African Americans, Festivals and Parades in the North, 1741–1834." *Journal of American History* 81, no. 1 (June 1983): 13–50.

———. "Pinkster: Afro-Dutch Syncretization in New York City and the Hudson Valley." *Journal of American Folklore* 102, no. 403 (1989): 68–75.

———. "A Question of Style: Blacks in and Around New York City in the Late 18th Century." *Journal of American Folklore* 102, no. 403 (1989): 23–44.

———. *Somewhat More Independent: The End of Slavery in New York City, 1770–1810.* Athens: University of Georgia Press, 1991.

———. *Stories of Freedom in Black New York.* Cambridge: Harvard University Press, 2002.

———. "'We Dwell in Safety and Pursue Our Honest Callings': Free Blacks in New York City, 1783–1810." *Journal of American History* 75, no. 2 (September 1988): 449–70.

White, Shane, and Graham White. *Stylin': African American Expressive Culture from Its Beginnings to the Zoot Suit.* Ithaca, N.Y.: Cornell University Press, 1998.

Wiggins, Rosalind Cobb. *Captain Paul Cuffe's Logs and Letters, 1808–1817: A Black Quaker's "Voice from within the Veil."* Washington, D.C.: Howard University Press, 1996.

Wilder, Craig Steven. *In the Company of Black Men: The African Influence on African American Culture in New York City.* New York: New York University Press, 2001.

———. "'The Guardian Angel of Africa': A Financial History of the New York African Society for Mutual Relief, 1808–1945." *Afro-Americans in New York Life and History* 26, no. 2 (July 2002): 67–94.

Wilentz, Sean. *Chants Democratic: New York City and the Rise of the American Working Class, 1788–1850.* New York: Oxford University Press, 1984.

Williams-Myers, A. J. "The Plight of African Americans in Ante-Bellum New York City." *Afro-Americans in New York Life and History* 22, no. 2 (July 1998): 49–58.

Wills, David W., and Richard Newman. *Black Apostles at Home and Abroad: Afro-Americans and the Christian Mission from the Revolution to Reconstruction.* Boston: G. K. Hall and Co, 1982.

Wilson, Carol. *Freedom at Risk: The Kidnapping of Free Blacks in America, 1780–1865.* Lexington: University of Kentucky Press, 1994.

Wilson, Rufus Rockwell. *New York: Old and New. Its Story, Streets, and Landmarks.* Philadelphia: J. B. Lippincott Company, 1903.

Wilson, Sherrill D. *New York City's African Slaveowners: A Social and Material Culture History.* New York: Garland Publishing, 1994.

Winch, Julie. *Philadelphia's Black Elite: Activism, Accommodation, and the Struggle for Autonomy, 1787–1848.* Philadelphia: Temple University Press, 1988.

Withington, Ann Fairfax. *Toward a More Perfect Union: Virtue and the Formation of American Republics.* New York: Oxford University Press, 1991.

Woodson, Carter G. *The African Background Outlined, or Handbook for the Study of the Negro.* 1936. Reprint, New York: Negro Universities Press, 1968.

———. *The Mind of the Negro as Reflected in Letters Written during the Crisis, 1800–1860.* New York: Negro Universities Press, 1969.

———, ed. *Negro Orators and Their Orations.* New York: Russell and Russell, 1969.

Wormley, G. Smith. "Prudence Crandall." *Journal of Negro History* 8, no. 1 (January 1923): 72–80.

Wyatt-Brown, Bertram. *Lewis Tappan and the Evangelical War against Slavery.* Reprint. Baton Rouge: Louisiana State University Press, 1997.

Yellin, Jean Fagan, and John C. Van Horne, eds. *The Abolitionist Sisterhood: Women's Political Culture in Antebellum America.* Ithaca, N.Y.: Cornell University Press, 1994.

Yoshpe, Harry B. "Record of Slave Manumissions in New York during the Colonial and Early National Periods." *Journal of Negro History* 26 (January 1941): 78–107.

Young, R. J. "The Political Economy of Black Abolitionists." *Afro-Americans in New York Life and History* 18, no. 1 (January 1994): 47–72.

Zilversmit, Arthur. *The First Emancipation: The Abolition of Slavery in the North.* Chicago: University of Chicago Press, 1967.

INDEX

Page numbers in italics refer to illustrations.

DR. LESLIE M. ALEXANDER is associate professor of history at the Ohio State University. She received her B.A. with honors from Stanford University, her M.A. from Cornell University, and her Ph.D. from Cornell University. She is the coeditor of *We Shall Independent Be: African American Place-Making and the Struggle to Claim Space in the U.S.* A recipient of several prestigious fellowships, including the Ford Foundation Postdoctoral Fellowship and the Ford Foundation Dissertation Fellowship, Prof. Alexander has presented her research at the annual meetings of the Association for the Study of African American Life and History, the Association for the Study of Worldwide African Diaspora, the American Historical Association, the Organization of American Historians, the African Heritage Studies Association, and the Caribbean Studies Association. In 1999, she was elected to the Executive Board of the African Heritage Studies Association. Her next research project, "'To Leave the House of Bondage': African American Internationalism in the Nineteenth Century," is an exploration of early African American foreign policy. This study seeks to investigate how African Americans in the antebellum and early postbellum eras viewed political issues throughout the African diaspora, particularly antislavery struggles and resistance movements in Haiti, Cuba, and Brazil.

The University of Illinois Press
is a founding member of the
Association of American University Presses.

Composed in 10.5/13 Adobe Minion Pro
at the University of Illinois Press
Manufactured by Thomson-Shore, Inc.

University of Illinois Press
1325 South Oak Street
Champaign, IL 61820-6903
www.press.uillinois.edu

DR. LESLIE M. ALEXANDER is associate professor of history at the Ohio State University. She received her B.A. with honors from Stanford University, her M.A. from Cornell University, and her Ph.D. from Cornell University. She is the coeditor of *We Shall Independent Be: African American Place-Making and the Struggle to Claim Space in the U.S.* A recipient of several prestigious fellowships, including the Ford Foundation Postdoctoral Fellowship and the Ford Foundation Dissertation Fellowship, Prof. Alexander has presented her research at the annual meetings of the Association for the Study of African American Life and History, the Association for the Study of Worldwide African Diaspora, the American Historical Association, the Organization of American Historians, the African Heritage Studies Association, and the Caribbean Studies Association. In 1999, she was elected to the Executive Board of the African Heritage Studies Association. Her next research project, "'To Leave the House of Bondage': African American Internationalism in the Nineteenth Century," is an exploration of early African American foreign policy. This study seeks to investigate how African Americans in the antebellum and early postbellum eras viewed political issues throughout the African diaspora, particularly antislavery struggles and resistance movements in Haiti, Cuba, and Brazil.

The University of Illinois Press
is a founding member of the
Association of American University Presses.

———————————————————

Composed in 10.5/13 Adobe Minion Pro
at the University of Illinois Press
Manufactured by Thomson-Shore, Inc.

University of Illinois Press
1325 South Oak Street
Champaign, IL 61820-6903
www.press.uillinois.edu